The Queen and the Torturer

The Queen and the Torturer

F. W. Brownlow

Cedar Hill Press
2019

The Queen and the Torturer by F.W.Brownlow
Published by Cedar Hill Press,
24 Cedar Hill Road, Holyoke MA 01040

© 2020 F.W.Brownlow

ISBN: 978-1-7359533-0-4

Contents

Acknowledgments	7
Preface	9
Prologue: An Arrest and a Letter	15
Two: Richard Topcliffe, Esquire	27
Three: Topcliffe, Esquire and Policeman	49
Four: The Habit of Torture	73
Five: Thomas Norton Raises the Stakes	91
Six: Master Topcliffe Takes Over	115
Seven: Hunting Vermin Northwards	145
Eight: "Black with Gibbets"	165
Nine: A Spider in the Cup	189
Ten: "Nowhere Left to Hide"	213
Eleven: "Very Vile Rumors"	235
Twelve: "Merciless Mr. Topcliffe"	259
Thirteen: "A Dishonest Man"	283
Fourteen: Twilight of a Torturer	307
Fifteen: Finale	335
Sixteen: Epilogue	351
Appendix I	
1 The Tortures, 1558–1603: General	363
II. The Tortures, 1558–1603: Topcliffe's Cases	369
III. Some Cases of Chronic Duress and Other Punishments	371
IV. Women	373
V. The Torturers	375
VI. Topcliffe at the Kill	377
VII. Live Mutilations	379
Appendix II	
Topcliffe: The Two Final Letters	385
Works Cited	397
Index	411

Acknowledgments

A fellowship at the Huntington Library enabled me to begin searching for material on Richard Topcliffe, and the research fund attached to my chair at Mount Holyoke College allowed me to visit essential manuscript repositaries and libraries: the National Archives, Kew; the Lincolnshire archives; the British Library; the Bodleian Library; Lambeth Palace Library; the Folger Library, and Exeter University Library, whose librarians, at very short notice, very kindly produced A.L.Rowse's copy of Girolamo Pollini's *L'historia ecclesiastica della rivoluzion d'Inghilterra,* owned and profusely annotated by Topcliffe, "Esquire of the body to Queen Elizabeth," himself.

I would like to acknowledge, too, the encouragement and advice of my friends Gary Bouchard, Richard Dutton, Kirby Farrell, Stephen Harris, John Klause, and Thomas Merriam; and I must thank my favorite artist, Elizabeth Brownlow, for painting the cover images for me. Clayton Beck painted the portrait sketch of myself on the back cover.

I need to explain to my friends, however, why it took such a long time to complete this book. I began the research for it in the beautiful surroundings of the Huntington Library as part of my long-standing work on Robert Southwell. Very quickly, though, it took on some of the qualities of a war-crimes investigation; and as the record of Mr. Topcliffe and Company's activities lengthened, I would have to break off work for a walk among the flowers in the sunshine. Six or seven years later, with the research more or less finished, I found myself in no doubt about the completeness of the Tudors' destruction of the English people's common law and statutory constitution, along with its remarkable protections of life and property, nor about the unpleasantness of the long-term effects.

For someone like me, who started out life as a Northern Irish Protestant, and was well-educated in a very good, but very conventional English school, this was a disconcerting conclusion. How was I to handle it?

After all, I was by no means the only 20th-century historian to come upon the fact. One writer was so upset by the staggering numbers of people judicially killed under the Tudors that he spent long hours trying to estimate the totals from court records. Most historians, though, end by shrugging their shoulders or, if they are looking for preferment in the English academic system, they learn quickly to moderate their criticisms of good queen Bess, her revolting father, and the creatures they both employed. After all, as one historian concluded, whatever happened, there is no point in crying over spilt milk: the English people are still there, and they are getting along just fine, in his case in "Anglican agnosticism in the serenity of Christchurch Cathedral"—a phrase that stuck in my mind. As my great friend William Coles likes to say, "Nice work if you can get it."

For me that approach was not an option, though I suppose it could have been easily enough. Having published a couple of essays and given a number of talks on the subject, I decided that there was an audience for at least some of the truth, and finally embarked upon the telling of it.

Holyoke, MA
2019.

Preface

There is a story that when Queen Victoria, paying a visit to the great Victorian painter Sir John Millais, set his little boy upon her knee, the child would have nothing to do with her. Asked why, he said, "You are wicked Queen Elizabeth, who cut off good Queen Mary's head." Coming from a well-brought-up Victorian child, that was an interesting reply, but the Queen's response was even more interesting. "No, dear," she is supposed to have said, "I am Queen of England, because I descend from good Queen Mary; and I have not a drop of wicked Queen Elizabeth's blood in my body."[1] And of course, Queen Victoria was right. Every English monarch since James VI and I, including the Hanoverians, descends from his mother, Mary Stuart, Queen of Scots. So much for William Cecil, Lord Burghley, and his creature Francis Walsingham's Babington Plot that enabled the pair of them to destroy Mary Stuart; and so much, too, for the English parliament and its statute, 23 Eliz. cap. 2, that made discussion of the succession a capital offense. And yet Cecil and Walsingham succeeded because they imposed their lies upon the narrative of English history. Not one in a hundred modern Englishmen knows that Elizabeth II is descended from Mary Queen of Scots.

In approaching the story of Richard Topcliffe and the torturing régime he served so well, the story-teller's great difficulty is the long-standing reluctance of English—and Anglo-American—historians to tell the truth about English history. Richard Topcliffe's career is one of the more notable examples of the "spun" or "elided" aspects of that history, and yet it is a mere detail in a much larger panorama. How is one to sketch in the lineaments of that larger story in a way that will enable one to make sense of Topcliffe's presence at Elizabeth I's court?

One could begin by noticing that it was Mary Stuart's misfortune, which she shared with the majority of English people at Elizabeth I's accession, that she was a Catholic. William Cecil, from the outset of his administration under Elizabeth I, was determined to eradicate Catholicism from England in favor of Protestantism, and as an essential strategy in that policy he decided upon Mary Stuart's deposition as Queen of

---

[1] Pollen 3, xiii.

Scotland before she had even returned to Scotland from France.

It was within the framework of that grand strategy or policy for the future of England and, indeed, of the entire British Isles, that the career of Richard Topcliffe, Elizabeth I's friend, servant, and policeman extraordinary, became not only possible but necessary if the policy was to succeed.

Who, then, was Topcliffe, and where did he come from? I first encountered him some years ago when, in a book about Robert Southwell's writings, I gave a short account of Topcliffe's capture of Fr. Southwell in which I quoted the letter he wrote to the Queen, announcing his capture and suggesting that he proceed to interrogate Southwell under torture. The book was finished and published when the question occurred to me: why was Topcliffe writing to the Queen, and in such informal terms? Why did he not report his catch to the Privy Council, to Robert Cecil as acting secretary, to his father, Lord Treasurer Burghley, or to Sir John Puckering, the newly-appointed Lord Keeper?

Southwell's biographer, Christopher Devlin, S.J., suggested that Topcliffe enjoyed the status of a kind of favorite with the Queen. James Heath, the historian of torture in England, proposed that, "he attained to a special working relationship with the Queen herself."[1] Yet apart from Topcliffe's letter no reliable evidence of any such thing had so far appeared. No-one knew what Topcliffe's position at court was, and further search into the available material about him revealed that more was assumed than was actually known, and that there were gaps and inconsistencies in the record.

I therefore set out on what I thought would be a short inquiry leading, I hoped, to an equally short but interesting essay. The brief inquiry metamorphosed into something more complex, and the essay became this book. The reason for that was that Topcliffe turned out to have left a bigger historical footprint than expected, also because his late-blooming career as Elizabeth I's chief enforcer of her laws mandating religious conformity takes us into the epicenter of a dark period in English history when the statutory protections of freedom, life, and property were in suspension because the government itself, both crown and parliament, had turned criminal.

That is a matter of fact, though very few historians can bring themselves to acknowledge it. The standard narrative of English history justifies Tudor law-breaking by the plea of necessity in a time of danger, and

---

[1]Devlin 1, 210; Heath, 139.

saves the appearance of criminality by arguing that since the illegal acts themselves, e.g., torture and summary imprisonment, were always carried out under the royal prerogative and usually with the Privy Council's authorization, they were consequently lawful, however unpleasant. Those who performed them, moreover, were protected from prosecution by the principle of sovereign immunity.

To accept the plea of necessity, however, is to accept the state's self-justifying propaganda, also to ignore the policies and actions that endangered the kingdom in the first place. It is a general principle, too—or it ought to be—that no statement made by the ministers of a criminal government should be taken at face value. As to the claim of sovereign immunity, by the fourteenth century English statute law, starting with Magna Carta, had established the principle that the Crown itself and Parliament were both of them subordinate to the law. The claim of sovereign immunity has never had any legal standing in England, however often it has been invoked.

The illegality of the Elizabethan government's proceedings is the grand, over-arching fact that enabled Richard Topcliffe's career as the untiring servant of the Elizabethan state and its Queen whom he adored, and to whom he reported personally.

That career began fairly quietly sometime in the late 1570s. By the later 1580s Topcliffe had become a kind of chief of police, "a primeval common ancestor," in James Heath's words, "of Pinkerton's and the FBI." Operating under a blanket commission that gave him extraordinary powers of search, arrest, and imprisonment, he investigated a number of ordinary criminal cases, but mostly he hunted, caught, and interrogated—frequently with torture—Catholics under the laws that criminalized dissent from the state's newly created Protestant Church of England.

Having made an arrest and prepared his case, he would attend the subsequent trial both as a witness for the prosecution, and as a kind of free-lance prosecutor himself. Then, since such trials always ended with a verdict of "guilty," he would attend the executions that followed as a kind of master of the ceremonies: he would harangue the victims and, in many cases, attach a *titulus* or placard to the gallows describing the victim's crime before giving orders that the killing should begin.

Although the fact is not generally known, Elizabeth I easily wins the prize among English monarchs for the largest number of her subjects interrogated under torture. Although such lists are never complete, we can now say that during her reign there were at least about 180 cases of torture or the threat of it.[1] During the period of most intense enforcement of the penal laws, from 1588 to 1595, there were 70 cases. Master Topcliffe was involved in at least 34 of them. In the course of his entire policing career, he attended 61 executions that we know about. Of these, more than half (37) took place in that same 7-year period between 1588 and 1595.

Nonetheless, despite Topcliffe's remarkable energy and his high personal score-card, he was not alone in his chosen line of work: there are 64 names in the list of Elizabethan torturers in the appendix to this book. Topcliffe, however, as he knew well, was the most visible and notorious of the state's enforcers, and what made him unique was that, as he liked to let people know, his authority came from the Queen herself, and he reported to her. Perhaps the most telling evidence of his real power is that on several occasions we find him writing his own orders and warrants through the medium of the Privy Council itself.

By 1595, when the Privy Council took back his commission, practicing Catholics had become a small minority of the population, and the extraordinary story of Richard Topcliffe's policing career goes a long way to explain that development. It also shines a light into an occluded place in English history as dark, in its way, as the underground pit in the Tower of London into which the Elizabethan authorities were so fond of dropping uncooperative prisoners.

*****

[1]The number of cases represents the individuals tortured, not the the number of torture sessions. Although Fr. Robert Southwell was tortured ten times over a period of about a week or more both by Topcliffe and the Privy Council's own torturers, his torture counts as one case.

A note upon forms of ecclesiastical address.

The habit of addressing priests as "Father" is comparatively recent. In the sixteenth century, after the schism with Rome, priests were addressed simply as "Mr." or "Master." Only members of religious orders, e.g., the Jesuits, were addressed as "Father" or described as "the father." In this book, therefore, only Jesuits and other religious are given the address "Fr."

Many of the priests and lay people here mentioned are now canonized or beatified martyrs of the Catholic Church, but again, for the purposes of this narrative they are named as they were known in their own time.

One

Prologue: An Arrest and a Letter

In the evening of Sunday, 25 June 1592, a man called Richard Topcliffe assembled a small force of men, and set out from Greenwich, just down river from London, for a manor house in Harrow-on-the Hill, Middlesex, called Uxenden or Uxendon. It belonged to a strongly Catholic family called Bellamy. Nothing remains of Uxendon now, which stood near the present-day Preston Road Tube Station, although the name is preserved in a couple of street-names and a local primary school.

In the late sixteenth century, though, Uxendon was a secluded place. In 1586 Anthony Babington had sought refuge at Uxendon in the aftermath of his failed plot: he had been captured there, bringing terrible misfortune to the family. On that evening in 1592, Topcliffe knew that he would find a young Jesuit priest at Uxendon called Robert Southwell, alias Cotton.

Robert Southwell had been in England since 1586. He was a good priest, an able manager and organizer, and—probably most important in the long run—a remarkable writer in both prose and poetry who had devoted his literary gift to his pastorate. During his time in England he had published two prose works, one, *An Epistle of Comfort,* on a secret press, the other, *Mary Magdalen's Funeral Tears,* publicly, and licensed for printing by no less a person than the archbishop of Canterbury himself. Three other prose works were circulating in manuscript, along with a collection of short lyric poems and a longer poem, *Saint Peter's Complaint,* which he had prepared for the press. For the Elizabethan Protestant government, determined to eradicate Catholicism from England, this poet-priest, if only they could find him, would be the most important catch since their agents caught Edmund Campion in 1581.

Richard Topcliffe, having discovered where and how to find

Southwell, now intended to capture him, and to take him back for interrogation to his own house in Westminster adjoining the Gatehouse
prison.

Stopping en route to add a Justice of the Peace to his posse (as he was
required and empowered to do by the terms of his commission),
Topcliffe arrived at Uxendon shortly after midnight. He positioned his
men round the house so that no-one could escape, then pounded on the
doors, demanding they be opened. Once inside the house, he found that
the owner, Richard Bellamy, was absent, the house in charge of his wife,
Katherine. He ordered his men to bind the men-servants, and told Mrs.
Bellamy to produce the priest. At first, and with great courage, she
denied that any such person was in the house; but when Topcliffe made
it plain to her that he not only knew about the priest's presence, but also
about the exact location of the secret place where he was hidden, Mrs.
Bellamy understood that she had no choice in the matter, and produced
Father Southwell.

When Topcliffe saw the priest, he made a run at him with a drawn
rapier, calling him, "Traitor!" The people with him restrained him.
Southwell replied that he was no traitor.

"What are you then?" asked Topcliffe.

"I am a gentlemen," said Southwell.

"You are a priest and a traitor," said Topcliffe.

"That is what you have to prove," said Southwell. The reply so infuriated Topcliffe that he made another lunge with his rapier, shouting that
Southwell was denying his priesthood. Father Garnet, Southwell's superior, whose account we are following, was not sure of the exact words of
Southwell's reply, but gives the gist of them:

> It is neither priest nor treason that you seek for, but only blood; and if mine
> will satisfy you, you shall have it with as good a will as ever any one's; and
> if mine will not satisfy, I do not doubt but you shall find many more as
> willing as myself; only, I would advise you to remember there is a God,
> and He is just in His judgment.

Topcliffe then sent his henchman, Thomas Fitzherbert, to Court with the
news of the capture. The Queen, according to Father Garnet's informant
at Court, received the news "with unwonted merriment."[1] Topcliffe,

---

[1] The researches of Patrick Martin and John Finnis have now told us who one of Father
Garnet's centrally-placed court informants was: William Sterrell, secretary to Edward,
Earl of Worcester, from about 1590 onwards. At the time of the Appellant controversy
he wrote a long series of letters to Fr. Persons under the name Anthony Rivers, S.J.
(M&F 2).

meanwhile, searched the house for "massing stuff, papistical books, and pictures," of which he seems to have found a good deal. He loaded his booty and the bound priest into a cart, and returned to his house in Westminster. There, after his first efforts at interrogating Southwell failed to produce any information at all (not even the priest's name), in the early morning of Monday, 26 June, Topcliffe wrote a letter to the Queen:

To your most excellent Majesty, my gracious Sovereign, in great haste.

Most gracious Sovereign, having Father Robert Southwell (of my knowledge) the Jesuit in my strong chamber in Westminster churchyard, I have made him assured for starting, or hurting of himself, by putting upon his arms a pair of hand gyves; and there and so can keep him either from view or conference with any but Nicholas the underkeeper of the Gatehouse and my boy—Nicholas being the man that caused me to take him, by setting of him into my hands, ten miles from him.

I have presumed (after my little sleep) to run over this examination enclosed, faithfully taken, and of him foully and suspiciously answered, and somewhat knowing the nature and doings of the man, may it please your Majesty to see my simple opinion.

Constrained in duty to offer it.

Upon this present taking of him, it is good forthwith to enforce him to answer truly, and directly, and so to prove his answers true in haste, to the end that such as be deeply concerned in his treacheries have not time to start, or make shift ——

To use any means in common prisons either to stand upon or against the wall (which above all things exceeds and hurteth not) will give warning: but if your highness' pleasure be to know any thing in his heart, to stand against the wall, his feet standing upon the ground, and his hands but as high as he can reach against the wall, like a trick at Trenchmore, will enforce him to tell all, and the truth proved by the sequel:

1. The answer of him to the question of the Countess of Arundel, and
2. That of Father Parsons, deciphereth him.

It may please your Majesty to consider that I did never take so weighty a man—if he be rightly used

Young Anthony Copley, the most desperate youth that liveth, and some others, be most familiar with Southwell. Copley did shoot at a gentleman the last summer, and killed an ox with a musket, and in Horsham Church threw his dagger at the parish Clerk, and stuck it in a seat in the church. There liveth not the like, I think, in England for sudden attempts, nor one upon whom I have good ground to have watchfuller eyes for his sister Gage's and his brother-in-law's, Gage's, sake, of whose pardons he boasteth he is assured.

So humbly submitting myself to your Majesty's direction in this, or in any service with any hazard, I cease, until I hear your pleasure, here at

Westminster with my charge and ghostly Father, this Monday the 26 of
June 1592.

your Majesty's faithful servant
Richard Topcliffe.[1]

This is an extraordinary letter in every way, decidedly brusque and
informal, considering the person to whom it is written. To begin with,
the writer launches into his subject assuming that his addressee, the
Queen of England, knows exactly what he is talking about, and will need
no long explanations. She knows all about Fr. Southwell the Jesuit,
about the house in Westminster and its strong chamber, and she is not
going to be in the least surprised to hear that Topcliffe has taken his prisoner there, or that—for the time being, anyway—he intends to keep him
there. Topcliffe seems to know, too, that the Queen will not need to have
the details of his request explained. Consequently, we cannot be quite
sure what he means by standing "upon or against the wall," as "in common prisons," although he seems to be referring to a way of frightening a
prisoner into confession by the threat of torture. Nor is his second proposal any clearer. If standing a prisoner against a wall with his hands
over his head is Topcliffe's method for finding out whatever secret stuff
may be lurking in the prisoner's heart, it does not sound all that terrible,
although standing against a wall with one's hands in the air would soon
become painful enough. In fact, though, we know—and everyone in
Elizabethan London, including the Queen, knew—exactly what
Topcliffe meant and what he actually did. He suspended his prisoners
by the hands, their feet barely touching the floor, and sometimes not
touching it at all. This posture very quickly became very painful indeed
and, continued long enough, was fatal.

Some people have thought that Topcliffe left the details of this procedure vague because he thought it best that the Queen not know too much
about what he actually did to his prisoners; but by midsummer 1592
everyone in London, including the Queen who authorized it all, knew
what Topcliffe did. It had become the standard torture in Bridewell
prison, and was being used in the Tower of London as well.

Besides, the whole tone of the letter makes that kind of interpretation
impossible. What, after all, is the letter really about? As a business letter
it asks the Queen for permission to torture an uncooperative prisoner, but
as a letter between two people who know each other well, and are on
good terms, it tells us that Topcliffe enjoys his work, and is keen to start.

[1]BL Ms. Lansdowne 72, No.39.

It tells us, too, that the Queen knows all about the work, and takes enough vicarious pleasure in it to think it is funny to joke about a prisoner under torture with his arms in the air looking like someone performing "a trick at Trenchmore"—Trenchmore being a rowdy, free-form dance popular at Court, and a "trick" being the kind of sprightly caper a dancer might perform, wagging his arms over his head. In fact, this letter assumes that its addressee knows all about torture and its methods, and will welcome the writer's professional assessment of the best path to take in this case.

To speak personally, it is not a letter I would want anyone to write to me. As originally sent, it included a transcript of the first interrogation, now lost, and intended, not for the Privy council, the Lord Keeper, or the principal secretary—the people one would expect a man in Topcliffe's position to write to—but for the Queen of England herself.

Meanwhile, off went the letter to Court, and Mr. Topcliffe waited with his jokingly-named "ghostly Father" in Westminster for the Queen's reply. That reply does not survive, but we can infer that it arrived because we know what happened next.

Robert Southwell spent the next forty hours being tortured in Richard Topcliffe's house.

As for the methods used, in the 1590s the favored English torture was the method already mentioned by Topcliffe: hanging up by the hands, an English variant on the Italian *strappado*, described in the Privy Council warrants as "the manacles." It seems mostly to have displaced the rack by the 1590s. The reason the torturers liked it was because it was simple to apply, far less labor-intensive than the rack, extremely painful, and—best of all—it left no permanent exterior physical mark—or as Topcliffe put it in his letter, "it exceeds and hurteth not."

To apply it, the torturer's men fitted to the subject's hands a pair of manacles or gauntlets with an iron ring attached to each. They passed an iron bar through the rings; then, after the subject raised his hands above his head—like a trick at Trenchmore—they made him climb a step arranged against the wall, placed the bar over iron staples driven into the wall, removed the step, and left him hanging with his feet barely supported. Then from time to time they would remove the support altogether.

John Gerard, S.J., who underwent two long sessions of "the manacles" in the underground torture-room of the Tower of London, has left a clear, precise description of the experience in his autobiography:

> Hanging like this I began to pray. The gentlemen standing around asked me whether I was willing to confess now.

"I cannot and I will not," I answered.

But I could hardly utter the words, such a gripping pain came over me. It was worst in my chest and belly, my hands and arms. All the blood in my body seemed to rush up into my arms and hands and I thought that my blood was oozing out from the ends of my fingers and the pores of my skin. But it was only a sensation caused by my flesh swelling above the irons holding them. The pain was so intense that I thought I could not possibly endure it....[1]

When they took Fr. Gerard for his second session, the manacles would only fit the "furrow" left in his arms by the first session, the flesh was so swollen on either side.

In this method of torture, the body's own weight produces the effect—and worse—of the rack. Prolonged much beyond ten minutes without support to the feet, the effect is permanent internal injury, then death caused by muscular spasms and a sinking of the diaphragm and liver that constricts breathing and blood circulation. In fact, it is the same death that a victim of crucifixion would suffer.[2] John Gerard passed out, he says, eight or nine times during his first session, and again in the second, but his torturers were careful not to prolong the complete hanging too much. Gerard believed that Sir Richard Berkeley, the Lieutenant of the Tower, took pity on him, and ended the second session after an hour. In fact Gerard heard that Sir Richard resigned his office after a very brief term of service because "he no longer wished to be an instrument in such torture of innocent men."[3]

The reason for the torture of priests was that the government wanted information about their contacts, the people who concealed and supported them, and for whom they said Mass. In Robert Southwell's case, in order to indict both him and the family in whose house he was captured, they also needed proof—preferably by his own confession—that he *was* a priest. Southwell, however, like Gerard, refused to speak. Henry Garnet, who had well-placed sources at court, informed Richard Verstegan at Antwerp, who passed the information on to Fr. Robert Per-

---

[1]Gerard, 109. Gerard was taken to the torture-room for a third session, but "when he entered the place he straightway threw himself on his knees, and with a loud voice prayed God that as He had given strength to some of His saints to be torn asunder by horses for the sake of Christ, so He would give him strength and courage to be rent in pieces before he should speak a word that would be injurious to anyone, or to the Divine glory, and so they did not torture him, seeing him so resolved" (Stonyhurst, Ms *Anglia* A. 2.27, printed in Gerard, 115).

[2]R.W.Hynek, 62–5, also cited by Devlin 1, 285–6.

[3]Gerard, 114.

sons, that, "The father refused to answer to anything, saying that if he should tell them any thing at all, yet would they not leave to torment him to know more, yea, to know more than himself did know:"

> Whereupon, one of the examiners did ask him whether he would confess if ever he had been in Paul's. The Father answered that he would not confess that neither, because he would confess nothing to them but they would still infer further matter upon it, and seek to get from him more than he knew. Upon this, he was hanged by the hands against a wall many hours together; and Topcliffe left him hanging, and so went abroad. After he had been a long time absent, one of his servants, perceiving the father to be in a swoon or in some danger to give up the ghost, called him hastily home again to let him down for that time.[1]

One of Verstegan's dispatches says that Topcliffe tortured Southwell "on four separate occasions, by hanging him up by the hands, and in other ways," and another dispatch mentions sleep deprivation as one of Topcliffe's methods.[2] The effect on Robert Southwell was permanent injury. At his trial, three years later, his enfeebled condition was very obvious, and his biographer Christopher Devlin quotes him—again on Garnet's report—asking his kindly keeper in Newgate "not to be too far away in case some accident should happen to him, or he should be in need of anything, because (as a result of his bitter tortures) his sides were not strong enough for him to shout."[3]

It is a remarkable fact, therefore, that Robert Southwell was in Topcliffe's hands almost two whole days, and spoke not one word that could be used against him or anyone else. Consequently Topcliffe had to notify the Queen and Council of his failure. Garnet's informant told him that the Queen called Topcliffe a fool, and ordered Southwell to be turned over to the Council's own interrogators. For this purpose, they moved him next door, to the Gatehouse Prison.[4]

Henry Garnet has preserved the names of the formidable team of interrogators that took over Father Southwell's case: Sir Henry Killigrew, Justice Young, Robert Beale, and William Waad, each of whom has his niche in the records of torture in England. The new

---

[1]Verstegan to Fr. Persons, Antwerp, 3 August 1592 (Verstegan, 58; Devlin 1, 280), adds the details that Topcliffe had "strapped [Southwell's] heels behind his thighs...When he was taken down and revived, he threw up a great quantity of blood."

[2]Verstegan, 52, 68.

[3]Devlin 1, 294.

[4]Verstegan, 68,

Oxford Dictionary of National Biography describes Sir Henry Killigrew as "diplomat," but he was more agent than diplomat. He began active political life by twice conspiring unsuccessfully to overthrow Mary I. Then, having gone to work for her sister, besides doing his best to destabilize the French government by supporting the Huguenots, he tried to arrange the murder of Mary, Queen of Scots. In 1591, towards the end of his career, we find him being instructed by the Privy Council, along with Topcliffe, Robert Beale, and the Bishop of London's brother, Dr. Fletcher, to interrogate—"aggressively" as we would say—a priest called Beesley and his friends.[1]

Robert Beale, named with Killigrew and Topcliffe as one of the interrogators of Mr. Beesley, was a clerk to the Council; he is best known because his delivery of the warrant for Mary, Queen of Scots's execution without Elizabeth I's knowledge landed him, for a time, in very hot water. Beale was Sir Francis Walsingham's brother-in-law, hence very much a man of the inner circle. Responsible for at least six tortures, *ODNB* describes him, too, as a diplomat and administrator.

As for Richard Young, justice and customer in the Port of London, he was one of the most feared enforcers of the penal laws prohibiting Catholicism. Robert Southwell himself had written in a letter to Claudio Aquaviva two years earlier, that Bridewell prison was, "the Purgatory that we all fear, where Topcliffe and Young, those two butchers of the Catholics, have complete freedom to torture."

William Waad, another "diplomat and administrator" according to the *Oxford Dictionary of National Biography*, was, like Beale, one of the clerks to the Council. A protegé of William Cecil, he was involved in at least eight torturings under Elizabeth, then as Lieutenant of the Tower under James I was responsible for the post-Gunpowder Plot tortures which included the crippling for life of the entirely innocent Thomas Strange, S.J., and the death, i.e., murder, of Nicholas Owen, the builder of ingenious hiding places in Catholic houses. It was Wade who administered the torture of John Gerard.[2]

These men continued to examine Southwell, singly and as a group—with torture—into the month of July. They had no better success than Topcliffe. Southwell remained silent, and so finally they quit, leaving

---

[1] *APC*, 20.18.

[2] For notices of Killigrew, Beale, and Waad, see *ODNB*. Heath, 138–9, has good accounts of Young and Waad. Pollen 1, 329–30, prints Southwell's letter, whose Latin original is "Unum istud purgatorium timemus omnes, in quo duo illi Catholicorum carnifices Topliffus et Youngus omnem habent cruciandi libertatem."

him to lie in the prison, injured and untended in his own filth, and infested with lice. Sir Robert Cecil (William, Lord Burghley's recently-knighted clever younger son), now secretary of state in succession to Sir Francis Walsingham in all but name, was among those who took part in the interrogation. His account of the scene was passed to Henry Garnet. "We have a new torture," Cecil is reported to have told a friend, "that is not possible for a man to endure. And yet I have seen Robert Southwell hanging by it, as still as a tree trunk, and none able to drag a word from his mouth."[1] By the interrogation's end, Southwell—as he said at his trial—had been tortured ten times. "I had rather have endured ten executions," he said.[2]

The difference between Robert Southwell and the average torture victim, however, was that he belonged to a rather wealthy, very well connected family. According to the old biographies, his family now intervened in an attempt to help him. Diego de Yepes, the Spanish author of the well-informed *Historia particular de la persecución de Inglaterra*, prints the text of a petition that his father, Richard Southwell, is said to have presented:

> That if his son had committed anything for which by the laws he had deserved death, he might suffer death. If not, as he was a gentleman, that her Majesty might be pleased to order that he should be treated as such, even though he were a Jesuit. And that as his father he might be permitted to send him what he needed to sustain life. This petition was granted, and thus his people visited him, and thenceforth sent him meat, and a Bible, and the works of St. Bernard, which he himself wanted for his solace.[3]

It seems likely that Richard Southwell had influential help in presenting this petition (Christopher Devlin, though, attributes the gift of St. Bernard's works, as well as clothes and bedding, to Southwell's former protectress, the Countess of Arundel). That there was a petition, and that it was successful in having him moved from the Gatehouse Prison, appears in a Privy Council order of 28 July 1592 addressed to the Lieutenant of the Tower of London:

[1] Devlin 1, 288, also Caraman, 80–81.

[2] From Thomas Leake's account of Southwell's trial and martyrdom (Pollen1, 335). Thomas Leake or Leake, born in Staffordshire in 1565, was not yet a priest when he attended Southwell's trial. He was ordained in 1596 at Valladolid, and sent into England. Though arrested more than once, he survived until 1638, when he died in a London fire. See Anstruther, 206–7.

[3] Quoted by Janelle, 68, and cited by Devlin 1, 289.

Her Majesty's pleasure is you shall receive into your custody and charge the person of Robert Southwell, a priest whom Mr. Topcliffe shall deliver unto you, to be kept close prisoner so as no person be suffered to have access unto him but such an one as the said Mr. Topcliffe shall appoint to remain with him as his keeper.[1]

Richard Verstegan sent a notice of the move to Father Persons, 15 October 1592:

Fr. Southwell by all likelihoods hath been very much tortured to confess, but hath said nothing. About the 1 of September he was removed to the Tower, when, as it was observed by some that saw him, that with close keeping and hard usage, wanting linen to shift himself, he was much troubled with lice. But since his being in the Tower, his father hath obtained leave of the Council to send him some necessary apparel, whereby he findeth himself in far better state than before he was, being in the custody of a merciless monster, one Topcliffe.[2]

As Southwell's biographer Christopher Devlin remarks, we can assess the horrors he suffered in the Gatehouse by the fact that his friends were relieved to hear of his transference to solitary confinement in the Tower.[3] Nonetheless, the Council's order reveals a sinister fact: however disappointed the Queen may have been by Topcliffe's inquisitorial skills, she allowed Southwell to remain his prisoner. Although the Council instructed the Lieutenant of the Tower to receive Southwell as a prisoner, he was to receive him from Topcliffe, and Topcliffe was to appoint his keeper. The presence of a peculiar—and to anyone familiar with his style, Topcliffian—descriptive note about Southwell added to the Council's order, also implies that the Council or one of its members (Robert Cecil's name comes to mind) allowed Topcliffe to write his own order:

Herein we are to require you to take that order for the safe keeping and close restraining of the said Southwell as appertaineth, being a most lewd and dangerous person, and this to be his sufficient warrant.

As we shall see, this was by no means the only time that the Council allowed Topcliffe to write his own warrant.

---

[1]*APC*, 23. 71 (28 July 1592).

[2]Verstegan, 79. Verstegan's date, 1 September, seems to be off by about a month, although it would not be surprising if it took that long for Topcliffe to act upon the Council's order.

[3]Devlin 1, 289.

Into the Tower, therefore, one of the most sinister prisons in Europe, and into the keeping of Richard Topcliffe, went Robert Southwell. He remained there for nearly two and a half years. Meanwhile, this sequence of events raises a whole set of questions. Who exactly was Richard Topcliffe? Just what kind of power did he have? How did he use it, and for what purpose?

Most important of all, why, in the early morning of 26 June, in the first exuberance of capturing his prisoner, did he write such a brusquely informal, joking letter to the Queen of England? Why did he not write to the Lord Keeper or to the Council? After all, it is not often that one finds a torturer writing directly to the head of state for his instructions.

Answers to all these questions will appear in due course.

*****

Two

Richard Topcliffe, Esquire

Richard Topcliffe, one of the most energetic agents of government in the last two decades of Elizabeth I's reign, is an absent figure in the mainstream history of the period. He seldom appears at all, and if he does, it is usually to be pigeon-holed with a phrase or two, "the notorious sadist," for example, or "the infamous Topcliffe."[1] More interesting than the phrases themselves, though, is the evasive historical maneuver they enable. When we diagnose a man as a sadist or describe him as infamous, we enroll him among the pathologically maimed, and thus remove him from the company and the counsels of the great, the good, and the normal. He is no longer a phenomenon to be observed, but an aberration to be explained away, and the explanations, naturally enough, tend to exculpate the society in which he found an outlet for his special tastes, and the employers who found his passions so useful.

"The Tudor monarchs generally observed the law," writes Penry Williams, the level-headed historian of Tudor government—always allowing, however, for a few exceptions, one of them being torture. In Williams's account, the power to inflict torture in England belonged to the Crown, acting through the Privy Council, "but there is some evidence that the official torturers, especially the infamous Topcliffe, sometimes acted without proper warrant."[2] The implication here is that Topcliffe had a liking for free-lance work, and so neither Crown nor Council can really be held responsible for his activities. James Heath, who has written the best study of torture and the law in Tudor and Stuart England, has nothing to say about free-lancing and torturing without warrant, but the career of Richard Topcliffe troubles him: "He was, however, fanatically hostile to Roman Catholicism and successful in attaching himself

---

[1]Weir, 50, 315; Williams 2, 393. Also Neale, 153: "that curious, sadistic gentleman, Richard Topcliffe;" Nicholl 2, 111: "We would call Topcliffe a sadist;" and Mathews, 293: "Topcliffe was a pathological sadist."

[2]Williams, 393.

to the highest centers of influence...he attained to a special working relationship with the Queen herself...."[1] This picture, too, portrays a
régime working for the most part benignly and within the law, but vulnerable to manipulation for his own peculiar ends by an unpleasant man
with a knack for ingratiating himself. "Attaching himself" is a nice way
of putting it: the Queen and her Council picked up Topcliffe the way
unwary ramblers in New England meadows pick up ticks in May.

This picture would have surprised Topcliffe's contemporaries.
Whether they liked him or loathed him, they would have been puzzled
by the implication that he was an outsider. From the moment he set foot
on the historical stage, Richard Topcliffe was an insider's insider, well-
born, well-connected, and knowing everyone of any importance there
was to know. They would have been equally puzzled by the suggestion
that a career pursued so publicly was in any sense illegal. A man with
some legal training himself, Topcliffe was always careful to have authority for his actions. Even the description "fanatically hostile to Roman
Catholicism" would have puzzled a contemporary. Calling someone a
fanatic, like calling him a sadist, marks him as unusual; these are isolat-
ing words, and in this case they segregate the man from the society in
which he was such an energetic, visible and successful actor. If
Topcliffe was a fanatic, so were the Crown's other servants, and so were
the people who gave him his instructions.

Understandable though the urge to segregate Richard Topcliffe from
English history is, a little reflection reveals the contradiction involved,
and Penry Williams, to his credit, states it, however reluctantly:

> Although legal opinion from Sir John Fortescue to Edward Coke unequiv-
> ocally stated that the use of torture was contrary to the common law, it was
> regularly used by the Privy Council in the sixteenth century...It is hard to
> reconcile this practice with a scrupulous regard for the law.[2]

So hard, in fact, that it cannot be done. Torture, which the Tudor monarchy used so freely against its own subjects, was—and is—illegal in English law no matter who authorizes it. It is one of the activities covered
by Magna Carta, specifically by its famous Cap.39, still, incidentally,
unrepealed:[3]

[1]Heath, 139.

[2]Williams, 398.

[3]Breay, 48.

> No free man shall be taken, imprisoned, disseised, outlawed, banished, or in any way destroyed, nor will We proceed against or prosecute him, except by the lawful judgment of his peers and by the law of the land.[1]

Magna Carta was renewed and confirmed under John's son, Henry III, and it was repeatedly confirmed under the succeeding reigns. Under Edward I, in 1297, it was entered into the statute books of the kingdom, and under Edward III the famous "six statutes" confirmed and emphasized the subject's rights as defined in the Charter's 39th article. Moreover, whereas the Charter had only guaranteed the rights of freemen, in 1331 the first of the six statutes (5 Edward III, cap.9) extended the Charter's protections to the people at large:

> It is enacted that no man from henceforth shall be attached by any accusation nor forejudged of life or limb, nor his lands, tenements, goods, nor chattels seized into the King's hands, against the form of the Great Charter, and the law of the land.

In 1354, the third of these statutes, 28 Edward III, cap. 3, not only spelled out unequivocally the extension of the subject's rights to all the people, but introduced the famous phrase defining proper procedure, "due process of the law:"

> Item, that no man of what estate or condition that he be, shall be put out of land or tenement, nor taken nor imprisoned, nor disinherited, nor put to death, without being brought in answer by due process of the law.

Finally, the sixth of these statutes, 42 Edward III, cap. 3 (1368), spelled out the full force of these protections:

> It is assented and accorded, for the good governance of the commons, that no man be put to answer without presentment before justices, or matter of record, or by due process and writ original, according to the old law of the land: And if any thing from henceforth be done to the contrary, it shall be void in the law, and holden for error.

Under the Great Charter and the confirming statutes, therefore, not only was the Crown subject to the law, but if Parliament enacted a statute in defiance of those statutes, it was "void in the law, and holden for error." Hence all those commissions to torture, whether Topcliffe's or anyone else's, all those summary imprisonments and punishments were in flagrant violation of the law no matter who authorized them. Magna Carta

[1]Howard 2, 43.

even forbade the imposition of ruinous fines that would destroy people's livelihoods, a key strategy in the Elizabethan state's push to impose religious conformity.

The principle of personal juridical right is so fundamental to English law that one can hardly imagine a worse offense against it than the torture of English subjects by agents of the sovereign power specifically charged with maintaining the laws intended to protect them. The government that does such things has itself turned criminal, and to call one of its most important agents a fanatical sadist is merely distracting. The fact to be noticed and recorded here is that in his own time and place there was nothing peculiar about Richard Topcliffe: that his was the face of his government in action, and the first question to be answered about him is: under what circumstances did a wealthy and respectable Lincolnshire gentleman embark on a career like that?

*****

Richard Topcliffe was born on 14 November, 1531, the eldest son of Robert Topcliffe of Somerby in the parish of Corringham, a village just outside Gainsborough, Lincolnshire.[1] The Topcliffes were originally from Yorkshire, from Topcliffe, in fact, on the River Swale, where Richard Topcliffe still owned property inherited from his father. The Topcliffes had acquired Somerby five generations earlier when a Walter Topcliffe married the daughter of Thomas Towers, whose family were the previous owners. Richard Topcliffe's grandfather John was a merchant of the Staple, presumably operating his business out of the port of Gainsborough, and he was a man of some wealth—it was he who depopulated the village of Somerby in order to raise sheep. He also brought a touch of genealogical glamor to the Topcliffes' pedigree when he married his son Robert to Margaret, daughter of his Gainsborough neighbor, Thomas, third Baron Burgh.[2]

The Burghs claimed descent from King John's justiciar, Hubert de Burgh (the Hubert of Shakespeare's *King John*), and they were intermarried with the Percies and the Nevilles—in fact, the Burgh's Gainsborough land came from the third Lord's great-grandmother, Elizabeth

---

[1]S.T.Bindoff, writing in Hasler, 3.513, is the authority for Topcliffe's birthday.

[2]Genealogical information about the Topcliffes is to be found in Maddison, 1000–01, "Topcliffe of Somerby in Corringham." Strictly speaking, Topcliffe's grandfather was the 1st baron, but since the revival of the title in 1916 he has been treated as the 3rd. For Burgh information, see "Burgh02," at: http://www.stirnet.com /main/index.php? option =com.wrapper& Itemid =79. Also *ODNB*, s.v., "Katherine Parr," and Rowse, 181–210.

Percy. Topcliffe's great-uncle Henry Burgh and his aunt Anne Burgh both married Nevilles. The third Lord Burgh himself, Topcliffe's grandfather, was chamberlain of the household to Queen Anne Boleyn, and Topcliffe's uncle, Sir Edward Burgh, was Queen Katherine Parr's first husband. Surviving evidence of Lord Burgh's dealings with other people suggests that he was a difficult man to get on with as well as a tyrant to his children. Eric Ives describes him as "an insignificant peer whose first achievement for [Queen] Anne was to vandalize Katherine of Aragon's barge for her use"—which he certainly did—but he was a keen supporter of the new approach to religion, and his Topcliffe grandson was intensely proud of him.[1]

The Burghs' Neville connections became important for young Richard Topcliffe when his father died in 1544.[2] The twelve-year-old heir's guardianship went to his uncle-by-marriage, Sir Anthony Neville of Leverton, Nottinghamshire, who was paid 20 marks a year (£6/13/4d) for his ward's upkeep. What happened to the heir himself is unknown, though the fact that years later (in 1568) he was to act on his aunt's behalf against the executors of his uncle's will suggests that the relationship was not an unpleasant one.[3] He seems not to have attended either university. In 1548, aged sixteen, he was admitted to Gray's Inn.[4] Then, on reaching the age of 21 in November, 1552, he "sued his livery," and entered into the possession of a considerable inheritance. The Topcliffe family property included lands in Nottinghamshire and Yorkshire as well as Lincolnshire, and seems to have comprised some 4,000 acres. It is not surprising that there was some family opposition to his inheriting such a large estate alone: an uncle and two cousins sued

[1]Ives, 264; James, 60–61. Rowse, 186, prints Topcliffe's marginalia about his grandfather found in a copy of Girolamo Pollini, *Historia ecclesiastica della rivoluzion d'Inghilterra*, Sig. B3, that Rowse owned, and bequeathed to the University of Exeter, where it now is: "Thomas Lord Burgh, my grandfather, being Lord Chamberlain, did openly pronounce him [Henry VIII] a villain in the Court, when his Queen was sent to the Tower, and did cast down his glove among such gentlemen and noblemen as did for popery speak against her fame. And for the same he was threatened to be sent to the Tower of London—which infamy was to like effect spoken of that godly Queen Anne, as here is printed." Since Topcliffe was four when this was supposed to have happened, the story is family legend at best.

[2]Bindoff says that Topcliffe's mother was already dead when his father died. This is not so. She had a long widowhood, and was buried at Louth, February, 1553 (Maddison, 1000).

[3]NA/REQ 2/130/16.

[4]Foster, Col.20.

him on the grounds that the family estate should have been divided between Richard's grandfather John's two sons, instead of descending to the eldest, Richard's father, Robert. The Court of Chancery finally dismissed the case in November 1560.[1]

At some point in this early period of his life, young Master Topcliffe made a good marriage. His wife was Jane, the daughter of Sir Edward Willoughby of Wollaton, whose family was as wealthy as it was well-connected. The Willoughbys were among the first English industrialists. Their money came from the Nottinghamshire coalfield under their land, and enabled Topcliffe's nephew, Sir Francis Willoughby, to build Wollaton Hall, his ostentatiously huge, and surely very ugly, house which survives as a museum belonging to Nottingham City Council.[2]

All of this information documents the growing-up of the rich heir of a propertied Lincolnshire family, and there is nothing particularly unusual about it. Towards the end of his life, though, writing to Robert Cecil, Richard Topcliffe made a statement about this early period of his life which changes the whole picture:

> Many envious eyes have beheld my plain doings, and would have been glad to have found some just cause to have exclaimed against me to her sacred Majesty or to her honorable Council, that either in heat, for malice, or through covetous corruption, I had stumbled, but I (knowing my own innocency from the first) and at my lxx[th] year of my age; and at the end of my xliv[th] year service of her sacred Majesty, and at the end of my xxxii[nd] year's service of this happy state (in which I am a simple freeholder), I do defy the malice and cankered hatred of the world, wherein none will wrong me, but traitorous Papists, atheists, or such as do countenance them for gain presently or for policy in time to come.[3]

In June 1601, when he wrote that letter, Topcliffe was indeed in his seventieth year. If he was then coming to the end of the forty-fourth year of

---

[1]NA/REQ 2/22/105; NA/C78/41/28.

[2]The marriage did not turn out well. The evidence for this is in letters exchanged between Topcliffe's niece Margaret Willoughby, married to Sir Matthew Arundell of Wardour, and her brother Sir Francis Willoughby. Unfortunately, the letters are undated, but were probably written in the later 1560s. In one letter, Lady Arundell is extremely worried about her "aunt Topcliffe" because Topcliffe "will not be got to pay his wife's portion," and in another she speaks of Aunt Topcliffe's "miserable condition, her husband not performing what he had promised for her maintenance." Lady Arundell even persuaded the bishop of London and others in commission with him to summon Topcliffe to appear before them, "and if this helps not,' she wrote, "I know not what will." The fate of the unfortunate Mrs. Topcliffe is unknown (Middleton, 530–1. The Middleton manuscripts are now at Nottingham University).

[3]Hatfield, 86/88. 11 June 1601.

his service to the Queen, he began serving her at the very outset of her reign, perhaps even a little before, since the forty-fourth year of her reign did not begin until 17 November 1601: if Topcliffe's forty-fourth year of service was ending in June 1601, then his service began in 1557, the year before Elizabeth I's accession. His third number is equally striking because it dates the beginning of what he calls his "service of this happy state" to 1569. That was the year of the Rising of the North, which gave such a shock to Elizabeth I and her advisers. It seems to have shocked Richard Topcliffe, too.

We do not know what network of patronage and affinity first led the twenty-six year-old Topcliffe into service with the young Queen who was so nearly his own age. The historian S.T.Bindoff thought the connection came through his wife's niece, Margaret Willoughby, who was one of the Lady Elizabeth's attendants at Hatfield. That is possible, though not very likely.[1] Topcliffe's own connections, through his grandfather Lord Burgh, with Elizabeth's mother, and through his uncle Sir Edward Burgh, with her step-mother, Queen Katherine Parr, who was his aunt, provide a more likely route for his acquaintance with her. One of Topcliffe's annotations to his copy of Pollini's *Historia ecclesiastica* implies that as a teenager he knew Queen Katherine Parr well:

> This lady Katherine Parr was first wife to Edward Burgh my uncle, he being son and heir of the Lord Burgh who was Lord Chamberlain to that godly Queen Anne Boleyn: whose virtues I have heard this lady my aunt Katherine Parr commend wonderfully.[2]

Young Topcliffe would have been fifteen when Katherine Parr died in 1548. Whatever the source of the relationship between himself and Elizabeth I, it began early and it lasted until the end of her reign. There is one hint of Topcliffe's early service with the Queen while she was still the Lady Elizabeth. Sir John Harington, writing to Prince Henry about his father's troubles for religion in Queen Mary's time, tells an interesting story:

> I may truly say, this prelate (Bishop Gardiner) did persecute me before I was born; for my father was by his command imprisoned in the Tower for

---

[1] "Richard Topcliffe," in Hasler, 3.513–15. (Topcliffe's brother-in-law, Sir Henry Willoughby of Wollaton, married Anne Grey, daughter of Thomas Grey, 2nd Marquis of Dorset: their daughter Margaret was Topcliffe's wife's niece. She married Sir Matthew Arundell of Wardour; their son was Sir Thomas Arundell, 1st Baron Wardour.)

[2] Annotation to p.174.

eleven months, for only carrying a letter to the Princess Elizabeth; and my mother was taken from her presence, and obliged to dwell with Mr. Topcliffe, as an heretic. My poor father did send many petitions to the Bishop, but in vain, as he expended one thousand pounds to get his liberty[1]

In another version of the story, Harington writes that, "My mother, that then served the said Lady Elizabeth, he caused to be sequestered from her as an heretic, insomuch that her own father durst not take her into his house, but she was glad to sojourn with one Mr. Topcliffe."[2] In the first version it sounds as if Gardiner had placed Harington's mother with Mr. Topcliffe in a kind of house arrest, and the implication, of course, is that Mr. Topcliffe was a sound Catholic. In the second version Topcliffe's house sounds more like a welcome refuge. Since both Topcliffe and Harington's mother served Elizabeth in the period just prior to her accession, that is the more likely version. One wonders if Topcliffe already owned his house in Westminster? Whichever version of the story one opts for, the implication is that Topcliffe was then—like the Lady Elizabeth herself— a conforming Catholic and a willing if half-hearted servant of Mary I's régime.

The exact nature of Topcliffe's early service of Elizabeth, once she became Queen, has also been a mystery. As early as 1573, the Council, acting on his behalf after a robbery, described him as "Her Majesty's servant," long before he was known as a hunter of Catholics.[3] Fortunately, Richard Topcliffe shared with his contemporaries a taste for litigation, and he has left quite a trail in the prerogative courts of Star Chamber, of Requests, and of Chancery. A feature of the procedure of those courts was that a complainant or plaintiff would initiate a case by presenting a "Bill of Complaint" to the court, and in the preamble to the Bill would often describe himself in some detail. Consequently, prerogative court cases can be a rich source of biographical information. In about 1589, Topcliffe sued William Robinson, an alderman of York, in the Court of Requests for money due him on land in Yorkshire. In

[1]Harington 3, 1.364.

[2]Harington 3, 2.67–8. Harington's story, though, has its own problems. Since he was baptized in August 1560, his mother cannot have been carrying him before the queen's accession. It is not even clear that his mother (née Isabell Markham) was married to his father then, since the first Mrs. Harington (née Etheldreda Malte) seems to have been still alive as late as 1559. Isabell, though, *was* in Elizabeth's service. See the entries for the Haringtons, father and son, in *ODNB*.

[3]See below, 49.

answering Topcliffe's Bill of Complaint, Robinson repeated Topcliffe's self-description, and in doing so answered the question that has puzzled historians for a long time: What, exactly, was Topcliffe's position at court? According to himself, it seems, his correct style was "Richard Topcliffe, esquire for the body to her Majesty."[1]

This is not the only example of his use of this surprising title.[2] There is no sign, however, of Topcliffe's name in the records of expenses of Elizabeth's Coronation, where all the members of the household and the Privy Chamber are listed, nor does he appear among the salaried members of her household. His position, therefore, was an honorary one.[3] His name is not in the few remaining lists of the New Year's gifts exchanged between the Queen and her household, either—although he was later to brag to one of his victims that the Queen had given him a gift of silk-embroidered white linen hose.[4] Nonetheless, the title describes his role in the Queen's entourage from the beginning. It certainly explains his standing at court, his presence on royal progresses, his free access to, and fiercely protective emotions towards, the Queen herself. The title also tells us that the young Topcliffe must have been a presentable fellow—Elizabeth Tudor liked to have handsome men around her, preferably with nice legs.

An esquire of the body's primary responsibility was the defense of his monarch's person; that attended to, his chief daily business, according to the "Black Book" of King Edward IV, was "many secrets."[5] Fittingly enough, therefore, Richard Topcliffe, Esquire for the Body, first stepped on to the historical stage as protector of the Queen and keeper of her secrets. In the autumn of 1569, the insurrection known as The Rising of the North or the Rebellion of the Earls broke out in the strongly Catholic

[1] NA/REQ 2/43/17.

[2] The label on the box containing A.L.Rowse's copy of Girolamo Pollini's *Historia ecclesiastica* includes the contemporary inscription, "Annotated by Mr Ric Topclyffe esquire of the body to Queen Elizabeth." The spelling of the name is Topcliffe's own, and the inscription is his own. Rowse had nothing to say on this subject in his 1987 essay on Topcliffe.

[3] NA/LC2/4/3. There were two salaried esquires for the body named, Robert Drury and Thomas Farnham, as well as a list of 4 "squires for the body ordinary": Roger Manners; James Marvyn; Henry Fortescue, and Richard Poynes.

[4] NA/C47/3/38 (anno 5); C47/3/39 (anno 19); C47/3/40 (anno 40); C47/3/41 (anno 45). Topcliffe's boast is printed in Verstegan, 97; the holograph is at Stonyhurst, *Anglia* I, no. 68, f. 119. See below, 222.

[5] Starkey, 34.

north of England. Its intention was to restore the Catholic faith and to remove the councilors responsible for its suppression. The Dudley brothers—Ambrose, Earl of Warwick, and Robert, Earl of Leicester, the Queen's favorite—were among those sent north to suppress it. By mid-December, when a large royal army under the Earls of Essex and Warwick and the Lord Admiral Clinton dispersed the rebels, any real danger to Elizabeth I's position had passed. All that remained for the government's officers to do, really, was to capture the leaders, and to terrify the northern counties into submission.[1] It was in that period, in January 1570, after the danger had passed, that the Earl of Leicester wrote affectionately to the Queen from Kenilworth Castle, complaining about the cold weather and an uncooperative messenger:

> The messenger I had thought to have sent to your Majesty found himself better at ease a great deal to remain where he is, and so wanting so fit a mercury as I made account of, was bold to send to your Majesty such one as I had of mine own, only that I might know and hear of your Highness' good estate...and fearing lest this hard weather will force messengers to be the slower, I have prayed this honest gentleman also to take the more pains, whose desire is as much to see your Majesty as my longing is to hear from you.

He then goes on to ask the Queen to remember her promise to send him a treasurer, and to say that his brother, Warwick, has arrived, cured of his gout by hard riding on the Queen's service "among your northern worse natured subjects." He then ends the letter with a postscript about the messenger who is so keen to see the Queen:

> If it please your Majesty for that Mr. Topcliffe is this messenger, my brother hath desired me, for that he thinks it good your Majesty should know who they are that have willingly and chargeably served in this journey against your rebels, that Mr. Topcliffe came to him with thirty horse and men all well appointed at his own charge and so continued all the time of service, without either requiring or receiving any wages or entertainment for himself or them, which he thinks fit your Majesty should know, for that it deserves your highness' gracious countenance.[2]

The willing messenger, then, was Mr. Topcliffe, who seems to have

---

[1]The chosen method of terror was summary executions in all the villages and towns of the affected areas. The Queen asked for 700 executions under martial law. Fortunately, her Provost-Marshal, Sir George Bowes, failed to meet that quota. Even so, "The bloodshed in the government's orgy of revenge was in marked contrast to the rebels' attitude to their victims" (Fletcher, 102).

[2]NA/ SP15/17/15b.

arrived at Kenilworth with Leicester's brother. It seems from Leicester's way of referring to Topcliffe that the Queen must know who he is, although she does not know about his remarkable gesture in equipping a troop of thirty horsemen for her service. A mere five days later, Topcliffe has been to court and back—quite a journey on horseback in winter[1]—and Leicester writes again to say that he is very glad to have news of the Queen:

> Now if it please your sweet Majesty that I may return to my wonted manner, your old [*eyes*] [a drawing of two eyes][2] are in your old ill lodging here, very well and much the better for the great comfort I have lately received, first by your treasurer, for whom I most humbly thank your Majesty, and next by Mr. Topcliffe, of your good and healthful estate, which is that above all earthly things I most pray for....[3]

Here then we have Topcliffe equipping a troop of horse in defense of the Queen, and riding a hundred miles each way to carry letters and messages between her and Leicester, the man who everyone agrees was her sweetheart. The only puzzle is Leicester's reference to him as "mine own." We have Topcliffe's own word dating his personal service to the Queen from before the reign's beginning. Yet there is now no doubt that Topcliffe served Leicester as well as the Queen. Years later, when he wrote offering his services to Gilbert, newly Earl of Shrewsbury following his father's death, Topcliffe explained his situation thus:

> For my part, if you will license me to honor you and love you still in that plain manner I have done, I shall not leave any faithful part or duty unperformed that shall become one of my profession to one of your state; and I was never so fit to offer and perform so much as now I am, for I that was entangled by many obligations (not long since) unto Leicester and Warwick (never for that lucre which was the lure to many followers) now am a freeman, and all bonds be cancelled by their deaths, and I at liberty to love whom, and where I list.[4]

Until very recently, despite this plain statement, there was no other evidence of Topcliffe's connection with the Dudley brothers; but now his name has appeared in the newly-discovered Leicester household accounts for 1584–86, and Simon Adams has inferred that Leicester's

---

[1] A round-trip of 200 miles.

[2] "Eyes" was Elizabeth's nickname for Leicester.

[3] NA/SP15/17/31.

[4] Talbot Papers, Vol. H (Lambeth MS 3199), f. 215.

patronage secured Topcliffe's seat in the Parliament of 1572 as a member for Beverley. Most striking of all, a letter that Topcliffe wrote to Leicester while he was in the Netherlands has surfaced in a Dutch library.[1] The significance of this Dudley connection is that for a long time some people have thought that Leicester was behind Topcliffe's more unsavory activities, and as we shall see in due course, the Dutch letter implies as much. It seems very likely, too, that Topcliffe's Dudley connection began, like his state service, with the Northern Rising and his rallying to the Queen's service with his thirty horsemen.

*****

When the Northern Rising ended in failure, the Nortons of Norton Conyers, a family of some consequence in northern Yorkshire who had been among its leaders, were among the gentry families whom its failure ruined. Attainted of high treason, Richard Norton, the head of the family, fled to Flanders with three of his sons, where he died in poverty, aged 91, in 1585. His son Christopher and brother Thomas, convicted of treason, were hanged, drawn, and quartered at Tyburn. His Yorkshire lands, Rylstone, Linton, and Threshfield, worth £110 a year, went to the Crown; and in 1570 Richard Topcliffe, no doubt thinking that he was owed something for his thirty horsemen, asked for them. The Queen, thrifty soul that she was, was not about to grant them outright. Instead, she gave Topcliffe the stewardship of the properties, and with that grant Mr. Topcliffe's service of the state began in earnest.[2]

He quickly found that administering forfeited rebel lands in his ancestral county of Yorkshire was not easy work. A string of lawsuits that he pursued in the courts of Requests and Star Chamber from the outset of his administration in 1571 until 1577 documents the local resistance he encountered. Lands were concealed, moneys withheld, produce removed, all with a surprising degree of violence. Local men attacked the Queen's keepers at least twice.

The leaders of the local resistance were "one Thomas Proctor of Cowpercote in Craven," an elderly man in his seventies, and his son, John. The Proctors, of whom there were several families dotted about the landscape of North Yorkshire, were a force in the district of Craven,

---

[1]In Adams 3, 218–9, Leicester pays Topcliffe £5 for "certain books." The letter to Leicester, which I owe to Roger Kuin, is in Teyler's Museum, Haarlem, Netherlands, MS Teyler 2376 fol. 53. See also Adams 1, 215, and below, 138.

[2]*ODNB*, s.v. "Richard Norton;" NA/SP12/75/31, 32; 152/54.

and they caused Topcliffe a good deal of trouble.[1] His sequence of Star chamber suits against them began in 1571 when he sued a pair called William Dunwell and Ralph Kighley.

Dunwell was Thomas Proctor's servant. Proctor had sent him and a party of other local men on a poaching raid into what was now the Queen's manor of Rylstone. There they met the Queen's newly-appointed keeper, William Ellsworth, who challenged them, whereupon they beat him up. In Topcliffe's vigorously phrased complaint, we hear his own prose style for the first time. As steward of her Majesty's manors of Rylstone, Threshfield, and Linton in Craven, and as overseer and keeper of her highness' woods and game, he begins, he had appointed William Ellsworth as keeper, a position he has enjoyed peaceably and quietly since. Notwithstanding, William Dunwell, Robert Morehouse, Ralph Kighley, William Kighley, Jeffrey Tenant & Stephen Halliday:

> being very lewd and disordered people and such as be obedient to no law, and the said William Dunwell partaker of the late rebellion in the north parts...did about the 23rd day of January now last past in very riotous, contemptuous, shameful, and rebellious manner assemble and gather themselves together about ten of the clock in the night, and with force and arms entered without any color or shadow of title in and upon your Majesty's said grounds and woods, and then and there with very unseemly and unlawful weapons invasive and defensive, that is to say with long pitchforks, pikes, staves, bows, and arrows, crossbows, swords, bucklers, forest bills, and other very unlawful weapons, and then and there having greyhounds, hounds, crossbows, and guns did not only in most contemptuous, lewd, and disordered manner hunt, course, kill, and chase the deer and game in your Majesty's said woods and grounds to the great destruction and spoiling of your Majesty's said game in the said grounds but also then and there finding the said William Ellsworth, deputed and appointed keeper under your Majesty's said subject in God's peace and your Majesty's then being, did very riotously and rebelliously and with a murderous and felonious intent, and in most foul and disordered manner violently assault, beat, wound, and evil entreat the said William Ellsworth in such foul and disordered manner that they left him for dead and in very great peril and danger of his life, contrary to your highness' laws and statutes...

---

[1] The best known and probably the nastiest of the Proctors was Stephen, son of Thomas Proctor of Friarhead, would-be courtier and pest to his neighbors, who made money collecting fines from prosecutions brought by informers under the penal statutes against the practice of Catholicism. He bought the Fountains Abbey estates, built Fountains Hall, and was knighted, but over-reached himself when an attempt to have two neighbors, Sir William Ingleby of Ripley and Sir John Yorke of Nidderdale, convicted of complicity in the Gunpowder Plot brought him up against Henry, Earl of Northampton. He died intestate and much indebted in 1614 (See Jensen, "Recusancy, festivity and community," in Dutton, 104–6; also *ODNB*, s.v. "Proctor, Sir Stephen").

In response to this explosion of Topcliffian legalese, Dunwell more or less admitted the truth of the complaint. He owned up to the grey-hounds, and he agreed that on the day in question, he and his compan-ions had indeed set off on Proctor's orders for a nocturnal hunting expe-dition. They met Ellsworth in Rylstone woods; he challenged them, they beat him up, and went home. The only difference between Topcliffe's complaint and their story was that according to them, their hunting desti-nation was not Rylstone, but a property belonging to the Earl of Cumber-land: they were merely passing through Rylstone woods on their way there, and beat up the keeper in self-defence when he challenged them—an unlikely story.[1]

This was the beginning of Topcliffe's Yorkshire problems. The Proc-tors, probably because of long-standing regional loyalties and seniorities, either saw themselves as in some sense surrogates for the Nortons in their absence, or—more likely—saw an opportunity to grab some of the Norton lands for themselves. Topcliffe accused Proctor of installing a former rebel, a man called Harrison, as keeper of Threshfield, and another rebel, his nephew, as tenant of Rylstone Tower. Then, when Topcliffe put his own man, Childe, in Harrison's place, Harrison and his supporters attacked him in Rylstone church. The Proctors also tried hard to keep some of the Nortons' property out of Crown hands by claiming prior usage agreements, and they removed tithe corn, turfs, and peat from one of the manors.[2]

Then, to complicate matters, there was—as one would expect—local feuding, even within the Proctor clan itself. By 1574, the Proctors of Cowpercote, father and son, were bound by recognizances of £100 each to keep the peace; nonetheless, on Whit Sunday, 1574, there was another riot in Rylstone Church, and although it had nothing to do with Topcliffe or his deputies, he prosecuted it in Star Chamber. William Proctor of Bordley Hall and his brother Jeffrey met on Whitsunday 1574 in Rylstone Church in the presence of Thomas Proctor of Friarhead to arrange a reassignment of the lease of Bordley Hall with John Proctor of Cowpercote. Why Proctor of Cowpercote was acting in this matter at all does not appear from the documents in Topcliffe's suit. The Proctors of Bordley had leased the hall for generations from its original owners, the monks of Fountains Abbey, and then from their lay successors. The lay

[1]NA/STAC5/T.5/14; T.28/30 (1571–2).

[2]NA/STAC5/T.33.5 (1572–3), Item 2 ("Interrogatories to be ministered unto Thomas Proctor of Cowpercote, yeoman, upon his answer unto the Bill of complaint exhibited in the Star chamber by Richard Topclyff Esquire"); NA/STAC5/T.10/29 (1575–6).

owner in 1574 was the estate of John White, alderman of London, but by the end of Elizabeth I's reign the Proctors of Bordley owned the freehold themselves, so it seems very likely that the transaction in Rylstone Church was a step in their acquisition of the property, with their kinsman, Proctor of Cowpercote acting as an intermediary.

In any case, the Proctors of Bordley produced their 200 marks earnest money, and it was placed in bags (that Proctor of Cowpercote brought for the purpose) on the board covering the church font. John Proctor then refused to hand over the lease, saying that he needed legal advice. When his man, Backhouse, looked into one of the money bags, a Londoner present promptly grabbed it, shouting that it belonged to his master and no-one else, and the riot broke out in earnest. John Proctor attacked Proctor of Friarhead, throwing him to the ground, and "sore wounding" him. Meanwhile, William Proctor of Bordley took the rest of his money back, and fought his way out of the church.[1]

It is true that the north of England was still a fairly wild place in the sixteenth century, and Topcliffe—though himself a northerner of Yorkshire origins on his father's side—strongly disapproved. Asked why he was prosecuting a riot in which he and his affairs had no part, he answered, in a replication written in his own hand, that since he took on the administration of the Norton lands, as appointed by the Court of Exchequer, John Proctor, Thomas Backhouse, and the other persons named in his bill of complaint have:

> committed and made divers riots, wrongful entries, and heinous misde-
> meanors in and upon her Majesty's lands aforesaid; and have quarreled in
> the Church of Rylstone (before the time of this riot committed) with her
> Majesty's keepers and officers; and (in great assemblies) they have been
> assaulted by them and put in great danger of their lives, and sore wounded.

And he went on to say he that he was prosecuting this riot because there was no other way of coping with the troubles that he had encountered as her Majesty's officer in the region, adding for the court's information that John Proctor caused the trouble in this case by refusing to fulfill covenants, and then by refusing to put the money paid in escrow until his doubts were satisfied.

Whatever views one comes to have about Topcliffe on the basis of his later career, it is apparent, on the evidence of these Star Chamber documents, that in Yorkshire he was doing his best to be a responsible administrator for the Queen. He was not alone in his opinion of the

---

[1]This story is told in NA/STAC5/T.32/18 (1575–6); NA/STAC5/T.18/7 (1576–7).

Proctors, either. Some of the local people agreed with him. One of them, asked as a witness in the suit that followed the attack on Childe the keeper in Rylstone Church, if John Proctor of Cowpercote was of quiet conversation and demeanor among his neighbors, answered that for many years he had been a "commersome" man, full of suits, a great vexer of his neighbors for his own gain—in fact he thought Proctor had troubled more people with suits in Craven than any other ten people. Other witnesses agreed that Proctor was "an unquiet man" and "given to suits." He and his father sound like a pair of local bullies. Topcliffe's energetic administration must have surprised them.

At one stage of Topcliffe's campaign to recover concealed lands, the older Proctor had been summoned to appear before a Parliamentary commission sitting at Ilkley to inquire into the concealment of rebel lands. He did not like Topcliffe's approach at all, and said so:

> And the said complainant [i.e., Topcliffe] being there present at the examination of this defendant, which is very rarely permitted, did himself read the interrogatories or the most part of them, and with eager and sharp countenance, unseemly speeches, and in taunting manner disturbed this defendant, saying at the first reading and answering of the said interrogatory to this effect, "Hear, masters, here is he perjured;" and divers times after, "Here he lies," and sometimes, "There thou art perjured," and with such lewd and disordered behavior entreated this defendant of intent to discountenance him and to drive him from his memory, then being a man of the age of threescore and thirteen years or more, and vexed with infirmity of sickness divers ways....[1]

Naturally, Topcliffe denied that he had been rude to Proctor (though this first report of his speech on record sounds very like him). The fact was, he insisted, that Proctor had perjured himself, and he went on to say exactly how. One of the witnesses, who had been on the commission's jury, agreed with Topcliffe's version of the matter; and one of the questions put to this witness indicates that Topcliffe himself persuaded the commission to suppress some of Proctor's testimony to protect him from the consequences of his perjury.[2] It was evidently more important to Topcliffe to secure the lands than to punish Proctor. A letter from him in the Hatfield papers to an unknown recipient (presumably William Cecil) indirectly records his success in this campaign, for it asks that none of the Norton lands in Craven under his stewardship should be sold

[1] NA/STAC5/T.18/21 (1572–3)

[2] NA/STAC5/T.20/23, items 3,4 (1573–4).

or granted to anyone else, because he had won them from the Proctors, father and son, after they had twice succeeded in concealing them.[1]

*****

Topcliffe's relationship to the Queen and Leicester explains his presence on the Nortons' Yorkshire estates from 1570 until at least 1577, but there was another important connection in his background that gave him influence and a measure of power in the north. This was his connection with the Talbots, Earls of Shrewsbury.

Bindoff thought that Topcliffe owed his intimacy with the Shrewsburys to his guardian during his minority, Sir Anthony Neville,[2] but Topcliffe mentions his family's long allegiance to the Shrewsburies in two letters. Writing to Gilbert, the seventh earl, upon his accession in December 1590, he mentioned "the old honor my foregone friends [i.e., my deceased relatives] have borne to your house;" and years later he had to remind the earl that "under [your] forefathers my ancestors have made proof of their loyal affections to their Sovereigns, and true love to the Earls of Shrewsbury."[3] There was evidently a long-standing Topcliffe-Talbot relationship, and the implication of the second statement is that at one time it had involved military service under the Talbots. In one of the marginal notes to his copy of Pollini's *Historia ecclesiastica della rivoluzion d'Inghilterra*, Topcliffe mentions his father's and Lord Burgh's service under the Earl of Shrewsbury against the rising of 1536 called the Pilgrimage of Grace.

George, the sixth Earl of Shrewsbury, was immensely wealthy, with three castles to live in (Tutbury, Pontefract, and Sheffield) as well as grand houses at Worksop, Sheffield, and Buxton. Not surprisingly, he was very powerful in the north midlands and Yorkshire. His wealth derived from hard-headed industrial and commercial exploitation of estates in Yorkshire, Derbyshire, and Nottinghamshire that were rich in coal, iron, and lead. When he acceded to the earldom in 1560, he was already a member of the Council of the North, constable of Pontefract Castle, and captain-general of the footmen in the army in the north. In 1565 he was named lord lieutenant of three counties: Yorkshire,

---

[1]*Hat. Cal.,* 13.102. This undated letter shows that Topcliffe prosecuted his cases against the Proctors to a successful conclusion.

[2]Hasler, 3.513.

[3] Talbot papers, Vol. H (Lambeth MS 3199), f.215, 8 December 1590; Vol. M (Lambeth MS 3203), f.184, 20 Feb. 1603/4.

Nottinghamshire, and Derbyshire. He joined the Privy Council in 1571. His active political life, however, came more or less to a complete stop when, in 1569, he found himself appointed keeper of Mary, Queen of Scots. The Queen chose him for this task because his wealth enabled him to afford it, and because the remote situation of his many properties kept Mary well out of trouble's way. Until Elizabeth relieved him of the assignment in 1584, it monopolized his time and resources. In fact, between Mary and his virago second wife, Elizabeth Cavendish—better known as Bess of Hardwick—not to mention Elizabeth I as well—the sixth Earl of Shrewsbury was probably the most hen-pecked nobleman in England.

This is the Earl of Shrewsbury with whom we find Topcliffe in regular communication in the 1570s and 80s. The first letter to survive, a very friendly one, shows him asking Shrewsbury in his capacity as an Elizabethan industrialist to supply him with four tons of lead.[1] It appears from the letter that Topcliffe had already bought iron from him ("so good as ever I did see"), and that the lead, which he had agreed to provide "unto the Councilors our partners," was "for the making of vessels for our work." Shrewsbury himself was not a partner in the "work," which was a speculative venture. Topcliffe had great hopes of it, but he had known better than to involve Shrewsbury in something so uncertain: "I was fearful to present an unknown, or uncertain thing to one who so greatly I honored, so was I cowardly to my repentance." In fact, the "work" was an alchemical scheme to turn iron into copper. Some time in 1574 Topcliffe, in company with William Humfrey, assay-master of the Tower mint, met with an alchemist called William Medley on behalf of Burghley and Leicester.[2] These were the "Councilors our partners" of Topcliffe's letter who had invested money in the scheme: in the previous September of 1573, Burghley had advanced Topcliffe £50.[3] Medley, whom Sir Thomas Smith had recommended, claimed to have a

---

[1]Talbot papers, Vol.F (Lambeth MS 3197), f.87, 26 May 1574.

[2]Strype 1, 2.1.521. Topcliffe seems to have been the author of a report of this meeting sent to Burghley.

[3]NA/SP12/92/31, Sept. 1573. (This note of a bond between Burghley and Topcliffe for the payment of £50 is incomplete. The dates when the money is to be paid are missing, and the signatures are lacking. But Burghley is to pay Topcliffe the money for the purposes spelled out in an indenture between A and B, dated Y, and if Topcliffe doesn't pay it back at a certain limited time, then the covenants are void. This is the payment that has led people to infer mistakenly that Burghley was Topcliffe's employer, but it seems pretty definitely to be an advance towards the copper-making project.

secret that would produce a ton of copper a week—but one imagines that despite Topcliffe's energy in rounding up lead and iron the partners never saw any copper.

It's hardly surprising that in pre-chemical England even the most powerful men in the country would cherish hopes of converting one metal into another by alchemy. Another alchemist whom Burghley took seriously was Dr. John Dee's associate, Edward Kelley, whom Burghley asked to supply him with a gold-making tincture to finance the war against Spain.[1] What is interesting about this episode for the student of Richard Topcliffe's rôle in Elizabethan life is that it shows him as the partner, associate, and friend of Burghley and Leicester, a man to be taken seriously, respected, and listened to, above all a man whose company is to be enjoyed. That is the way he appears in his correspondence with the Shrewsburys, too.

One of Shrewsbury's many estate-development projects was the exploitation of the medicinal springs at Buxton in Derbyshire. The Talbots had owned the springs since 1461, but their use had been prohibited under Henry VIII as part of the general closing down of all pilgrim sites, including holy wells. Mineral water springs, Buxton among them, came back into use for medicinal purposes under Elizabeth I, and at Buxton the Earl of Shrewsbury built a grand, battlemented mansion house of four stories to house the noble and fashionable visitors who flocked to the springs there. The building included a great hall and lodgings for thirty.[2] The Earl of Leicester was among Buxton's patrons, and in the summer of 1577 Topcliffe was there with him. Following the visit, as he moved on from one house party to the next, he wrote a familiar, chatty letter of social news and gossip to the Countess of Shrewsbury:

> We did yesternight come to Rycote, my Lord Norris's, where late did arrive the Countesses of Bedford and Cumberland, and the Earl of Cumberland, the Lord Wharton and his wife—the fat earl cometh this day—my Lord of Leicester being departed toward the Court to Sir Thomas Gresham's thirty-three miles hence (whereby you may perceive of his health), only a little troubled with a boil drawn to a head in the calf on the leg, which maketh him use his litter. The Countess kept him over long waking, asking him if Buxton sent sound men halting home—but I never did hear him commend the place nor the entertainment half so much.[3]

[1] Nicholl 2, 259.

[2] Hembry, 3, 9–11.

[3] Folger MS X.d.428, No.125 (9 July 1577).

"My Lord Norris" is Henry, first Baron Norris, whose very grand Oxfordshire house, Rycote, came to him as part of his wife's inheritance. She was Margery, daughter of Sir John Williams, a man who became rich under Henry VIII out of the sale of confiscated Church properties: he probably built the house. The Norrises were great friends of Elizabeth I, who nicknamed Lady Norris "Crow." The rest of the house party were a family group, all of them in high favor at court. The Countess of Cumberland was Margaret, daughter of Francis Russell, second Earl of Bedford, newly married to George Clifford, third Earl of Cumberland, who was also one of the party. The marriage turned out badly. She was a high-spirited, very bright young lady—she will have been the countess who made the joke about the effect of Buxton on Leicester's health. The Countess of Bedford was her father's second wife, hence her step-mother. Lord Wharton was Philip, third Baron Wharton (1535–1625), named after his godfather, King Philip of Spain; his wife, Frances Clifford, was the Earl of Cumberland's sister, and so sister-in-law to the newly married Countess of Cumberland. And who was "the fat earl," hourly expected to join this family party? It was presumably the head of the family, the great Earl of Bedford himself, magnate, Privy Councilor, and keen Protestant. He certainly looks plump enough in his portraits. If it was Bedford, then Topcliffe felt no qualms about sharing what must have been a standing joke about Bedford's girth with the Countess of Shrewsbury. Perhaps they had all been at Buxton together.

One suspects, though, that these people never did anything for the mere fun of it. A short concluding paragraph to this letter implies that the Shrewsburys wanted something from Leicester in addition to his company, and that Leicester wanted something from them in addition to the medicinal effects of the Buxton springs, also that whatever Leicester wanted, Shrewsbury was not enthusiastic about it. Hence the letter to the wife:

> I can send your Ladyship no more unpleasant news but that his Lordship hath said with many vows that he will be as tender over your Lord and yourself, and both yours as ever his own health. And my Lord is very careful over his two young cousins Mr. Edward and Mr. Henry, to have them placed in Oxford, wishing that he may find of his kindred to work his good will upon, as he hath done hitherto of many unthankful persons. Good madam, further you my good Lord your husband's disposition that way. For your son Charles, my Lord will bring his old dead suit unto a new life....

Nonetheless, here is Topcliffe taking part in, and chattering and joking about, mutual back-scratching in the highest zones of Elizabethan society. It may have been on this visit to Buxton that he added his name and motto or "device" to a large window in the great guest hall at Buxton. Though the window itself is long gone, a diagram of the inscriptions on it survives. They include verses by Mary, Queen of Scots (who was allowed to visit Buxton for her health) and her secretary Nau, as well as the Earl of Pembroke (Shrewsbury's son-in-law), and others. Topcliffe's device is an erupting volcano accompanied by the words, "Ætna mons. Dulcior vitæ finis" ("Mount Etna. A sweeter end to life"). The implied reference is presumably to Empedocles, the philosopher who was supposed to have flung himself into Etna to prove his immortality; perhaps Topcliffe's image plus motto means "A death like that of Empedocles is desirable, being quick and merciful." If it does mean that, or something like it, then it is the first sign we have of a quirk in his psyche.[1]

A year or so later, when Shrewsbury was having alterations made to his London house, Topcliffe was on hand with Gilbert Talbot, Shrewsbury's eldest son, to check up on the quality of the work, even calling on "Mr. Clarentius" (Robert Cook, Clarencieux King of Arms), who had designed a heraldic decoration for the roof of one of the rooms:

> This afternoon, I called upon Mr. Clarentius and had sight of that work he hath set out for the roof of your chamber besides your gallery, which as it shall exceed in rareness of device and beauty, so is it thought no two of any estate in England can be able in honor to reach to perform the like.

—and went on to chat about the looming appointment of a successor to Lord Keeper Bacon, and a visit to England by the German Calvinist prince, John Casimir.[2] During this period, too, Shrewsbury was in difficulties with his tenants in Glossopdale in the High Peak district of Derbyshire whose rents he had raised. With the backing, apparently, of his wife and one of his sons, the tenants had appealed to the Privy Council. Unable himself to go to London (because of his responsibilities towards Mary, Queen of Scots), Shrewsbury needed agents to speak for him before the Council. He therefore sent his son, Gilbert, accompanied by Topcliffe. According to Gilbert, writing to his father on Easter Saturday, 1579, he and Topcliffe had met with the tenants at Barnet on their way to London, and tried, ineffectually, to reason with them. Then, when the case went to formal hearing before the Council, first Gilbert

---

[1] Bath, 2.22: "1573–1582. 'A note of things written in the glasse windowes at Buxtons.'" I owe the suggested interpretation of the device to John Frodsham.

[2] Talbot Papers, Vol.F (Lambeth MS 3197), f. 291. 28 Feb. 1578/79. Richard Topcliffe to Earl of Shrewsbury, Earl Marshal, from Mr. Talbot's house.

spoke to the Council, then four tenants' representatives were called in, and then Topcliffe, whose performance on Shrewsbury's behalf certainly impressed Gilbert: "I protest to your Lordship before God," Gilbert writes to his father, "that Mr. Topcliffe hath taken as very great care and pains therein, as if it had lain upon his own estate and all the friends he hath besides in England."[1]

At this period of his life, when Topcliffe was busying himself with gossip and business for the Talbots, he was in his mid-to-late forties, a good age in Elizabethan times. He was evidently a man of some presence, extremely well-connected, energetic and useful to his friends. There is no sign in his activities or his letters of the interests that would soon make him notorious. In fact, in all this chatter about windows, boils, court news and fat earls, there is no sign of a consistent career or avocation at all. Administering the Norton estates for the Queen, managing an alchemical project for Leicester and Burghley, and running interference for Shrewsbury in his troubles with tenants all look like the activities of a middle-aged man who is still in search of a career that he can call his own. Yet he has told us himself that his service of the state began in 1569. In his own mind, therefore, when he scratched his peculiar motto into the window at Buxton he was well embarked upon his mid-life career of state service, and the question is, how did a career of state service that began with administering the Norton estates lead him to the torture chamber?

*****

---

[1]Talbot Papers, Vol. P (Lambeth MS 3206), f. 951 (Easter Eve, 1579). For an account of the Glossopdale dispute, see Stephen E. Kershaw, "Power and duty in the Elizabethan aristocracy: George, earl of Shrewsbury, the Glossopdale dispute and the Council," in Bernard, 266–95.

Three

Topcliffe, Esquire, and Policeman

We do not know how or when Richard Topcliffe first discovered that he was one of nature's policemen. Although his activities at the height of his power are so well documented that it would be possible to compile a near-daily record of them, the record toward the outset of his career is naturally much sparser. We know that crime crossed his personal door-step in the early 1570s when, by an odd coincidence, he was twice robbed. In 1571, someone broke into his house in Westminster, and stole £50 worth of clothing—from which S.T.Bindoff inferred that he was something of a dandy.[1] Then in early 1573, thieves broke into his Lincolnshire house as well. We know this because the Privy Council wrote instructing the Lincolnshire assize justices to examine a burglary committed by a pair of Irish brothers "in the house of Richard Topcliffe, her Majesty's servant." Quite apart from the fact of the robberies them-selves, we learn from the first of these records that in 1571 Topcliffe already owned the house in Westminster where he would later interro-gate prisoners, and from the second we learn that in 1573 he was suffi-ciently important among the Queen's servants for the Privy council to write to the Lincolnshire justices on his behalf. It seems a fair inference, too, that he supplied the information contained in the Council's letter, both the fact that he had been robbed, and that the perpetrators were a pair of Irishmen called Walter and Daniel Dwiggen. By 1573, then, he had begun to develop an interest in catching and punishing law-breakers.[2]

A document in the Shrewsbury papers, probably written in February, 1579, reinforces this conclusion because it shows Topcliffe acting as the senior partner of a pair of detectives. The writer of the document, a man

---

[1]Which indeed he was. The culprit, one Mathew Bowcher, was caught and prosecuted, 30 December 1571. Among the stolen items was a a black velvet coat laid with gold and silk lace and lined with taffeta, an embroidered guard of silk, a black doublet, two pair of velvet breeches, two pair of black satin and silk stocks, and garters (Jeaffreson, 1.75).

[2]Hasler, 3.513; *APC*, 8. 213 (21 March 1573).

49

called Richard Cotts, one of the Earl of Shrewsbury's staff, tells the Earl that he has been at Lincoln with Master Topcliffe:

> ...where I heard (at large) the second examination of that prisoner there which your honor doth know of. And although Master Topcliffe (very wisely) persuaded the party rather to unsay that which he had said, than with deceitful and false words seek to prolong his life contrary to all honesty and truth, he did then not only offer to pawn his life in gage upon the trial of his first examination, but also could readily repeat unto us the very self-same words set down before in writing....

Cotts then goes on to describe the evidence of this man whom Topcliffe had persuaded to talk, how "within this twelve month" he had "been at sundry robberies." Then:

> Master Topcliffe hath taken his journey to Grimsby, and to other places adjoining upon the sea coast, only to lay wait and see if he can hear of any of the suspected persons. As time doth serve, so your honor shall have further intelligence.[1]

Here, then, we find Topcliffe interrogating a suspect in a case involving multiple robberies. Acting upon information received in the interrogation, he goes off alone, with an enthusiastic thoroughness that we will come to recognize, to hunt for the rest of the gang. As for his methods, there is no hint of violence or coercion, and his partner Cotts is full of admiration for his approach.

*****

As we have already seen, Topcliffe's administration of the Norton estates, beginning about 1570, involved him in a certain amount of detective work as he went about looking for concealed lands and diverted revenues. It was a quest that took him into the heart of the northern Catholic resistance that produced the Rising of 1569, and, of course, he was always acting as an agent of the Crown. William Cecil shared his interest in the Catholics of North Yorkshire; there is a docu-

---

[1] Talbot, Ms. 704, f. 51 (11 February [n.y.]. The verso of this document, like many of the others, is covered in tiny, scratchy writing by Nathaniel Johnston, the 17th–18th-century antiquarian who had access to, and indeed owned, some of the Talbot papers now at Lambeth. There is a "Burnelo" mentioned in the letter who may be Edward Burnell, whose case figures in letters from Lord Gilbert and his wife, 6 March 1578/79 (Ms. 697, f.53, with a ref. to "The obtaining of the judges' opinion on [Edward] Burnell's matter") Burnell was an Irishman arrested in Canterbury for smuggling Catholic books. The Council instructed Thomas Norton to interrogate him (*APC*, 10. 246).

ment among the Burghley papers in the Lansdowne manuscripts giving a genealogy of the Nortons and their relations the Mortons, Plumptons, and Thurlands under the heading, "A tribe of wicked people." These are the very people among whom Topcliffe made his first catches for the state.[1]

The story begins in 1575 when a man called Afferton, a servant of Samson Morton, a nephew of Nicholas Morton, was arrested in the north. Topcliffe examined this man "so closely...that he was brought to reveal strange conspiracies."[2] The full story behind this cryptic note emerges some\ years later in another of Topcliffe's letters to Robert Cecil.

In 1575, Nicholas Morton, a Yorkshire-born, Cambridge-trained English priest who began a promising ecclesiastical career under Mary I was the most famous, or notorious, member of the Morton family. Upon the accession of Mary's half-sister, Elizabeth, he went into exile at Rome, where he became the English penitentiary at St. Peter's, and later joined the staff of the English College. In the mid-60s he began lobbying for Papal action against Elizabeth's régime. In February 1569 Pius V sent him to England to gather information, perhaps also to work as a penitentiary, but definitely not to engage in political activity. Nonetheless, once in England he went into his native north country, where he met the Earl of Northumberland, Thomas Markenfield, and his kinsman, Richard Norton, all three of whom played leading roles in the Northern Rising that developed soon after Morton returned to Rome.

Markenfield later said that he had asked Morton whether the Queen was excommunicated, and that Morton had told him she was excommunicated in law because she had refused to admit a Papal nuncio. Naturally enough, the government concluded that Morton's visit had contributed to the Rising.[3]

Nicholas Morton had a brother, Robert, whose second wife was Richard Norton's sister, Anne. This couple had three sons, Robert, Daniel, and Samson, the employer of Afferton. Robert left England about 1568, went traveling about Europe, and then spent three years in Rome with his uncle Nicholas. In October 1573, he entered the college at Douay to begin the study of theology, presumably intending to become a priest, but instead, probably owing to his father's death, he returned to England,

[1]BL Ms. Lansdowne 27, No.?, cited by Stapleton, cxxxii-iii.

[2]Strype 1, 2. 577–78.

[3]*ODNB*, s.v. "Nicholas Morton;" Hughes, 3.273n.

where he married Ursula, the sister of a kinsman, Edmund Thurland. A few years later, he and his wife decided to leave England. By July 1578 they were on shipboard on the point of leaving to join their uncle Nicholas in Rome when Richard Topcliffe arrested them.[1]

After Burghley committed Robert Morton to the Gatehouse prison, Ursula wrote to him, 18 July, petitioning for his liberation. On 30 July, though, the Council wrote to Bishop Aylmer of London, Sir Owen Hopton, the Lieutenant of the Tower, and Recorder Fleetwood, instructing them to examine Morton. Topcliffe had arrested him "upon notice of his intention to depart out of the realm with his wife, whereof there was cause to suspect some ill meaning of him," and so the three examiners were required to send for him and examine him "for the discovery of his intention...*and if Mr. Topcliffe be in the City to use some conference with him, and after examining of the said Morton to advertise what they find*" (my italics).[2]

The examiners did not consult Topcliffe, who was not in the city, and they made no dramatic discoveries. The hum-drum substance of Robert Morton's examination was that, intending to go abroad, he had sold his goods and land for £91, and that his wife would not let him go without her. Friends at court added their voices to his wife's petition, and he was released. Had the examiners conferred with Topcliffe as instructed, perhaps he would have told them the same startling story that he told Robert Cecil nearly twenty years later: that Robert Morton had been:

> a practicer for his uncle in a conspiracy for the stealing away of the Scottish Queen from the old Earl of Shrewsbury, and murder of the Earl, which practice intended I revealed to her Majesty, and have the confessions of the parties extant for proof.[3]

This dramatic and surely unlikely story is probably the substance of the "strange conspiracies" revealed in the examination of the mysterious Afferton three years earlier. If so, then it looks as if neither the Queen nor Burghley was impressed by the evidence, even though they thought well enough of Topcliffe as an expert on the Yorkshire Catholics to instruct their examiners to consult him.

Topcliffe, in fact, ran into opposition over Robert Morton's arrest. Writing to the Earl of Shrewsbury, 30 August, from the Queen's prog-

[1]Topcliffe to Robert Cecil, 12 June 95 (Hatfield, 32/94); Anstruther, 238–9; Pollen 1, 135–6.

[2]*APC*, 10. 295; NA/SP12/125, No. 31.

[3] Hatfield 32/94.

ress that year, Topcliffe thanked him for backing him up over Morton: "Your Lordship's countenancing me about Morton is well taken of her Majesty."[1] As the Oxford Dictionary tells us, "to countenance" used in this sense means "to favour, patronize, sanction, encourage, back up, bear out." Topcliffe, therefore, had needed authorization and support to act against Morton, and had received it from Shrewsbury, with the Queen's approval.

He was annoyed to hear that Morton was released; but ten years later Topcliffe—who had an elephant's memory and a long reach—had his revenge. Robert Morton's wife who could not bear him to leave without her died, probably in 1586, and he left England again, successfully this time, joining his uncle in Rome in April of that year. Nicholas Morton, though, was in failing health, and died January 1587. Robert, who must have been fond of his uncle, arranged for a memorial tablet to be set up in the English College chapel, where it is still to be seen. In April 1587, he entered the College himself, and received all the orders as far as deacon. He then left Rome for Rheims, was ordained to the priesthood, 14 June 1587, and set off for England 2 July 1587 where, as Anstruther laconically puts it, "Topcliffe was waiting for him."

By 1587, Topcliffe was sufficiently well-informed about the movements of English Catholics to have notice of Robert Morton's arrival. He tracked him to his wife's family's house at Gamston, Nottinghamshire, then picked him up back in London, where he was arrested and later condemned, 26 August 1588. He was executed two days later, one of twenty-eight Catholics, both priests and lay people, killed in the autumn of 1588 following the Armada victory: "He was prudent in action; about thirty years of age [actually forty]; a good height, his hair and beard inclining to red."[2]

The significance of this case for us is that it records Topcliffe's first recusant catch, which developed from his administration of the Norton estates. It also tells us that because of his standing at Court the Council was prepared to use him as a consultant. Robert Morton, of course, was a layman when Topcliffe first caught him in 1578. When Topcliffe caught his first priest four years later in 1582, he too was a man with Norton connections, actually born on the Norton estates.

A letter to the Earl of Shrewsbury in the Hatfield papers, dated 12 April 1578, provides another sign of Topcliffe's emergence at this time

---

[1] Lodge, 2.187–91.

[2] Hatfield 32/94; Pollen 2, 273.

as an expert on northern Catholics. The writer—presumably Burghley—had received an interesting, if puzzling, bundle of letters from Shrewsbury:

> My very good lord, I have received your lordship's letters of the 9th of this present, with others to Mr. Topcliffe which, because he is not here about the court, according to your lordship's request I have opened. And for that I neither know or heretofore have heard anything of the same Matthew Throwpe of whom you write to Mr Topcliffe, neither the said Topcliffe is here to make me acquainted with the man or matter, I cannot as you desire deliver my opinion what were fittest for you to do herein, further than that I think it convenient, having the said Throwpe's hand, being a suspected person it were not amiss he were detained in safe custody until he be sufficiently examined and discovered at what time Mr Topcliffe shall come hither, or that I may be more perfectly informed from your lordship of this man and matter. I will not fail to send you my opinion accordingly what I judge meetest by you to be done with him.
>
> For the other matter your Lordship writeth of in your said letter, touching Mr Cumberford, I will think how the access to him where he now is in custody may be cut off. And so humbly commending your lordship to God I take my leave. From Greenwich the 12th of April 1578.[1]

The letter is unsigned, perhaps never sent, but from it we learn that the absent Topcliffe is the expert on this unfortunate man Throwpe (or Thorpe) whom Shrewsbury is here instructed to keep in custody until Topcliffe "examines and discovers" him. The implication is that Thorpe was a Topcliffe catch. The Mr. Comberford referred to at the letter's end is the old Marian priest Henry Comberford, the deprived precentor of Lichfield cathedral who was to spend twenty years in prison without trial, dying 4 March 1586 in the Hull Blockhouse in his late eighties. A further implication of the letter might be that Topcliffe was interested in Comberford, too.

*****

When the Council wrote instructing their examiners to consult Topcliffe about Robert Morton, the court was staying at Audley End, Essex, during the 1578 royal progress into East Anglia. The progress had started in early May, and was to last until late September. By the beginning of August, when the Queen and her court reached Sir William Cordell's house at Long Melford, Suffolk, Topcliffe—as we learn from his long letter to Shrewsbury—had joined them.[2] If the opening of that

---

[1] Hatfield 161/10.

letter means what it seems to mean, he did not travel north from London to join the progress, but south from somewhere in the north, visiting the earl *en route,* and taking in a detour to Kenilworth with Gilbert Talbot. If that was his itinerary, then his shipboard capture of the Mortons will not have happened in the Port of London, but in some northern, east coast harbor, probably Grimsby or Whitby.

Topcliffe's long letter to Shrewsbury from the progress, like his arrest of Robert Morton, is an important marker in the early stages of his career as the Elizabethan state's policeman—not that he had joined the progress in that capacity. He was there as Topcliffe of Somerby, honorary esquire of the body, with his sixteen quarterings, and as such he received privileged treatment. When Elizabeth visited Burghley's house, Theobalds, in 1572, the esquires of the body were lodged near to the Queen's withdrawing room and dining gallery; their neighbors were the lords Warwick, Oxford, and Rutland plus Sir Thomas Heneage, the treasurer of the household.[2] As an esquire, then, Topcliffe was one of the inner circle, and in 1578—if we judge by his letter—he enjoyed himself immensely in their company.

It is common knowledge that the Elizabethan court regularly spent its summers on "progress" into the southern English countryside, and that these progresses gave the Queen an opportunity to present herself to more of her people, and to enjoy their adulation. Zillah Dovey's wonderfully detailed account of the 1578 progress reveals the extraordinary amount of administrative organizing that went on behind the scenes to produce the required effects.[3] To begin with, entertainment of the Queen on a progress was not simply a matter of wealthy proprietors along the way opening their houses and buying new bedclothes for the occasion—as popular history would lead one to believe. Once a progress began, alternating teams of privy chamber staff under the supervision of a gentleman-usher requisitioned the houses where the Queen would stay, often spending as long as six days there to prepare them for the residence of the Court and Council. Then, while the Queen was stay-

---

[2]For a chronology of the progress and a list of the houses visited, see Cole, 191–91. Topcliffe's letter is printed in Nicholls 1, 2.215–19.

[2]*Hat.Cal*, 13.110–11 (22 July 1572).

[3]*An Elizabethan Progress: The Queen's Journey into East Anglia, 1578* (Frome, Somerset, UK: Alan Sutton Publishing Ltd., 1996). I have adapted the following account of events on the progress, with permission, from my "Performance and Reality at the Court of Elizabeth I," in Kirby Farrell and Kathleen Swaim, eds., *The Mysteries of Elizabeth* (Amherst, MA.: University of Massachusetts Press, 2003), 3–20.

ing in a house, it was hers, not the owner's. The rooms she used were furnished with her belongings for her purposes, including her tableware. For as long as she stayed there, the house became the Court, and therefore came under the rule of the Lord Chamberlain and his staff. Consequently, with the exception of palaces belonging to very grand hosts like Leicester or Cecil, who were themselves part of the inner Court circle, the Queen probably never saw much of her host's houses as they lived in them themselves, and certainly didn't see much, if anything at all, of her less important hosts. But then she probably never saw the provincial towns and cities she visited as they really were, either.

Norwich, the second largest city in the kingdom, was the destination of the 1578 progress, and as one reads Dovey's account of the preparations required there, the suspicion intensifies that an Elizabethan progress was a forerunner of the Potemkin Village phenomenon. First, the city council was required to clean the place up, widening and graveling the roads. Then, for the month of August they had to be sure that the city was clear of livestock (cows, pigs, and horses), that no cows were milked in the city, and that all butcher's waste was carted away and buried. As for the inhabitants, they had to repair and paint their houses "towards the street's side," and repair the pathways outside their doors. They had to see that their privies were emptied and their chimneys swept. Once all that had been taken care of, there was the equally carefully regulated interaction between the Queen and the city to be provided for, consisting mostly of congratulatory shows and performances, and gifts for the Queen and her more important courtiers and servants. To arrange the performances at Norwich, the court provided three writer-impresarios, Thomas Churchyard, Bernard Garter, and Henry Goldingham. As for the gifts, there were probably very precise specifications for them, too, to judge from the level of detail the courtier planners were prepared to handle in all other aspects of the progress. Even the cathedral, which was an independent jurisdiction within the city, operating under Crown oversight, had to submit to courtly supervision. Chief usher Anthony Wingfield spent two days at the cathedral, making sure, as Dovey remarks, "that the Dean's preparations were adequate."[1]

---

[1] All these details are from Dovey's book, where the account of the doings at Norwich occupies Chapter 4 and makes very amusing reading. For the bishop, Edmund Freake, whom the Queen and Council thought too soft on Catholics and too hard on Puritans, the progress will have been a trying experience. He was the Queen's own appointment, but how was he to know that the royal "line" on Catholics and Puritans in East Anglia had changed for this progress?

The government, however, did not expend the time and treasure a progress demanded solely for pleasure and mutual congratulation. A progress was also a projection of royal power into the districts visited. In 1578, the first clear sign of this aspect of the progress appeared during the Queen's two-night stop at a house in Euston, Suffolk, belonging to a young Catholic gentleman, Edward Rookwood. During the Sunday, or perhaps the Monday morning, of the Queen's stay, the young man was brought into her presence, either by arrangement or by her own request (the account is not clear on that point) to receive her thanks for the use of his house, and to kiss her hand. The men in the Queen's entourage construed this as a liberty on Rookwood's part, and the Earl of Sussex (acting as Lord Chamberlain, the officer responsible for regulating admission to the Court) called him before him, and berated him, as a Catholic, for having the nerve to kiss the Queen's hand. He then dismissed Mr. Rookwood from the Court (which meant, at that moment, dismissal from his own house), and commanded him to await the Council's pleasure at Norwich. Then, a piece of the Queen's plate being missed, there was a search of the hayrick to find it. Whether they found the plate (which was probably never missing in the first place) is doubtful; instead they found, hidden in the hayrick, a very beautiful image of the Virgin. The finders brought it to the Queen as she was watching a dance of country people, and she commanded it to be burnt.

One detects the hand of the scenario-writer as clearly in this incident as in any of the later shows at Norwich. The whole sequence of events, including the search, has the appearance of a put-up job. Moreover, the basis of the scenario behind this display of power was a routine played over and over by Elizabeth and her councillors, known to modern journalists as the good cop/bad cop routine. In this case the Queen graciously extended her hand to be kissed; the Lord Chamberlain then swung the truncheon, so to speak, and there is no record of any demurral on the Queen's part at so gross a breach of hospitality as the arrest of her host while she was staying in his house.

This very public disgrace of a young Catholic landowner in his own house was the first move in a considerable show of power in East Anglia. Before the court left Norwich itself a couple of weeks later, the Council had interrogated nine wealthy local Catholic proprietors. They imprisoned Rookwood and another man in Norwich gaol; the remaining seven were put under house arrest with reliable local citizens, and required to post £200 bail guaranteeing that they would take daily instruction from the bishop or a deputy until such time as they were willing to conform to the state's own Church of England. At Woodrising on

their way home out of Norfolk, the Council interrogated two more gentlemen, Edmund Wyndham, formerly Professor of Civil Law at Cambridge, and Sir Henry Bedingfield. Wyndham received the same punishment as the Norwich seven, but Sir Henry—who had been a major figure
at the court of Mary I—was required to post £500 bail. There was no
reason to suspect any of these gentlemen of political crime. One explanation for the government's severity is that it was part of a steady inten-
sification of anti-Catholic measures that would continue into the last
years of Elizabeth I's reign.

A more specific reason was that it was only six years since the execution of the fourth Duke of Norfolk had left a power vacuum in East
Anglia that the government was anxious to fill and be seen to fill.
Although the Duke himself had been a Protestant—in name at least—the
Catholic sympathies of his family, their friends and dependents, were
well-known. Moreover, the interrogation of East Anglian Catholics was
not the Crown's only means of displaying its power over the Howards
and their affinity in their own country. The same point was made
through the symbolism of the progress itself when the Queen's officers
requisitioned the great Howard palace of Kenninghall to house the
Queen and her entourage.

Kenninghall had been closed, and its contents inventoried, at the time
of the arrest of the fourth Duke in 1571. Its opening in 1578 to house the
Queen and Court was probably its first use since then. In principle the
Duke's young heir Philip Howard was the Queen's host both at
Kenninghall and later at the Howards' town house in Norwich, but this
was not a matter over which he had much if any say. The visit cost him
upwards of £10,000, an enormous sum, and left him with heavy debts.[1]
It would be hard to imagine a more complete enactment of the substitu-
tion of royal power for ducal influence.

Topcliffe's letter written to Shrewsbury from the Progress, 30 August,
is our source for the narrative of the hazing—for that is what it was—of
Edward Rookwood. The whole letter, which is partly personal, partly
official, and partly a newsletter, is a fascinating projection of court policy as it was developing at the time, though so far it has not been read in
that light. Helen Hackett used Topcliffe's gloating account as the opening incident of her *Virgin Mother, Maiden Queen,* where she was not at
all happy about the story because it places responsibility for an unpleas-

---

[1]Dovey, 56–9. Philip Howard's title, earl of Surrey, was forfeited with his father's
execution in 1572. In 1580, upon the death of his maternal grandfather, he became earl of
Arundel.

ant incident on the Queen herself;[1] but then she reassures her reader that it is only Topcliffe's version, and that as a man "notorious for his pursuit and persecution of Catholics...he had his own reasons for wanting to stress Elizabeth's active participation." Zillah Dovey, otherwise so level-headed, shares Hackett's response to Topcliffe's story. Topcliffe, "extremely anti-Catholic," is "the arch-enemy of Catholics and authorized torturer;" hence he wrote with a bias, and it is "unfortunate" that his is the only account we have[2].

It is a measure of the enduring power of the Elizabethan myth that two scholars should so mistake Mr. Topcliffe and his letter. To begin with, in 1578 Topcliffe had no reputation at all as the arch-enemy of Catholics, and he had not tortured anybody. Nor was he "with the royal entourage" in East Anglia, as Hackett put it: he was *part* of it. It's important, too, to insist that he wrote as a witness, not a participant; he claimed no role in the affair for himself.[3] Even the language he uses is not necessarily his own. He does, however, give an impression of authority, and it is worth pausing a moment to see how he does this: he frames his account of Rookwood and his image of the Virgin with private conversations between himself and the Queen which would have left Shrewsbury in no doubt that the letter was a bulletin from the innermost circles of the progress.

He begins by telling Shrewsbury—who, we should remember was an extremely senior earl and Privy Councilor—that besides ordinary news, some of it probably old, some new, he has a personal message for him from the Queen that he will "keep in store:"

> having charge from her Majesty to your good Lordship all tending towards her gracious favor and affiance in your Lordship, of whom her Highness saith she hath daily most faithful trial, which the Lord knows I joy at, next some comfort I received of her for myself that must ever lie nearest my own heart.

One is bound to wonder how the earl reacted to this curiously packaged

---

[1]Hackett, 2. "Topcliffe attributes agency to her," is the way she puts it.

[2]Dovey, 37, 54.

[3]Hackett even wonders whether Elizabeth was being "manipulated by Topcliffe and his cronies," but this speculation is probably only mischievous fabling in defense of Gloriana. If serious, it reveals considerable ignorance of the way life was arranged at the Elizabethan court. If anyone other than the Queen and Council was responsible, then on the basis of Topcliffe's letter one would say it was Sussex, who may have wished to reingratiate himself with the Queen after a humiliating reprimand he received at Long Melford. See Dovey, 45.

royal testimonial. One implication of the phrasing might be that the earl's reputation at Court needed bolstering; another that Topcliffe had a royal command to convey that the earl would have to attend to. Yet another implication might be that Topcliffe was outgrowing any dependence he had on the Shrewsburys. It appears, too, that the Queen liked him, and had something very nice to say to him as one of her attendants. This mildly sinister prelude out of the way, Topcliffe moves quickly to the letter's real subject, which is the political business accomplished on the progress.

> The next good news (but in account the highest) [is that] her Majesty hath served God with great zeal and comfortable examples;[1] for by her counsel two notorious Papists, young Rookwood (the Master of Euston Hall, where her Majesty did lie upon Sunday now a fortnight, and one Downes, a Gentleman, were both committed, the one to the town prison at Norwich, the other to the county prison there, for obstinate Papistry; and seven more gentlemen of worship were committed to several houses in Norwich as prisoners; two of the Lovells, another Downes, one Bedingfield, one Parry, and two others not worth memory, for badness of belief.

The words "by her counsel" (orig. "Cownsaille") are ambiguous. Does the phrase mean that the Queen herself advised the commitment of the two notorious Papists, or does it mean that her Council committed them? When Topcliffe refers unmistakably to the Council in the next paragraph, he spells the word "Counsell." In this sentence both the spelling, "Cownsaille," and the idiom suggest that the word's meaning is "advice." That being so, Topcliffe is letting Shrewsbury know that this policy he approves of so strongly is the Queen's own. The detailed account of the Rookwood affair, which follows, makes the same point:

> This Rookwood is a papist of kind newly crept out of his late wardship. Her Majesty, by some means I know not, was lodged at his house, Euston, far unmeet for her Highness, but fitter for the black guard;[2] nevertheless (the gentleman brought into her Majesty's presence by like device) her excellent Majesty gave to Rookwood ordinary thanks for his bad house, and her fair hand to kiss; after which it was braved at. But my Lord Chamberlain, nobly and gravely understanding that Rookwood was excommunicated for papistry, called him before him; demanded of him how he durst presume to attempt her real presence, he, unfit to accompany any Christian person; forthwith said he was fitter for a pair of stocks; commanded him

---

[1]"To serve God" in Topcliffe's language is to be a good Protestant.

[2]"Lowest menials of a royal or noble household, who had charge of pots and pans and other kitchen utensils" (*OED*).

out of the Court, and yet to attend her Council's pleasure; and at Norwich he was committed. And, to decipher the gentleman to the full: a piece of plate being missed in the Court, and searched for in his hay house, in the hayrick such an image of Our Lady was there found, as for greatness, for gayness, and workmanship, I did never see a match; and, after a sort of country dances ended, in her Majesty's sight the idol was set behind the people, who avoided: she rather seemed a beast, raised upon a sudden from Hell by conjuring, than the picture for whom it had been so often and long abused. Her Majesty commanded it to the fire, which in her sight by the country folks was quickly done, to her content, and unspeakable joy of every one but some one or two who had sucked of the idol's poisoned milk.

Topcliffe here describes a carefully scripted little play with two scenes. The first, "The discovery of Edward Rookwood," begins when the young man is brought to receive his guest's thanks for her use of his house. The house and the entertainment have been more modest than the visitors expect, and the Queen's "ordinary thanks" cues the men in the audience to protest Rookwood's admission to "the real [i.e., 'royal'[1]] presence," whereupon Sussex, as chamberlain, using extremely insulting language, calls him before him, and dismisses him from the court—in other words orders him out of his own house. Was Topcliffe one of the audience who "braved at" Rookwood's being admitted to kiss the royal hand? His account reads like the work of an eye-witness, and his language communicates vividly the atmosphere of bullying humiliation; it's like a scene from an Elizabethan forerunner of *The Godfather*, or a foretaste of Cornwall's and Regan's behavior "on progress" at Gloucester's house in *King Lear*, Act 3, scene 7.[2]

Scene two, "The Discovery of an Idol," follows very naturally. One thing the Queen and her entourage knew was that in a Catholic house there were Catholic things to be found by a person who knew how and

---

[1] Some recent commentary (e.g,. Montrose, 83) has made heavy weather of this phrase as Topcliffe's bad-taste pun on the doctrine of the "real presence" in the sacrament of the altar. But "real presence" was not Topcliffe's phrase. It was the Lord Chamberlain's, and there's no reason to doubt that he was using it literally to mean simply "the royal presence." *OED* indicates that the primary meaning of "real" was "royal," and the primary meaning of "presence" was "the place or space in front of or around a person; the immediate vicinity of a person...frequently with reference to ceremonial or formal attendance on a distinguished, esp. royal, person." Had the Lord Chamberlain intended some kind of clumsy pun on the dogma of the real presence, his theologically discriminating Queen, already seriously irritated by him during the progress, might well have boxed his ears.

[2] As Regan says, Gloucester's house, like Rookwood's, "is little, the old man and's people / Cannot be well bestowed" (2.4.288).

where to look for them. Young Rookwood's image will have been one
of his family's treasures. No doubt he hid it in his hayrick—one understands why—and someone among his people, perhaps unintentionally,
had betrayed him to a court snoop.[1] Once again we are experiencing a
scripted performance, and again the Queen initiates the real action when
she commands the burning of the image. Topcliffe strongly approves of
the action and the policy behind it, though how much his language
reflects his own beliefs, and how much his obsequiousness to the Queen
is hard to tell. It would be a mistake to treat his language as entirely his
own. At this stage of his career, Topcliffe was a follower, not a leader,
an observer, not a participant. What we hear in his letter is the mood
and tone of the court on that progress.

   He then announces to Shrewsbury the corollary of the anti-Catholic
policy, which was to encourage the more extreme Protestants in the
region:

> Shortly after, a great sort of good preachers, who had been long com-
> manded to silence for a little niceness, were licensed, and again com-
> manded to preach, a greater and more universal joy to the countries, and
> the most of the Court, than the disgrace of the Papists; and the gentlemen
> of those parts, being great and hot Protestants[2] (almost before by policy
> discredited and disgraced) were greatly countenanced.

   Then, just as the letter began with the Queen speaking to Topcliffe, this
part of it ends with her speaking to him again, and we discover the letter's real purpose:

> I was so happy lately, amongst other good graces, that her Majesty did tell
> me of sundry lewd Popish beasts that have resorted to Buxtons from these
> countries in the south since my Lord[3] did come from thence: Her High-
> ness doubteth not but you regard them well enough; amongst whom there
> is a detestable Popish Priest, one Dereham, or Durand, as I remember, at
> the bath, or lurking in those parts after the ladies. Mr. Secretary hath writ-
> ten to your Lordship as he said, in this his letter here enclosed, to wish

---

[1]The destruction of Mr. Rookwood's picture of Mary is another example of the careless
criminality of this régime. Neither the Queen nor her Council have any memory, sense,
or understanding of the constitutional limitations on their behavior written into the kingdom's statute books.

[2]In using this phrase to describe the kind of Protestants called Puritans, Topcliff was
anticipating Robert Persons, to whom it is usually attributed, by a couple of years. In *A
brief discours* (1580), Persons defined Puritans as "the hotter sort of Protestants." See
Clancy 1, 22 and n.26.

[3]The Earl of Leicester.

your Lordship to apprehend him; to examine him of his coming to the Church; and, upon the least or lightest occasion, to commit him, and to certify the Lords thereof; and they mean to send for him, as Mr. Secretary said, upon further causes. Hereof he did give me charge to signify your Lordship besides his letter. It had comed to your Lordship's hands ere now, but that my best nag by chance did break his leg, wherefore I trust your Lordship will pardon me.

Here, and for the first time at the very outset of Topcliffe's new career we find the Queen discussing the behavior of "lewd Popish beasts" with him; and since these particular beasts are lurking at the bath at Buxton, which belongs to Shrewsbury, and since Topcliffe worked for Shrewsbury as well as the Queen, we can infer that this was not merely a moment's social gossip. The Queen was giving Topcliffe a job.

One of the houses visited on this progress was Costessey Hall, home of the widowed Lady Jerningham. Lady Jerningham's husband, Sir Henry, had been a strong supporter of Queen Mary, and one of her Privy Councilors. The Jerninghams were Catholic, and as Edward Rookwood found out, a visit from the Queen at a Catholic house was not necessarily a sign of favor. The priest called Dereham, who was now so much on the Queen's and the Council's mind, was schoolmaster to Lady Jerningham's grandchildren, and a member of her household. He must have been at Costessey on 19 August when the Court was there, because the Council summoned him to appear before them at Norwich.[1] When he failed to appear, they brought Topcliffe in, presumably because of his Shrewsbury connection and his knowledge of Buxton. The Queen spoke to him personally, and Secretary Wilson instructed him to instruct Shrewsbury to arrest the priest—he even wrote his own letter which he enclosed with Topcliffe's.[2]

One has to wonder what Shrewsbury made of all this. Earls, generally speaking, did not care to take instruction from their inferiors, no matter how many quarterings they had. Besides, as Topcliffe's letter acknowledges, not everyone on the progress approved of the image-burning, the treatment of the Catholic gentlemen, or the encouragement of the Puritans. From what we know of Shrewsbury, had he been with the progress he might have been one of them. Topcliffe's letter, *enclosing* Secretary Wilson's with his own, is designed to let Shrewsbury know that

---

[1]*Hat. Cal.*, 2.194.

[2]Dereham went free a little longer. Two weeks after Topcliffe wrote, the Council heard he was back in Norwich, "attendant for the most part about the Lady Jerningham's," and instructed Bishop Freake to arrest him (Dovey, 76–7).

Topcliffe is intimate with the Queen and her ministers, that he feels free
to pass on a number of their personal remarks, and that while he may
feel required to caress Shrewsbury with flattery, he is also letting him
know what is expected of him as a representative of the government in
his country. In fact, this letter could be construed as a rather sinister
document, especially in view of Topcliffe's later career and dealings
with Shrewsbury. Sometime before his death in 1590, Shrewsbury sev-
ered his connection with Topcliffe; it would not be surprising if the
seeds that grew into this change of mind were planted with this letter.
"Mr. Topcliffe is in favor," the earl may have said to himself, "and it is
going to his head."

*****

The next three to four years pass with no sign of Topcliffian
policework.[1]

Then, early in 1582, the picture changes entirely.

In 1580, Thomas Alfield, son of an usher at Eton, himself a graduate
and fellow of King's College, Cambridge, left England for the college at
Rheims. He was ordained priest at Châlons and was back in England in
time to be present at the execution of Edmund Campion and his companions, 1 December 1581. He wrote an account, *A True Report...Observed
and Written by a Catholic Priest, which was Present thereat,* which
Richard Rowland printed in late February 1582[2] on a secret press in
Smithfield. The little book included four poems, one of them Henry

---

[1]There is one possible exception. More, Bk. 2, Sec. 19, prints an undated letter from
Thomas Pounde, the Jesuit lay-brother who, after being imprisoned by Horne, bishop of
Winchester, in 1576, was to spend the remainder of the reign in one prison or another. In
the letter, Pounde describes being examined by Justice Young and five or six commissioners, Topcliffe among them, whom he describes (in More's Latin translation of his letter) as *Toplifus quæstionibus præfectus,* translated back into English by Edwards 2, 59,
as "in charge of examinations." Simpson 3, 30, describes the letter as written to Pounde's
companions in Winchester gaol shortly after his committal to the Marshalsea, 11 March
1576. This date, though, cannot be correct, because 1576 is far too early for Young and
Topcliffe to be acting together as interrogators, or for Topcliffe to be described as
quæstionibus præfectus. Young's first appearance in State Papers as an examiner of
Catholics is 9 October 1584 (*CSPD 1581–90,* 205), his first commission by the Council
as a torturer on 24 April 1587 (*APC,* 15. 51).

[2]Recorder Fleetwood's report dates the printing to the first week of Lent, 1582. Ash
Wednesday fell upon 28 February that year. The full title is *A true reporte of the death &
martyrdome of M. Campion Iesuite and preiste, & M. Sherwin, & M. Bryan preistes, at
Tiborne the first of December 1581. Observid and written by a Catholike preist, which
was present therat. Wherunto is annexid cetayne verses made by sundrie persons.*

Walpole's "Why do I use my paper, ink, and pen," which William Byrd set to music. (The authorship of the other poems is uncertain: Walpole, Rowland/Verstegan, and Stephen Vallenger have all been suggested.) Alfield's book found a ready audience. William Allen incorporated his narrative into his own *A Brief History of the Glorious Martyrdom of Twelve Reverend Priests*. In this form, and translated into Latin and Spanish, Alfield's work went on to reach a large continental audience, and caused the English government severe embarassment.[1]

Their first reaction was to instruct William Fleetwood, the Recorder of London, and Richard Topcliffe to look for the original book's author and printer. After the search was over, Fleetwood wrote Burghley, bragging that he "pursued the matter so near" that he found the press and a number of the books, and he mentions that in the process of the search it just so happened that, "one Osborne a Seminary priest came dropping into a chamber, where Mr. Topcliffe of the Court" and he were rooting about looking for incriminating papers and books. So, of course, they arrested him.[2]

Topcliffe had already filed his own very prompt report of the same incident. It is much more detailed, and says nothing about Recorder Fleetwood's role in the search.[3] The chamber was in Symons Inn, and it belonged to a man called Norwood who, Topcliffe says, was the publisher of the book. Like Fleetwood, he says that Edward Osborne, "did by great fortune come to one Norwood's chamber whiles I was searching of his study, books, and papers:"

> And starting suddenly from thence (loath to be known), I caused him to be pursued and taken. He confessed that he was a seminary priest returned from Rheims a little before Christmas. He had received six of the traitorous books of Campion's, Sherwin, and Brian's martyrdom, as they term it.

In this account we hear for the first time the clear tones of a policeman's voice. Osborne's capture, though, was an accident.

How did Topcliffe come to be in Norwood's chamber in the first place? The first part of his report describes another priest, William Deane, whom Fleetwood had committed to Newgate prison, 21 February 1582. Topcliffe had captured Deane a little while before he caught Osborne, no doubt as part of the same operation. He was a Yorkshire man from

[1] For Alfield, see *Anstruther*, 3.

[2] BL Ms. Lansdowne 35, No. 26. Transcript in Pollen 1, 27–28.

[3] NA/SP12/152/54. Transcript in Pollen 1, 26–7.

Linton in Craven on the Norton estates, and Topcliffe knew a great deal about him. He had been a Church of England curate at Monk Fryston, North Yorkshire, until Thomas Alfield, the author of the Campion book, reconciled him to the Catholic Church. He then left England for Rheims, intending—according to Topcliffe—to serve his old master, Richard Norton; but Alfield gave him a letter of introduction to William Allen, and with it he entered the seminary at Rheims, 9 July 1581. He was ordained at Soissons in December, and left for England 25 January 1582, where Topcliffe caught him just a few weeks later.

Deane was the first priest Topcliffe caught. The case gave his employers proof, if they needed it, of his skill in detection. The Alfield-Deane connection makes it likely that Deane's arrest led Fleetwood and Topcliffe to the press and the other distributors: threatened with torture, Deane and Osborne both broke down and told all they knew.[1] Norwood tipped off the printer, Rowland; he escaped to his native Netherlands, where he resumed his original family name, Verstegan, and went on to a remarkable career as publisher, prose writer, poet, scholar, engraver, and intelligencer. Topcliffe then found forty more copies of the book in a desk belonging to Edward Cooke, a clerk employed by Proctor Smythe in Paternoster Row. They arrested him, and went on to raid the house of a man called Stephen Vallenger, whom they suspected of complicity in the writing of the book. They found a manuscript copy written in his hand, but he denied authorship.

Vallenger was tried as author in Star Chamber, 16 May 1582, and sentenced to the maximum that Star Chamber could impose: imprisonment in the Fleet during pleasure, a heavy fine, exposure in the pillory, and his ears to be cropped.[2]

By then they had caught Alfield himself, 7 April, whose own father may have had a part in turning him in.[3] It seems likely that, under tor-

---

[1] For Deane and Osborne, see Anstruther, 100, 261–2, and Burton-Pollen, 351–9. Deane's lapse into co-operation was brief; he was indicted in King's Bench in 1583, and was banished in 1585. Both priests named the people for whom they had said Mass, and Osborne gave evidence against Lord Vaux and Sir Thomas Tresham at their trial. He too recanted, and went back to Rheims where Allen could find no place for him. He then went to Rome, and eventually fetched up in Spain, where he was dead by 1600. A sad story: Osborne, as Allen should have known, was quite unsuited to the dangers of the English mission.

[2] He may have written one of the poems. Fr. Persons thought he had been punished for writing the poems (CRS 4.38; also see Petti, 248–64). Vallenger was a Church of England clergyman; he held the prebendal stall of Selsey in Chichester Cathedral until his deprivation in 1582 (Questier, 160).

[3] Anstruther, 3.

ture, he admitted his authorship, but this knowledge did not lead them to mitigate Vallenger's sentence. Earless, Vallenger spent nine years in prison, dying there in November 1591. Alfield survived to be arrested again, tried, and sentenced to death in 1585 for distributing yet another book, William Allen's *A True, Sincere and Modest Defence of English Catholiques.*

From the government's point of view, the investigation had gone extremely well: in Topcliffe they had a new, very effective agent. Not surprisingly, they appointed him, 15 March 1582, along with Recorder Fleetwood and Dr. Hammond, to examine Lord Vaux and Sir Thomas Tresham about the Mass that Edward Osborne confessed to saying for them in the Fleet prison; and it was probably in connection with the final stages of the same Alfield book-ring investigation that the Council gave Topcliffe his first personal commission, 8 April. It required "the justices and other her Majesty's officers in the county of Essex to aid and assist Richard Topcliffe, esquire, this bearer, in his secret and diligent search of certain houses." They were charged to enter into and search any houses he named to them, "what and wheresoever they be," and to "follow such advice and direction as he shall prescribe unto them."[1]

With a commission like that in his hand, Topcliffe became a man to be feared. There is evidence that in Osborne's case he was willing to use the threat of torture—presumably on his own initiative—to extract a confession, and it seems very likely that he did the same with Deane. So far, though, he had not himself stepped into the torture chamber. Alfield was racked, but the presiding interrogators were Hopton, Randolph, Hammond, and Owen, operating under a Council warrant of 29 April 1582.[2] Nonetheless, though not yet a torturer himself, by the spring of 1582 Topcliffe had joined the state's policing apparatus.

Another sign of his new employment was his attendance at executions. Court observer-participants were a feature of Elizabethan executions for treason, but it was a new rôle for Topcliffe. He had been present as a spectator at the execution of Dr. John Storey,[3] but he became a vocal participant for the first time with the executions of Fathers William Filby, Luke Kirby, Lawrence Johnson, and Thomas Cottam, 30

---

[1] *APC*, 13. 382.

[2] *APC*, 13. 400–1. Under torture, Alfield agreed to attend the state church. Osborne, threatened with *Sir Owen Hopton's School*, i.e., with racking in the Tower, of which Hopton was Lieutenant, denied his faith and abjured his priesthood (*A true report of the late apprehension and imprisonment of Iohn Nichols* [*STC* 18537], Sig. E3).

[3] Rowse, 190–1.

May 1582. At these executions Sheriff Martin did all he could to persuade the priests to abjure their religion and accept the Queen's mercy.
Left to himself, the sheriff might even have spared them on their assur-
ance of loyalty. Topcliffe's rôle, to judge from his reported questions
and comments, was to make sure that nothing of the sort happened without a complete abjuration. For example:

> Then Mr.[*Johnson*][1] was willed once again to confess and ask pardon of
> the Queen: he answered, that he never offended her to his knowledge.
> Then *Topcliffe* said, the like mercy was never showed to any offender, and
> if you were in any other commonwealth you should be torn in pieces with
> horses. Then he was willed to pray; he prayed, desiring all Catholics to
> pray with him; he said his *Pater noster*, his *Ave,* and his *Creed*, and when
> the cart passed, *Lord, receive my soul.*[2]

The ferocity of Topcliffe's intervention was a sign of things very shortly
to come.

The Jetters of Lowestoft, Suffolk, had two sons, George and John.
Both went to the seminary at Rheims. George was there by 25 March
1581, when he was ordained deacon. Priest's orders followed at
Soissons in September, and he left for England the same month. The
government knew of his existence, but never caught him; he died in
Sussex in 1608–9 of natural causes. John Jetter followed his brother to
Rheims, but returned to England in May 1582 without taking any orders.
A couple of months after his arrival home, he was arrested, briefly
imprisoned in the Clink, then sent to the Tower:

> John Jetter, late servant unto one Mr. Higgins of London, Scrivener, com-
> mitted vii[th] day of August 1582 and sent for from hence to the Tower by
> the Right Worshipful Sir Owen Hopton, and there remaineth.[3]

No reason for John Jetter's arrest is given in the documents, but it seems
likely that the authorities picked him up as a way of finding his brother.
That motive would go some way to explain his atrocious treatment. He
was not indicted or convicted of any offense, but he was so savagely tortured that his tormenters must have been after information they thought
he had.

The Tower prisoner who kept the record known as "The Tower
Diary"[4] wrote on 1 September that John Jetter had been put in the

---

[1]Allen's text names this priest by his alias, which was Richardson.

[2]Allen 1, 81.

[3]Pollen 4, 227–8.

"Scavenger's Daughter," then thrown into the "pit" for eight days, and finally racked almost to death.[2] The case was so pitiful that other accounts made their way out of the Tower, one of them preserved in Father Grene's Collectanea M, now at Stonyhurst:

> You shall understand that one Jetter hath been monstrously racked, he showed great patience and courage. In the extreme of torment he never ceased to call upon the name of Jesus, so that Topcliffe in a great fury said, "What in the devil's name! Here is such a mumbling of Jesus Psalter[3] as I never saw...."
>
> His extremity was such, that being all in a burning heat, which proceeded in the stretching of his limbs to their highest power (unless they should have rent him in pieces), they poured upon his breast out of an ewer cold water, whether for a further torment, or *ad refocillandum*, I leave it for others to judge.
>
> The poor man is in such misery that he is able to receive nothing in his body but with a quill at the hand of his keeper, who, God knoweth, looketh but slenderly to him. I think, notwithstanding this, he had been racked again had they not feared he would die of this already done.
>
> There is another now that far passeth the old rackmaster, Mr. Topcliffe.[4]

Topcliffe's rôle in Jetter's case is puzzling. The Council registers are missing from June 1582 to February, 1586; consequently no warrant for Jetter's torture, if there was one, survives. Hopton, as Lieutenant of the Tower, was responsible for his prisoners, and could only administer torture in the Tower under a Council warrant. For Topcliffe to play his part in Jetter's torture, he would have to be named in the warrant. We can

---

[4]Formerly attributed to Edward Rishton, and first printed in Dodd, 3, 155. The author is now known to have been Fr. John Hart; see Pollen 5, 4; also DT, 19.

[2] The "Scavenger's Daughter" was an invention of Henry VIII's time, attributed to Leonard Skeffington, a Lieutenant of the Tower, and sometimes called "Skevington's irons." It was an iron hoop: "When this device is to be used, the body of the examinate is folded into three, shins to thighs, thighs to chest, and in this state put within two iron arcs, the ends of which are forced together by the labour of the executioners so as to complete a circle, the body of the examinate meanwhile being almost crushed by the horrid pressure...some as a result bleed from the extremities of their hands and feet; other, their rib-cages broken, lose much blood from their noses and throats" (Heath, 191, quoting Tanner, *Societas Iesu usque ad sanguinis et vitae profusionem militans*).

[3]The "Jesus Psalter" was a very popular English devotion ascribed to the sixteenth-century English Brigittine of Syon, Richard Whitford. Its first petition is, "Jesus, Jesus, Jesus: have mercy on me," repeated ten times. It is likely that Jetter *was* remembering the "Jesus Psalter." Topcliffe, who had been Catholic himself as a child and under Queen Mary, recognized it.

[4]Printed in Pollen 2, 222–3.

therefore be sure, I think, that there was a warrant, and that Topcliffe's name was in it. The real puzzle is in the reporter's last sentence: "There is another now that far passeth the old rackmaster, Mr. Topcliffe." The Oxford Dictionary, which knows all about the rack but knows little about the rack's master, defines "rackmaster" as "an officer having charge of the rack," and quotes the sentence above about Topcliffe as the earliest example of its use. Thomas Fitzherbert, writing about the torture of Edward Squire in 1598, speaks of rackmasters in the plural, the implication being that whoever was in charge of the infliction of torture was a rackmaster, and that there could be more than one of them.[1] "The old rackmaster" to whom Topcliffe is being compared is no doubt Thomas Norton, about whom we shall hear in the next two chapters. Nonetheless, read carefully, the sentence about Topcliffe means neither that he has joined the rackmasters, and is a particularly nasty one, nor that he has succeeded someone else as the only rackmaster. The sentence puts him in a class by himself, and has no word for him except *another*— "There is another now that far passeth the old rackmaster, Mr. Topcliffe." Topcliffe is both a rackmaster and more than a rackmaster, and our writer is horrified.

In the early 1580s, the authorities were still restricting torture to the Tower, where it was authorized only by Conciliar warrant to the Lieutenant—in this case Hopton—and any other interrogators associated with him. As Heath says, the actual physical infliction of torture was the work of the yeoman warders. Only a few months before Jetter's torture, Topcliffe—or someone associated with him—had broken Edward Osborne's nerve by threatening to send him to "Sir Owen Hopton's School," a threat which certainly implies that Hopton was the man in charge of torture. Yet here we have Topcliffe, operating under Hopton's titular authority, but supervising the infliction of Jetter's torture. That is what a rackmaster did, and to do it with such ferocity under the Lieutenant's supervision he must have had special authorization. By August 1582 the title "Esquire of the body" as applied to Topcliffe had acquired a new and sinister significance.

Despite the torture, John Jetter, by the way, seems to have told them nothing. Perhaps he had nothing to tell, but if he knew anything about his brother's whereabouts, his silence saved his brother's life. No evidence survives to associate John Jetter with any plot or crime against the state. He remained in the Tower until late July 1583, when he was

---

[1]Thomas Fitzherbert, *An Apology of T.F. in Defence of Himself* , 4. The *Apology* is appended to his *A Defence of the Catholyke Cause,* Antwerp, 1602.

moved to Newgate. There he was kept in irons, "his flesh nearly eaten away by the constant chafing of the irons," until his treatment killed him some time in 1585. The irony is that the brother whose whereabouts his torture was intended to reveal was able to visit him in prison before his death.[1]

---

[1] The documents bearing on Jetter's case are brought together by Pollen 2, 221–5.

Four

The Habit of Torture

Torture may be one of those things, like the poor, that we shall always have with us; it has certainly been with us for a long time. A famous passage towards the end of the Anglo-Saxon Chronicle tells how some of the Norman magnates, finding King Stephen to be a good-natured, easy-going man, broke their oaths to him and ensconced themselves in castles from which they terrorized the surrounding country. To pay for the castles and their garrisons, they imposed forced labor and confiscated people's goods; and when people, naturally enough, hid any wealth they possessed, they used torture to force them to produce it.

The outraged Chronicler provides a list of the tortures used: hanging by the feet, by the thumbs, or the head; using coats of mail to add to the body's own weight; fumigation with foul smokes; twisting knotted cords round the head, and confinement in a narrow chest (*crucethus*) lined with sharp stones. For more chronic torture they used infested dungeons—adders and snakes are mentioned—and a device that held the victim immobile by the neck.[1]

Some historians believe that the clerical author of this passage was exaggerating or even fabling. For the historian of torture, though, his list is evidence of the deep conservatism of the torturer's trade. The various modes of hanging described, as well as the methods of confining or immobilizing the body under stress, all had their versions in use at the Tower of London, along with its more notorious rack, over four hundred years later in the sixteenth century. Calculatedly uncomfortable or infested cells remained popular at the Tower, and elsewhere as well. Thomas Cromwell is said to have tortured Mark Smeaton with a cord knotted around the head.[2]

What is odd about the Chronicle account is that we normally associate the development, manufacture, maintenance, and use of such devices

---

[1] G.G.N.Garmonsway, trs. *The Anglo-Saxon Chronicle* (London: J.M.Dent & Sons Ltd, 1953), 263. The year is 1137.
[2] Heath, 60.

with government, whereas the torturers of Stephen's unhappy reign were free-lancing aristocratic thugs; and while one should never under-estimate the human capacity for mischief, it seems unlikely that these people invented their methods and devices all by themselves, *ad hoc*. Since all their methods have a subsequent history, it seems likely that they had a previous history, too, and that although we do not associate torture with Anglo-Saxon or Norman rule, something of the sort must have gone on from time to time.

Torture made its way formally into European legal proceedings with the revival of Roman or Civil law, beginning with the recovery in the eleventh century of the Emperor Justinian's *Corpus iuris*. Civilian learn-ing came to England when Archbishop Theobald of Canterbury brought over the legal scholar Vacarius from Italy, who composed his *Liber Pauperum* (1149) in England. This work became the standard textbook on the subject of Civil law: at Oxford they called law students *pauper-isti*.[1] This revival of Roman Law was not the result of academic whim or historical curiosity: it answered to the needs of the more centralized, autocratic monarchies that were emerging all over Europe. As Heath puts it, "From the eleventh century, ascendancy of the royalist star is increasingly apparent...We may suppose that some importance attached to the boost inevitably given to the morale of royal governments by acceptance of political absolutism that permeates the *Corpus iuris*."[2] A monarch who wished to improve on the medieval system of justice by accusation and ordeal, found in the *Corpus iuris* a rational approach that encouraged investigation. For instance, in the pursuit of evidence, it per-mitted, with limitations, the torture of witnesses as well as of the accused before and after a conviction. Consequently, as Heath in his dry way writes, "There may, therefore, seem little cause for surprise that, before the end of the thirteenth century—indeed by early in its fourth decade—judicial torture was certainly again being used." He thinks that its use might even have begun in the twelfth century.[3]

The situation in England, however, was rather different from that on the continent. Henry II, the first Plantagenet king, was certainly auto-cratic, and he was determined to improve the administration of justice in the kingdom; but in Henry's England the civilians ran into opposition, and the expanded judicial activity of Henry's courts led to the develop-

[1]Heath, 13ff.

[2]Heath, 14.

[3]Heath, 16.

ment of a large body of national customary law, which Ranulph de Glanvil, the King's justiciar, described in his *De legibus et consuetudinibus regni Angliæ* (1187). In fact, Ranulph almost certainly wrote this famous treatise on English law to counter the civilians' ambitions. It contains the origins of what came to be called in England the Common Law, and from that point of view its most interesting provision is that Henry vested the presentation of cases to the royal justices in local juries. This method of popular accusation, fundamental to Common Law, and the origin of the American grand jury, may have originated before the Norman Conquest, either with the Old English kings or the Danes; but whatever its origin, the use of a jury to find the facts of a case rendered the civilian use of torture, whether for evidence or confession, unnecessary. There is no evidence of torture in Henry's judicial system.[1]

In fact the conflict between Civil Law and the Common Law that the existence of Glanvil's treatise indicates became a perennial fact of English legal life, emerging finally in the conflict between the Common Law courts and the Prerogative courts—of Star Chamber and High Commission in particular—under the Stuarts.

Consequently, when Pope Clement V, under pressure from Philip IV of France, tried to extend the Inquisition's prosecution and suppression of the Templars to England, the English took the position that the Inquisition's ways of proceeding, especially its use of torture, were illegal. In the end, faced with the threat of Papal sanctions against the kingdom and themselves, and accepting the principle that in Church matters Canon Law took precedence over local law, the king (Edward II) and his advisers gave in, but reluctantly and with a minimum of cooperation. Torture, or the threat of it, may have been used in the province of Canterbury in the matter of the Templars, but the northerners of the province of York continued to resist. It is fascinating—and heartening—to see how tenaciously the English—the king, the bishops, the sheriffs, the city of London, and, it seems, the populace at large—resisted the Inquisition's claims and authority, and always on the basis of the illegality of torture in England.

In England, the real move to exploit civilian procedure, and with it the use of torture, was a fifteenth-century phenomenon, and it originated with a group of humanistically educated magnates, among them Duke Humphrey of Gloucester, John Holland, Earl of Exeter, and John Tiptoft,

[1]Heath, 17–19.

Earl of Worcester. To Holland, probably, goes the credit—or infamy—of introducing the rack—or rake, or brakes, to give it its other names—to the Tower of London. Since its popular name in the earlier years was "The Duke of Exeter's daughter,"[1] he is its most likely father. Of these men, Tiptoft, appointed Constable of England and Constable of the Tower in 1461 under the Yorkists, is the most notorious, earning himself a thoroughly bad reputation for dispensing cruel and summary justice under civilian procedure or "law of Padua" as the English called it. When Tiptoft lost his Constableships in 1467, the letters patent issued to his successor in office, Richard Woodville, Lord Rivers, describe in amazingly candid terms the office as Tiptoft held it. He was authorized to try cases of high treason, proceeding in the civilian and canonical manner either upon formal accusation or *ex officio*, and he was instructed to act "summarily and without judicial pomp, fuss, or artificiality," a phrase which, according to Heath, is "an established canonical/civilian formula." Exactly the same authority was then conferred on Lord Rivers.[2]

Three years later, Tiptoft became Constable for a second time. When Lord Sales defeated Clarence's and Warwick's ships, and took his prisoners to Southampton, the king ordered Tiptoft to judge them. He condemned twenty prisoners to be hanged, drawn, quartered, and beheaded, adding impalement to the punishment.[3]

Heath sums up the implications of Tiptoft's career rather tentatively, saying that although we do not really know the extent of Tiptoft's innovations, the record provides grounds for suspicion: "All that can be said is that the impression he left behind makes him—and so the Yorkist administration—a natural object of suspicion in the matter of responsibility for instituting torture at the Tower"[4] What these fifteenth-century developments show, unmistakably, is that an ambitious executive, operating with and for the Crown, could sidestep, and even co-opt the law.

---

[1] It is fitting that people should name such machines after their inventors, even though in time the real name can be lost, as in the case of "The Scavenger's Daughter," a device used in the Tower, and named after Sir Leonard Skeffington, a Lieutenant of the Tower under Henry VIII.

[2] Heath, 55.

[3] *ODNB*.

[4] Heath, 56. Arrested and arraigned by John de Vere, the Lancastrian earl of Oxford whose father Tiptoft had condemned, he was beheaded on Tower Hill.

It was a development that did not go unnoticed. After all, the mere fact that the Tower's rack had a nickname is evidence that people knew what was going on. There were important people who disapproved, too. The distinguished Common Lawyer, Sir John Fortescue, Chief Justice of the King's Bench, and named Chancellor under Henry VI, wrote his *De laudibus legum Anglie* (c.1470)—like Glanvil before him—to defend English Common Law against civilian encroachment, including the practice of torture, which he despised. As we shall see, he had sixteenth-century successors who continued to insist that English law neither needed nor permitted torture; and it is an odd fact that the use of torture never seems to have become an accepted principle of English law even under Elizabeth I, who tortured far more of her subjects than any of her predecessors or successors—including her father. Nonetheless, those fifteenth-century humanists with their civilian training opened a wide door through which, under the protection of sovereign immunity, a determined executive could march. And march they did, in increasing numbers, as the next century proceeded. These are the people who inaugurated the Tower of London's bad reputation.

*****

No doubt a general decline in civil decency caused by "the cruel rage of the late mortal wars within the realm of England"—as Sir John Fortescue describes the euphemistically-named Wars of the Roses[1]—underlay the Yorkist magnates' use of torture. With the return of stable government, the torturing seems to have stopped. There are no records of it from the reigns of Richard III or Henry VII. Nonetheless, the precedent had been set, and at least one machine for the purpose existed in the Tower, ready for use when its time came again.[2]

That time came when the crown decided to extend its absolute power to include the Church, in effect nationalizing it, and turning it into a department of state. The ostensible cause of that development was Henry VIII's determination to have his marriage to Catherine of Aragon annulled. The historian John Guy, though, believes that from its beginnings in 1485 the Tudor dynasty began to think about asserting royal authority over the clergy, and that Henry VIII, in particular:

---

[1] *De laudibus legum Angliæ* (London, 1660), opening sentence.

[2] Absence of records does not guarantee absence of torture, however. According to Sir Thomas Wyatt, Richard III had his father, Sir Henry, racked, though a later Wyatt family tradition identified the torture as "the barnacles " (Muir, 1, 40).

had decided from the beginning of his reign that he meant to control and manage the English church; for fourteen years he ran the church and clergy through Wolsey, and the clergy connived, because it was better to be ruled by a churchman, however abrasive, than more directly by the king—and Wolsey certainly protected the clergy from the full force of Tudor policy between 1515 and 1529.[1]

Then came the business of the annulment and "the King's great matter." Wolsey fell from power, indicted under the statutes of *praemunire,* which forbad dealings with a foreign power, in this case the Church at Rome. As a cleric, let alone as Papal Legate, Wolsey could have refused to accept the jurisdiction of the King's court; but for his own reasons (he preferred to throw himself upon the King's mercy rather than face his peers) he accepted the summons, and by that act destroyed the independence of the Church of England, which until then had been the one institution in England able to stand up to the crown.

Wolsey's surrender, writes the Catholic historian, Philip Hughes, "was a great defeat; it was the reversal of all that St.Thomas of Canterbury signified."[2] And so in a new age of absolute monarchies, the Church in England found itself naked of protection from the Crown, despite the fact that Magna Carta's first article guaranteed its freedom:

> We have, in the first place, granted to God, and by this Our present Charter confirmed for Us and Our heirs forever—That the English Church shall be free and enjoy her rights in their integrity and her liberties untouched. And that we will this so to be observed appears from the fact that We of Our own free will...granted, confirmed, and procured to be confirmed by Pope Innocent III the freedom of elections, which is considered most important and necessary to the English Church.[3]

It was one thing for Henry VIII to assert his royal supremacy over the Church, sweeping up the entire religious, educational, and social system of the kingdom, with its accumulated wealth, into his own greedy royal hands; it was another to convince the English people to applaud the fact. After all, they had been Catholic for nearly a thousand years, and—if we

[1] http://www.tudors.org/undergraduate/thomas-cromwell-and-the-intellectual-origins-of-the-henrician-revolution/

[2] Hughes, 1.208–9.

[3] Howard 2, 34. Oddly enough, this is one of the three articles of Magna Carta still unrepealed, even though the head of the Church of England is legally still the ruling monarch, and its bishops are appointed by the prime minister. One concludes that in English ruling circles "freedom" and "liberty" are words understood only in a Pickwickian sense.

are to judge by the churches they built, the religious houses and colleges they endowed, the religious literature they produced, and the liturgical music they composed—enthusiastically Catholic. Moreover, they were still building, rebuilding, writing and composing at the very moment that Henry struck.[1] In a matter of months, all that activity, from the most modest parish churches to the grandest abbey and cathedral chancels, became illegal, its practice an invitation to terrible punishment.

Given the arrival of centralized, autocratic government, it was probably inevitable that the Church, by its very existence a challenge to the claims of a monarchy like Henry VIII's, would sooner or later lose its independence. Nonetheless, Henry's *nationalization* of the Church of England by the Act of Supremacy in 1534 was a revolutionary act, and the assertion of the royal supremac*y in matters spiritual as well as temporal required a kind of total allegiance from his subjects that very few English people have ever been able to offer without some kind of mental reservation. For many of them, Henry's uniting of Church and state in his own person created for the first time in England a clearly-drawn line of separation between the allegiance owed to the temporal power of the crown and the allegiance owed to the things of God. To erase that line, Henry had no compunction whatever about using all the powers of state available to him, torture among them.

With Henry's break from Rome, torture became a common, regularly-used weapon in the arsenal of royal power. Only a small list of cases from Henry's time survives, but there is no reason to believe it is complete. The surviving cases, though, are typical and representative; nearly all of them involve the kind of politico-religious offense that Henry's announcement of his religious supremacy created. Disagreement with the King's religious pretensions was now treason. Hence, when a local parson speaks out against the suppression of a priory, he is "pinched with pain" by two local justices on instructions from Thomas Cromwell. When a Herefordshire man prophesies that Henry's actions will cause him to lose his realm, Cromwell sends him to the Tower with instructions that he be threatened with the rack. Cromwell himself oversees the torture of an Irish monk. At Norwich, a hermit is convicted of high treasons—no doubt because he spoke his mind about religious matters—and the Duke of Norfolk asks whether he should be sent to the Tower for torture. Most notorious of all, the authorities torture a reform-minded

---

[1]At Ripon the central space under the tower of the minster has two rounded Norman arches and two pointed arches because Henry's takeover stopped the restoration of the church in mid-course.

gentlewoman, Anne Askew, to make her reveal the identities of her fellow-believers, and if John Bale's account of her case is to be believed, Chancellor Wriothesley and Sir Richard Rich worked the rack themselves with great enthusiasm.[1] In all these cases, the King was consulted and consenting. In fact there can be no doubt that this kind of executive torture was always carried out under the royal prerogative and by its protection. And of course there were people who welcomed it. A sentence in a letter to Cromwell from his protégé Stephen Vaughan, an enthusiastic reformer very much in favor of the royal religious policy, encapsulates the whole attitude of mind and approach behind the approval of torture: "If the friars, which were taken in London before my coming hither, were brought to the brake, their counsel should shortly be bewrayed."[2]

During the short reigns of Edward VI and Mary I it is apparent that torture has become one of the ordinary tools of government. In both reigns we find the Council ready to use torture on prisoners taken in response to political disturbance, as at the time of Protector Somerset's fall and alleged treason under Edward, and following the Wyatt and Dudley conspiracies against Mary. But the Council ordered torture, or the threat of it, in ordinary criminal cases of sedition, robbery, and murder as well. In Edward's time we find the lieutenant of the Tower instructed to torture a pair of suspected murderers, presumably to inculpate themselves by confession. Two other men, suspected of stealing hawks from the Princess Mary's land, were to be examined by the Council, and if they refused to confess, to be tortured "to the example of others."[3] This is the first instance of torture being used in a case of theft of royal property.

Under Mary this pattern continues. Several cases arose from the Wyatt and Dudley conspiracies, but most uses of torture under Mary occurred in ordinary criminal cases: five robberies (one of royal property), one murder, and two cases of counterfeiting. One of the latter took place in Bristol, whose mayor was instructed to rack the suspects, leaving us with the interesting implication that Bristol owned a rack. There is just one alleged instance of torture being used in a religious case—one would have expected more.

[1] Elaine V. Beilin, ed., *The Examinations of Anne Askew* (New York: Oxford University Press, 1996), 127ff.

[2] Quoted by Heath, 60, who lists all of these Henrician cases.

[3] Heath, 76.

Elizabeth I, then, inherited a situation in which the use of torture under the prerogative had become increasingly normal. In the first year of her reign the Council authorized the torture of a pair of thieves, but then, until they tortured a man accused of murder in 1570, Elizabeth's Council evidently felt some embarrassment about the practice, in one case ordering torture to be used "without any great bodily hurt," in another prescribing the rack as a last resort, and in another using it as a threat.[1] But they soon overcame these scruples, and over the course of the reign about a hundred and eighty suspects or potential witnesses were tortured or threatened with torture in ordinary criminal and political cases, the great majority arising from the criminalizing of religious nonconformity.[2]

All three of Henry VIII's children shared their father's belief that the determination of the country's religion was a prerogative of the crown, and all three had their own strong opinions on what that religion should be. In the case of the first of them, the boy king Edward VI, one sometimes sees it argued that he and his Protestant clerics tolerated dissent.[3] That may have been true of the first couple of years of the reign when they all thought that no reasonable person could possibly disagree with them, but once the strength of popular opposition to their policies appeared, the Edwardian government showed itself willing enough, on both the secular and the spiritual side, to impose conformity, violently if necessary. The western rising in 1549 to restore Catholicism was savagely suppressed, and the new code of canon law produced under Cranmer's direction at the end of Edward's short reign spelled out the new church's readiness to kill disssenters and heretics as necessary. The Duke of Northumberland shelved Cranmer's code, but the young king's attempt to exclude his half-sisters from the succession for religious reasons was a sign of enforcements that would have come.

As a Catholic, Mary I, whose accession in 1553 was a very popular event, would not have allowed Parliament to name her supreme governor of the Church in England, but she had not a moment's doubt that she had the right to return it to the fold of Western Catholicism. As it happens, the great majority of the population agreed with her, but one suspects

---

[1]*APC*, 7. 66–7 (15 March 1559); 7. 222 (22 June 1565); 7. 324 (28 November 1569). A threat of torture is, nonetheless, a use of torture.

[2]See Appendix I. This is by far the largest number of documentable cases in any English monarch's reign, and it is not to be taken as a complete list.

[3]E.g., MacCulloch, 133.

that the population's agreement or disagreement held little interest for Mary. She did not come to the throne intending to kill people who disagreed with her about religion, but when the Protestant minority proved unpersuadable, she, her husband and Council, under the revived laws of Henry IV, executed some 273 of them by burning over a period of about four years.

These Marian executions are the reason the adjective "bloody" became attached to Mary's name. Yet it is one of the little-noticed ironies of the period that only a few months before Mary's accession, Archbishop Cranmer had been trying to enact new heresy laws as fierce in principle as the old ones,[1] but favoring the Protestant side. A couple of years later, he saw the old laws revived under which he himself suffered.

With Mary's death in November 1558, and the accession of her half-sister Elizabeth, the pattern of events repeated itself. Elizabeth and her Council set about revoking her sister's enactments and inaugurating her own approach to the royal management of religion, which was settled fairly quickly with the passing of the acts of Supremacy and Uniformity (29 April 1559). The act of Supremacy required virtually everyone in a position of any importance to subscribe to an oath acknowledging Elizabeth to be "supreme governor of this realm, and of all other her highness' dominions and countries, as well in all spiritual or ecclesiastical things or causes as temporal."[2] The act of Uniformity reinstated the 1552 Edwardine Book of Common Prayer (with a few revisions) as the only liturgical text authorized for use in the Church of England.

Both acts spelled out sanctions for the disobedient. Refusal of the oath brought loss of any office held, and disqualification for life. The punishment for defending the Papal authority which the act of Supremacy repudiated was loss of goods for the first offense. A second offense added imprisonment for life to loss of property, and a third offense was considered high treason. Under the act of Uniformity, any cleric who used a form of service other than that in the Prayer Book, or who criticized the Prayer Book, was fined six months' income, and imprisoned for six months. A second offense brought a year's prison and loss of benefices. The punishment for a third offense was life imprisonment. There were penalties for lay people, too. Anyone speaking or writing

---

[1] It seems likely that most of the Marian victims, concentrated in the counties of Essex and Kent, were either Anabaptists, universally execrated, or holders of equally radical views. This being so, Smyth, 3, suggests that two-thirds of the Marian victims would have been burned under Edward, had he survived.

[2] Peers (the lords temporal) were exempt from the oath.

against the Prayer Book, encouraging a priest to use a different form of service, or interrupting or hindering a service was liable to a fine of 100 marks (£66. 13s. 4d) for the first offense. The fine for a second offense was 400 marks (£266.13s.4d), and a third offense entailed loss of goods and life imprisonment. Lay people were required to attend service in their parish churches. The fine for missed attendance on Sundays and holy days was one shilling for each absence, to be collected by the church wardens and distributed to the parish poor.

It has become one of the clichés of English history that these punishments were comparatively mild, and that during the earlier years of the reign the government's reluctance to enforce them effectively rendered them even milder. Yet to mere commonsense they seem severe enough, and in 1563 Parliament made them more severe. A first refusal of the oath brought loss of all property and life imprisonment. A second refusal was treason, punishable by death; and the same penalty applied to a defense of Papal jurisdiction over the Church. The same statute extended the reach of the oath to all members of the House of Commons, all barristers and attorneys, court officers, and schoolmasters, public and private. Meanwhile, enforcement had begun immediately, the first commission for administration of the oath being issued 23 May 1559, three weeks after the first act of Supremacy passed.

Signs of the government's determination and portents of things to come appeared very quickly. The commissioners began with the 16 Marian bishops who were still alive. By November, all but one of them had refused the oath, and were deprived of their sees.[1] By early 1560, five more of them had died, and one (Goldwell of St. Asaph) had left England. By the summer six of them were in the Tower, Scott of Chester was in the Fleet, and Bonner of London in the Marshalsea. They would spend the remainder of their lives either in prison or under house arrest with their Protestant successors, not the kindest of hosts.[2] John Jewel, newly appointed Bishop of Salisbury and literary champion of the new church, delivered his opinion of them in a letter to Peter Martyr, February 1562:

[1] The exception was Anthony Kitchin of Llandaff, a remarkable survivor from Henry VIII's time, who held on to his bishopric through all the changes, dying in his eighties in 1563. See *ODNB* for a sympathetic account of his career. Kitchin, who refused to take part in Matthew Parker's consecration as archbishop of Canterbury, never actually took the oath. The queen allowed him to sign a general undertaking to follow the form of religion now required.

[2] In 1563, Scott escaped to the continent. See Hughes, 3. 245–46.

The Marian bishops are still confined in the Tower, and are going on in their old way. If the laws were but as rigorous now as in the time of Henry, they would submit themselves without difficulty. They are an obstinate and untamed set of men, but are nevertheless subdued by terror and the sword.[1]

After dealing with the bishops, the commissioners turned to the rest of the clergy and the laity, many of whom must have been not at all clear about what they were being asked to sign. The minority who refused—instead of merely staying away—quickly found themselves in hot water. John Bolton, a priest who refused in 1559, was imprisoned first in York Castle, then in Ousebridge, York, for about twelve years, then moved to the Hull Blockhouse for another eight years before being finally banished. Another priestly refuser, Henry Comberford, precentor of Lichfield cathedral, described as "learned but wilful [i.e., he would not sign] and meet to be considered," seems first to have been put under house arrest with leave to make two journeys a year home. But by 1566 he was in York Ousebridge where he spent 6 years before being moved, like Bolton, to the Hull Blockhouse where he died in his eighties in 1586.[2]

These must have been fairly old men when they were first imprisoned, and there is nothing in the records to suggest that they were guilty of anything except refusal to take the oath. They are two of many, and they are mentioned here to show that from the beginning the government was prepared to be uncompromising with dissenters.[3] Among laymen, Sir Thomas Fitzherbert of Norbury in Derbyshire provides an example. Having refused the oath, he was in the Fleet prison by 1561, and he was to spend the rest of his life without trial in one prison or another, eventually dying in the Tower thirty years later for nothing except refusing to take the oath and attend the nationalized Church of England. To demonstrate his loyalty to the Queen in temporal matters, he volunteered twice

---

[1]*Zurich Letters,* 101. Notice Bishop Jewel's readiness to enforce agreement by judicial and civil violence.

[2]NA/SP15/11/45; Morris, 3. 300. The first priest killed under this legislation seems to have been a Dominican, William Blagrave, executed in York, 10 May 1566; though according to Strype his real offense was pretending to be a Protestant, and preaching doctrines intended to causes confusion (Strype, 1.1.342–43).

[3]Excellent correctives, both to the common notion that the Marian clergy offered no resistance to the Elizabethan settlement of religion, and to the related belief that English Catholicism was moribund until the influx of seminary priests and Jesuits beginning in the late 70s revived it, will be found in McGrath 1 & 2.

the amount levied on his estate at the time of the Armada, but his gesture cut no ice with the government.[1]

The government was equally prepared to enforce the act of Uniformity. Again, a couple of examples will make the point. In April 1561, officers at Gravesend searched the baggage of a priest called Cox or Devon *en route* for Flanders, and found a rosary and a breviary. They sent the priest to a local justice, and under questioning, presumably with threats, he accused a number of people, including Sir Edward Waldgrave and Sir Thomas Wharton, of hearing Mass and possessing Catholic service books. In the upshot, the Council ordered bishop Grindal of London to examine the priest. They also commissioned the Earl of Oxford, Lord Lieutenant of Essex, to search Wharton's and Waldgrave's houses, and to arrest them and the other people whom the priest had named. On 20 April several people, including two priests, were sent to the Tower.[2]

A second example, occurring a year later, has even more interesting implications. On 8 September 1562, certain "promoters" or informers and the bishop of Ely's men arrested a priest named Haverd or Havard in the act of saying Mass at Lady Cary's house in Fetter Lane. They led him in his vestments through Holborn, Newgate Market, and Cheapside to the Counter in the Poultry, his missal, "porttoys" [breviary], chalice, and pax carried before him. A crowd followed, "mocking, deriding, cursing, and wishing evil to him, some wanting him pilloried, some hanged, some hanged and quartered." Lady Cary, Lady Sackville, Mrs. Pierpoint, a man called Sherwood and his wife, were all arrested, brought before Cox, bishop of Ely, their houses searched, and books confiscated. They were all then taken to prison, the women to the Fleet (where they would have joined Bishop Scott of Chester and Sir Thomas Fitzherbert), the Sherwoods and the priest to the Counter. On the 2 October, they were all arraigned at the Newgate sessions "amongst thieves and murderers," and found guilty under the statute, the priest for preparing to say Mass, the others for being willing to see and hear it. They all received the statutory punishment: 12 months in Newgate for the priest; 3 months in the Fleet for Lady Cary and Mrs. Pierpoint plus 100 marks fine, and 6 months for the Sherwoods plus the fine as well.[3]

---

[1] For Sir Thomas, see Camm 2, 1–74, and Cox 1.

[2] Bayne, 99. Bayne is inclined to write this episode off as a flexing of political muscle to influence the queen, but seen in a longer perspective, it is a good example of the Council's selective enforcement.

[3] Stow, 121–22. The Sherwoods were Henry Sherwood and his wife Elizabeth, née Tregian. He was a woolen draper, recently returned to London from Mechlin. Thomas

There are several interesting features to this case. First we have "promoters" or professional informer-accusers in action.[1] Then although Lady Sackville seems to have escaped unscathed, Lady Cary, "being of the Queen's blood" as Stow remarks, went to prison notwithstanding. The priest, Thomas Haverd, was a Marian, home-born and bred, yet we find a pair of Anglican bishops, Grindal and Cox, encouraging the Council to torture him, and making a bad joke about it: "Some think that if this priest, Haverd, might be put to some kind of torment, and so driven to confess what he knoweth, he might gain the Queen's Majesty a good Mass of money by the Masses he hath said: but this we lay to your Lordships' wisdom."[2] The Haverd case, in fact, is a model in little of things to come. There are informers at work, there is money to be had, there are jokes to be made, and there is torture to be inflicted, all under the authority of the acts of Supremacy and Uniformity, and there is no hint of subversive politics or conspiracy by way of justification. It is entirely a matter of enforcing religious conformity.

The government evidently thought that the legislation, backed by selective but high-profile enforcement, would be enough to secure the establishment of the new religious arrangements. In fact, and as they should have expected, the people proved quietly unwilling because, as all historians of the period now somewhat belatedly agree,[3] and as contemporaries knew well at the time, the reformers were a tiny if vocal minority even in the city of London. Except for that minority, there was no general enthusiasm for the changes. Besides, in a little over twenty years, the Crown had mandated four changes of religion. People had no reason to expect that the current arrangements would last any longer than the new Queen, and no-one in 1559 expected her to last for nearly forty-five years. But then, at the end of the Queen's first decade, four dramatic events changed the whole picture.

One predictable effect of the 1559 legislation had been to cause a flight of religious refugees overseas to France, to what is now Belgium, and to Spain. There were some lay people among them, but many were

---

Sherwood, now beatified, killed 7 Feb. 1578, was their son (Pollen 2, 2–4, 7–8, and see below, 89–90). Elizabeth Sherwood, Henry's widow, died in the 1590s after fourteen years in prison (Pollen 2, 7–8).

[1] They received their pay or fee (1/3) out of their victims' fines.

[2] Haynes 2, 395, quoted by Hughes, 3. 255.

[3] Even Diarmaid McCulloch, himself strongly in favor of the changes, acknowledges that the people he calls "evangelicals" were a minority (McCulloch, 115).

clerics and scholars, ejected from their benefices and university places and forced to set about making new professional lives for themselves on the continent, a process that included the founding of schools, colleges, and religious houses.[1] Over the years they were remarkably successful in doing this, so that when the French Revolution brought with it the suppression of religious houses, there were over forty English foundations in existence overseas. Historically speaking, though, the first of them was the most important: this was the seminary that William Allen founded at Douay in September 1568. It was partly a school for educating Catholic boys, but most famously—or notoriously—it was a seminary for the training of a new generation of English priests to minister to English Catholics. Its very existence told the Queen and her Council that English Catholicism was not going to die, as they hoped and expected, from inanition and the passage of time. In 1573, the first 4 seminary priests were ordained, and the first priests were sent into England. By the time the college moved temporarily to Rheims in 1578, 75 men had been ordained, 52 of them sent into England.[2]

The second situation-changing event of 1568 was the arrival in England of Mary Queen of Scots after her defeat by the Confederate Lords at the Battle of Langside. Like her cousin Elizabeth I, Mary was a grandchild of Henry VII, and so an entirely legitimate claimant to the English throne. Unlike her English cousin, she was Catholic, and so her presence in England set up a situation that had become something of a paradigm—in fact the only effective paradigm—for régime change in England: a viable claimant, a significant body of disaffected nobility and gentry, and powerful overseas backing, in Mary's case from her Guise relatives in France. Just such an alignment of forces in the past had already put three kings on the throne—Henry IV, Edward IV, and Henry VII—and Cecil, Walsingham, and Elizabeth I were acutely aware of the possibility that it might happen again. Unlike those claimants, though, Mary, having fled into England, was a prisoner in her enemies' hands, isolated from her friends and supporters. Even so, her captors could not prevent her from representing an alternative to the current scheme of things, and so becoming a focus for conspiratorial activity.

The third event was the Northern Rising of late 1569, when the Earls of Northumberland and Westmorland found themselves forced into

---

[1]This should not surprise the reader. There was nothing insular or provincial about the pre-schismatic Church of England.

[2]Hughes, 3. 293.

unenthusiastic leadership of what proved to be a popular but very short-lived rebellion in favor of the removal of Cecil and the restoration of Catholicism. The earls' half-heartedness and military incompetence plus the government's quick response easily defeated the poorly-armed rebels, and prevented the rebellion from spreading south. Nonetheless, it gave the Queen and Council an unpleasant shock, and frightened them badly, as their savage response showed.

Finally, there was the papal bull, *Regnans in excelsis*, that Pope St. Pius V signed on 25 February, 1570, delivering the judgment of a papal court that Elizabeth I was a heretic who had forfeited her right to rule and whose subjects were therefore released from their allegiance. The bull was never formally published in England (how could it be?), but on 25 May 1570 a layman fastened a copy to the Bishop of London's door. No-one knows what Pius V expected the bull to achieve, but its first and lasting effect in England was to confirm the government in its belief that a Catholic and a traitor were potentially the same thing.

During the years 1568–70, therefore, a confluence of events told an already jittery English government that English Catholicism was not only not dead, it was not even moribund, and was showing definite signs of life. An immediate response was to bring out the torturers. Although John Felton, the man who fastened Pius V's bull to the bishop's door, had made no secret of his action, the Council, wanting to know more about the network of associations that had made his act possible, decided to extract the information from him by torture. Felton was racked in the Tower, June 1570, by warrant from the Council.

The next year, as a result of the complex of events known as the Ridolphi Plot (a fantastic scheme thought up by the Florentine banker, Robert Ridophi and the Spanish ambassador, Guerau de Spes, which involved invading England, releasing Mary Stuart, and marrying her to the duke of Norfolk[1]), the Council brought out the rack again as an instrument of policy. A Burgundian courier in the service of the bishop of Ross, Charles Bailly, having first been threatened with the rack by William Cecil, was racked in the Tower by the lieutenant, Sir Owen Hopton, April 1571, and put into the notorious punishment cell called

---

[1]Like all the later Elizabethan plots, the Ridolphi Plot resists simple explanation. As managed and developed by Cecil and Walsingham its true purpose seems to have been the removal first of Norfolk, inevitably the focus of aristocratic opposition to Cecil's influence, and then of Mary Stuart. They succeeded in the first aim, but not the second. There is little doubt that Ridolphi, while under house arrest with Walsingham, was "turned," and became a double agent. See the accounts in Williams 3, Read, and Edwards 1.

"Little Ease." In the autumn of that same year, Cecil used the threat of the rack to set Mary's representative, the bishop of Ross, talking, and actually racked two of Norfolk's servants.

As we learned long ago in school, *facilis descensus Averno*. Once started, the intermittent use of the rack continued, in ordinary criminal cases as well as state cases, all through the 1570s until it really blossomed in the 1580s.

The first use of torture in a case involving enforcement of the statutes of Supremacy and Uniformity was that of Thomas Sherwood, a young man reported for keeping company with priests and for going overseas. He was arrested in 1577. Brought before Recorder Fleetwood, he was easily tricked into saying that Elizabeth would not be lawfully Queen if the Pope had excommunicated her. Fleetwood then sent him to the Council, who put him in the Tower and instructed the Attorney General to see that he was arraigned. They added a further instruction that Mr. Attorney should first examine him to find out from whom he received his ideas, and then, should he refuse to answer the questions, to put him in the dungeon amongst the rats. Meanwhile, finding himself under interrogation again, and having had time to reflect upon what had happened to him, Sherwood retracted his previous words and refused to give any information incriminating others. The examiners—Hopton, Gerard, Bromley, and Fleetwood—reported their failure to the Council, who thanked them for their report, and replied that:

> Where they signify by their said letter that Sherwood doth not only stagger in his first confession, and fain would retract his words, in respect he affirmed her Majesty to be an heretic and usurper, but also will in no case be brought to confess or answer such interrogatories as they have propounded unto him, their Lordships are of opinion that, if he be used thereafter, he can discover other persons as evil affected towards her Majesty as himself; they are therefore to assay him at the rack upon such articles as they shall think meet to minister unto him for the discovering either of the persons or of further matter.

According to the report of his case, young Sherwood was racked three times, and sufficiently injured to lose the use of his limbs. When his tormenters failed to elicit any information from him, they left him in the darkness of a fetid dungeon without food, clothing or a bed. He was brought to trial 1 February 1578, convicted, and shortly afterwards killed at Tyburn in the usual manner.

This first case of its kind is paradigmatic. The torture is not intended to incriminate the victim, but to force him to incriminate others; and when the torturers fail, their response is to punish the victim with no regard for law or humanity.[1]

There is no sign, however, of Topcliffe in the torture rooms of the seventies. Hopton, the lieutenant of the Tower, was the chief supervisor of the torturing, in association with the law officers and others, not all of whom enjoyed the work. Sir Thomas Smith, the scholar-lawyer, for instance, had bragged that torture was unlawful in England:

> Likewise, torment or question which is used by the order of the civil law and custom of other countries to put a malefactor to excessive pain, to make him confess of himself, or of his fellows or complices, is not used in England, it is taken for servile. For what can he serve the commonwealth after as a free man, who hath his body so haled and tormented, if he be not found guilty, and what amends can be made him? And if he must die, what cruelty is it so to torment him before?...The nature of Englishmen is to neglect death, to abide no torment: And therefore he will confess rather to have done any thing, yea, to have killed his own father, than to suffer torment, for death our nation doth not so much esteem as a mean torment...There is an old law of England, that if any gaoler shall put any prisoner being in his custody to any torment, to the intent to make him an approver, that is to say an accuser or Index of his complices, the gaoler shall die therefore as a felon....The nature of our nation is free, stout, haut, prodigal of life and blood: but contumely, beatings, servitude and servile torment & punishment it will not abide....[2]

When Smith was employed in the torture of the duke of Norfolk's servants, he was not very happy about it. Others were less reluctant, and one detects a kind of zest in the sadistic treatment of Thomas Sherwood.

In 1574 the name of Thomas Norton, poet, lawyer, parliamentarian, and pamphleteer, appeared for the first time in the torture records, and although Norton did not have a very long career as a torturer, his enthusiastic participation in some high-profile cases earned him a bad reputation, and lead Robert Persons to describe him as "Rackmaster Norton." In fact, if one figure stands out as Topcliffe's role-model and predecessor, it is Thomas Norton.

*****

---

[1] *APC*, 10. 92, 94, 111; Pollen 2, 1–20; Camm, 234–48.

[2] Sir Thomas Smith, *De republica Anglorum* (1583), Bk.II, Chap. 24 (pp.84–86), "Certain orders peculiar to England, touching punishment of malefactors." Smith must have known that by the time he was writing (ca. 1562–66), torture had become fairly common. One wonders whether Smith wrote as he did in an attempt to call the likes of Cecil, Leicester, Walsingham—and Elizabeth I herself—to order. If so, he failed.

Five

Thomas Norton Raises the Stakes

Thomas Norton (1530–1584) was born in London, son and heir of a wealthy London Grocer who acquired property in Bedfordshire, including the rectory, church, and advowson of Streatley, which Thomas in time inherited. In 1544, he went up to Michaelhouse, Cambridge as a fellow-commoner. He declared strong Protestant loyalties very early on. By 1550 when the twenty-year-old Norton was in service with Edward Seymour, Duke of Somerset, as secretary and tutor to his children, the direction of his life was already taking shape. In Seymour's household he met his future father-in-law, Henry VIII's founding archbishop of the Church of England, Thomas Cranmer, and his future patron and employer, William Cecil, Elizabeth I's Lord Treasurer to be.[1] He married Cranmer's daughter Margaret sometime in the 1550s. Later on, his Protestant printer-friend Whitchurch married Cranmer's widow, so that Whitchurch became Norton's stepfather-in-law, and they all lived together until Whitchurch died. After Margaret Cranmer's death, Norton married as his second wife another Cranmer, Margaret's cousin Alice, daughter of Edmund Cranmer, archdeacon of Canterbury. In short, young Norton, having envisaged himself as an important player on the religious field, positioned himself accordingly by marrying into the Protestant purple.

He served the cause first as a writer. He contributed to the translation of Erasmus's *Paraphrases upon the New Testament* that his stepfather-in-law Whitchurch printed, and that was later (1559) ordered to be placed in every church in England. He contributed to the Sternhold collection of metrical psalms, and translated Calvin's *Institutiones* (1561). Richard Tottel's inclusion of two of his poems in *Songes and Sonettes* (1557) was a sign of his growing fame as a writer, and a few years later, Jasper Heywood, the translator of Seneca and future Jesuit, praised him as one of the Inns of Court poets.[2] But of course his most famous pro-

---

[1] *ODNB*, s.v. "Thomas Norton."
[2] See Rollins, 2.81. Rollins attributes Tottell's nos. 257 and 289 to Norton. Graves, followed by Axton in *ODNB*, thinks that No.253, "An epitaph of maister Henry Williams," is Norton's, but this attribution is based on a misreading of Rollins's note (2.325) pointing out that 289, 'An other of the same,' is Norton's elegy on Williams (Rollins, 2.325).

duction, for which he is remembered in all the histories of English literature, is his share of *Gorboduc* or *Ferrex and Porrex*, the first blank-verse
tragedy in English, written with Richard Sackville for production in the
Inner Temple revels, December 1561, then performed again at court,
1562.

Norton, though, had more important activities in mind than writing.
He entered the Inner Temple in 1555, and by the time he was called to
the bar in 1563, was already a member of Parliament, where he became
one of the most active members. During the crisis years of 1568–71, he
turned political pamphleteer, publishing attacks on Mary Stuart and the
Duke of Norfolk, on the northern rising and the Earls of Northumberland
and Westmorland, and on the papal bull of 1570 that excommunicated
Elizabeth I. At the same time, in the parliament of 1571, he revived
Cranmer's code of canon law, and John Foxe published it, but both it
and Norton's other ideas for church reform ran into the Queen's firm
opposition, and so went nowhere. He had more success with a
"treasons" bill, and in 1572 argued strenuously (and successfully) for
Norfolk's execution, equally strenuously, but unsuccessfully, for Mary
Stuart's death, too.

So, given his connections, principles, and qualifications, Norton was a
natural choice when the government, i.e., the Queen and his patron
Cecil, decided that the country's religious policy needed more muscle.
During the 1570s the Council commissioned him intermittently as an
interrogator in a number of ordinary criminal cases involving theft,
fraud, receiving stolen goods, and coin-clipping. One of these cases
brought him into the torture room for the first time.

A man called Humphrey Needham had wangled money out of archbishop Parker by persuading him that he had correspondence and information that would lead to the capture of the Puritan Thomas Cartwright
(sometime Lady Margaret professor of divinity at Cambridge), wanted
for his attacks on the established church. In November 1574, the Council commissioned Norton along with Thomas Randolph and Henry
Knollys to examine Needham, adding as a postcript the instruction to
"bring him to the rack without stretching his body in the intent he might
discover the truth." To threaten Needham with the rack in a case like
this, the Council must have been seriously irritated with him.[1]

Then, towards the end of the decade, panicked by the arrival of
newly-ordained priests from Allen's seminary, and especially by the arri-

---

[1]*APC*, 8. 319; NA/SP12/93/4. See also Heath, 95.

val of the two Jesuits, Campion and Persons, in the summer of 1580, the Council began to use Norton in religious cases. The existence among Norton's papers of materials bearing on the case of Cuthbert Mayne (the proto-martyr of the seminary priests, killed in 1577), implies that the Council began by consulting him about Mayne.[1] Then in 1578 and 1579, the Council instructed him to examine a number of lay people arrested for offenses against the laws enforcing religious conformity, among them an Irishman, Edward Burnell, picked up for importing Catholic books, and Sir John Throckmorton's son, who had attended a mass. There is no hint of torture in any of these cases. In late 1578, though, Recorder Fleetwood and Norton arrested a young man called John Tippet, newly returned from the Douay-Rheims seminary, and their treatment of him so shocked local observers that accounts were sent overseas for distribution through the exiles' news services. Tippet had matriculated at the seminary in 1577–8, but as Fleetwood and Norton soon discovered, his early return home before completing the course had nothing to do with a change in his opinions. His refusal, under interrogation, to disown his Catholicism drove the pair into a typically Elizabethan fit of rage. They "condemned him to be whipped at a Cart's tail, and to be bored through the ear with a hot iron." Then, after this public and, for a young man of good family, disgraceful punishment, they imprisoned him, in rags, without food, in "the horrible cold, stench and terrible darkness of the pit or dungeon in Newgate" where he remained for a couple of months. Upon his release he promptly returned to the seminary.[2]

The Privy Council first commissioned Norton to examine a priest in January 1580. Lord Cromwell had arrested "a mass priest" called

---

[1] A disagreement among the assize judges had brought Mayne's case before the Council (Graves, 202; Camm, 217).

[2] In 1580, John Tippet moved to the English College at Rome, was ordained there in 1584, became a Carthusian, and was made Procurator-General of the order. He died in Rome, 24 August 1593 (Douay, 160; *CRS* 2.191). Norton's biographer writes of this episode, "If a foreign Catholic report can be believed, Fleetwood and Norton supervised the administration of the punishment," and proceeds to suggest that this "unsubstantiated report' was "incorrect or mere invention." This will not do. First, letters between Tippet and his distressed father, Mark Tippet, substantiate the report. Second, this was not a foreign report. Its authors were (a) Alban Dolman, an English Marian priest writing from London at the time of the events, and (b) Robert Persons, writing retrospectively, both of them English. Dolman's account pairs Recorder Fleetwood with the bishop of London, ("the biteshipe of London," Dolman calls him) and does not mention Norton. Persons's account, mentioning Norton, is based on Tippet's own narrative after he returned to the seminary (Graves, 246; *CRS* 2.77, 80–82, 149).

Edward Jackson in Norfolk, and after examining him sent him up to the Council in Whitehall, who put him in the Tower and commissioned Lord Hunsdon, Hopton the Lieutenant of the Tower, Secretary Wilson, Recorder Fleetwood, and Mr. Norton, or any two of them, to draw up interrogatories and to re-examine him:

> using their best endeavor to bolt out from him such matter as the circumstances of his confession may induce them unto, as well to think him guilty concerning reconciling of her Majesty's subjects to the See of Rome, as to discover with what persons and in what places he hath been most conversant within the Realm, and who may have been receivers and maintainers of him.

We can assume, I think, that Fleetwood and Norton were the two members of this commission who actually carried out the interrogation, no doubt under Hopton's supervision or with his assistance. There is no explicit mention of torture, but the expression "bolt out" has a sinister ring to it, and we can be sure that the Council was very interested to discover who had been helping Jackson, and whom he had reconciled.[1]

The torturing began in earnest with the next group of commissions issued shortly after 9 November 1580, when Norton along with the knight marshal and the civil lawyer Hammond was required to examine "a dangerous Papist named Nicholas Roscarrock not long since arrived here from the parts beyond the seas, and one Ralph Sherwin, a massing priest."[2] Three weeks later the torturing began to come into the open with a commission issued on 30 November to Lieutenant Hopton, the attorney-general (Gerard), and solicitor-general (Popham):

> that considering the number of English priests, Jesuits as they be termed, to come into this realm, and of other persons their confederates, her Majesty meaning to make some example of them by punishment, to the terror of others, their Lordships do require these said Commissioners to bring them to the Tower, there to be committed, and then to acquaint Sir George Carey, Mr. Doctor Hammond and Mr. Thomas Norton, having taken pains in their former examinations, with the matter of their assistance, and to certify their Lordships what they shall further draw out of those men than is already confessed.[3]

---

[1] *APC*, 11. 255–6, 257, 263. Jackson cannot have been long in the Tower, since his name does not appear in the Tower Bills. He was moved to the Marshalsea, and was still there in June 1583, but had gone by October. What happened to him is unknown (*CRS* 2. 231, 233). He was a Marian priest, resident at one time with Viscount Montagu (Questier, 185).

[2] *APC*, 12. 264.

According to this warrant, the Queen's end or purpose in deciding to move the priests—and the laymen associated with them—to the Tower was to punish them and terrorize others; the strongly implied means of terror is torture, and her agents are to be Carey, Hammond, and Norton.

Sure enough, torture and other forms of rough treatment soon followed. Fr. John Hart's Tower Diary tells us that on 10 December two priests, Thomas Cottam and Luke Kirby, were "placed under compression in the Scavenger's Daughter for more than one hour." Then Robert Johnson and Ralph Sherwin were racked on 15 December, Sherwin again on the 16th, presumably under the warrant of 30 November.[2]

The Council issued its next explicit torture warrant on Christmas Eve, and again it speaks of terror: it instructed Hopton, Carey, Gerard, and Popham to interrogate John Hart, James Bosgrave, priests, and John Pascal, layman, and as necessary "to bring them unto the tortures, and by terror thereof wring from them the truth of such matters as they shall find most necessary to be discovered."[3] This warrant does not name Norton, but we know that he was involved because William Allen published a circumstantial account of a conversation between Norton and John Hart after the torture:

> And when *M. Hart* was taken from the rack, the commissioners talking with him after a familiar manner: *Norton* asked him, saying, *Tell truly Hart, what is the meaning of the coming in, of so many priests into England?* who answered, *To convert the land again to her first Christian faith and religion, by preaching and peaceable persuasion, after the manner that it was first planted.* To which *Norton* said: *In my conscience Hart, I think thou sayest truth*"[4]

This conversation must have taken place on 31 December, when Hart, according to his own Tower Diary, was "led to be tortured on the rack" along with a layman, Henry Orton. Its comparatively genial tone is to be explained by the fact that although Hart was led to the rack, he was not actually put on it: this was the first of at least three occasions when

---

[3]APC, 12. 271.

[2]DT, 38.

[3]*APC*, 12. 294–5. The choice of Christmas Eve seems not to have been accidental. As Allen noticed in his *Brief History*: "And which is worth the marking, or rather lamenting of all Christian hearts, that for our more affliction, they profanely make choice to give the torture to our brethren upon Sundays and high holydays in God's Church, after the old manner of the heathen persecutors, rather than upon working days" (Sig. B3).

[4]Allen 1, Sig.B4–B4v.

either Hart's nerve failed him and he offered to cooperate, or Secretary Walsingham, for reasons of his own, intervened.[1] Henry Orton, arrested with the priest, Robert Johnson, was tried with Campion and the rest in the grand show-trial, November 1581, and convicted but not executed. John Pascal, also named in the Christmas Eve warrant, was a young layman, a student at the English College, Rome, who had accompanied the Campion party into England. He was brought to the rack on 15 January 1581 along with another layman, Jerome Stephens. The experience frightened both of them into agreeing to go to the Protestant services of the national church, and so they were released. Another layman, George Dutton, no doubt arrested because of association with one of the priests, was similarly frightened into submission, 10 February 1581.[2] As we learn from the threatened racking of Orton, Stephens, and Dutton, none of them named in a warrant, the torturers did not necessarily follow the letter of the warrants, but allowed themselves a degree of improvisation.

Nicholas Roscarrock, who had found himself named in the same interrogation warrant as Ralph Sherwin, was a Catholic gentleman from Cornwall who visited Rome and Douay in the summer of 1580. When the authorities captured Sherwin in the act of preaching in Roscarrock's London house they arrested him, too. He was moved to the Tower from the Marshalsea along with Sherwin, and remained there for five years.[3] He was racked 14 January 1581.

All these men—Thomas Cottam, Luke Kirby, Nicholas Roscarrock, Ralph Sherwin, Robert Johnson, Henry Orton, John Hart, James Bosgrave, John Pascal, Jerome Stephens, and George Dutton—were linked in the Council's mind with the mission party led by Robert Persons and Edmund Campion that had left Rome on 18 April 1580. There

---

[1] Hart's is an interesting, virtually unique case. See note at the end of this chapter.

[2] *DT*, 40, 41. Young Pascal belonged to a family of Much Baddow, Essex. "This young man was named John Paschall, a gentleman as I take him, born in Essex, who had been scholar to Mr. Sherwin in Oxford, and dearly beloved of him; and being young and sanguine of complexion, and fervent in his religion, would oftentimes break forth into zealous speeches, offering much of himself....but Mr. Sherwin would always reprove him, say 'O John, John, little knowest thou what thou shalt do before thou comest to it.' And so it fell out with no little grief of the martyr, who had been in the same prison with his scholar, to wit in the Marshalsea, and was no sooner removed from him to the Tower but that the other fell" (Morris 1, 2.295).

[3] Hopton, the Lieutenant of the Tower, wrote to the Council, 6 March 1586, renewing his "old suit" that Roscarrock should be released on bond, having been in prison five and a quarter years, and owing the Lieutenant £140 (NA/SP/12/187/19).

had been fourteen in the original group: three Jesuits (Robert Persons, Edmund Campion, and Br. Ralph Emerson), three English priests (Ralph Sherwin, Luke Kirby, and Edward Rishton), and two lay students (John Pascal and Thomas Briscoe). There were also four older Marian priests (Edward Bromborough, William Giblet, Thomas Crane, and William Kemp) plus Bishop Thomas Goldwell and Fr. Nicholas Morton. The last two, being older men, turned back at Rheims, and returned to Rome, their places being supplied by Dr. Humphrey Ely, still a layman, and John Hart. Thomas Cottam joined the party in Rheims, and set out for England 5 June 1580 with Ely, Hart, and Edward Rishton. He was arrested on landing.

When Campion came to trial, November 1581, charged with conspiring at Rome and Rheims to overthrow and assassinate Elizabeth I, nineteen others were indicted with him: Robert Persons, William Allen, Nicholas Morton, James Bosgrave, Alexander Briant, John Colleton, Thomas Cottam, Humphrey Ely, William Filby, Thomas Ford, John Hart, Robert Johnson, Luke Kirby, Henry Orton (layman), George Ostcliff, Lawrence Richardson/Johnson, Edward Rishton, John Shert, and Ralph Sherwin.

Only four of these men had been in the party that left Rome with Campion and Persons: Morton, Kirby, Rishton, and Sherwin. The rest were a miscellaneous group. Cottam, Hart, and Ely had joined the group at Rheims. Alexander Briant, who had come to England from Douay back in August 1579, had been arrested in London by Thomas Norton, March 1581. He was a pupil of Persons at Balliol College, hence the authorities' keen interest in him. Thomas Ford, William Filby, and John Colleton were arrested with Campion at Lyford Grange. John Shert, who had been in England since August 1578, was captured in London in July 1581. Lawrence Johnson was a Lancashire man, sent into England a second time in early 1580, arrested in Lancashire, 1581, and sent up to London just in time to be tried and convicted with Campion. Robert Johnson, racked 15 December 1580, had no connection with Campion's mission, either. He had studied at the German College, Rome, and been ordained at Brussels in 1576. He crossed over to England in the early summer of 1580, and was arrested almost immediately. He said he never saw any of his companions in misfortune until he met them at the bar. James Bosgrave, S.J. had become a Jesuit in Rome in 1564, and after ordination in Austria had spent his professional life teaching in Poland and Lithuania. He was in England because his superiors had sent him home to recover his health. *En route* he met an English diplomat who intercepted his mail, discovered he was a Jesuit, and sent word about him ahead to England so that he was arrested on arrival. Although he had no connection whatever with any of the Campion group, he was tried and convicted with them. The king of Poland, however, intervened on his behalf, and he was spared the gallows. Banished in 1585, he returned to Poland, where he died in 1623.[1]

Even though the charge that all these men had conspired together was a manifest fiction, only one of them, Colleton, was able to produce witnesses to prove he had never been at Rheims or Rome, and was in England on the dates specified in the indictment. The rest were convicted, and sentenced to death. When the trial began, however, William Allen, Nicholas Morton, and Humphrey Ely were not in England, Robert Persons had escaped, and George Ostcliff, though arrested, may not have been tried.[2] Like four of his trial-mates (Hart, Bosgrave, Rishton,and Orton), he spent five years in prison until exile in 1586. The rest were all executed.

During their imprisonment in the Tower, eleven of these men (Briant, Campion, Colleton, Cottam, Ford, Hart, Robert Johnson, Kirby, Orton, Shert, Sherwin) were interrogated either under torture or the threat of it. Council torture warrants survive for seven of the cases, and John Hart's Tower Diary is the evidence for the others.[3] Four of the warrants name Thomas Norton as one of the torturers. But as we have already seen, Hart's diary tells us that torture could be inflicted without a specific instruction; and William Allen's account of the conversation between Norton and Hart similarly tells us that Norton could take part in torture without being named in a warrant. Consequently, when we find Norton named as the interrogator of Roscarrock, Sherwin, Johnson, and Orton,[4] and when Hart tells us that all four were tortured, it is a reasonable inference that Norton was involved in the torture; and when one of Norton's warrants quite specifically authorizes the torture of other prisoners besides those actually named, one begins to suspect that he was involved in all these cases.[5]

---

[1]*ODNB*.

[2]Anstruther, 262, says he was tried and condemned, but not executed.

[3]Although James Bosgrave is listed in the Christmas Eve warrant, I am assuming that the absence of his name from the lists of those tortured in Hart's diary means that he was not tortured.

[4]*APC*, 12. 264; *CRS* 1.67.

[5]*APC*, 13. 249, 29 October 1581. "A letter to the Attorney and Solicitor General, the Lieutenant of the Tower, Doctor Hammond, Thomas Wilkes and Thomas Norton for th'examining of Edmund Campion, Thomas Ford and others, prisoners in the Tower,

This is not surprising, since Norton, as client and "man of business" associated with Burghley, Walsingham and other councilors, was a keen proponent of strong measures against Catholics. In Parliament he worked energetically on the Council's behalf for passage of the 1581 "Act to retain the Queen's Majesty's subjects in their obedience" (23 Eliz. c.1). This statute made it high treason either to reconcile or to be reconciled to "the Romish religion;" prohibited the mass under penalty of two hundred marks fine and a year's imprisonment for the celebrant, and one hundred marks fine and a year in prison for the attenders; and increased the penalty for not attending the state church to a monthly fine of twenty pounds or imprisonment until either the fine was paid or the offender went to the church. As the Council's campaign to suppress Catholicism intensified, the councilors came to rely on Norton and his colleague Dr. Hammond to frame the questions to be put in the interrogation of priests and laity, and they repeatedly commissioned both of them to do the interrogating. There is no sign that either man was reluctant to do the work.

An interesting aspect of the torturing was that although the Council was secretive about details, there was nothing secret about the fact itself because, as a case that involved Norton reveals, torture could not be kept secret. In early 1580, on the advice of Lord Grey de Wilton, the Council arrested an Irishman called Thomas Myagh or Meagh because they suspected him of involvement in Kildare's rebellion. They instructed Hopton and Hammond to interrogate him, which they did. In their report they said that although they had examined him twice, they got nothing out of him because they had been unable to put him in the Scavenger's Daughter (which they call Skevington's Irons). And why had they not used the Scavenger's Daughter? The Council had instructed them to work secretly, and "that manner of dealing required the presence and aid of one of the jailors all the time that he should be in those irons," and, of course, the jailors would talk. Preferring information to secrecy, the Council ordered torture, 30 July 1581, and put Norton in charge.[1] Even so, they got nothing out of Myagh.

---

upon certain matters, and to put them unto the Rack, &c., according to the minute thereof in the Council Chest."

[1]Dick, 17; *APC*, 13.147. Myagh carved the following inscription on the wall of the Beauchamp Tower, where it is still to be seen:

> Thomas Myagh, whiche lieth here alon,
> That fayne wovld from hens be gon,
> By tortyre straynge mi troyth was
> Tried, yet of my libertie denied. 1581, Thomas Myagh.

Not only was the use of torture public by its nature, but in the case of
the Catholic prisoners, the whole process of capture, interrogation, trial,
and execution was intended to expose and degrade the defendants as
well as to inculpate them. Hence managed publicity at every stage of the
proceedings formed part of the Council's strategy, as the case of
Edmund Campion demonstrates.

Campion was arrested, along with Thomas Ford and John Colleton, at
Lyford Grange, Berkshire, 17 July 1581. Three days later, under orders
from the Council, the sheriff of Berkshire set off for London with his
prisoners. On Friday, 21 July, they arrived at Colnbrook, about fifteen
miles from London, where the Council required them to stay so that they
would enter London at noon on the Saturday when the streets were
crowded with people. Whereas the sheriff had treated his captives like
gentlemen, the Council now began the process of degrading them into a
public spectacle: they were to ride under a guard of fifty, their hands
tied, and their legs tied under the horses' bellies. Fr. Campion was to
ride first, with a paper fastened round his hat that read in large letters,
"Edmund Campion the seditious Jesuit." In this style they rode through
London to the Tower on 22 July.

The next step in the Council's publicity campaign was to announce
that Campion had denied his religion and was about to recant, and
though the rumor was short-lived, it had its effect in leading people to
doubt his reliability under pressure. On 30 July, the Council issued its
first commission to Hopton, Hammond, Beale, and Norton authorizing
them to interrogate Campion with torture: "...and in case he continue
willfully to deny the truth, then to deal with him by the rack." That day
or the next, Campion went on the rack, and—as Simpson puts it—"by
the 2nd of August the Council had somehow acquired a flood of light
about his doings."[1] During the next week they sent out a stream of
instructions ordering the arrest of people whom he had visited, and
began to circulate rumors that his nerve had failed on the rack, and he
had betrayed the people who had welcomed him into their houses.

Yet despite these rumors, on 6th August Burghley wrote telling the
Earl of Shrewsbury that "Campion is in the Tower, and stiffly denieth to
answer any question of moment," and on 7 August the Council wrote
again to Hopton, Hammond, and Norton asking them to interrogate
Campion and his fellows further "upon such points wherein their

---

[1]Simpson 1, 343. The day was probably 31 July, anniversary of the death of St. Ignatius
Loyola, already observed by the Jesuits, though Ignatius was not beatified until 1609. As
we have already seen, torture tended to take place on Sundays and holy days.

Lordships are desirous they should make a more plain and direct answer."[1] As a result, on or shortly after 14 August, he was racked again, along with Ford and Colleton, because "they refuse to confess whether they have said any masses or no, whom they have confessed, and where Parsons and the other priests be." So: did Campion give up the names of his hosts or not?

At the first of the Tower conferences between Campion and some picked Protestant divines that began almost immediately after the second racking, the subject of torture came up when Campion said that he "had been twice on the rack, and that racking was more grievous than hanging, and that he had rather choose to be hanged than racked." To this Hopton, the lieutenant, replied:

> that he had no cause to complain of racking, who had rather seen than felt the rack: and admonished him to use good speech, that he gave not cause to be used with more severity. For although...you were put to the rack, yet notwithstanding you were so favorably used therein, as being taken off, you could and did presently go thence to your lodging without help, and use your hands in writing, and all other parts of your body, which you could not have done if you had been put to that punishment with any such extremity as you speak of.

When Robert Beale, one of the torturers, asked if he had been examined on points of religion, he answered that although he had not been asked directly about religion, he had been racked to make him to name the places and people whom he had visited. He had not done this, he said, because "he might not betray his Catholic brethren which were (as he said) the temples of the holy Ghost."[2]

Neither Hopton nor Beale made any answer to this, and neither did their fellow-torturers Norton and Hammond, both of them present at the conference. Had Campion revealed the names of his hosts under torture, they would surely have challenged his denial. Lord Hunsdon, the Queen's first cousin (and very possibly her half-brother), who was present at some of the torturing, is reported to have said, "You can pluck out his heart more easily than we can find words to express what religion meant to this man," a remark implying that the torture failed.[3]

[1]Simpson 2, 349–52, 360–66; *APC*, 13. 165.

[2]Simpson 1, 350–1.

[3]Edwards 2, 138. Translated from the Latin translation of the original in Henry More, *Historia Missionis Anglicanae Societatis Jesu* (1660).

Perhaps the most striking evidence of the torturers' failure to elicit the information that the Council wanted is that on 29 October Hopton, Hammond, Wilkes, and Norton were ordered to torture Campion, Ford, and others again "upon certain matters."[1] The torture followed on 31 October and 2 November and, in Campion's case, was conducted with a savagery that reveals the torturers' rage and frustration, presumably because of his refusal to tell them what they wanted.[2] Yet he must have said *something*, probably in the October racking. On the scaffold he asked "all them to forgive him whom he had confessed upon the rack," and according to reports of a letter he wrote to Thomas Pounde, distressed by the rumors of his betrayals, he said that he had revealed nothing unknown to his interrogators.[3] The strong implication of recently-discovered manuscript material is that the government lied about Campion's supposed confessions, both to discredit him and to trap his hosts. One suspects that Campion's mistake, insofar as he made one, was to have said anything at all, a lesson well learned by Robert Southwell who, finding himself similarly tortured, refused to answer even the simplest question.[4]

The Council's campaign to expose and vilify the missioners came to a climax with the grand show trial mounted in November, followed by the first executions on 1 December. In the short run, however, the outcome for the government both at home and abroad was a public relations disaster. Robert Persons, who left England in late August after Campion's capture, had already published at Rouen his Latin *De Persecutione Anglicana, Epistola* (1581), a very effective little book that went into two more editions, and was translated into French and English. Thomas Alfield, a priest who had been present at the executions, wrote up his detailed eye-witness account that was printed so quickly that Richard Topcliffe was already searching for it in February 1582. Alfield's little

---

[1]*APC*, 13. 249.

[2]The dates are recorded by Hart (DT, 47) and Fr. Persons (Hicks, 118–19). 31 October is the vigil of All Saints' Day, 2 November All Souls' Day.

[3]Alfield, Sig. C1; Simpson 1, 415. The letter was read at his trial, and included this sentence: "It grieveth me much to have offended the Catholic cause so highly as to confess the names of some gentlemen and friends in whose houses I had been entertained; yet in this I greatly cherish and comfort myself that I never discovered any secrets there declared, and that I will not, come rack, come rope."

[4]On this whole difficult question, see especially Kilroy 1, in particular his superb chapter 5, "Within these Walls: the Interior Life of Sir Thomas Tresham," and Kilroy 2, 255–7, 313–14.

book was distributed in Europe, and William Allen incorporated it into his *A Brief History of the Glorious Martyrdom of Twelve Reverend Priests,* published later in 1582. Allen's book, translated into Latin, Spanish, and Italian, circulated widely, and did the reputation of Elizabeth I and her government no good at all.

Well-informed as Allen was, both by Alfield's book and by his own contacts in London, he gave detailed accounts of Fr. Campion's and Fr. Briant's torture.[1] One name stands out: Thomas Norton, the Council's chief interrogator in these cases, and hence the man most responsible for directing the torture, in short the "rackmaster" as Fr. Persons called him.

Because Fr. Alexander Briant had been Robert Persons's pupil, and knew him and his family well, Norton and his fellow-commissioners had great hopes of eliciting from him information about Fr. Persons's habits and whereabouts. When they saw that Fr. Briant was not about to tell them anything of the kind, they turned nasty, sending him to the Counter with orders that he be deprived of food and water. Real torture then followed in the Tower. When Briant refused to say where he had last seen Persons, how he was maintained, where he had said mass, and whose confessions he had heard:

> They caused needles to be thrust under his nails, whereat *M. Brian* was not moved at all, but with a constant mind and pleasant countenance said the Psalm *Miserere,* desiring God to forgive his tormentors. Whereat *Dr. Hammond* stamped and stared as a man half beside himself, saying, "What thing is this? If a man were not settled in his religion, this were enough to convert him."...He was even to the dismembering of his body rent and torn upon the rack because he would not confess where *F. Persons* was.[2]

The most dramatic story about Norton's treatment of Fr. Briant appears on the last page of the English translation of *De Persecutione Anglicana* in a letter that he wrote to the Jesuits asking to be admitted to the Society. He described his torture, how he had prepared himself with prayers, and how it seemed to him that his prayers had been answered:

> Whether this that I will say, be miraculous or no, God he knoweth: but true it is, and thereof my conscience is a witness before God. And this I say:

---

[1] Since mainstream English historians often write dismissively about Allen's and Persons's accounts, it is worth repeating that they were well-informed, by letters from prisoners as well as by their own sources at court and on the council. Allen wrote to Agazarri in March, 1583 telling him that he had received many letters from the Tower prisoners, but could not publish them without raising questions about their sending (Morris 1, 2.33).

[2] Allen 1, Sig F5.

that in the end of the torture though my hands and feet were violently stretched and racked, and my adversaries fulfilled their wicked lust, in practicing their cruel tyranny upon my body, yet notwithstanding I was without sense and feeling well nigh of all grief and pain: and not so only, but as it were comforted, eased, and refreshed by the griefs of the torture bypassed, I continued still with perfect and present senses, in quietnesses of heart, and tranquillity of mind. Which thing when the commissioners did see, they departed, and in going forth of the door, they gave order to rack me again the next day following, after the same sort.[1]

Fr. Persons printed this letter, and responded to it on the last page of the English version of his book. He could not understand, he wrote, how human nature could bear such pain unless helped by divine grace:

And that our Lord did concur with extraordinary comfort, in their torments, it may appear in this epistle going before of Master Briant: whom Master Norton the Rackmaster (if he be not misreported) vaunted in the court to have pulled one good foot longer than ever God made him and yet in the midst of all he seemed to care nothing, and therefore out of doubt (saith he) he had a devil within him to bear witness, and the Judge both of devils and devilish men, shall be at hand to give sentence.[2]

Michael Graves, Norton's admiring biographer, says of Allen's account of the torture-by-needles-under-the-nails that "The accuracy of such detail cannot always be authenticated," and of Persons's story about Norton's boast of pulling Briant a foot longer than God made him that Persons had "picked it up," and that his sources "were sometimes unreliable."[3]

Again, this will not do. Hart's Tower Diary verifies the needle torture. Norton himself verified the accounts of Briant's starvation in his pamphlet, *A Declaration of the Favourable Dealing of Her Majesty's Commissioners*. In a personal letter to Walsingham, he even verified, with modification, the cruelty of his treatment of Briant as well as the boast reported by Persons. As he told Walsingham, he did not say that he *had* stretched Briant a foot longer than God made him, but rather that

---

[1]John Hart (DT, 42) records this experience from Briant's own account: "The same Briant was thrown into the Pit: then, after eight days, was taken to the rack on which he suffered very severely, once that very day, and twice the next day; after which last stretching of his body, as I heard from his own mouth (shortly before his death) he felt no pain at all even when the torturers were at their cruelest and inflicting the greatest tortures on him."

[2]Robert Persons, *An Epistle of the Persecution of Catholickes in Englande*, Sig. M3.

[3]Graves, 272, 273.

if Briant persisted in refusing to answer the questions put to him, he *would* "be made a foot longer than God had made him." And he added that because of his "apparent obstinacy in matters that he well knew," he was "racked more than the rest." As for the deprivation of Briant's food, it was entirely the fault, said Norton, of his own "cursed heart." Had he only provided the writing sample they asked for, he could have had all the food he wanted.[1]

By the time these books appeared to embarrass the English government generally and Thomas Norton in particular, Norton had found himself committed to the Tower of London, occupying the room recently vacated by Edmund Campion. If the spy Sledd is to be believed, the keeper responsible for the room was going about saying that having had a saint in his keeping, he now had a devil.[2]

The exact date of Norton's committal is not known. It used to be thought that he owed his downfall to disobliging remarks about the bishops, but Roger Manners, son of the Earl of Rutland and an esquire of the body, and therefore in a position to know, wrote that Mr. Norton, the great Parliament man, had been committed "for his overmuch and undutiful speaking touching Monsieur's cause."[3] In other words Norton, as one would expect, given his religious views, was one of those opposed to the proposed marriage between Elizabeth I and "Monsieur," the Duke of Anjou, brother of the French king, and it seems that he had spoken too freely on the subject. Roger Manners's letter, announcing Norton's arrest as news, is dated 5 December. Norton, therefore, had been picked up as soon as the Campion case concluded with the executions of Campion, Sherwin, and Briant on 1 December, and there can be no doubt that his arrest was the doing of the Queen herself. She had already expressed displeasure at some of the things he had said in the Parliament of 1581; she disapproved strongly of his well-known views on the bishops, and word of indiscreet remarks about her marriage negotiations was probably the last straw. It is likely that she had wanted to move against Norton some months earlier, but had been persuaded—by

[1]NA/SP12/152/72, quoted in Graves, 275–6. In the letter to Walsingham, Norton—by now a connoisseur in these things—paid Briant an interesting compliment by intervening in a discussion of Campion's courage to say that "there was more courage of a man's heart in one Briant than in ten Campions"—the implication being that torture had defeated Campion. For Norton's account of the starvation, see *A Declaration of the Favourable Dealing of Her Majesty's Commissioners,* Sigs A2v–3.

[2]Allen 1, Sig. B2.

[3]Graves, 388, 391.

Burghley and Walsingham—to wait until his work on the Campion case was finished.

One has only to recall the case of John Stubbs to realize how dangerous it was to go about speaking "undutifully" about the French match. Stubbs's own strong opinions, encouraged by powerful figures careful to keep themselves in the shadows, betrayed him into writing and publishing his obscenely titled pamphlet, *The Gaping Gulf* (1579), attacking the Queen for even thinking about such a marriage. This genuinely offensive book infuriated Elizabeth so much that she wanted him executed for it, but settled instead for the "merciful" alternative of having the offending hand that wrote it cut off with a meat cleaver. After losing his hand, Stubbs spent eighteen months in the Tower.

Norton was lucky to get off as lightly as he did, but then he had powerful if discreet support, from Walsingham and Hatton especially. At the time of his arrest, Monsieur was in England, and until he left there was nothing that Norton's backers could do to help him. Anjou left in February, 1582. By March, Secretary Walsingham had succeeded in having Norton moved from the Tower to house arrest. He was released from all restraint in April.

Alfield and Allen both knew about Norton's downfall when they were writing their books, and understandably enough took some pleasure in it. Allen, as usual, seems to have been extremely well informed—in fact if English historians had paid more attention to Allen's book, they would have known sooner why Norton was arrested. Allen was too discreet and protective of his sources to speak plainly, but he knew that Norton was in trouble for his opinions about the French marriage, and he knew, too, that Norton and Secretary Walsingham saw eye to eye in the matter:

> This same man [Norton] not discovered only of ill affection, but justly put into the Tower for seditious words and plain treason (so much as would have hanged an hundred Catholics and honest men) yet much complained that he was so unkindly dealt withal, that a few rash words which of many wise men were not misliked of, as he saith, could not be forgiven, but with such difficulty. Specially to him that was so necessary for their service...
>
> And *Mr. Norton's* wife, if she will be as plain to the Council, as she is to some of her neighbors, can tell (if Mr. Secretary himself remember it not) who put unto this same *Norton*, being then for the said treasons in the Tower, and justly in disgrace with her Majesty, to pen matters of state, and to set down orders and articles to be treated of against Catholics in the parliament, and other places...
>
> The said *Mistress Norton* can tell also, where her husband did lay up *Stubbs's* book against her Majesty for a secret treasure, which gear well sifted would bewray worse affection and intention too, then they shall ever find in Catholics whilst they live.

This is fascinating. Allen knew that Norton was in the Tower for seditious and treasonable speech of a kind that plenty of people agreed with, that he had Walsingham's backing, and was even, at Walsingham's bidding, drawing up proposals for further anti-Catholic measures during his imprisonment. And then the *coup de grace*: Stubbs's book was one of his secret treasures, carefully hidden.[1]

Although Norton continued to work for Walsingham after his release, the Queen seems to have put her foot down. He took part in no more interrogations of Catholics until, in November 1583, Walsingham brought him back as an expert to rack Francis Throckmorton. In March, 1584, he died.[2] His last service had been to conduct the prosecution of the Catholic printer William Carter, condemned and executed 10 and 11 January 1584. Carter had been severely racked, but the identity of the commissioner in charge is not known. It is unlikely to have been Norton.[3]

Were the Catholics justified in focusing their exposure of the English government's methods on Norton? His biographer, Michael Graves, thinks not. Referring to an engraving portraying Norton as torturer, he suggests that the Catholics had unfairly fixed upon him as a cartoon-figure embodying their pain and distress:

> Rackmaster Norton. Archicarnifex. The cartoon, the visual image, completed the transformation from man to monster. Moreover he was now the master-tormentor, assisted by satellites; no longer just one of a team of examiners commissioned by the privy council....[4]

Graves begins his account of Norton's torturing career by reminding us that after living through the twentieth century we should understand that, "Any lingering notions that the sixteenth century was a more barbarous age do not warrant serious consideration." The implication of this argument is that, having the examples of Hitler, Stalin, and Mao to guide us, we should moderate our condemnation of the Elizabethans.[5] But does

[1] Allen 1, Sig. C5-C5v.

[2] Graves, 269, 407.

[3] Graves, 248; Pollen , 30; CRS 4. 74; *ODNB*. It was probably Topcliffe. See below, 121, 141.

[4] Graves, 274. This line of defense—that he was merely a conscientious crown servant carrying out instructions dutifully—is one we shall encounter again. A.L. Rowse used it of Topcliffe himself, and Claire Cross uses it of the Earl of Huntington (Rowse, 193; Cross 2, 139–40).

[5] Graves, 244.

this argument work the other way, one wonders? Given the example set for us by the Elizabethans, should we perhaps moderate our criticisms of Hitler and Co.?

The English Catholics, as we have seen, were well-informed. They knew that for the brief period of the investigation into the Campion mission, Thomas Norton—whoever his fellow-commissioners might have been—was the chief executive of the Council's determination to suppress the mission and the Catholics who welcomed it. They knew, too, that Norton had consistently put himself forward as theoretician and executive of the Council's policy, and they knew too—as we do from his own words—that he had a relish for the work. He enjoyed doing it.[1]

The final effects of Norton's enthusiasm were apparent in the pathetic appearance of Edmund Campion at his trial. At his arraignment, his hands and arms were so injured that he could not raise his arm to take the oath until one of his fellow prisoners held his arm up for him. He could only hold a cup of water by taking it within his two hands, and both the Spanish and Venetian ambassadors reported home that his fingernails had been taken off in the torture.[2] William Allen's reports of the last tortures that produced these results complete the picture:

> He was so cruelly torn and rent upon the torture the two last times, that he told a secret friend of his that found means to speak with him, that he thought they meant to make away with him in that sort...He used to fall down at the rackhouse door upon both knees to commend himself to God's mercy and to crave his grace of patience in his pains...He said to his keeper after his last racking, that it was a preface to death.
>
> And his said keeper asking him the next day how he felt his hands and feet: he answered, not ill, because not at all.[3]

This was a man, we should remember, who had been called in his time "the flower of Oxford," and who had a European reputation as a writer, teacher, and scholar.

---

[1] When the Jesuit lay-brother Thomas Pounde was imprisoned in Bishop's Stortford Castle in the early 80s, Walsingham sent Norton to make an assessment of his case. Norton's recommendation to Walsingham was that Pounde should be treated as a lunatic, and put in Bedlam. Even Walsingham was not prepared to do that (Simpson 3, 99).

[2] Simpson 2, 439; Morris 2, 459. The Spanish ambassador's secretary writes, "the tortures...were so great that, as was seen when they produced him, they had torn his nails off in them." Mendoza, the Spanish ambassador, went in disguise to witness Campion's execution. John Morris suggests that Campion's nails came off because of the swelling caused by the racking.

[3] Allen 1, Sigs D6–D7.

Stung by the publicity given to his activities, Norton wrote a short pamphlet, *A Declaration of the Favourable Dealing of Her Majesty's Commissioners*, in justification of his own and the Council's proceedings. His hand is detectable, too, in the longer work published under Burghley's own name a year later, *The Execution of Justice in England.* Just one sentence from Norton's own *Declaration* is sufficient to represent the man :

> That very Campion, I say, before the conference had with him by learned men in the Tower, wherein he was charitably used, was never so racked, but that he was presently able to walk, and to write, and did presently write and subscribe all his confessions, as by the originals thereof may appear.[1]

That may have been true after Campion's first rackings, before the Tower conferences or debates took place in August, but by the time Norton was writing in self-defense it was a lie, and he knew it.

About a month before Norton died, the Queen whom he had served so faithfully, but who had never approved of him or his opinions, finally spoke out in his praise, no doubt persuaded to do so by Burghley or Walsingham, or both of them. Her little speech on the subject survives in a newsletter to the Earl of Rutland, 6 February 1584:

> I forgot in my last to report these good words which it pleased her Majesty to bestow upon Norton on Sunday last...by the which, with great and vehement protestation, her Grace pronounced him a most faithful and loyal servant to her, and such a one as had done many good services, alleging further that howsoever his adversaries did slander or libel against him, yet true it was that he never touched any that had not before deserved to be hanged.[2]

Considering how much Norton had done in a life of hard work for his conciliar patrons, for the city of London, and in parliament, and considering how little Elizabeth I liked his religious and political views, this was a decidedly back-handed compliment. Ignoring everything in his voluminous *curriculum vitae* except his anti-Catholic activity, the Queen singled him out for his work in that one field. In fact her speech was not so much a compliment to Norton as it was an endorsement of the persecution, of its agents, and its methods. She praised him for pursuing, arresting, interrogating, torturing, and killing Catholics, and that only.

---

[1] If there were any signed confessions, they have long since disappeared.

[2] Quoted by Graves, 278, from *CSP. Dom., 1547-80*, Vol. 133, no.45.

Having disposed of him, moreover, at the time of her speech she was grooming his successor.

*****

John Hart: Apostate or Hero?

John Hart, born to a gentleman's family of Eynsham Ferry, near Oxford, matriculated at Louvain in 1569, and is next heard of in Rome, 1575, when bishop Goldwell admitted him to minor orders at the English Hospice. He received his bachelor of theology degree from Douay in January, 1578, and was ordained priest at Cambrai, March 1578. When the Campion party arrived at Rheims, May 1580, its two elderly members, bishop Goldwell and Dr. Nicholas Morton, decided to go no further. John Hart and the lay scholar, Dr. Humphrey Ely, took their places. Hart was sent to England, 5 June, ahead of Campion and Persons. He was arrested on landing at Dover, and sent to the court at Nonesuch. There Walsingham interviewed him, and instead of immediately imprisoning him, sent him to Oxford to confer with the puritan, John Reynolds.

This unusual treatment leads one to infer either that Hart communicated a willingness to be influenced or that Walsingham had his own reasons for sparing him. Hart remained faithful, was brought back to London, and imprisoned in the Marshalsea. Then, like other priests, he was moved to the Tower, 24 December, where he spent five days sleeping on the bare earth before being led to the rack. Once again, he either indicated willingness to cooperate, or else Walsingham intervened.

Norton examined him on 31 December. In the surviving extracts from his examination, he gives his understanding of the current inoperative state of Pius V's notorious bull of excommunication against the Queen, and explains the faculties given by Gregory XIII to Frs. Persons and Campion governing their interpretation of the bull. If we are to judge from these extracts, Hart said nothing useful to his interrogators.[1]

---

[1] NA/SP12/144/64,65. A couple of years later Norton, preparing his "Chain of Treasons," attributed to Hart's examination a fantastically detailed cock-and-bull story implicating Allen in an alleged Papal League against England of 1580, now known to have been a fabrication by the English for their own propaganda purposes. For a detailed account of this episode and its uses, including an analysis of the contradictions and inconsistencies in the material attributed to Hart, see Hicks 2, Appendix 1, "The Bogus Papal League of 1580," 223–34. It is just possible that Hart made the story up himself, though had that been the case, one would have expected the government to use such dramatic material at his November trial, along with Campion and the rest, including Allen himself *in absentia*, for just that kind of conspiracy.

He had disappointed his captors again, and when we next hear of him, he is being tried and convicted with Campion and the others. He was arraigned 16 November, 1581, convicted and sentenced to death, 21 November. On the morning of 1 December, he was supposed to share Fr. Campion's hurdle to Tyburn, but evaded his captors yet again, this time, it seems, by promising conformity. That same day he compounded his fall by writing a letter to Walsingham offering to spy on William Allen. The letter, though, may be a forgery.[1]

During the whole period of his captivity in the Tower, he kept a diary recording the treatment of Catholic prisoners there, lay and clerical. On 11 January, six weeks after his escape from Tyburn, he wrote that, "John Hart, priest, because he refused to co-operate with the heretics in any way after his condemnation, was sent to the pit for nine days."

William Allen, at Rheims, did not know why or how Hart had escaped death, but in a letter, 2 February, he wrote that Hart's brother William was upset that he had not died with Campion, also that his mother had urged martyrdom upon him. Allen knew nothing about an apostasy; five days later he described Hart as a "brave athlete of God."

As Hart's nine days in the pit indicates, he had again refused to co-operate, and in the spring of that year he was again scheduled for execution, this time with Thomas Ford, John Shert, and Robert Johnson, who were all three killed 28 May. The day before, though, 27 May, the Council wrote to the Lieutenant of the Tower, "that whereas the sheriffs of London were tomorrow to receive certain seminary priests lately condemned, he should for certain good considerations stay John Hart and signify so much on their Lordships' behalf unto the said sheriffs." John Hart had escaped death again.

Evidently he had agreed—again—to enter into discussions with the Protestants. Sometime in 1582 Walsingham arranged for him to have talks with John Reynolds, but once again he disappointed the Council, for as his diary says (1 December), "John Hart, priest already condemned to death, was punished with twenty days in irons because he refused to agree with the minister Reynolds." Six months later, in June 1583, he was given another forty days in the pit for the same offense. Meanwhile, he had succeeded in converting his keeper, a young man

---

[1]This letter is so peculiar in its claims of intimacy with Allen, and so unlike other statements by Hart that it may, in fact, be a forgery. But to what end? Walsingham could never use it without exposing his agent, and Hart, once out of English hands, could always deny it. For the text of the letter, see TD, 163, and for skepticism about its genuineness, see Hicks 2, 226–7.

called Samuel Kennet. In a letter, 23 June 1582, Allen told Agazzari that "this morning a young man has come to us with letters from John Hart," that the young man was Hart's keeper, and that Hart had converted him and reconciled him to the Church. Hart's relationship with his keeper no doubt explains how he came to have access to pen and paper, to receive information, and to write his diary.[1]

In October, Allen wrote telling Agazarri that Hart, in prison, was daily expecting martyrdom, and that he wished to become a Jesuit. At about that same time, he must have been having the conversations with Reynolds that put him in the pit. In mid-1584, Reynolds published those discussions as *The Sum of the Conference between John Reynolds and John Hart*. Dedicated to Leicester, this book had prefatory letters by both men. From Hart's we learn that beginning with his arrest, Walsingham had shown him "great favor...in granting me liberty of conference at home, first in mine own country and afterward in prison;" that after he was sentenced, Walsingham had continued to offer him "the same favor if I would admit it," and had arranged the meetings with Reynolds. Walsingham must have had some personal reason for so persistently intervening in Hart's fate, although he will also have hoped for a propaganda advantage from any concession that Hart might make. But Hart consistently disappointed him, and conceded nothing.

No explanation of these extraordinary proceedings survives, but it looks as if Hart's escapes from punishment and death had as much to do with Walsingham as with himself, and the only explanation is either that Hart was a remarkably persuasive, plausible man, or else as Hart later told Persons, Walsingham took a personal interest in his fate. Hart certainly had no intention at any time of apostatizing.

In June 1585, the Council sent Hart into banishment with twenty-one other prisoners. He made his way to Rome, where he was formally admitted into the Society of Jesus. In 1586, Edward Rishton printed Hart's diary, *Diarium rerum gestarum in Turri Londinensi*, in his edition and continuation of Nicholas Sander's *De origine ac progressu schismatis Anglicani,* but when Robert Persons edited a third edition in 1587, he omitted the diary.[2]

In the spring of 1586, Hart's Jesuit superiors sent him to Jaroslaw, Poland, where he died almost immediately, 19 July. There is a surprising

---

[1]The keeper went to Rome, was ordained in the Lateran, May 1589, and eventually became a Benedictine (Anstruther, 195).

[2]The author of the article on Hart in *ODNB* suggests that Persons had discovered Hart's apostasy. If this was so, nothing was said about it by Persons or anyone else.

coda to this extraordinary story. In 1594, Hart's body was found to be incorrupt, a phenomenon that Catholics consider to be an indication of unusual sanctity.

His younger brother William, who had been so upset to hear of his escape from death in 1581, was himself admitted to the Society in Rome, where he died as a novice in 1584.[1]

*****

[1]The materials for this account of John Hart's career are taken from Anstruther, 153–5; *DT*, passim; *CSPD 1581–90*, 32, 56, 69, 144, 223; *LM*, 113–14, 146, 166, 167, 199; McCoog, 203; *ODNB*.

Six

Topcliffe Takes Over

With Edmund Campion dead and eight other priests whom they associated with him under sentence of death, the Queen and her Council must have thought they had dealt satisfactorily with that aspect of the Catholic problem. Then, early in 1582, they had news that a Catholic priest had written a book describing the executions as martyrdoms, and realized that a whole new chapter of the Campion story had opened. That is why, with Norton disgraced and in the Tower, they brought in Richard Topcliffe to join Norton's old colleague Recorder Fleetwood in searching for the printers and distributors of Alfield's book.

But why Topcliffe? Norton, a successful lawyer, was Walsingham's and Burghley's client and "man of business," and they were the men in charge of this kind of operation. Topcliffe was nobody's "man of business." Like many Elizabethan gentlemen, he had some legal training, but he was no lawyer, and he had never completed a degree course at either university. As we have seen, he hobnobbed with Burghley, and he came to do fairly regular business with Walsingham, but it is most unlikely that either of those characters would have commissioned him as a replacement for Norton. Topcliffe's connections were elsewhere, with the Dudley brothers and the Queen herself. His own court connections therefore explain why this man who had already shown interest in what we would call police work now emerged as Elizabeth I's chief detective.

Following his success at dispersing the Alfield book ring, and on the very day of Alfield's arrest, the Council gave Topcliffe his first personal commission, 8 April 1582, in the form of a warrant to "the justices and other her Majesty's officers in the county of Essex:"

> to aid and assist Richard Topcliffe, esquire, this bearer, in his secret and diligent search of certain houses and places within that county, and to apprehend and seize sundry persons and things according to such particular direction as he hath in that behalf received, the same being of great importance for her Majesty's service. They are required and in her Majesty's name straitly charged to enter into and search such houses and places as the said Topcliffe shall name unto them, what or wheresoever they be, either within liberties or without, and therein, as in the conveying of them hither unto the Court, shall follow such advice and direction as he shall prescribe unto them.[1]

The warrant restricted his movements to the county of Essex, but was otherwise a forerunner of the kind of blanket commission under which he later operated. The Council's instructions ("such particular direction as he hath in that behalf received") were of the most general kind, since they leave *all* the detail—the places to be visited, the houses to be raided, the people to be arrested, and the goods to be seized—entirely to his discretion. What is more, the law officers of the county—all of them—are to submit to his direction. How did such a warrant come to be issued? It seems likely that Topcliffe, having been instrumental in Alfield's arrest, had other, related objectives in mind but, knowing there were security leaks on the Council, asked for a commission in a form that would preserve secrecy.

Commission in hand, five days later he went into Essex looking for Sir Thomas More's grandson, Thomas More II (1531–1606). Topcliffe found him at a house belonging to a Mr. Wayfarer, where he maintained a study, and he came away from the search with a manuscript copy of Nicholas Harpsfield's life of Sir Thomas More. He endorsed the manuscript's first leaf in his distinctive handwriting, "This book was found by Rich: Topcliffe in Mr. Thomas More's study amongst other books at Greenstreet, Mr. Wayfarer's house, when Mr. More was apprehended the 13th of April 1582."[2] He also came away with Mr. More himself, a man over fifty, who spent the next four years in the Marshalsea prison because he owned a biography of his grandfather as well as "other books."[3] Such was Topcliffe's new-found power. There is no hint in this operation of the treasonable behavior that, according to Burghley in his pamphlet *The Execution of Justice in England,* published for the whole of Europe to read, was the sole reason for the molestation of Catholics. The sole reason for Thomas More II's arrest was the possession of Catholic books, a subject that was to become a Topcliffe specialty.

If, however, Topcliffe was to be riding out into the counties, searching houses and arresting people, he would need assistance, and so it was probably during these early months of 1582 that he began to put together the squadron or platoon of helpers whom he was to call his "instru-

---

[1]*APC,* 13. 382–3.

[2]The manuscript is now in Emmanuel College Library, Cambridge, Ms. 76. See Montague Rhodes James, *The Western Manuscripts in the Library of Emmanuel College: A Descriptive Catalogue* (Cambridge, U.K.: Cambridge University Press, 1904), 69.

[3]The younger More was proud of his family's tradition of fidelity to his grandfather's memory. He purchased the Holbein portrait of Sir Thomas More and his family (now lost), and had at least three copies made of it (Honigmann, 80–82).

ments."[1] It has been thought that one of his recruits may have been Anthony Munday, dramatist, poet, anti-Catholic pamphleteer, turncoat, and spy. Munday had played an important role in the government's campaign to blacken Edmund Campion's reputation, whereas Topcliffe, as far as we know, had no part in the Campion affair until he went looking for the people responsible for publishing Alfield's book. Both men, however, were present and vocal at the deaths of four priests (Filby, Kirby, Richardson, and Cottam) on 30 May 1582, and although Topcliffe may have been present merely as a court observer, the fact that he spoke up suggests that he was there in a more official role, and it is just possible that he and Munday attended the executions as employer and employee.

In 1588 Munday dedicated a collection of poems, *A Banquet of Dainty Conceits*, to Topcliffe as an acknowledgment for "manifold good turns and deeds of friendship;" but although the phrase suggests an association of some standing, unfortunately we have no way of knowing Munday's real reasons for dedicating a book to Topcliffe. There is no sign of his presence in Topcliffe's operations until 1592, when Topcliffe sent him to arrest Ralph Marshal.[2] Munday's anti-Catholic activities predated any association with Topcliffe, and continued long after his death. He was still hunting Catholics in 1612 when the poet Hugh Holland was indicted as a recusant on his evidence,[3] and so we should probably resist the temptation to enroll Munday in Topcliffe's band of "instruments."[4]

Topcliffe's next venture into bibliographical detection took him to the home of the printer William Carter on Tower Hill. Carter, born ca.1549, had already been in trouble for printing Catholic books. He was first imprisoned in the Poultry, September 1578, then again in the Gatehouse, December 1579, when John Aylmer, bishop of London, wrote to Burghley describing how he had not only found Carter's press, but

---

[1] E.g., BL. Ms. Lansdowne 72, no. 40.

[2] See below, 245. This is Topcliffe's only mention of Munday.

[3] *ODNB*, s.v. "Anthony Munday."

[4] There is no evidence for the statement in *ODNB* that Topcliffe was Munday's mentor in "papist-hunting," nor is there any evidence to support the argument in John Jowett's Arden edition of the play *Sir Thomas More* (London: Arden Shakespeare, 2011, 10, 419–20) that Munday was able to borrow Harpsfield's life of More from Topcliffe some fourteen or fifteen years after Topcliffe confiscated it from Thomas More II. There is no evidence of his presence on that occasion, and it is most unlikely that Topcliffe would lend such a Ms. to a man like Munday.

searched his house, and found "naughty, papistical books." In June 1581 he was released on condition that he remain within three miles of his house, and conform himself to the state church.[1]

Topcliffe raided Carter's house in July 1582, looking for more Catholic books. He arrested Carter, and imprisoned him, initially in the Gatehouse; then, 19 July, Carter was moved to the Tower.[2] No reason for the search of Carter's house appears in the surviving accounts of his fate, but it is likely that Topcliffe, after his success with Thomas More II, was looking for more writing by Nicholas Harpsfield.

Harpsfield, archdeacon of Canterbury in Queen Mary's time, was an important scholar-writer on the Catholic side. During Mary's reign he completed his life of More, and produced two other works, *Cranmer's Recantations* and *A Treatise of the Pretended Divorce*. In 1562 his refusal to accept the new ecclesiastical arrangements led to his imprisonment in the Fleet Prison, along with his brother John, archdeacon of London. The brothers remained there for twelve years. During that time, Nicholas produced his immense *Dialogi sex* published in Antwerp, 1566, as well as a Latin history of the English Church. The former included a detailed criticism and rebuttal of John Foxe's *Acts and Monuments* (the Protestants' famous "Book of Martyrs"); the latter, circulating widely in manuscript, was meant to be a corrective to the Protestants' revisionist church history. The *Treatise of the Pretended Divorce* was perhaps the most influential of all because Nicholas Sander took from it some of the information in his extremely successful Latin history of the religious changes in England, *De origine et progressu schismatis Anglicani* (1573). For Topcliffe, the most offensive passage of Harpsfield's book was probably his mention of the story that Henry VIII had slept with Anne Boleyn's sister Mary, and with her mother too.[3]

It is hardly surprising that Topcliffe was interested in tracking down

---

[1]*ODNB*.

[2]Hart's diary dates Carter's arrival in the Tower. Robert Persons, though, modified Hart's account to say that Carter had been brought to the tower from another prison. The Gatehouse, adjoining Topcliffe's own house, was likely to have been that prison (TD, 55, note 2).

[3]"For now, to be plain with you, the said Lady Anne was sister to her whom the King had carnally known before. Wherefore, after that he minded this divorce, and had a while some comfort thereof, he labored to the Pope to have a dispensation to marry that woman whose sister he had carnally known before...Yea, I have credibly heard reported that the King knew the mother of the said Lady Anne Boleyn, which is a fourth impediment, and worse then the precedents; of the which impediment Sir Thomas More was not by likelihood ignorant..." (Harpsfield, 236–7).

copies of Harpsfield's books. He learned that during Harpsfield's imprisonment William Carter had served him as a secretary-amanuensis, and inferred (correctly) that given Carter's record as a Catholic printer and publisher it was likely he would have Harpsfield manuscripts in his possession. It was a successful search. Topcliffe not only found Harpsfield's *Treatise of the Pretended Divorce* and his *Historia ecclesiae Christi;*[1] he also found that Carter had been selling manuscript copies at £20 each. We learn this from Topcliffe's own marginalia, bragging that it was he who had discovered and arrested Carter. In fact, Topcliffe was so proud of taking Carter that he wrote three notes on the subject in the margins of his copy of Pollini's book, and he was equally proud that he had shown the manuscript of the *Historia* to the Queen, and that she had allowed him to keep it:

> This William Carter I did discover & apprehend. He was Doctor Nicholas Harpsfield's boy who did bring him up with old Cawood the printer, & he became skillful in the art of printing, & was learned in the tongues: he did print many traitorous books...I did take him and he was executed for his publishing and selling divers traitorous books, amongst which was Doctor Nicholas Harpsfield's book, of which he sold written copies for £20 a copy...That same original written book by Doctor Nicholas Harpsfield I did find in this William Carter's custody, which the Queen's Majesty hath seen and hath read of, and her highness did command me to keep, which I have extant still for her Majesty's service. Ric: Topcliffe.[2]

These annotations alert us to an interesting feature of Topcliffe's activities, that he made a collection of the books and manuscripts that he had confiscated, asserting his ownership by endorsements and marginalia.

The Carter raid produced two other items for the Topcliffe collection. First there was a group of three manuscript transcripts of Edmund Campion's disputations with Protestant ministers, held in the Tower. A Mr. Whiting from Lancashire had given them to Carter, who said that Stephen Vallenger (the prebendary of Chichester who lost his ears over the Alfield book) had written out two of them. Topcliffe gave these manuscripts to John Foxe.[3] The other item was a book that Carter had published in 1578, Gregory Martin's *Treatise of Schism*, written to per-

---

[1]*A Treatise on the Pretended Divorce*, ed. Nicholas Pocock (Westminster: Camden Society, 1878), 4; Topcliffe, note in Pollini, 666.

[2]Notes to Pollini, 575, and Index.

[3]These manuscripts survive, BL MS Harleian 422, nos. 22–5. The historian John Strype acquired them, and they passed from him, via the Harleian collection, to the British Museum.

suade Catholics to stay away from Protestant services. Topcliffe kept this book too, annotating it as usual, first with a small tipped-in leaf at the beginning, separately stitched, telling us that:

> William Carter hath confessed he hath printed of these books + 1250...This was found at Wm. Carter's:—In his house at the Tower hill. With the original copy sent from Rheims allowed under Doctor Allen's own hand....

Topcliffe, then, found the author's manuscript bearing Allen's *imprimatur* as well as the printed book. The copy he found is now in the Bodleian Library.[1]

It seems likely that the authorities had known about this book for some time—it may have been one of the publications that got Carter into trouble with the bishop of London, although Aylmer does not specify it in his letter to Cecil. It took Topcliffe, though, to find the sentence in it that would kill William Carter, and to comment upon it. The marginal note that was to cause poor Carter such trouble appears on Signature D2:

> A Traitorous meaning of the author and printer to our gentlewomen Catholic to become like Judith to destroy Holofernes: to amaze &c.

The troublesome sentence itself appears in a paragraph praising various Old Testament worthies for refusing to compromise their religious obligations by eating with, consorting with, or worshipping with gentiles:

> Judith followeth, whose godly and constant wisdom if our Catholic gentlewomen would follow, they might destroy Holofernes, the master heretic, and amaze all his retinue, and never defile their religion by communicating with them in any final point.

In Topcliffe's mind, this sentence could only mean that Martin and his printer were encouraging Catholic ladies to play Judith and assassinate Elizabeth I, alias Holofernes.

After Carter had been in the Tower for a year and a half, someone decided that he should be indicted for treason on the basis of that reading of the sentence. He was therefore moved to Newgate, and brought up for trial, 10 January 1584. The Council brought Thomas Norton out of retirement to conduct the prosecution, and Carter was found guilty despite his attempt to show that the passage did not mean that at all. The next day, 11 January, he was killed in the usual way.

Very soon after Carter's arrest, one of Walsingham's spies, known only as P.W.H., inveigled himself into the confidence of Carter's wife

---

[1] 8C 95(3) Th.

Jane, who in her distress told him that she hoped Lord Lumley would intercede for her husband, and that the Mass furnishings Topcliffe had found in their house actually belonged to him. P.W.H. sent all this off to Walsingham with the comment that very important Catholics of all kinds trusted Carter, who was therefore a repository of secrets that should be "ripped to the bottom." In consequence, Carter was put to the torture sometime between his move to the Tower in July and 15 November, when John Hart wrote to William Allen telling him that Carter, like his fellow layman John Jetter, had been "racked nearly to death," but that his torturers had got nothing out of him.[1]

Since the Council's records are missing after the end of June 1582, no warrant survives to tell who tortured Carter. Hart's letter links his torture with Jetter's, and we know that Topcliffe was responsible for that, so it seems reasonable to add William Carter to the list of Topcliffe's victims, and to conclude that Walsingham, acting upon his spy's information, was a party to the decision to use Topcliffe in that capacity.

The next item from Topcliffe's library of contraband texts to be noticed is now in the Huntington Library, California, acquired with other items from the Egerton family's collections. It is a copy in unbound sheets of William Allen's *A True, Sincere and Modest Defense of English Catholics,* printed on Fr. Persons's press in 1584. Although the book is unbound, the gatherings are folded, cut, pierced for stitching, and held in a loose vellum wrapper made from a waste legal document. Since the wrapper is pierced with holes matching those of the sheets, it appears that Mr. Topcliffe, the book's original owner, began the process of binding, but never completed it. He did, however, annotate the book, starting with the title-page, which he modified parodically in a way that Max Beerbohm would have admired, writing across the top:

A False, Seditious, and Immodest Offense, Set out by English Traitors, Some Abroad and Some at Home, Groaning for the Gallows, under Color and Shadow of —[2]

The original language of the title-page then follows: "A True, Sincere

---

[1] Burton-Pollen, 26–7; *CRS* 4.75 (Persons's copy of Hart's letter). T.A.Birrell, who gives an excellent account of Carter's trial, assumes that the "well-known team" of Norton, Hammond, and Beale supervised Carter's racking, but there is no record of this (Birrell, 25).

[2] Since Topcliffe's spelling is in a class by itself, the reader might like to see the original form of these words: "A false Sediceoos & Imodest offense Sett ovt by Englishe Trators ([some] / abroade & svme at home) Groaning for the Gallows, vnder Cvllor & / Shaddowe off —"

and Modest Defense of English Catholics." Then, in the middle of the page, he wrote, "To be read and used for the service of God, Q. Elizabeth, and the peace of England, and for no other purpose, or cause."

To follow his markings and marginalia through the book is to begin to understand the peculiar obsessiveness of his personality. He underlines text very neatly, and draws delicate pointing hands in the margins. He glues pink thread, very carefully, in the margins to draw attention to the passages that really outrage him, and from time to time he writes a comment. All this took time and work, especially the threads.

Allen's book was a beautifully written, thorough, eloquent reply to Lord Burghley's pamphlet in defense of the government's treatment of the Catholics, and one can see why it enraged Topcliffe. A curious feature of his markings is that they only appear in the book's political chapters, no doubt because those chapters, in his mind, convicted Allen of treason. Chapter Five, "Of Excommunication and Deprivation of Princes for Heresy and falling from the Faith..." really catches his interest, so that we have a flurry of glued pink thread in the margins. He neglects those parts of the book—the first chapter, for instance—in which Allen enumerates and describes, in unsparing detail, the atrocities committed in the Tower and elsewhere.

It is not known where Topcliffe found Allen's book, but since more than one copy survives with Topcliffe's modifications to the title-page, he evidently seized a cache of them, and it seems likely that besides keeping a copy for himself he would have lent or given copies to friends at court concerned, like himself, in prosecutions under the penal laws.[1]

The best-known distributor of this book in England was Thomas Alfield, author of the book that had been the object of Topcliffe's first book-hunt, *A True Report of the Death & Martyrdom of M. Campion, Jesuit and Priest.* After Alfield's release from prison, probably in the late summer of 1582, he had crossed over to the continent again, then returned to England in September 1584 via Newcastle, bringing copies of Allen's book with him. He made his way to London, where he set about distributing his books from the parish of All Hallows, Bread Street. He was arrested in the spring of 1585, and sent to the Tower, where he was interrogated, under torture, about political matters that he probably knew nothing about. He was then charged with "dispersing of slanderous books against the execution of justice," brought to trial 5 July 1585, indicted for "bringing into the Realm and uttering of a certain

---

[1]There are two copies with Topcliffe's title-page alterations in the Bodleian Library, and more may come to light.

slanderous and lewd book against her Majesty and the Realm, devised by one Doctor Allen." Condemned along with his lay helper, Thomas Webley, he was killed the next day.[1]

Alfield brought five or six hundred copies of Allen's book over with him, and Topcliffe's books may have been among them, although there is no sign of him in the proceedings against Alfield. Had the Council's records for the period survived, we would know whether he was one of Alfield's interrogators.[2]

Another possible source of Topcliffe's copies was the French embassy. In the summer of 1584 Walsingham heard from his sources in the embassy that the butler, Girault de la Chassagne, who was running a book-smuggling operation, was distributing copies of Allen's *Defense* along with the sensationally popular character-assassination of Leicester, *Leicester's Commonwealth*. John Bossy interprets an August 1584 reference to Topcliffe in Walsingham's memorandum book to mean that Topcliffe was to be asked to help in searching for the books. If Bossy is right, then Topcliffe could have acquired his copies in that search. [3]

Four more of Topcliffe's books can be mentioned here. When Sir Francis Drake returned from Santo Domingo in 1586, among the spoils he brought back with him was a Latin bible, printed in Paris, 1541. He gave the Bible to Topcliffe, of all people, who characteristically noted the fact of the gift on the title-page:

> This book was found, and taken, by my right worthy friend Sir Francis Drake, Knight, when he was in the Indies at Santo Domingo, where he and our nation did win great fame: Amongst other favors he bestowed this Jewel upon me. Which will endure for ever, and his fame long: Ric: Topcliffe.[4]

---

[1]Burton-Pollen, 145–63; Pollen 1, 112–20. A Newcastle merchant, Robert Heathfield, had brought Alfield and his books over from the continent (Pollen 1, 127).

[2]Some of Alfield's books went to Oxford, sent to a man called Barber, whose wife "conveyed the books into a privy where by the said Vice-chancellor's means they were found, and after burned in the open street" (Pollen 1, 109). The image of the vice-chancellor of Oxford University rooting for books in a privy in order to burn them stays in the mind.

[3]Bossy, 126, 146. Fr. William Weston, SJ, and Brother Ralph Emerson ("Little Ralph"), his companion, also brought copies of Allen's book into England with them in 1584. The books were discovered in Norwich, and Emerson was arrested. He remained in prison until he was banished in 1603. Topcliffe was one of his interrogators, but he was not involved in the discovery and arrest (Weston, 1–3; *CRS* 2.249).

[4]The Bible is now in the Huntington Library. See Sherman, 78.

A friendship between Drake and Topcliffe comes as a surprise.

Sometime after his arrest of Robert Southwell in 1592, Topcliffe acquired a copy of Southwell's *A Humble Supplication to Her Majesty*, which was then circulating in manuscript. He lent it to Francis Bacon, who mentioned it in a letter to his brother, admiring the style if not the subject-matter. R.C.Bald dates the loan to 1594 when Bacon and Topcliffe were interrogating Fr. Henry Walpole.[1] The implication of the loan is that Topcliffe knew Bacon well enough to know that Bacon would be interested in Southwell's writing, also that Topcliffe knew enough about writing to recognize its quality.

Topcliffe acquired another important manuscript in 1594 when he arrested a gentleman called Robert Barnes. This was the so-called "Book of Miracles," a narrative description of a series of exorcisms that took place in various houses between late 1585 and the spring of 1586. This manuscript, though, did not remain in Topcliffe's collection. It went to Richard Bancroft, Bishop of London, and served as the basis of the Bancroft-Harsnett inquiry into the exorcisms, which produced Samuel Harsnett's book, *A Declaration of Egregious Popish Impostures* (1603), which in turn had such a strong influence on Shakespeare's writing of *King Lear*. The manuscript itself was destroyed along with the other records of the Ecclesiastical Court of High Commission during the civil wars.[2]

At about the same time or a little later, Topcliffe acquired his copy of the second, 1594, edition of Girolamo Pollini's history of England's "ecclesiastical revolution," *L'historia ecclesiastica della rivoluzion d'Inghilterra,* published in Rome. Pollini was a Dominican friar belonging to the great convent of Santa Maria Novella in Florence. A Catholic book like his, telling the whole story of the English religious revolution from its beginnings in Henry VIII's divorce to recent events under Elizabeth, was bound to cause offense in England; but what really infuriated the Queen was Pollini's repetition of the story current in England and France since Henry VIII's time, that Henry had not only slept with Anne Boleyn's sister Mary, but with their mother as well. In fact, as some versions of the story went, Henry was Anne Boleyn's father.[3] Elizabeth

---

[1]Bald, xii.

[2]For an account of this inquiry, see Brownlow 2, 49–90.

[3]Pollini took his version of the story from Sander 1, ff.15–17, who gives William Rastell's lost *Life of More* as his source. But the story was well-known. See Lewis's Introduction to Sander 2, xxiv–xxxvii, for an account of the story's dispersion. Henry himself, told by Sir George Throgmorton that, "It is thought ye have meddled with the

wrote personally to the Grand Duke of Tuscany, Ferdinando de' Medici, in Italian, asking him to suppress the book, but although there were rumors of the book's having been burned in both London and Rome, there is no actual evidence that Ferdinando did anything in response to Elizabeth's letter. Why would he? Pollini's publication of his second, enlarged edition in 1594 aggravated his original offense; but when he left Santa Maria Novella it was to be promoted prior of the Dominican house at San Gimignano.[1]

Topcliffe was as upset by Pollini's book as his mistress, and for the same reasons. Consequently his marginalia, apart from a few interesting personal notes, are more than usually vituperative. He starts off with Pollini's dedication to Cardinal Allen, first calling Allen "a viperous traitor," then revenging Pollini's tales about Anne Boleyn's parentage by going on to write that "gentlemen of good worship" had told him that "Doctor William Allen (after Cardinal at Rome) or his father was begotten and was the bastard of the Abbot of Delachrist or Delacruze, Staffordshire, of the body of one Nan or Bess Bradshaw, when she was the wife of one Allen, when he, Allen, was the bailiff of husbandry, or [*illegible*] of the Abbot, who was godfather to his own son." In later notes mentioning Allen, he always changes the title "cardinal" to "carnal," e.g., "O villany, villany, villany, Carnal Allen!" He draws a gallows for Allen and the Pope on p.88, another gallows for Allen on p.90, one for Clement VII on p.89, and two for Pius V on pp.445–6. On p.520 he writes that Edmund Campion was a foundling whom desperation made a Jesuit, and on p.556 that, "I will allow him to be no ghostly father who was *filius populi* in London in an hospital and a foundling in the streets, and after a venomous traitor at Rome." The whole latter part of Pollini's book, he says, is devoted to "their stinking martyrs," and he mentions that he was present at the execution of the first of them, Dr. John Storey, another "viperous traitor."

Obsessively annotated though the book is, one notices that there is no note this time to say that the Queen had instructed him to keep it for use in her service. Pollini's *Historia* was one book that even Elizabeth's favorite policeman might not have been encouraged to keep in his collection.

---

mother and the sister,' excluded Lady Boleyn (née Lady Elizabeth Howard) with the memorable words, "Never with the mother" (*L&P* 4, cccxxix–cccxxx).

[1] There is some account of Pollini and his book's reception in England in Michael Wyatt, *The Italian Encounter with Tudor England* (Cambridge: Cambridge University Press, 2005), 128–30.

In January 1593, Topcliffe sent Lord Keeper Puckering a "vile, trai-torous book" in unbound sheets that he had recently intercepted. To pre-pare Puckering for the proceedings against the "bringers-over," evidently in custody, he annotated the significant passages of "treason and vil-lainy," and gave him a list of pages. This book has so far not turned up.[1]

No doubt other items from Topcliffe's collection will appear in due course. He was an unusually energetic collector.

*****

In the 1580s, Topcliffe applied himself to a good deal more than book-collecting, and by the summer of 1588, when the Armada arrived, he was becoming the chief agent of the government's determination to eradicate Catholicism in England. Before giving a description of the range of his activities, it is necessary to clear up a misconception about his standing and employment.

English writers on these Elizabethan undercover activities, rendered uneasy by the subject, do their best to save the appearance of rectitude at the center of things by erecting a kind of moral barrier between the Queen and her Council and the various agents—spies, informers, "pro-jecters," pursuivants—whom they employed, among whom they invari-ably include Topcliffe. There is a fundamental misconception here.

There is general agreement that Sir Francis Walsingham, the Elizabe-than government's spymaster, ran a remarkably successful intelligence network and, in association with his colleague Lord Burghley, was the executive in charge of Elizabethan foreign policy. There is also general agreement that, as Christopher Devlin put it, Walsingham "had a certain grim sense of propriety," and that he would never have employed a free-booter like Topcliffe. Another writer on these undercover matters remarks that Topcliffe did not flourish until Walsingham was dead and out of the way, the implication being that Topcliffe was not up to Walsingham's moral standards, and that Walsingham, as long as he was alive, kept him in check.[2] For Charles Nicholl, giving an account of Walsingham and his operatives in his book on Christopher Marlowe's death, "With Topcliffe we scrape the bottom of this barrel," and he goes on to say that although Topcliffe, "provided intelligence to Walsingham

[1]NA/SP12/244/4 (Topcliffe to Puckering, 6 January 1593). It was a long book, at least 777 pages. Pollini's first edition (1591)?

[2]Devlin 2, 65; Haynes, 52.

and others...he was not primarily a spy...He was chief of the pursuivants."[1]

Operating through his own "instruments," Topcliffe did indeed gather intelligence; and acting in command of his own platoon of searchers, he hunted and caught suspects, but it is unlikely that any of his court friends would ever have called him either a spy or a pursuivant. His social and courtly standing was too high for that. For the same reason there would never have been any question of Walsingham *employing* Topcliffe. Walsingham did not *employ* wealthy gentlemen with sixteen quarterings who had the Queen's ear. He employed scallywags and apostate Catholics.

As we have seen, it is likely that Walsingham consulted Topcliffe over the French embassy book-smuggling operation, and that he was responsible for the torture, probably by Topcliffe, of William Carter. Then, when in June 1586, Walsingham was clearing out the London prisons in preparation for the glut of prisoners following the dénoument of the Babington Plot, Topcliffe's name turns up several times in the prison lists as an examiner of prisoners whom Walsingham had committed,[2] and Topcliffe committed one of the priests to prison himself.[3] In that same June, Topcliffe sent Walsingham information about the arrival of a Scottish priest *en route* to Scotland from Picardy, who had been spreading rumors of invasion in the west country. It appears from Topcliffe's letter that his information came from his own sources, and that he had spoken to Walsingham about the same kind of activity the previous February. He concludes by suggesting that he and Walsingham should have a talk about these matters.[4] Walsingham and Topcliffe, between them, killed Thomas Clifton whom the Council had ordered to be banished.[5]

What the records show, then, is that when their interests overlapped, Topcliffe cooperated with Walsingham, and Walsingham, on his side, was happy to use Topcliffe's developing expertise. What the records do not show is that Walsingham or Burghley or Elizabeth I—or anyone else in a position of real power—ever found it necessary to disassociate him-

---

[1]Nicholl, 110–12.

[2]Topcliffe examined John Lister, Nicholas Knight, John Bolton, William Clargenet, Thomas Bramston, Ralph Crocket, and George Stranshsm, alias Potter (*CRS* 2.242–3).

[3]This was Edward James, whom Topcliffe committed to the Clink (*CRS* 2, 246, 268).

[4]NA/SP12/190/15.

[5]See below, 134.

self from Topcliffe or thought for a moment that "With Topcliffe we scrape the bottom of this barrel."

The sheer range of his activities is proof enough of that. He quickly became one of the authorities' ranking experts on, and participants in, the campaign to eradicate English Catholicism. So we find him among the searchers in the great coordinated midnight raid ordered by the Lord Mayor on London's Catholics, 26–27 August 1584. He raided Mrs. Mainey's house, and was excited to find a warm bed, recently slept in:

> To prove that some person lay there who was removed in haste it seemeth apparent, for that there was a pair of Jersey nether-stocks and garters, and a pair of socks foul, the waist girdle of velvet, and falling short band of the person that is supposed to lie there, left in the chamber, and no one of the house would declare directly to whom they did belong.[1]

His expertise was generally acknowledged. In July 1586 as the Babington Plot was coming to the boil, Sir Thomas Heneage, treasurer of the household, writing a memorandum on the Queen's safety, and wondering how to keep recusants out of the court, thought of Topcliffe:

> ...And care would be had and used, that recusants should not presume to come into her Majesty's court; and specially not into her Majesty's presence, for which purpose such ferreters in that behalf by secret inquisition, as Mr. Topcliffe is, would be comforted.[2]

Heneage, by the way, who prided himself on being a puritan, thought that people became recusants not only because of "Jesuits and seminaries," but also because of "over-stiff maintenance of popish ceremonies, set out in the Book of Common Prayer, but exacted more than the law doth require by our bishops." Why the bishops' keenness on keeping up ceremonial should turn people Catholic, he does not say.

When the Council appointed a commission, including Topcliffe, to examine Jesuits and seminary priests in the London prisons to persuade them to conform in religion, they gave instructions that if they refused to conform, then Mr. Barker and Mr. Topcliffe:

> being acquainted with such persons and causes, do consider in what sort the said persons may stand charged with any misdemeanor towards the estate, or otherwise to sound their opinions touching such questions as are extant in print, and have been propounded unto others of that sect.[3]

---

[1] NA/SP12/172/112, quoted in Foley 6.710/

[2] BL Ms. Lansdowne 51. Nos. 12 & 18.

Topcliffe's fellow-expert Edward Barker was register of the Court of Delegates. He prepared a "breviate" of the Babington conspiracy, and was present at the examinations, but does not otherwise appear in the records of the enforcement of the penal laws. He was probably a civil lawyer. About a year later he and Topcliffe were to be associated on a similar commission.

In this same period Topcliffe began to be a familiar, vocal, figure at executions, sometimes as one of the court observers, but often—especially in the later stages of his career—because he had a personal interest in the execution, having himself caught, imprisoned, interrogated, and seen the victim condemned. He attended the executions of the fourteen condemned Babington plotters, although he had played no part in rounding them up (the Babington Plot was a Walsingham operation). He was present both days (20–21 September 1586), on the first day speaking to Robert Barnwell, on the second to Robert Gage, in both cases urging their guilt upon them.[2] About a month later, 8 October, he attended the executions of three seminary priests, John Low, John Adams, and Robert Dibdale, chaplain to the Peckhams of Denham, who was one of the priests who conducted exorcisms at Denham and at Lord Vaux's house in Hackney. He had been arrested in the general roundup that accompanied the dénoument of the Babington Plot. At his execution, Topcliffe accused him of conjuration, also of acting on diabolically inspired delusions.[3] Since Topcliffe had no part in Dibdale's arrest or condemnation, someone at Court or on the Council must have encouraged him to attend the execution, and to bring up the subject of the exorcisms. Walsingham? Very probably. It was Walsingham's men, the pursuivants Newall and Worsley, operating under the instructions of Francis Mills, Walsingham's secretary, who had arrested Dibdale in Tothill Street.[4]

One of Topcliffe's most interesting interventions occurred at the execution of William Parry, 2 March 1585. Parry was a spendthrift Welshman who had hoped to recoup his fortunes by a career in spying and "projecting," i.e., cooking up conspiracies out of which he might

---

[3]*APC*, 15. 122 (10 June 1587).

[2]BL Ms. Additional 48027, ff. 265, 271.

[3]Pollen 2, 285. Dibdale was from Stratford-upon-Avon, perhaps related to Shakespeare. For an account of the Denham exorcisms and Shakespeare's interest in them, see Brownlow 2.

[4]Morris 1, 2.165

profit.[1] After a shaky start, which included imprisonment on a charge of murder, and after turning, or pretending to turn, Catholic to give credibility to his activities, he returned to the continent, and began a correspondence intended to inveigle Pope Gregory XIII himself and his secretary of state, the Cardinal of Como, into an assassination plot against Elizabeth I by offering them his services for an unspecified enterprise. He then returned to England to report, in audience with the Queen and Burghley, that the Pope, the Scottish Queen's friends, and the Jesuits, had sent him to kill Elizabeth and put Mary on the throne. With a reply from Como in hand, approving of his "good disposition and resolution," encouraging him to persevere in whatever he had in mind, and offering him the plenary indulgence he had asked for, Parry's fortune seemed to be made. He found himself on familiar terms with the Queen and Burghley, and became a member of Parliament, where he caused some trouble for himself by speaking out on behalf of the Catholics.

Unfortunately Parry, not the most stable of men, wanted more. In a fit of grandiosity he wrote to Burghley, in unacceptably familiar language (e.g., "Remember me, my dearest Lord"), asking for the wardenship of St. Catherine's Hospital. When the wardenship went elsewhere, and he realized that pensions and preferments were not about to rain down upon him without further exertions on his part, he made a huge mistake. He cooked up another project, aimed this time at a fellow spy, Edward Neville. Neville claimed to be the heir of the last Lord Latimer, whose daughter had married Burghley's son Thomas, taking the Latimer property with her. Parry, a protegé of Burghley, must have seen a perfect target in Neville, and so he set about trying to entrap Neville into agreeing to join him in a plan to assassinate the Queen, his idea being, of course, to reveal the "plot" by denouncing Neville.

What happened was that Neville denounced Parry, who had made two of the cardinal mistakes of the secret service game. Not only had he shown himself to be unreliable, he had tried to destroy an agent who was someone else's asset—Neville had been working, however unsatisfactorily, for Walsingham, and to Walsingham Parry found himself required to explain his activities.[2] The predictable outcome was that Parry was charged with treason as a Catholic who planned to kill the Queen, and—of course—was found guilty. The Queen, who seems to

---

[1]Parry's story is an extraordinarily convoluted one which can only be touched upon in outline here. Detailed accounts are to be found in Hicks 3, Edwards 1, 100–24, and Bossy, 96–99, 132–4, 142–3.

[2]Edwards 1, 108, links Neville with Walsingham, citing Hicks 3, 362, n.77.

have liked him, and who certainly knew that he had no intention to harm her, either could not or would not intervene to save him, even though he appealed to her personally from the Tower.

Topcliffe, along with Sir Francis Knollys and Lord Treasurer Burghley attended Parry's execution, and for anyone present who knew the real story of Parry's career the exchange between him and Topcliffe at the beginning of the proceedings would have raised an eyebrow:

> William Parry being lifted up at the place of execution, and standing on the hurdle in his gown, beheld round about him, and espying Mr. Topcliffe standing very near, besought him to tell the Queen's Majesty that he would die her true subject: to whom Mr. Topcliffe answered, I cannot do so, I have seen and heard too much to the contrary.

Standing there, then, and looking around at the people who had come to see him die, Parry recognized in Topcliffe the one spectator who might take a message for him directly to the Queen.[1]   Later, in his speech avowing his innocence, Parry confessed that he had been wrong to conceal his exchanges with Neville, but that he had done so "upon confidence of her Majesty, to whom he had before bewrayed what he had been solicited to do." Topcliffe then reminded him of the letter from the Cardinal of Como in which, said Topcliffe, he had promised to "destroy her Majesty, and was by him as from the Pope animated thereunto:"[2]

> "O Master Topcliffe," said he, "you clean mistake it. I deny any such matter to be in the letter; and I wish it might be truly examined and considered of."

That was true, strictly speaking; but Parry had been too ingeniously ambiguous, and for their own reasons the powers in charge had decided to be rid of him. His support in Parliament for the Catholics would certainly have turned Burghley against him.

After brief speeches by Sir Francis Knollys and Burghley, the sheriff then told him to confess and make an end. When Parry still protested his innocence, Topcliffe intervened once more:

> Mr. Topcliffe answered him, "You are neither true to her Majesty, to your own religion, cardinals, or pope, and therefore you cannot justify your truth to any party: God forgive you."

---

[1]BL Ms. Additional 48027, f.244. There are two complementary accounts of Parry's death, this and Lansdowne Ms. 43, No. 53, printed by Strrype 1, 3.1, 362–4.

[2]Ms. Lansdowne 43, no.53.

"O urge me not, Mr. Topcliffe," said Parry, "I pray for you all."[1]

When the chaplain urged him to be sorry for his sins, and to pray for mercy, Parry said the Lord's Prayer in Latin and some other private prayers. Finally—the moment one finds hardest to face in these accounts —"The people then cried, 'Away with him, away with him'." And so, after a pause and a little more talk, "He was turned from the ladder, and after one swing was cut down. When his bowels were taken out, he gave a great groan."

This was the kind of event of which Topcliffe was to become a connoisseur in the next ten years.

There were interesting sequels to the Parry case. In June 1585, Neville was pardoned and given a large pension of £100 per year—though they kept him in the Tower until early 1598. In the Parry case, then, we have an example of the hunter hunted, or the projecter projected. But who set Neville on? As we have seen, he was Walsingham's man, and many years later after Walsingham's death, Thomas Harrison, one of his former operatives, confessed that Walsingham, Thomas Phelippes, and he had "wrought" the Parry plot.[2] Parry, then, was telling the truth when he said he had told the Queen "what he had been solicited to do."

The Queen evidently knew nothing about the underside or back-story of Parry's so-called plot, but she found thoughts of Mary Stuart's helper Thomas Morgan sitting in Paris discussing plots to murder her infuriating. So she asked the French king, Henri III, to imprison and extradite Morgan. In March 1585 the French put him in the Bastille, and kept him there until August 1587; but he was never in any danger from them. In fact, they made sure that none of his important papers fell into English hands.

The Queen, therefore, decided to take matters into her own hands, and took a step or two of her own into the muddy waters of international intrigue. We know this because among the few Morgan papers that the French handed over to the English ambassador was a confession by a man called Lewis whom the French had picked up. Asked to explain himself and his reasons for being in Paris, Lewis said he was there

---

[1] Ms. Additional 48027, f.244.

[2] Hicks 2, 69, n.207. Walsingham's motive in cooking up the Parry plot was to intensify the atmosphere of fear and panic, of "plotmania," that Parry's own prior shenanigans had done much to create. His trial and execution constituted a classic false-flag operation. Walsingham (and Burghley) needed a political context in which Mary Stuart could be plausibly killed. See Edwards 1, 106.

because Richard Topcliffe, with the Queen's consent, had sent him over to assassinate Thomas Morgan.

This was a deeply embarrassing confession. Stafford, the ambassador, knew that the French were playing with him over the whole business of Morgan's arrest and his papers, and thought they had sent him Lewis's confession to see how he would take it. He protested in the strongest terms that the Queen would never dream of doing such a thing, however badly she wanted Morgan punished. Unfortunately Lewis, whom the ambassador now had in his own custody, stood to his confession, saying that "Topcliffe used all manner of speeches to him as are there, and that Charles Burgh can testify the same, to whom he told it when he would needs know the cause of his coming away." As for Topcliffe, he had written recommending Lewis to the ambassador's wife, but he had not written to the ambassador himself about that or anything else. All the ambassador could do was hope that Walsingham would have a talk with Topcliffe about the whole embarrassing affair.

The French must have been in stitches over this business, and one detects a tone of quiet irony in the French king's response, as reported by Stafford:

> For the man [Lewis], the King was willing that I should do with him what I would, but in his opinion, it was of no use to have him kept, "being but a knave's speech, whom nobody would nor did believe, and that there could be but his yea and another's nay about the matter, which would never come to trial;" that the King and everybody else knew her Majesty too well....

We can be sure of just one thing: Topcliffe would never have done such a thing on his own initiative. The only explanation is that—as Lewis said—the Queen put him up to it.[1]

*****

In this same period, when Topcliffe became a regular examiner of Catholic prisoners, he was involved, by the Council's order, both as examiner and custodian, in the puzzling and pathetic case of Thomas Clifton.

Clifton was a seminary priest ordained at Laon, December 1579, and sent into England in January 1580. He was captured in November 1580,

---

[1]Hicks 2, 180–81, n.522. The ambassador's letter to Walsingham, 4 May 1585, is calendared in *State Papers Foreign, Elizabeth*, Vol. 19, p.457. The irony of this affair is that Morgan, unknown to the Queen, was probably a double-agent.

and according to a contemporary account published by bishop Challoner was led through the streets to his trial laden with chains. Then, instead of being condemned to death under the treason laws, he was condemned to perpetual imprisonment and loss of goods under the statute of *præmunire*. He was returned to Newgate where they chained his hands, feet, and neck "in such sort that he could neither sit down nor stir out of his place all the day, and every night being put down into a horrid and darksome dungeon." They then moved him to King's Bench prison, where he stayed until June 1586 when, by order of the Council, he was delivered to the custody of Mr. Topcliffe "to be banished." Banished, however, he was not, but moved to the Marshalsea, where he is found in a prison list of July 1587. About a year later, they moved him to the worst prison of all, Bridewell. A petition that the governors of Bridewell sent to Walsingham sometimes after 1589 for relief of poor prisoners names Clifton first, "sent in by your honor, 1 April 1588."

So between them Topcliffe and Walsingham unloaded him on to Bridewell, where he died. Henry Garnet announced his death in a letter dated 17 March 1593:

> Mr. Clifton, who after suffering bonds for ten years and injuries unspeakable, was killed by the miseries of his prison.[1]

*****

In the absence of Council records for the mid-1580s, we cannot be sure just how Topcliffe was instructed or to whom he regularly reported, but a pair of letters from Sir Thomas Heneage, Chamberlain of the household, to Sir Christopher Hatton provide evidence of the Queen's interest in the suppression of the priests as well as her use of Topcliffe to accomplish that end. Heneage's first letter, 2 April 1585, ends: "The Queen is glad with me that the priest is taken; I pray God you may make him open all truth that may advance her surety...." The captured priest was Isaac Higgens, and Hatton must have replied, because Heneage's next letter, 2 May, passes on the Queen's own instructions:

> Sir, I have showed her Majesty your letter, this bearer brought me for answer, whereof her Highness's pleasure is, I should let you know, that she would have Isaac Higgens, now in your custody yet detained three or four days, and in the mean season, that he should be again better examined; and

[1]Challoner, 17; Anstruther, 80–1; *CRS* 2, 220,236,237,244,267,274,277,279; *CRS* 5, 230, 233,

that Mr. Secretary should be sent to, and likewise Mr. Topcliffe with those in that commission, to know if the name of this man be in any of their rules, which they keep of such bad fellows as carry and re-carry books and letters into this Realm, and out of it, which being certainly known, that he be kept or let go, as shall be thought best by you for her Majesty's service.

From this we learn that the two names in the Queen's mind for this work are Walsingham and Topcliffe, though there are others in the "commission" besides them. We also learn that at the time of this instruction, she was still associating Topcliffe with keeping track of "such bad fellows as carry and re-carry books and letters into this Realm, and out of it."[1]

If there was now a standing commission for such work, then Topcliffe, as its most energetic member, will have acted both on instruction and, to some extent, on his own initiative.

He certainly enjoyed the police work of detection and arrest. In June 1584 one of his "instruments" informed him that a priest called Thomas Worthington had come to London with a small party consisting of three nephews whom he was taking to Rheims, another priest, and an alumnus of the English College at Rome, Humphrey Maxfield. They were all staying at an inn in Islington. Topcliffe raided the inn early on a Sunday morning, 19 June 1584, and caught Mr. Worthington while he was still in bed. A few weeks later, Topcliffe was bragging of his exploit to the Lords of the Council in a letter complaining bitterly about the number of seminary priests in London:

> About twenty days passed, one *Thomas Worthington*, a notorious seminary priest, did resort thither, a stirrer of sedition as ever haunted Lancashire, Cheshire, Shropshire, Staffordshire, Derbyshire, Yorkshire, &c; and one *Revell,* a seminary priest, his companion; one *Humphrey Maxfield,* a seminary scholar of Rome and Rheims, a great companion, conveyer, and intelligencer to and from Worthington; and three boys to be conveyed beyond seas to be made priests, stolen by their uncle Worthington from the Bishop of Chester.

[1]Nicholas, 415, 426. Isaac Higgens had been ordained at Rheims in March 1584, left for England in February 1585, and was soon caught at Sir John Arundell's, Clerkenwell. The Council committed him to Newgate 1 July. He was in Newgate in December 1586, described as a "bad fellow" in Walsingham's prison list of July, and marked for hanging in a similar December list. But they sent him to Wisbech instead where he caused as much trouble as possible. He was still there in December 1588, but then disappears from the record. As early as August 1585 Richard Barrett was describing him as an apostate, accused of betraying his father (Anstruther, 166–7; Foley, 3.277; *CRS* 2, 256, 270, 273, 278).

These three men and one of the boys (being the eldest) I did apprehend at Islington the 25th of July. *Worth*ington *worth*ily is committed to the Tower by my Lord Treasurer's direction, Revel and Maxfield to the Clink, and the boy to the Gatehouse; of which boy I beseech you to have consideration, such as I shall humbly move you to. Worthington, Maxfield, and Revell have been twice examined by Sir Owen Hopton, Mr. Doctor Hammond, Mr. Rokeby, and myself; and Worthington hath been once examined before by myself.

We all agree that there never did come before us so arrogant, willful, and obstinate persons, as all those three men, impudently denying any acquaintance or familiarity betwixt them, or that any one of them had seen another before they last met together at Islington before their last apprehension....[1]

Worthington was badly treated in the Tower, where he was put in the Pit for over two months. Then six months later, to Topcliffe's intense disgust, he was included in the group of twenty-one priests sent into banishment, 21 January 1585, by order of the Queen. He made his way back to Rheims, and was briefly chaplain at Deventer to the English soldiers fighting in the Netherlands on the Spanish side. From 1599 until 1613 he was president of the Rheims seminary; then after two years in Rome he returned to England, where he died at Biddulph Hall, Staffordshire. One sees why Topcliffe regretted his banishment.[2]

At about the same time, a pair of letters that he wrote the Council about a couple of other operations reveal the reach of his intelligence system. The first letter was about a man called William Price, Apreece, or Ap Rhys who was a prisoner in the Tower. It appears from the letter that Topcliffe had raided Washingley Hall, Huntingdonshire, belonging

---

[1] BL MS. Lansdowne 72. No. 40. "Revel" was the alias of Thomas Brown, ordained at Cambrai, May 1578. Foley, 2.116–32 tells the story of the boys' adventures before arriving in London. Thomas, the eldest, was in the Gatehouse until at least December 1586 (*CRS* 2.271). What became of him after that is not clear. The two who escaped capture joined up with a fourth brother, and made it to Rheims. Two of them became Jesuits. They were also Cardinal Allen's nephews. His sister Mary was their mother (Foley, 2.76).

[2] DT, 64, 131; Anstruther, 387–88. Topcliffe recorded his disgust over the banishment in a memorandum written probably to Burghley, c.1590, arguing in effect that it was a mistake to allow any Jesuit or seminary priest out of one's sight. "When I was ridden into the north about service of her Majesty's Doctor Worthington was banished with 20 other priests, & immediately after his banishment he recompensed her Majesty's mercy with monstrous treasons: for first he caused Sir William Stanley to give over the Queen's town of Deventer in the Low Countries into the hands of the Spaniards..." (NA/SP12/235/8). Stanley surrendered Deventer and took his regiment over to the Spaniards in January 1587; Worthington did not become their chaplain until May.

to a Catholic family of Welsh origin called Price. William, a kinsman of the owner, Robert, was the steward, and Topcliffe arrested him because:

> William Ap Rhys [or Price], being longtime an obstinate recusant and papist, he was steward and principal entertainer, receiver, and secret conveyor of all such traitorous seminaries as resorted to Washingley, his master's house; whereof himself hath confessed ten by name under his hand, besides recusants and fugitives whose like resorted thither as well when his master was from home as to a harburrow, college, or sanctuary, passing from north to south, & to the perilous example and infection of those countries
>
> He received of them & kept for them their traitorous and seditious books, and trumpery for massing; and was of counsel with the making of a secret conveyance in a double wall wherein they used to hide the same, and the priests when need required.[1]

There was a boy too, called Jackson, whom Topcliffe thought was a priest's boy or companion, and so he arrested him as well. William went to the Clink, the boy to Bridewell. The boy then "grew conformable" and was put to a Protestant master. The reason Price was now in the Tower was that, according to Topcliffe, he had conspired to remove the boy from his master, and had now either had him murdered or sent overseas to prevent him from revealing more information. The letter to the Council seems intended to justify Price's detention in the Tower. The idea that Price had murdered the boy was presumably a fiction invented for the occasion. The Tower Bills show that William Price came to the Tower sometime between midsummer and Christmas 1584. He was still there at Michaelmas 1585, but was out by Christmas despite Topcliffe's representations.[2]

The second of these letters asks on behalf of "a gentleman of a good family who then served in those parts" [Spain] that a pair of ship's captains, Robert Walter of Liverpool now on his way to Spain, and John Man, master of the Marigold out of Harwich, be "regarded as persons dangerous to their native country," and in particular that "authority may be given to some such as shall be thought most fit for every respect in Cheshire and Lancashire to apprehend Robert Walter of Liverpool so shortly as he shall arrive, and set foot on land from Spain." According to Topcliffe's letter, an English agent, David Gwyn, boatswain of

---

[1] NA/SP12/175,87, tentatively dated in the Calendar 1584?

[2] *CRS* 3.18-21. He may be the same William Price mentioned in "An Old Editor's Notebook" (Morris 1, 3.27), who was arrested by a Puritan and put in Shrewsbury gaol sometime before 1591.

another ship, entrusted a letter of information about Spanish preparations against England to Man. Walter and a confederate called Boone had taken the letter from Man and given it to the Conte di Lima, who then pursued Gwyn, and eventually caught up with him at The Groyne (i.e., Corunna):

> There David Gwyn was by their means apprehended; and by Conte de Lima sent to the Holy House at Saint James in Galicia where the Lord knoweth his end.

True or false, Topcliffe could only have had this information from an agent in place in Spain.

*****

On 8 October 1586 Topcliffe wrote from Leicester House to "his singular good Lord" the Earl of Leicester, then commanding the English troops aiding the Dutch Protestants in the Netherlands, to inform him of a plot being investigated back home in England. The authorities had arrested a young man called Roger Walton on his return from Cologne. Interrogated, he had told quite a story: that a pair called Owen and Meredith had brought:

> an Italian being a low thick man with a foul face and a yellow beard who intended to go to my Lord of Leicester and there to kill him by some device.

Topcliffe, not knowing whether Leicester had heard this, thought it his duty to tell him about it. Walton had then gone on to talk about another young man, John Digby, with whom he had been in Cologne, and to accuse him of intending "the highest treasons." "Digby," writes Topcliffe, "denieth the substance, but enough to hang him as a traitor. I am but entering into th'examination of the matter by her Majesty's appointment in the tower."[1]

Sure enough, this affair left its traces in the official records. On 26 September, the Council instructed Sir Walter Mildmay to appoint his son Anthony to apprehend John Digby, "that should come forth of Denmark through Scotland into this realm," and on 8 October they wrote again to Sir Walter, "signifying in how gracious part her Majesty did take the care both he and his son used in the apprehending and sending up of

---

[1]Topcliffe's letter is in Teyler's Museum, Haarlem, Netherlands, MS Teyler 2376 fol. 53, where it was found by Roger Kuin, to whose generosity I owe a transcript.

John Digby." On the same day, Sir Thomas Heneage, having already paid John Marshal ten pounds for "helping to bring hither out of Germany one Walton, a lewd fellow, and aiding to the discovering and apprehending of him," paid another ten pounds to Mildmay's servant Leonard Doddington, "being used in the apprehending and conveying hither of John Digby, apprehended in Northamptonshire." A warrant to Hopton, lieutenant of the Tower, "to receive of Richard Topcliffe, esquire, the person of John Digby, and to see him kept close prisoner" completed the business. Digby was still in the Tower in July 1588: "John Digby gent., prisoner one year seven months, indicted of treason."[1]

In a marginal note to his letter, Topcliffe identifies John Digby as the "second son to old Everard Digby of Rutland, father to Savage alias Digby the late traitor." If Topcliffe was right, these are the Digbys of Stoke Dry, Rutland, and John Savage the Babington conspirator will have been a brother to Everard Digby the future Gunpowder Plotter. But is he right? John Savage, whose antecedents have always been a mystery, had been executed as a Babington conspirator just a few weeks earlier. If he too was a Digby, that family produced a triple in conspiracy.

John Digby, though, was probably innocent of everything except being a Catholic. Roger Walton was another "projecting" rascal, and the Elizabethan authorities, including Topcliffe, knew that. A couple of years later, in March 1588, Walton was reporting back to Walsingham from France, claiming to have talked to Fr. Darbishire and other Catholics in Paris.[2] At that same time, the English ambassador in Paris, Edward Stafford, wrote a summary description of him:

He lieth here not far from me...To some he showeth himself a great Papist, to others a Protestant; but as they take him that haunteth him most, he hath neither God nor religion, a very evil condition, a swearer without measure and a tearer of God, a notable whoremaster...This Walton is young, without any hair of his face, a little above twenty, lean faced and slender, somewhat tall, complexion a little sallowish, most goeth apparelled in a doublet of black carke cut upon a dark reddish velvet.

In short, a vile character. The ambassador thought he had been a page to Lady Northumberland; Verstegan thought he had been a page to the Earl of Northumberland "that was slain in the Tower." Verstegan had also been told that "Walton did in England make an occupation of accus-

[1] *APC*, 14. 235, 236, 241, 242; *CRS* 2. 281.

[2] His report is in NA/SP12/209/57.

ing men, and that he had brought five or six to the gallows."[1]   Indeed,
in September 1588, according to the official published account, he was
called in evidence against the seminary priest William Hartley, claiming
to have seen a letter written by Hartley to Paris to "certain seminary
priests there, importing the full resolution of the said Hartley, and some
other his confederates, immediately upon the landing of the Spaniards, to
have supressed her Majesty's Tower of London, and to have fired the
City." The letter wasn't produced, and Hartley denied writing it. But of
course they hanged him all the same.[2]

Walsingham, Essex, and Cecil all used Walton's services. When he
was produced as a witness at the trial of the Earl of Arundel, April 1589,
the earl challenged him as "a very lewd fellow in that he had accused
Digby." His career as an informer may have begun with accusing John
Digby.[3]

*****

The one Topcliffean activity of which we have no record between
August 1582 and September 1588 is the one for which he is most
famous, torture—not that the absence of records means that he did no
torturing. For one thing, the Privy Council records are missing from
June 1582 until February 1586, and for another, as we have seen, torture
could be administered, even in the Tower, without specific authorization.
Of nineteen known cases during the period of the missing Council
records, it is likely that Topcliffe was responsible for at least one that
took place besides John Jetter's, that of the printer William Carter. As
we have seen, he had played a major part in Carter's arrest and condemnation.

There are two further reasons for thinking that Topcliffe was responsible for Carter's torture. First, from Topcliffe's point of view Carter's
offense—the publication of the incriminating sentence that Topcliffe had
found in Gregory Martin's book—was aimed directly at the Queen,
whom Topcliffe considered it his duty to protect. Secondly, Carter, like

---

[1]Verstegan, 204, 205.

[2] *A true report of the inditement, arraignment, conuiction, condemnation, and execution of Iohn Weldon, William Hartley, and Robert Sutton. Who suffered for high treason,
in seuerall places, about the Citie of London, on Saturday the fifth of October. anno
1588.* (London 1588), Sig C4v.

[3]*CRS* 21, 244. Walton was still active in 1596 when he accused a man called John
Berrrington, lately arrived in England, "of many criminal causes against the state."
Berrington described him as "a notorious evil-liver" (*CSPD 1595–97*, 294).

Topcliffe's earlier victim Jetter, was treated with extreme cruelty. As John Hart wrote, linking the cases together in his letter to William Allen, they were both racked "nearly to death."[1]

These two men were tortured in the Tower of London, which was a military installation, governed from day to day by a lieutenant who was answerable to the Queen and Council for the maintenance of proper order and discipline. Whatever the Tower's bad reputation, there were some limits to what could be done there with a free hand. Something more easy-going was needed for the kind of social control at which the Elizabethan authorities were aiming. And so, in this same period of the mid-80s, they began to use an institution called Bridewell for the punitive detention of priests and lay recusants. Bridewell gave far more scope than the Tower for freely improvised interrogation and punishment.

Bridewell, named in one of those moments of cosmic humor after the nearby holy well of St. Bride,[2] was not a prison at all in the ordinary sense of the word. There had been a royal residence on the site since the middle ages, and Cardinal Wolsey had begun to build a residential palace there, adjacent to the Fleet River, in 1510. Henry VIII then took the project over, completing it in 1523. For a while the palace was an important royal residence. Then in 1553 Edward VI gave Bridewell to the city of London to be a "workhouse" for "the poor and idle persons of the city."[3]

As the London chronicler John Stow describes it, the result was a curiously mixed institution, partly a workhouse for the poor and partly a house of correction for people considered to be social refuse—beggars, vagrants, and prostitutes—and the place quickly acquired an extremely unsavory reputation.[4] It was never one of the ordinary London prisons.

One of the first Catholics to be sent there was John Jacob, an Oxford musician who had been captured at Lyford Grange with Edmund Campion. He was first imprisoned in the Marshalsea, where John Gerard, S.J., met him. But then they moved him to Bridewell, presumably because he could not pay for his keep, and there Gerard succeeded in visiting him, ca. 1583:

[1]See above, 121.

[2]St. Bride or Brigit, "the Mary of the Gael," is one of the most famous and revered of Irish saints. Her feast day is 1 February.

[3]Stow 2, 340.

[4]Stow 2, 414.

> When I visited him...he was wasted to a skeleton and in a state of exhaustion from grinding at the treadmill, a most pitiful sight. There was nothing left of him except skin and bones and I cannot remember having seen anything like it—lice swarmed on him like ants on a mole-hill[1]

No record survives of John Jacob's transfer from the Marshalsea prison to Bridewell, and nothing is heard of him after John Gerard's visit. One can only presume that he died. As far as we know, John Jacob was never charged with any offense. He was simply arrested and, finally, left to die in Bridewell of hard, pointless labor and starvation. In Elizabethan Bridewell, "a loathsome prison" as John Gerard described it, we have a forerunner or anti-type of Auschwitz.

The first priest we hear of in Bridewell is Roger Dickenson, a Lincolnshire man ordained at Laon in April, 1583, and sent to England, where he was soon arrested, and sent to Bridewell for interrogation. There, according to Pollen, "he was very barbarously used." The implication is that he was tortured, although Pollen gives no reference. Since there was no rack at Bridewell, "barbarous usage" there had to take other forms.[2]

Just what those forms were we learn a few years later when a lay Catholic, Thomas Felton, was captured in the spring of 1588 and put in Bridewell. He was the son of John Felton, executed in 1570 for nailing Pius V's bull of excommunication, *Regnans in excelsis*, to the bishop of London's door. He had been sent as boy to Rheims where, aged sixteen, he had been tonsured and become a postulant of the Bonhommes or Friars Minor; but finding that the strict life and diet did not agree with him, he returned to England to recover his health. Then, attempting to return to France, he was arrested at the seaside, sent to London, and committed to the Counter Prison in the Poultry where he remained two years. Upon release he tried again to go to France, was arrested again, and sent to Bridewell, released again, arrested again, and returned to Bridewell.

There he was first imprisoned for three days in a cell too small for him either to stand or lie down, and fed bread and water. He was then put to hard labor, grinding in the mill, still on a diet of bread and water. Finally, determined to discover what priests he knew in England and overseas, his captors resorted to other means: "He was hanged up by the

---

[1]Gerard, 5.

[2]Pollen 2, 84; Anstruther, 103. Dickenson was moved to the Gatehouse, January 1584, and presumably exiled. But he returned, was captured again at Winchester, and after trial and conviction under the act of 1585 was executed at Winchester with a lay helper, Ralph Milner.

hands...which punishment was so grievous that therewith the blood sprung forth at his finger's ends."[1]

At about the same time, there was another Rheims alumnus in Bridewell, the seminary priest William Watson. Sent into England in June 1586, he was soon arrested and imprisoned in the Marshalsea. He was still there in July 1587, even though an annotated prison list of December 1586 said that he was to be banished. According to his own account, he was released on the condition that he leave the country in a specified time, but before the given time had expired, Topcliffe arrested him again, committed him to Bridewell, and proceeded to mistreat him:

> All the plagues and torments of that place were inflicted upon me (whereof few I think were left out, and some I dare say unknown to her Majesty or Council that ever I suffered, as whipping, grinding in the mill.[2]

After he had been in Bridewell some time, a lady called Margaret Ward, taking pity upon him, smuggled a rope to him, and in March 1588 he succeeded in escaping. The gaoler traced the rope to Margaret Ward. The authorities arrested her at her house and put her in Bridewell where, wanting to know Watson's whereabouts, they tortured her:

> She was flogged and hung up by the wrists, the tips of her toes only touching the ground, for so long a time, that she was crippled and paralysed.[3]

Here, then, we have two definite cases of torture in Bridewell by the manacles, with a possible third and fourth in the cases of Dickenson and Watson. It is not too surprising, therefore, in June 1589 to find the Privy Council instructing Justice Young to remove an unnamed goldsmith

---

[1]Challoner, 138–40. Challoner's source was a manuscript written by Felton's sister. See also Burton-Pollen, 402–3. Thomas Felton, convicted of the felony of being reconciled to the Catholic Church, was hanged at Brentford, 28 August 1588, one of twenty-eight priests and lay people executed in the wake of the Armada crisis.

[2]*ODNB*. There are good accounts of Watson in both *ODNB* and the old *DNB*. After a later escape from prison in 1599, he left a letter for William Waad, secretary to the Council, saying among other things that, "towards such as yourself in authority, so far as I ever have found favor, I will make known a difference from others of Topcliffe's stamp, that dishonor her Majesty, her Highness' Council, and defame all..." (*Hat. Cal.* 9.214). He became one of the principal writers against the Jesuits in the Appellant controversy, was arrested for his role in the Bye and Main Plots, and executed, 9 December 1603.

[3]For Margaret Ward, canonized 25 October 1970, see Challoner, 142–5; Burton-Pollen, 430–37. The quoted passage is from Burton-Pollen, 435, where it is taken from a letter of Robert Southwell to Claudio Aquaviva, the Jesuit Father-General in Rome, also available in Pollen 1, 327.

accused of robbery to Bridewell, and to "use towards him the torture of the house in such sort and measure as you in discretion shall think fit."[1]

By the end of the decade, then, Bridewell had become a place for the rigorous treatment of certain prisoners, and the routine "torture of the house" was the manacles, along with other punishments, including whipping and hard labor. One wonders who introduced the manacles to Bridewell. Was it Topcliffe? He was not the first to use the manacles: Richard White or Gwyn, tortured at Bewdley and Bridgnorth in 1583 under the authority of the Council of Wales, was "laid in the manacles."[2] Topcliffe did not invent the manacles, but it became his preferred method of torture, and he may have introduced it to Bridewell.

One would like to know for certain, too, who was responsible for the cruel treatment of Thomas Felton, and the barbarous treatment of Margaret Ward. Topcliffe is the most likely suspect. By then he was the government's principal agent in the enforcement of the anti-Catholic laws. When in January 1590 Robert Southwell wrote describing the horrors of Bridewell to Father General Aquaviva he ended his account with a chilling sentence; "It is the Purgatory that we all fear, where Topcliffe and Young, those two butchers of the Catholics, have complete freedom to torture."[3]

---

[1] *APC*, 17. 310.

[2] Burton-Pollen, 134–5.

[3] *Unum istud purgatorium timemus omnes, in quo duo illi Catholicorum carnifices Topliffus et Youngus omnem habent cruciandi libertatem.* Printed in *CRS* 5, 329–30.

Seven

Hunting Vermin Northwards

Letters tell one almost as much about the person written to as about the writer, a principle that applies to the letters that Topcliffe wrote to people with whom he felt at ease, such as Leicester and the Queen. For example, his letter of 8 October 1586 to Leicester ends with a sentence one cannot imagine him writing to Burghley, Walsingham, or the Earl of Shrewsbury: "I cannot write at large thereof as I would," he wrote, "the rather because I am hunting northwards for more vermin in post." Walsingham and Burghley would have agreed with Topcliffe's assessment of the people referred to, but would never have used such language about them publicly, and perhaps not in private either. Leicester was less discriminating, and so Topcliffe could write to him confident that his opinions and his language would find a welcome.

No record of Topcliffe in the hunting field survives, though as a connoisseur of venison and a man with large land-holdings he knew that in hunters' language "vermin" described an animal to be taken and killed by any means possible. And of course, there was fun to be had from hunting vermin. In medieval times, aristocrats had coursed foxes with greyhounds, more for sport than for any useful purpose such as protecting people's lambs and chickens. Fox-hunting as we know it is a much later invention, although sixteenth-century English farmers were beginning to hunt foxes by way of pest-control.[1]

Topcliffe's talk of hunting vermin is one of those window-opening passages in these manuscripts that tells us exactly what went through the minds of these people.[2] As for hunting vermin northward, the question

---

[1] *MG*, 213.

[2] Topcliffe was not alone in treating people he disagreed with as vermin. During proceedings against the Earl of Strafford in the Long Parliament, Oliver St. John said that in their pursuit of Strafford the members should not treat him "as a stag or a hare, to whom some law was to be given, but as a fox, to be snared by any means and knocked on the head without pity"(*MG*, 65–66n.).

is, whom did Topcliffe have in mind? Topcliffe was a northerner. His family's origins were in Yorkshire; his estates were in Lincolnshire and Nottinghamshire; he was related to the Percies and the Nevilles, and he had ties of affinity with the Talbot Earls of Shrewsbury. In 1586, his friend George Shrewsbury, the sixth earl, was Lord Lieutenant of Yorkshire, Nottinghamshire, Derbyshire, and Staffordshire.

The north was Topcliffe's natural hunting ground. His career as the state's enforcer had begun with his arrests of Robert Morton and William Deane, both of them men from Yorkshire with connections to the Norton family, and hence to the Rising of the Earls. But in 1586 the beam of Topcliffe's attention northwards was focused elsewhere, and the vermin he had in mind were members of a family called Fitzherbert, with extensive land-holdings in Derbyshire and Staffordshire.

The Fitzherberts could trace their ancestry in a straight line back to the Norman Conquest, when a character called Herbert came into England as a retainer of Henry de Ferrers, one of the Conqueror's barons. In 1125, the prior of the Benedictine Abbey of Tutbury that Henry de Ferrers had founded granted the manor of Norbury on the River Dove in south-west Derbyshire to Herbert's son William Fitz (i.e., son of) Herbert, subject to certain rents. Norbury, on the border of Staffordshire, remained the Fitzherbert family's chief seat until 1649, and was in the family's possession for over 750 years, until 1881.[1]

The family's most famous member in the sixteenth century was Sir Anthony Fitzherbert (ca.1470–1538), a distinguished judge of the court of common pleas in Henry VIII's time, and a much-respected authority and writer on English law. Although he had been the youngest son of a large family, he ended up owning a great deal of property. This was because he acquired his family's estates, including Norbury, under the will of his eldest brother John Fitzherbert, and because his marriage to Maud, daughter and heir of Richard Cotton, brought him the considerable manor of Hamstall Ridware, south of Norbury, in Staffordshire.

True to his family's habits, Sir Anthony himself produced a large family, of which four sons and three daughters survived. His second but first surviving son, Sir Thomas, born ca. 1518, was his heir. Like his father, he married advantageously. His wife was Anne, daughter and heir of Sir Anthony Eyre of Padley, and through her the Fitzherberts were able to add the manors of Padley and Hathersage in the Derbyshire Peak to their holdings. On his father's death in 1538, Sir Thomas suc-

---

[1]On the Fitzherberts, including Sir Thomas, see Cox 1 and Camm 2.

ceeded to the estates, and still in his twenties became Sheriff of Staffordshire in 1543 and a member of the last Henrician parliament, 1545–7. Under Philip and Mary he was knighted, and was sheriff again in 1554.[1]

With Elizabeth's accession his fortunes changed. When at the outset of her reign, she and her Council set about enforcing the Acts of Supremacy and Uniformity, Sir Thomas Fitzherbert was among those who refused the oath of supremacy when the local commissioners tendered it to him. Did local animosities play a part in what then happened to him? In 1561 he was sent to London and imprisoned in the Fleet Prison, and for the next thirty years, until he died in the Tower in 1591, seventy-four years old, Sir Thomas was under one kind of imprisonment or another.

John, Sir Thomas's next brother, married Catherine, daughter of Edward Restwolde of the Vache, Buckinghamshire, near Chalfont St. Giles. He lived at Padley, which he managed for his brother. Since Sir Thomas had no children of his own, his heir was John's eldest son, also named Thomas. The third brother, Richard, had gone overseas when Sir Thomas was first arrested, but had then returned. He lived on another family property, Hartsmere, part of their holdings at Hamstall Ridware. Both John and Richard were to die in prison, like their brother. The fourth brother, William, married Elizabeth, daughter and heir of Humphrey Swynnerton of Swynnerton. He seemed set for a career of some distinction, becoming a bencher of the Middle Temple and member of parliament for Lichfield, but he died, sometime between December 1558 and August 1559, before the imposition of the penal statutes. William Fitzherbert's marriage, though, brought Swynnerton into the family, and when the senior branch failed in 1649 with the death of Sir John Fitzherbert of Norbury, William's great-grandson, also William, succeeded as head of the family.

Swynnerton then became the family's chief seat. The Fitzherberts, moreover, are still there, still Catholic, and the head of the family is now the fifteenth Baron Stafford. This was not the outcome foreseen by Richard Topcliffe when he set off hunting for vermin among the Fitzherberts of Derbyshire and Staffordshire in 1586.[2]

*****

[1] "Sheriffs of Staffordshire, 1086–1912," *Collections*, 284.

[2] For William Fitzherbert, see Hasler, 2. 139–40.

We do not know just what it was that first drew Topcliffe's attention
to the Fitzherberts. One would naturally tend to assume that his interest
originated with his connection to the Shrewsburys, especially since the
Earl of Shrewsbury was lord lieutenant of both Staffordshire and
Derbyshire. Yet although old George Shrewsbury was a time-server
who knew very well on which side his bread was buttered, there is no
sign that he had any wish to see the Fitzherberts molested. He left them
alone until Topcliffe, with the backing of the Privy Council, forced him
into raiding Padley and Norbury.

As usual with Topcliffe, his own court connections provide the likeli-
est source of his interest. We have already seen the Queen discussing
the presence of "lewd Popish beasts" in Derbyshire with him.[1] The
Earl of Leicester, Queen's favorite and privy councilor, is a likely source
of Topcliffe's midland activities, too. Leicester had territorial and political ambitions in the region, and there was no love lost between him and
the conservative, mostly Catholic, midland gentry. When in 1579 he set
about gaining a foothold in Staffordshire by acquiring the manor of
Drayton Bassett through proxies, the result was a series of violent con-
frontations in which his people found themselves up against a coalition
of midland gentry that included Harcourt of Stanton Harcourt, and
Topcliffe's nephew by marriage, Sir Francis Willoughby of Wollaton. It
took the full weight of the Privy Council to install Leicester in Drayton
Bassett.[2]

One of the gentlemen opposed to Leicester's midland ambitions,
including his takeover of Drayton Bassett, was Shakespeare's kinsman,
Edward Arden of Park Hall, Warwickshire, and former high sheriff of
the county. Like the Fitzherberts he was strongly Catholic, and he came
of even more ancient stock. When his son-in-law John Somerville of
Edstone, Warwickshire, went crazy and set off for London waving a pistol and saying he was going to shoot the Queen, Arden and his wife
found themselves in the Tower, charged with treason. Arden was tortured in the Tower—by whom we do not know—tried, convicted,
hanged, drawn, and quartered. *ODNB* describes him as a "convicted
conspirator," but he was guilty of absolutely nothing, as he said at his
execution, except being a Catholic, and contemporaries agreed that it
was Leicester, bent on revenging Arden's contempt for him, who
brought about his ghastly end.[3]

---

[1]See above, 63–3.

[2]For an account of the Drayton Bassett affair, see Peck 1, Appendix D (5), 182–3.

Although no Fitzherberts were involved at Drayton Bassett, they, their kin and friends, were a force to be reckoned with in Staffordshire and Derbyshire. As the Queen and Council were well aware, they were also a presence on the continent. Of the younger generation, John Fitzherbert's son Nicholas, having left England in the 1570s, was associated with William Allen, becoming his secretary after Allen was made a cardinal in 1587. He was to be attainted of treason *in absentia* in 1589.[2] William Fitzherbert of Swynnerton's son Thomas, in exile in France, was connected with the group that produced the wonderfully scandalous book known as *Leicester's Commonwealth* that everyone wanted to read and that upset Leicester and the English court so much.

The Queen and Council, therefore, and Leicester in particular, had every reason to encourage Topcliffe to bring down the Fitzherberts, and it is a very reasonable presumption that Leicester understood exactly what Topcliffe meant when he wrote that he was about to ride north hunting for vermin.

We do not know exactly when Topcliffe began his operation against the Fitzherberts, but it must have been some time in the early 1580s. In 1583, Sir Thomas's nephew and heir was in Derby gaol, presumably for recusancy.[3] Derby gaol was a notorious place. It was built over the town sewer and, as Topcliffe himself later said, it was a "foul hole...that always stank and bred corruption in the prisoners."[4] Topcliffe, who may have put the nephew there in the first place, quickly entered into an understanding with him. He seems to have told him that, quite apart from the dangers of the prison itself, if he persisted like the rest of his family in religious obstinacy, he would lose any inheritance he might expect from Sir Thomas. If, on the other hand, he threw his lot in with Topcliffe, not only would Topcliffe see to it that he got out of prison, but with Topcliffe's help and influence he could be sure to keep his property from sequestration. Thomas Fitzherbert, therefore, reneged upon his family, and became one of Topcliffe's henchmen. He worked with him for the next decade.

---

[3]*ODNB*. Arden was tortured 23 November 1583 (DT, 58).

[2]Topcliffe, writing to Cecil 11 October 1600 (Hatfield 250/20.) seems to take credit for that.

[3]Camm 2, 34.

[4]Cox 1, 253, quoting from the Chancery suit, "Fitzherbert v. Topcliffe, *Calendars of the Proceedings in Chancery, in the Reign of Queen Elizabeth*, Vol 1 (London, 1827), p.320 (F.f.9, No.63).

He did more than that. Sometime in the 1580s, probably earlier rather than later, he entered into a bond to pay Topcliffe £3,000—a huge sum of money—if Topcliffe would persecute[1] to death his uncle Sir Thomas, his father John, and his cousin, William Bassett of Langley and Blore in Staffordshire, who was another of Sir Thomas's nephews.[2] The nineteenth-century writers who mention this bond all tend to sympathize with the "wretched young man," and put the blame for the whole transaction upon Topcliffe. The terms of the agreement itself, though, linked to Thomas Fitzherbert's later history, show that he was one of nature's born criminals and, like most criminals, not terribly bright. Nor was he all that young: he was in his thirties when he took up with Topcliffe.

One can't help wondering, though, did the thought not cross his mind that Topcliffe was in this for himself? Topcliffe was well-off, but like Walsingham he was spending his own money on police activities for the Queen that he could not afford. The Fitzherberts were a great deal richer than he, and one or two of their properties would make up the deficit in his accounts very nicely. The agreement over the bond between him and Thomas Fitzherbert no doubt began with a discussion between the two of them over the best way to secure the Fitzherbert property before Thomas's father's and uncle's recusancy led to its final sequestration. But from Topcliffe's point of view the £3000 was a kind of downpayment on more profitable transactions.

Why, though, did Thomas want Topcliffe to go after cousin William of Langley and Blore as well? One suspects that cousin William had spoken his mind too freely on the subject of Master Thomas's moral character.

News of his nephew's betrayal came quickly to Sir Thomas. As early as October 1583 he constructed an elaborate series of legal maneuvers designed to bypass his nephew and to keep the family's property secure in the hands of his brothers John and Richard and their heirs.[3] In the

---

[1]This word is ambiguous. The abbreviation used in the manuscript can be expanded either as "prosecution" or "persecution."

[2]Sir Thomas's sister Elizabeth had married William's father, also called William. The younger William had been brought up by his Fitzherbert uncles. He proved to be the last of the male line of the Bassetts of Blore. His fine alabaster effigy is to be seen in Blore Church. Camm 2, 35, confuses him with his father. Foley, 4.49–50. prints Fr. Garnet's letter to Robert Persons telling him about the bond and Topcliffe's Chancery suit for payment.

[3]Camm 2, 36.

short run, the attempt failed. With Topcliffe's backing the younger Thomas enlisted the Queen and the Privy Council on his side, as a letter sent from the Council to the judges of the Staffordshire assizes, 6 September 1587, reveals:

> That whereas their Lordships are informed there are divers suits and controversies depending between Sir Thomas Fitzherbert, knight, and Thomas Fitzherbert, his nephew, concerning certain fraudulent estates pretended to be made of all the inheritance of the said Sir Thomas, only to defeat the said Thomas, who ought to have the same by way of remainder, and that there is extraordinary proceeding against him for that purpose by Privy Sessions held in Staffordshire and otherwise; their Lordships did think good to signify...that they thought her Majesty would take it well if they took due regard and care at the assizes next to be holden at Stafford, and at all other times hereafter, that he were dealt withal in every of his causes according to conscience and the equity thereof.[1]

In short, the Council was telling the judges to settle the case in the younger Fitzherbert's favor—by no means the only case of Council interference in the course of justice, as we shall see. Topcliffe had used his influence well. Sure enough, the judges, sitting at Stafford, "in obedience to the orders of the Council," as Camm puts it, threw out Sir Thomas's arrangements, so that when he died, Thomas the younger inherited the property under Sir Thomas's original settlement of 1578, drawn up after the death of his wife when it was apparent that he was a childless widower.

Topcliffe, in the meantime, had been preparing to earn his three thousand pounds. He set about drawing up a set of questions to be put to Sir Thomas Fitzherbert, accusing him of a long series of treasonous acts, starting with a visit to the Earl of Northumberland and Sir John Neville on the eve of the Rising of the North in 1569, and including a mass at Norbury with Fr. Robert Persons in 1580, as well as dealings with Anthony Babington in 1586. Sir Thomas, continually imprisoned since 1561, and in increasingly poor health, could not possibly have done any of these things. Other questions accuse him of maintaining, and encouraging his servants and tenants to maintain, a number of priests. These questions, which include the names of the priests—Sir Richard Arnold, Abraham Sutton, Robert Gray, and "one Francis"—probably Francis Ridcall[2]—are probably accurate enough, though it would not have

---

[1] *APC*, 15. 226.

[2] See below, 250.

been easy, given Sir Thomas's continued imprisonment, to prove his responsibility.[1]

The object, of course, was to have Sir Thomas indicted, tried, and convicted of treason. One of Topcliffe's henchmen, Edmund Browne, delivered his questions to the Council, and on 26 March 1587, the Council instructed Messrs. Rokeby and Herbert, the Masters of the Requests, to bring Sir Thomas before them, and put the questions to him.[2] For the time being, nothing seems to have come of this initiative, perhaps because of Sir Thomas's ill-health, perhaps because most of the questions were manifestly absurd.

One of the signers of this letter was the Earl of Shrewsbury, who, though always happy enough to act upon Council instructions, had hitherto shown no interest in harassing the Fitzherberts and their friends on his own initiative. When, early in 1588, he began taking unusually vigorous action against the local Catholics in general and the Fitzherberts in particular, it is very likely that Topcliffe, who had little confidence in Shrewsbury's eagerness for the job, had brought pressure to bear on him through his Council friends, Burghley and Leicester in particular.

Shrewsbury first publicized his willingness to proceed against the local Catholics by writing to the Council (of which he was a member), 5 January 1588, reporting the arrest of a seminary priest, Richard Simpson, and asking what he should do with him. In reply his fellow-councillors told him to commit the priest to prison in readiness for trial at the next assizes. This, of course, is something that Shrewsbury could have done on his own initiative, and one suspects him of angling for the gratifying compliment with which the Council ended their letter:

> And for that his Lordship's great care and travail in this and other her Majesty's good services, especially in these times of danger and peril, as their Lordships doth greatly commend his Lordship, so will they not fail to make it known unto her Majesty, who no doubt will graciously accept of the same to his Lordship's comfort.[3]

Shrewsbury's next move, 29 January, was to write instructing John Manners and Roger Columbell of Derby to search for seminary priests and other recusants residing or lurking in houses belonging to ill-affected

---

[1] The articles are in NA/SP12/194/75, and printed in Cox 1, 256–59.

[2] *APC*, 15. 3.

[3] *APC*, 15. 333. Simpson, a Yorkshireman, was arrested *en route* from Lancashire to Derbyshire by a trickster pretending to be a Catholic (Foley 3.229).

persons in the hundred of the High Peak. In particular they were to arrest John Fitzherbert of Padley and Richard Fenton of North Lees hundred, and commit them as Queen's prisoners.[1] The next day, 30 January, he wrote to the Staffordshire commissioners for recusants, reprimanding them for negligence in not certifying the names of the recusants in their county, and he ordered them to arrest and imprison some of the more important among them.[2]

Then, early in the morning of Candlemas Day, 2 February, Roger Columbell went, as instructed, with twenty men to Padley, where he found John Fitzherbert's son Anthony, two of his daughters, Thomas Fitzherbert's wife, and about twenty other people, but failed to find any priests or John Fitzherbert himself. Anthony was imprisoned in Derby gaol, and his two sisters were delivered into the keeping of a pair of local Protestant ministers.[3]

There matters lay for a few months. Topcliffe, meanwhile, had been busying himself with other aspects of the case. He was almost certainly the agency behind Shrewsbury's letter chiding the Staffordshire authorities for not reporting, arresting, and prosecuting the local recusants, and he understood that to enforce the law there effectively he would need agents of his own in the area. Consequently, he had taken up with at least two local men interested in making themselves a nuisance to their neighbors: Edmund Browne of Yoxall, Staffordshire, and a man known variously as Edward Thorne, Edward Thornes, and Old Thorne, a character one could fairly describe as a thug. He proved very useful to Topcliffe, who even used him to keep the Shrewsburys up to the mark.

One of Thorne's first jobs for Topcliffe was to investigate the Staffordshire recusants' strange immunity from the law. Who was protecting them? Thorne thought he had found out. The clerk of the peace for Staffordshire was a lawyer called Nicholas Blackwell who lived at Hamstall Ridware, a Fitzherbert property. It seems he had been "winking at" (Topcliffe's expression) recusants brought up before the local assize courts. He had not turned their names over to the exchequer at London, and so no fines had been collected. We know this from a letter that Topcliffe wrote to Richard Bagot of Blithfield, 4 March 1588.

[1]Cox 2, 259.

[2]NA/SP12/208/37. For the named recusants and their fates, see Greenslade, 59.

[3]Cox 2, 260, 257. When after about a year the two girls proved unpersuadable, the Council wrote, 21 August 1589, telling Shrewsbury to sell off some of the Fitzherbert's property in order to recompense their Protestant hosts for their upkeep.

The Bagots of Blithfield had a pedigree as long as the Fitzherberts, and like the Fitzherberts, were a force to be reckoned with in the midlands. Unlike the Fitzherberts, though, they had decided to cooperate with the regime, and Richard Bagot was well-connected at court. He corresponded with Sir Francis Knollys. His older son married Burghley's niece, and his younger son was one of Essex's entourage. He served twice as sheriff of Staffordshire, and so he was one of the people the Council called upon to implement its policies in the county. Yet although one local historian describes him as "a notable hammer of the Staffordshire recusants and their priests,"[1] the family's position was rather more complex than that. Willing though Mr. Bagot was to do the Council's bidding if ordered to do so, left to himself he had no more interest in irritating his neighbors than old George Shrewsbury himself.

After all, if Nicholas Blackwell had been "winking" at the local recusants, Richard Bagot had been "winking" at Nicholas Blackwell as well as the Fitzherberts and their Hamstall Ridware tenants. A careful reading of Topcliffe's letter to him reveals that Topcliffe understood this aspect of local politics very well:

> To the right worshipful my very good friend Mr Richard Bagot, Esq.
>
> After my right hearty Commendations unto you I am very glad that your son is settled, and now at rest in his office of the Clerkship of the Peace, by whose, or his deputies' diligence (as small a while as they have exercised that office) I have been an eyewitness in the records of the Exchequer lately, that divers recusants and fugitives be returned into the Exchequer, indicted etc., who for a long time have (by that lewd fellow Blackwell) been winked at.
>
> I had occasion to shew to my Lord Treasurer how divers of those who by negligence (as Blackwell will excuse it), but by corruption (as I take it) were never certified, but now by your son certified. As this bearer can tell you, who was the finder out of the matter, in whose behalf (Mr. Thorne's I mean) I must thank you for the great pains you did take in the commission that was prosecuted by him, wherein my Lord Treasurer found himself your travail to be very diligent, with special words of affection towards you for your zeal in all good services, and surely for I hear and partly know, that you have not that assistance of any great number; but much of the weight of that backward shire lieth upon your shoulders, if I may speak it without flattery. And if your son hold on that course it seemeth he beginneth, and yourself see that the fattest be not spared, and the poorest sent into the Exchequer, it will breed a good alteration in your country. And so desiring the continuance of your favour towards Mr Thorne in all his hon-

[1]Greenslade, 41.

est services, as you shall be assured of me to requite the like unto any
friend of yours, I end. At the court, the 4th of March 1588.
                    Richard Topcliffe

This letter is a characteristic Topcliffe performance. From it we learn
that Thorne, who is the bearer of the letter, had presented himself to
Bagot carrying a commission, and that Bagot had, as required by its
terms, assisted him to carry it out. As a result, Bagot's son (which son
the letter does not say) is now clerk of the peace, and Topcliffe, having
personally visited the Exchequer to check up on the results, tells Bagot
something he must have known already—that the convicted recusants'
names had been turned over to the Exchequer. He then goes out of his
way to let Bagot know that he has discussed the whole subject with
Burghley—who was the most powerful man in England, let us
remember—and to pass along Burghley's compliments upon his "zeal in
all good services." The letter ends with Topcliffe more or less ordering
Bagot to continue helping Thorne "in all his honest services" in
Staffordshire.

The obvious purpose of the letter is to recognize and acknowledge
Bagot's cooperation with Thorne, and to let him know that he is
expected to keep it up. Its less obvious purpose is to make sure that
Bagot understands that in dealing with Thorne he is dealing with
Topcliffe, and that in dealing with Topcliffe, he is dealing with Burghley
and the Council. It was one thing for a man of Richard Bagot's standing
to carry out requests from the Council. It was another thing entirely for
him to take orders from a man like Thorne, no matter whose commission
he was carrying, and it is a measure of Topcliffe's own power by this
time, and the length of his arm, that he was able to write like this to
Richard Bagot.

The attack on Blackwell must have begun several months earlier,
probably at the same time that Topcliffe began planning his first moves
against John Fitzherbert and his people in Derbyshire. Blackwell was
now out of his position as clerk of the peace, but even so Topcliffe and
Thorne were not finished with him and all that he stood for. Shortly
after Thorne delivered Topcliffe's letter to Bagot, he and one Caudwell
(or Caldwell), operating still with Bagot's approval, arrested a man
called William Deeg for recusancy. According to the published transcript of the manuscript narrating what then happened, Deeg was the servant of a man called Bakewell; but—especially given the timing of the
arrest—it seems likely that this is a copyist's mistake for Blackwell.
Thorne and Caudwell took Deeg to Caudwell's house, "where he was
most strictly examined, threatened, and most barbarously used:"

For it is most constantly reported, because they could get nothing out of him by any speech, they tormented him with a hot iron. Yet not thus contented they further threatened to hang him, although, peradventure they had no such meaning, for in truth, they hanged him. Then, to save their credit, gave it out that he had hanged himself, and buried him as if he had so done; but without a 'crowner,' which is a thing not lawful in such a fact. They kept him three days. This was done in 1588, the 14th of March.[1]

There was only one reason for this kind of interrogation, which was to force the witness to incriminate someone else, in this case Deeg's master, Blackwell. When he refused to tell them anything they wanted to hear, they resorted to torture, and being a pair of amateurs, they killed him.

According to the same witness, a few weeks later, on 8 April in Easter week, Thorne and Caudwell raided Comberford Hall, then tenanted by Mr. Thomas Heath, and caught a priest, James Harrison. Again, it is worth reading the contemporary account of what happened during the raid:

They so cruelly used Mrs. Heath at that time, tossing and tumbling her, that she, thereby frighted, died the Friday following.

Thorne sent both Harrison and Heath to London. Harrison was imprisoned in the Tower, Heath in Newgate.[2]

This arrest had an unusual sequel that has some bearing upon Topcliffe's own later fortunes. Although Heath was indicted for harboring Harrison, he seems not to have been condemned. Harrison too, although he was in the Tower until July 1590, and then sent to the Marshalsea, was not convicted, but somehow regained his freedom. The explanation of this unusual outcome is that Shrewsbury's eldest son, Gilbert, Lord Talbot, took an interest in Harrison because his brother, Humphrey, was one of Gilbert's servants. Gilbert explained all this in a letter, 23 May 1589, to Richard Bagot, asking for his help in relieving the hardships of James Harrison's imprisonment:

Mr Bagot: Whereas one James Harrison was about Easter last was a twelve-month apprehended as a seminary priest in the house of one Mr. Heath, tenant there to Mr. Comberford in the county of Staffs., whereupon the same Mr. Comberford seized upon such apparel, linens, and furniture as belonged to the said Harrison, holding it as an escheat fallen within the

[1]Foley, 3.227.

[2]Morris 1, 3.16.

liberty of his manor. Now for that Harrison hath in effect ever since lain prisoner in the Tower, utterly void of all relief, save only from this bearer his brother, my servant Humphrey Harrison, who, upon special licence is admitted to relieve him with apparel and such necessaries as he wanteth, I am therefore very heartily to desire you to deal with the said Mr. Comberford (with whom I am not acquainted) and earnestly entreat him to render the said apparel, linens, and furniture to this said bearer, that he may therewith relieve the wants of his brother, which act no doubt shall be a part of commiseration and charity done by Mr. Comberford (though this[1] fellow in respect of his function deserve no favor) and for mine own part I shall be ready to requite his courtesy therein as any good occasion might offer. And so desiring your effectual and best furtherance herein I bid you very heartily well-to-fare. From my lodging at Mr. Bosville's house near Clement's Inn, this xxiii[rd] of May 1589.

> Your very loving friend
> Gilb: Talbot

I pray you conmmend me
very heartily to good Mrs.
Bagot, who made me better
entertainment than I deserved
when I troubled you at your house.[2]

Oddly enough, the Mr. Comberford who took the priest's belongings was himself a Catholic, and was imprisoned in 1592.[3] Eighteen months after the date of this letter, Gilbert Talbot became the seventh Earl of Shrewsbury on the death of his father. He obviously knew Richard Bagot well, and was well-disposed towards him. Nonetheless the letter conveys the kind of strong request that is virtually an order, and its language tells us pretty clearly that in Gilbert's mind personal and local loyalties took precedence over the demands of a Council-inspired ruffian like Thorne. The letter also implies that it was through Gilbert that Humphrey Harrison had access to his brother, and that Gilbert's sympathies were with the brothers. In fact, it is very likely that his intervention saved the priest and his harborer, Mr. Heath.[4] As we shall see, Gil-

---

[1] Miswritten in the Ms. as "they." This parenthesis, politically prudent, is inserted over a caret.

[2] Folger Ms. L.a.828. The body of the letter is in a secretary's hand. Gilbert wrote the postscript himself.

[3] Greenslade, 69.

[4] The Council drew up instructions sending them both back to Staffordshire for trial, but the letters were never sent (Pollen 1, 162–5). James Harrison went free for more than ten years. Sir Stephen Proctor then captured him in Nidderdale, Yorkshire, in the house of a

bert's sense of personal loyalty did not extend to Richard Topcliffe.

Meanwhile in June 1588, three months after Topcliffe wrote to Richard Bagot, Blackwell, the ex-clerk of the peace, was himself examined in London on the Council's behalf. He told his questioners that he had taken the Oath of Supremacy twenty years earlier, at his admission to Clement's Inn, but that none of his family received communion in the Church of England, although his servants did. As the examination proceeded, it emerged that its real object was the Fitzherbert family, and that Blackwell was suspected of using his position to help them defer fines and confiscations. One thing that emerges from Blackwell's examination is that it was common knowledge among Sir Thomas Fitzherbert's friends and dependants that his nephew had accused him of the things laid out in Topcliffe's list of questions to be put to him. Blackwell told his examiners that he had tried to reconcile Thomas with his uncle, using the argument that he would lose his inheritance were he to prove him guilty of treason.

Blackwell's examination also shows that the local people made some attempt to fight back against their tormentors. The eleventh question is all about Edmund Browne of Yoxhall, Staffordshire. Browne was the local agent who carried Topcliffe's questions for Sir Thomas Fitzherbert to the Council. Some time in early 1587, Blackwell had Browne arrested in Westminster for a felony, and imprisoned in the Gatehouse prison by a warrant from the Lord Chief Baron. Topcliffe promptly had him bailed out. Later that year Browne went back to Staffordshire, and was re-arrested on orders from Sir Walter Aston and Richard Bagot. The Council then wrote to the assize justices in Staffordshire, telling them to suspend proceedings against Browne:[1]

This instruction formed part of the Council's letter instructing the justices to settle the suits between Sir Thomas and his nephew in his nephew's favor.[2] What happened then is not clear, but Browne was still in prison in Stafford in February 1588, and had not delivered his "informations" to their Lordships. Their Lordships therefore intervened once again, instructing the Lord Chief Justice (Sir Christopher Wray) to release him:

Whereas Edmund Browne of Yoxall in the county of Stafford, remaining

---

poor farmer, Anthony Batty. Both Harrison and Batty were martyred at York, 22 March 1602 (Anstruther, 151).

[1] Blackwell's examination, Folger Ms. L.a.1038; *APC*, 15. 226 (6 September 1587).

[2] Above, 151.

prisoner in the common gaol of the said county, being committed thither upon suspicion of felony, forasmuch as the said Browne was to prosecute here before their Lordships divers accusations of seditious persons for matters which concern the Queen's Majesty and the present State, which could not be done without his presence to such effect as was determined, their Lordships required him, with convenient speed after the receipt hereof to award out of that court of King's Bench a writ of *habeas corpus* for the removing of the body of the said Browne from the said gaol where he remained, and that bands may be taken of him to her Majesty's use as well for his good behavior as his forthcoming at all times as for his speedy and personal appearance before their Lordships.[1]

Blackwell—and, one presumes, his local supporters—did not let this action of the Council pass unchallenged, either. When his examiners "charged" him with telling the justices of the peace that they should not deliver Browne on bail or by any other means, he told them plainly that he had indeed either written a letter or sent a message to that effect, that his action was justifiable, and that should Browne reappear he would promptly prosecute outlawry against him.[2]

Thorne, too, ran into opposition. In July 1589 we find the Council responding to complaints that Thorne had seized the house and possessions of an eighty-year old widow, "besides divers other outrages which he committed"—not that that prevented the Council from commissioning him again on Topcliffe's behalf.[3] Then a man called Warde "conceived and commenced" an action against Thorne in the court of King's Bench "for words supposed to be spoken by Thorne, in doing her Majesty' important services." Once again, the Council's response was to protect Topcliffe's man, and they wrote telling the Lord Chief Justice "to stay further proceedings." Even so, the case came to a hearing. Thorne lost, and was assessed twenty marks damages (£6/13s/4d). So the Council wrote again to the Lord Chief Justice, 24 May 1590, this time in strong language—

> to signify unto you that in no case you proceed to judgment in that matter, but to stay all other proceedings against him before you until you hear further from us. And so not doubting of the due performance hereof as appertaineth we commit you to God..

Mr. Bagot's role in these events is interesting. He and Sir Walter

---

[1] *APC*, 15. 363.

[2] The text of Blackwell's examination is in Folger Ms. L.a.1038.

[3] *APC*, 17. 337–8.

Aston had arrested Browne, and though as a justice of the peace he found himself required to assist, even take part in, Thorne's proceedings, he cannot have enjoyed the experience. Writing to him in January 1590, Blackwell reminded him how he had reacted to the suggestion that Richard Fitzherbert should be reported to London as a recusant:

> At one of the same assizes, the name of Richard Fitzherbert without any presentment was by me preferred, and yourself upon sight thereof, told me that I did him wrong, for that he was not, nor had been of long inhabiting in this shire, and thereupon he was left forth of the indictment.[1]

This was not the action of a "hammer" of the local recusants. In fact this same letter leaves one with a strong impression that although Bagot's son might now hold the clerkship in name, Blackwell was still doing the work, and for all we know enjoying the salary.

All this activity in Staffordshire and Derbyshire originated with Topcliffe, including the intervention of the Council on behalf of Browne, Thorne, and Thomas Fitzherbert in the local assize courts and the Court of King's Bench. Even so, from Topcliffe's point of view, as long as there were still three Fitzherbert brothers alive, nothing had been achieved.

On 12 July 1588, however, Shrewsbury himself, acting on a tip from Thomas Fitzherbert that his father would be at Padley, raided the house again. This time he not only caught John Fitzherbert but two priests, Nicholas Garlick and Robert Ludlam, as well. All three prisoners were put in Derby gaol. Shrewsbury wrote promptly, 15 July, to the Council, announcing his capture; and the Council replied, equally promptly, to congratulate him:

> We have received your letters of the 15th of this month certifying the apprehension of two seminary priests and of other recusants, and we observe your zeal for the advancement of true religion by the rooting out of such seditious and traitorous persons. Her Majesty sends you grateful thanks, considering the notable mischiefs wrought by such lewd and wicked persons and the hurt and danger thereof in these doubtful times. We have written to the Justices of Assize of the county of York to proceed with the said priests at the next assizes according to the law, for their conviction, condemnation and execution. Please send them at once under a safe guard to the sheriff of the county, the place of execution to be as you shall direct. The rest are to remain as they are until we send further order....[2]

[1]Folger Ms. L.a.207.

[2]Bath, 5 (*Talbot, Dudley and Devereux Papers 1533–1659*), 92–3.

On 23 July the two priests, along with Richard Simpson, already in prison, were indicted and condemned for high treason for being priests in England. John Fitzherbert, convicted of felony for harboring them, was also condemned to death. On 25 July the three priests were hanged, drawn, and quartered at Derby. Immediately after the trial, John Fitzherbert, his son Anthony, and "an old massing priest," i.e., a Marian priest, were in held in Shrewsbury's own house, and once again, he wrote to the Council asking what he should do with them. In reply the Council told him to put them in Derby gaol until they had time to decide upon their fate.[1]

As for the manor of Padley, liable to forfeit as the residence of convicted felons, the Council's letter instructed Shrewsbury to appoint "meet persons" to keep the house, "to take the harvest and other profits," and to send an assessment of the value of the contents to them. Thomas Fitzherbert had written, probably well ahead of the arrest, assuring the Council that his uncle had long since conveyed half of Padley and two thirds of another manor to him.[2] Meanwhile Shrewsbury had already taken possession of Padley, not for the Council, but for himself. Nor could he resist sending his own letter to the Queen, bragging of his arrest of John Fitzherbert:

> On Sunday last I was in those parts of Derbyshire, where I lately took John Fitzherbert and the other seminaries, of purpose only to reduce into some good order the multitude of ignorant people heretofore by them seduced. Where at one sermon before me came above two hundred persons, whereof many had not comed to church twenty years before, and as many not since the beginning of your Majesty's reign. Beside them be two hundred and twenty which came not as yet, but I hope ere long, seeing their Captain is caught, they will generally become more obedient subjects.[3]

Sir Thomas Fitzherbert naturally enough wrote a pained letter to Shrewsbury about his appropriation of Padley:

> Very good Lord, with all humble duty I crave leave in lowliness to open my griefs unto you. I suppose your honor hath known me above fifty years, and my wife that was daughter and heir unto Sir Arthur Eyre; I trust I have been dutiful unto my lords your grandfather, your father, and your honor and so have found your honors all my good lords till now of late your

[1]Camm 2, 43–6; *APC,* 16. 286.

[2]*APC*, 16. 169.

[3]NA/SP12/214/51 (quoted by Camm, 46). Since the letter is in the State Papers, it is possible the Queen never saw it.

lordship entering into the house of Padley found two seminaries there, all unknown unto my brother, as was confessed at their deaths and is well approved since by good testimony, since which time your Lordship also hath entered upon my house of Padley and the demesne thereof, seized all the goods of my brother's and mine, that was in that house, amongst which I had certain evidences, of a wood, and meadows, under Levin house called Faultcliff which as I am informed your honor hath entered upon and occupieth wholly to your use though I have been possessed and my wife's ancestors thereof, time out of mind. Very good lord, these things are greater than my present poor estate can suffer or in any wise bear, I paying her Majesty the Statute of Recusancy, being £260 by year, which is more than all rents yearly rise unto. Loth I am to complain of your honor any way, wherefore I complain me first unto your lordship, hoping you will deal so nobly and charitably with me as I shall be restored to my house, lands, and goods, by your honor, so as I shall be fully satisfied, and be able to pay her Majesty, and for ever bound to pray for your lordship's long life, in all honor long to continue.[1]

Getting no response from Shrewsbury, Sir Thomas petitioned the Council, and they—no doubt to everyone's surprise—ordered Shrewsbury to return Sir Thomas's property to him. It appears, too, from their reply that Thorne had also appropriated two of Sir Thomas's properties, Hartsmere and Bancroft, occupied by Richard Fitzherbert. The council asked Shrewsbury to see that those were returned, too.[2]

Instead, Shrewsbury wrote explaining that it would be better all round to keep things as they were, and that he would see to it that any tenants he installed would pay the recusancy fines. The Council agreed, and told him to keep the property. In Thorne's case, he confessed to taking the properties, but since he had acted under a commission out of the Court of Exchequer, and stood charged to hand over the profits to her Majesty, those properties, too, were to stay as they were. As for Sir Thomas, he was "to be left to his remedy by traversing the proceedings in that behalf held in her Majesty's Court of Exchequer," and one can imagine the laughter at the Council table over that suggestion. As Bede Camm remarks, the Council's only interest was to keep the fines coming in.[3]

Sir Thomas's letter reveals that the Fitzherberts were a part of the Talbot affinity, and had been for a long time. This no doubt explains why, as long as no-one instructed him otherwise, Shrewsbury, like Rich-

---

[1]28 From London, May 1589. Talbot, Vol G (Ms. Lambeth 3198), f. 456.

[2]*APC*, 17. 357 (7 July 1589).

[3]*APC*, 18. 139–40 (22 September 1589); 18. 286 (28 December 1589); Camm 2, 48.

ard Bagot, had left them alone. In fact, he may have been motivated to seize the property himself in order to protect the family's longer-term interests. Indeed, that proved to be the effect of his seizure of the property, whereas any return of Padley to Sir Thomas would have been short-lived.

John Fitzherbert's arrest and Shrewsbury's appropriation of Padley ended the first episode of Topcliffe's campaign to destroy the Fitzherberts. It was Topcliffe's favorite project at this period of his career, and he evidently had the complete and well-informed support of the Queen for it. The Council told the Staffordshire Assize judges that it was the Queen who would be pleased if they settled the suits between Sir Thomas Fitzherbert and his nephew in the nephew's favor, and the Queen thanked Shrewsbury personally for his arrest of John Fitzherbert. This pattern would continue.

Topcliffe's behavior earned him enemies. On 12 January 1585, he was walking along the Strand just outside Temple Bar, going towards Leicester House, accompanied by a servant with a sword, and a page carrying his rapier, when he encountered one of the earl of Shrewsbury's gentlemen, Mr. George Benthall. Benthall, who was wearing a gold chain, had with him a red-faced man with a sword, and a man in a blue coat with sword and dagger (One of these two was Benthall's brother, Richard.) When Topcliffe, being the older man, "took the wall," Benthall "jostled" him so that his cloak fell off. Topcliffe picked up his cloak, and asked Benthall, "What he meant to jostle him," to which Benthall replied, "Amend it if thou darest." Something of a fray then ensued in the yard of The Ship inn nearby. The red-faced man seized Topcliffe's rapier from the page, and Benthall made a move towards Topcliffe, who said, "Let go my rapier, wilt thou see me murdered having no weapon but my dagger? Deliver it or it shall cost thee thy life, for I will not be killed." He then punched Benthall in the face, and swords were drawn on Benthall's side. Topcliffe's rapier was broken in the tussle, so his page started throwing stones—when the people restrained him, he asked if they expected him to see his master murdered weaponless. The people then separated the brawlers.

That was not quite the end, though. Benthall shouted out to Topcliffe:

"Thou darest not go with me into the fields." "Yes," said Topcliffe, "if thou wilt lead the the way, for thou art nearer to the door and fields." But he cried still, "Thou darest not, thou darest not," very often. With that Topcliffe ran out through the press of the people saying. "Follow me, I will go into the fields by God's leave, and so will not thou, I dare be bound," going forthwith indeed into the lane near the fields. But missing the point of his rapier, and seeing the other not to come and follow him, turned to the people and said, "I am, masters, ashamed that you should see me in this sort like a ruffian, in my doublet and hose, and with a gray head." The people and boys cried, "Well said, old gent, follow him for shame, follow!"

Topcliffe then made his way to a chamber in the George where his friend Bushie was, and there he stayed. Benthall, looking in, shouted that "Mr. Topcliffe durst as well eat a load of logs as come out of the doors," and he spent the evening (according to one of Bushie's servants), striding up and down outside, "seeming to be in a great rage." Even so, one has the impression that he was as careful as Topcliffe to avoid a real fight. The whole episode reads like a scene from an Elizabethan play—it reminds one of Falstaff and Pistol in Shakespeare's *II Henry IV*, even down to Falstaff's telling his page-boy, "Give me my rapier, boy."[1]

The witnesses' statements suggest that Benthall was spoiling for a fight which, however, he was careful to avoid. No hint is given of the underlying cause of the fray. It may be that as one of Shrewsbury's people, Benthall knew all about Topcliffe's activities, and was offended by them on the Earl's behalf.[2]

*****

[1] *II Henry IV,* 2.4.201.

[2] Benthall may have had a private reason for disliking Topcliffe in addition to his loyalty to Shrewsbury. Benthall had paid for the reversion of the office of Garter King of Arms, but the Earl of Leicester procured a grant of the office from Shrewsbury, the Earl-marshall, for Robert Cooke, Clarencieux King of Arms. Benthall protested to Leicester that the grant had cost him £100, and Leicester replied that Cooke would pay Benthall the money, but keep the office. So Cooke gave Benthall £20 in cash and a bond for £80. On the death of Sir Gilbert Dethick, Garter King at Arms, October 1584, Cooke became acting Garter, but Dethick's son William was appointed to the office, April 1586. Benthall, nonetheless, sued Cooke for his bond. Topcliffe as both Leicester's and Shrewsbury's man may have been the agent of Shrewsbury's grant to Cooke. As we have seen, he admired Cooke's work. This might go some way to explain Benthall's hostility (*AC,* 1.145; *ODNB,* s.v. "Robert Cooke").

Eight

"Black with Gibbets"[1]

When the Earl of Shrewsbury arrested John Fitzherbert on 12 July 1588, the great Spanish Armada was within a week of being sighted off the coast of Cornwall. Its arrival was the culminating event in a decade of intensifying hostility on the part of the English government towards Catholics at home and towards Catholic powers overseas, especially Spain. That was the context in which Topcliffe rose to power.

The decade had begun with the executions of Cuthbert Mayne (1577), John Nelson, and Thomas Sherwood (1578), but its first major events were the Jesuit mission of 1580, the great show-trial of Edmund Campion and the others in November 1581, and the following executions. In 1581, Parliament enacted the statute of 23 Eliz. c. 1, making it high treason to reconcile anyone or to be reconciled to "the Romish religion," and imposing very severe fines for the celebration and hearing of mass, and for not attending the state Church. This statute also divided the fines so received three ways: a third to the Queen, a third to the poor, and—most sinisterly—a third to the informer.

In 1582–4 there were the anxieties of the Guisean "Enterprise of England" which came to center, in England, upon the arrest, torture, trial, conviction, and execution of Francis Throckmorton. Then in July 1584, a Frenchman, Balthasar Gérard, shot William of Orange, the leader of the Dutch Protestants in revolt against Spanish rule of the Netherlands.[2] In response Burghley and Walsingham concocted the "Bond of Association," creating a kind of brotherhood devoted to the destruction of anyone planning to supplant the Queen and her current government, and of anyone—Mary, Queen of Scots, for instance—in

[1]Pollen 2, 314.

[2]The classic account of the assassination and ensuing trial is in Motley, 3.608–13. The sickeningly cruel process of interrogation and execution that the Dutch authorities inflicted on Balthasar Gérard gives one some idea of what Elizabeth I had in mind when she asked for unprecedentedly cruel punishments for the convicted Babington plotters.

whose favor such an attempt might be made. The bond was offered for signature at the opening of Parliament, November 1584, and subsequently in churches in a kind of religious ceremony. The first act of the Parliament was a statute turning the declarations of the Bond into law.[1]

In the winter of 1584–5, the Parry plot developed, and Parry himself was executed in March. Although there was no real substance to the "plot," it had the effect, as Francis Edwards pointed out, of stirring up the plot-mania that now settled over the country, and that came to its first boil with the Babington Plot in the summer.of 1586.[2]

If the 1584 Parliament's Bond of Association and associated statute had amounted to "a declaration of lynch law" against Mary Stuart,[3] in 1585 Parliament issued another against Catholics and their priests in the form of the act of 27 Eliz. c. 2, "Against Jesuits, Seminary priests and other suchlike disobedient persons." This was the statute that made it high treason for a seminary priest or a Jesuit merely to be in England at all, and as a corollary made it a felony for anyone to harbor or relieve one. Under this law, to give a priest a glass of water, or to put a bandage on a sore foot brought a death sentence. The statute imposed the penalties of *præmunire* on anyone contributing money to support the seminaries overseas, and a fine of £100 on anyone who sent a child overseas without licence.[4] This law was in effect a hunting licence for informers, projecters, and other trouble-makers, its purpose to drive people into the state church by terror and despair.

Meanwhile the English had intervened in the Netherlands, sending the Earl of Leicester there with a small army in late 1585. Leicester's incompetence, whether as military commander or as statesman, doomed this expensive gesture to pointlessness. Its one dramatic military outcome was the surrender of Deventer and Zutphen by their English Catholic commanders, Stanley and York, to the duke of Parma, and the transference of themselves and their soldiers to his service.

The Babington Plot, a much controverted episode in the history of the period, emerged in the summer of 1586. It was the most important com-

---

[1]Hughes, 3.374–5.

[2]Edwards 1, 106: "Certainly by the end of 1584, it was due as much to Parry as any that England was in the grip of plotmania."

[3]The phrase is from Neale 2, 290, cited by Hughes, 3.375n. This association had its origin in a proposal by William Cecil in 1569 for a "general association" for the protection of the Queen and the Protestant religion (NA/SP12/51/6; see Simpson 1, 205).

[4]The texts of the statutes are readily available, in Stephens, 1.440–47.

plication of its kind until the Gunpowder Plot of 1605. Looked at empirically and objectively as a work of political art, one sees that it was the political equivalent of a double fugue with two subjects, both working in elaborate counterpoint towards a common end or object, which was the removal of Mary Stuart from her captivity. On the one hand there was Anthony Babington and his band of conspirators and their wholly fantastic, largely imaginary scheme of assassinating Elizabeth, liberating Mary, then crowning her Queen of England with French and Spanish backing. Opposing them and managing them was the Queen's spymaster, Mr. Secretary Walsingham, who deployed the whole course of the plot from its obscure beginnings to its tragic conclusion in order to secure his own wholly serious object, which was the removal of Mary not only from captivity, but from England and its royal succession by death.

In due time, Walsingham brought the plot, a freely developing, extemporal form always under his control, to its desired conclusion with the deaths of the conspirators at Tyburn and of Mary herself on a scaffold in Fotheringay Castle, 8 February 1587—an outcome that the Bond of Association and its associated statute had been designed to ensure.

Three years later, Walsingham was dead himself, knowing that in her last moments Mary, despite the most careful preparations, had escaped his direction. Acting with superb courage and dignity on the scaffold, she had clothed herself, to the shock of the Protestant onlookers, in the colors of Catholic martyrdom. What Walsingham could not know was that Mary's real triumph lay in the future when her son became king of England, and moved the body of Elizabeth I, re-interring his mother in the central place of dynastic honor in Westminster Abbey.[1] All later English monarchs descend from her, and when her great-grandson brought Catholicism back to England, Walsingham's successors had his work of intrigue and violence to do all over again.

As for the management of the plot, Walsingham's agents were all over it from the start: Gilbert Gifford,[2] Bernard Maude, Robert Pooley,

---

[1] For a fascinating account of this rearrangement of the Westminster tombs, see Walker.

[2] All Walsingham's agents were extremely shady characters, but Gilbert Gifford was a uniquely shady character whom Ambassador Stafford described as "the most notable double treble villain that ever lived." A Catholic student expelled from both the Rheims seminary and the English College at Rome, he prevailed upon the forgiving William Allen to re-admit him; but by the time he took deacon's orders, April 1585, he was already engaged in conspiratorial discussions with people later to be implicated in the Babington Plot: John Savage at Rheims, and Paget and Morgan in Paris. When he arrived in England in December 1585 he was taken straight to Walsingham, and if he was not

and Solomon Aldred were the major players, but Walsingham's men were present at every stage, including the brewer ("the honest man") who carried Mary's letters in his barrels, and Gilbert Gifford's stand-in as postman, Barnes. Even the spy Nicholas Berden had a part. The mainstream view is that the plot was real, that Walsingham discovered it, monitored it, and prevented it.[1] The opposing view, whose first representative was Fr. Robert Southwell, is that Walsingham, working through *agents provocateurs,* invented the plot, then nurtured it to its climax.[2] A realistic, disenchanted view would treat the plot as a sting operation, its purpose for Walsingham (and Cecil) being the destruction of Mary, Queen of Scots, and the infliction of maximum damage on the English Catholics as a body. After nearly thirty years of suffering, there were certainly people hoping fervently for Elizabeth I's removal. All Walsingham had to do was find them, encourage them, and monitor them—and the more amateurish and incompetent they were, the better from his point of view.

It is hardly surprising that Philip II of Spain should have decided, after years of English attacks on his New World settlements and his treasure fleets, after the English attempt, however botched, to help the Dutch, and finally after their killing of Mary Stuart, that he had no alternative to attacking England itself, and that he proceeded to assemble forces for the purpose. The English Council knew all about his plans, and in the spring of 1587 Sir Francis Drake brought off his famous raid on Cadiz, "singeing the King of Spain's beard," and causing enough damage to Spanish ships to delay the attack on England by a year.

Then on 28 May 1588 the great fleet finally sailed from Lisbon into defeat at the battle off Gravelines, 28 July, by superior English maneuverability and gunnery, and then into destruction by Atlantic gales off the west of Ireland. By the time the Queen made her famous speech to her soldiers at Tilbury, 8 August, the danger had passed. Lord Admiral

---

already one of Walsingham's men, he worked for him thereafter. He became the chief agent in Walsingham's management of Mary Stuart's correspondence, and when the Plot began to ripen he left England again, July 1586, fearing for his own skin. He was ordained priest in March 1587, but continued to act for Walsingham, leading one to infer that his ordination was merely cover. Fittingly, the French authorities arrested him in a brothel, December 1587, and he died in prison, 1590 (*ODNB*; Anstruther, 152).

[1]See, for example, *ODNB* (Penry Williams) and Bossy among more recent writers..

[2]Southwell 3, 17–22: see his report to Verstegan (Verstegan, 3–4) for his more detailed analysis; Edwards 1, 125–68. One of Walsingham's agents, Thomas Harrison, claimed that he and Thomas Phelippes forged the letters that convicted Mary and the plotters, and that he, Walsingham, Phelippes, and Bernard Maude invented the plot (Martin, P, 53–4).

Howard had recalled the English fleet from pursuit of the Spanish, and there was no likelihood at all that either the Queen, her commander Leicester, or her soldiers would be required to meet a Spanish army in battle.

*****

The first surviving torture warrant issued to Topcliffe originated with the Armada defeat. It concerned a man called Tristram Winslade, and the Council issued it to Topcliffe along with Hopton, Justice Young, and James Dalton on 8 September.[1] On 30 July, Sir Francis Drake had captured a Spanish galleon, Nuestra Señora del Rosario, under the command of Don Pedro de Valdés. Tristram Winslade was among the prisoners. The Spanish had him listed as an Irishman, but Drake's people quickly identified him as English, and his first interrogation took place that day.

Winslade was the son of a well-to-do Cornish family. His grandfather, who had been executed for his part in the 1549 western rebellion, had prudently settled his property on his wife. She, unfortunately, married a man called John Trevanion who, on her death, seized the properties, and sold them, leaving the Winslades penniless. Young Tristram entered the service of Sir John Arundell. When trouble came to Sir John with the arrest of the seminary priest Cuthbert Mayne, Tristram—as he told his questioners—left England for the Low Countries, traveling from there into Germany, Italy, and Spain.

What his questioners wanted to know, of course, was what he was doing on board a Spanish ship. He told them candidly that he was a Catholic, but insisted that his only intention was "to die for her Majesty and his country against any invasion that the Pope or any others shall make against England." Unsatisfied, his captors sent him to London, where he was committed to Newgate prison. There he remained until the torture warrant of 8 September ordered his removal to the Tower.

No record of his interrogation under torture survives, but his interrogators probably wanted to know not only his real reason for accompanying the invading force, but what he knew about the part played by the English in Spain in the planning of the Armada. Whatever they wanted to know, Winslade told them nothing except his original story, and that he had been brought against his will. Over a year later, having found out nothing, the Council drew up his discharge, upon bond to appear at ten days' notice.[2]

---

[1] *APC*, 16. 273.

By then he had been examined "often" by Sir George Carey, Sir Walter Raleigh, Sir Richard Grenville, the attorney-general, Justice Young and others, and had also been "upon the rack to draw from him his knowledge of the intended invasion." His first action on being released was to try to have himself named as heir to the earldom of Devon. When that came to nothing, he left England once again for Brussels where, in 1595, he drew up a report urging Philip II to plan for a new attempt at invading England whenever Elizabeth I should die leaving a vacant throne. One naturally concludes that the failure of the first Armada had disappointed him. If that was so, it is all the more remarkable that the Council's examiners, including Topcliffe, got nothing out of him. Winslade was evidently a tough character. He died in 1605, and was buried in the chapel of the English college at Douay.[2]

Despite the activities of Tristram Winslade and like-minded exiles, a striking feature of the Armada crisis was that the English Catholics proved entirely—and strikingly—loyal to the country and their Queen. Even old Sir Thomas Fitzherbert, imprisoned and heavily fined because of his religion, volunteered to pay double the amount levied upon his estate for the defense of the country.[3] Burghley could not resist crowing about this to the French and the Spanish, but being Burghley he did not broadcast the news in a straight-forward way. Instead he composed a letter supposed to have been written by a disappointed English Catholic and found among the effects of a priest executed for treason: *The Copy of a Letter sent out of England to Don Bernardine Mendoza Ambassador in France for the King of Spain.*[4] Even the Catholic gentlemen, wrote Burghley in this piece of disinformation, who had been interned in the bishop's palace at Ely had offered to give their fortunes and their lives in defense of the Queen. In fact, had the Council not thought it best to keep them there for their own safety, they would have set them free. As it was, they were being treated virtually as guests of the bishop, and they were even allowed to maintain their religion on payment of a small fine:

And so they do remain in the Bishop's palace there, with fruition of large

---

[2] *APC,* 18. 387 (24 February 1590).

[2] For a good account of Winslade, see Hayden. Hyland, 194–5, prints the text of Winslade's first examination, preserved in the Loseley Papers, now held at the Surrey History Centre.

[3] Camm 2, 50.

[4] *STC* 15412.

walks about the same, altogether without any imprisonment, other then that they are not suffered to depart into the town or country: and yet for their religion, I think surely they do, and will, remain constant to the obedience of the Church of Rome: for the which nevertheless they are not impeached to any danger of their lives, but only charged with a penalty of money, because they will not come to the Churches: whereby, by the law, a portion of their revenue is allotted to the Queen, and the rest left to the maintenance of them, their wives, and children.[1]

The substance of that final clause was to be repeated in the royal proclamation of 1591 against Jesuits and seminary priests in a sentence that Geoffrey Hill described as "the most willful and monstrous cant."[2] The letter also repeats Burghley's favorite justification of the penal laws against Catholicism: that no Catholic was punished for religion, but only for treason.

Since the Catholics had just proved their loyalty so dramatically, one might have expected that the government, including the author of *A Letter*, might now begin to think seriously about relaxing the penal laws, especially since the *Letter* implied that it was only with the greatest reluctance that the government punished Catholics at all. The truth was that as the Armada was approaching England the Council was already consulting the lawyers about measures for distinguishing between dangerous, "traitorously-minded" Catholics and the merely ignorant and mislead.[3] As soon as the danger was passed, the government promptly set about killing Catholics, but without bothering about distinctions between the dangerous and the ignorant.

The first step was to identify the available prisoners on hand, and so the Council wrote, 14 August, to nine people, Hopton, Topcliffe, Francis Bacon, and Justice Young among them, instructing any six or seven of them to find out the names of recusants in the London prisons:

And for that her Majesty's pleasure is they should be proceeded with according to the law and as the quality of their offenses shall have

---

[1] 9–10 (Sig B2–B2v).

[2] Hill, 24. For the sentence, see H & L, 3. 88: "And of this that none do suffer death for matter of religion there is manifest proof in that a number of men of wealth in our realm professing contrary religion are known not to be impeached for the same either in their lives, lands, or goods or in their liberties, but only by payment of a pecuniary sum as a penalty for the time that they do refuse to come to church." The proclamation's loutish, vulgar style marks it as Burghley's own composition.

[3] NA/SP12/212/70, a letter, 20 July, from William Fleetwood and Thomas Egerton to the Council.

deserved, to consider in what sort the examinations may be most speedily taken for th'understanding with what matters they may be lawfully charged; and thereupon assembling themselves in two or three companies as they shall think most convenient in respect of the multitude of the prisoners, to proceed thereunto according to their good discretions, but especially that they enquire which of them be Jesuits or Priests, and either have not departed out of the realm or have returned hither again contrary to the Statutes made in that behalf....[1]

This commission was really an order to draw up a list of candidates for execution. The commissioners finished their work quickly, and their papers were in the hands of Sergeant Sir John Puckering by 20 August, who decided who would be tried and where, and what the punishment would be. He then consulted with Burghley, and the proceedings began, 26 August, at the Sessions Hall, Newgate, with the condemnation of fourteen people (nine priests and eight lay people) to be hanged in and about London, some of them on gibbets specially erected for the purpose. The reason for these dispersed hangings was presumably to spread terror. Why else erect a gallows outside the Theatre in Shoreditch?

The hangings began on 28 August when the first eight victims were carried, pinioned in carts, to the new gallows. The first cartload, consisting of William Deane and William Gunter, priests, plus Henry Webley a layman, set off for Mile End Green, a suburb on the road out of London towards Colchester, where Deane and Webley were hanged.[2] The cart then went on to the new gallows outside the Theatre in Shoreditch, where they hanged William Gunter, another priest from Allen's seminary, arrested in London in June after about a year's activity.

The sheriffs then went back to Newgate for their next load of three: Robert Morton and Thomas Holford, priests, and another layman, Hugh Moore This time the cart went to Lincoln's Inn Fields, where Morton and Moore were hanged. Morton was the priest whom Topcliffe had arrested after his return to England in 1587 by tracking him to his deceased wife's family's house; Hugh Moore was a layman who had gone to Rheims to become a priest, but whose poor health had brought him home. Those two disposed of, the cart went on to Clerkenwell, where they hanged Thomas Holford, who had been arrested in London,

---

[1]*APC*, 16. 235.

[2]Not much is known about Webley. He was probably from Gloucestershire, and was evidently a poor man. He had been caught on board ship in Chichester harbor, about to go over to France. Bishop Challoner thought he was executed with Deane because he had assisted him (Burton-Pollen, 360–5; Challoner, 135).

where he had gone to buy a suit of clothes. The last two victims, Thomas Felton and a priest called James Claxton, were taken on horseback, their hands tied behind them and their feet tied under the horses' bellies, to be hanged together at Brentford, then a village just west of London.[1]

Thus died the first eight of the Armada victims. The mode of death was plain hanging—there was no bowelling and quartering although that was the normal sentence in these treason cases. The victims were not allowed to speak. Robert Southwell, writing to Claudio Aquaviva, 31 August, said that William Deane was roughly gagged for attempting to speak. John Gerard's catalogue adds the detail that, "as he sat in the cart...he was sore hurt by an officer with a bill upon his head."[2]

The hangings continued on 30 August when the remaining six people convicted at the Newgate sessions were hanged at Tyburn: one priest, Richard Leigh, and five lay people, Richard Lloyd or Flower, Richard Martin, John Roche, Edward Shelley, and Margaret Ward. Richard Leigh was the priest on whom Burghley fathered his bogus *Copy of a Letter sent out of England to Don Bernardine Mendoza.* The lay people were all convicted of helping a priest. Edward Shelley had helped William Deane. Richard Martin was convicted of being in Robert Morton's company, and paying sixpence for his supper. Richard Lloyd or Flower, a twenty-two year-old Welshman from Anglesea, was convicted for supporting a priest called Horner. John Roche was an Irish friend of Margaret Ward, who had helped her assist William Watson to escape from Bridewell.

After a month the killing resumed. This time the candidates for death were sent to provincial towns for trial. Their executions took place on 1 October, and the full sentence for treason (hanging, drawing, and quartering) was carried out. Three priests and a layman were executed at Canterbury, of all places, at a site called Oaten Hill. Two priests died at Chichester, one at Kingston-upon-Thames, and one at Ipswich. We should probably include among these deaths a layman, a glover called William Lampley, who died at Gloucester in 1588.[3]

---

[1]For details of the executions, see *A brief treatise discovering in substance the offences of the late 14 traitours...Who were all executed* (London, 1588). For Robert Morton, see above, 51–3. For brief accounts of these priests, see Anstruther, 78, who also gives a good account of the procedures. Burton-Pollen gives more detailed accounts of all the victims, including the laymen.

[2]Pollen 1, 288, 325, prints the catalogue and the letter.

[3]Accounts of all these executions will be found in Burton-Pollen, 408–542.

On 5 October, the executions returned to London. Two priests and two laymen died. This time the Queen commuted the sentences to plain hanging. One layman, Robert Sutton, was hanged at Clerkenwell, the other, John Harrison alias Symons, at Tyburn. The priests, John Hewitt and William Hartley, were hanged at Mile End and the Theatre. The theatrical entrepreneur James Burbage had built the Theatre on the site of a dissolved priory of Augustinian canonesses, and this fact led the Shakespeare scholar T.W.Baldwin to think that Shakespeare was remembering this execution in *The Comedy of Errors*, 5.1.119–22, probably written shortly afterwards in 1589:

> Anon I'm sure the Duke himself in person
> Comes this way to the melancholy vale,
> The place of death and sorry execution,
> Behind the ditches of the abbey here.

Not everyone agrees with this suggestion, even though the topography of the Theatre's site corresponds to the "place of death and sorry execution," including the abbey (or priory) and even the ditches. Besides, it is hard to believe that anyone could hear those lines spoken at the Theatre in 1589 and not think of the recent executions. It is not every day that priests are hanged outside a theatre.[1]

Topcliffe, as one would expect, was present at some, probably all, the London executions. According to an account written up by Fr. Henry Walpole, before Richard Leigh was hanged at Tyburn, he asked if he could pray:

> Being in his meditations his color changed and his legs began to bend, insomuch that it was thought his soul had been already in Heaven; whereupon Topcliffe cried out very loud, saying, "Lee, Lee!" divers times, "It is the devil that doth deceive thee." The hangman pulling him by the sleeve, he came to himself, and looking about demanded what the matter was.[2]

Topcliffe, then, was at the Tyburn hangings. He was also at the hangings of John Hewitt and William Hartley at Mile End and the Theatre on 5 October. These two were carried by cart, first taking Hewitt to Mile End, then Hartley to the Theatre. Topcliffe will have ridden in the cart. At Mile End he told Hewitt that the Queen was merciful, and, "whereas by his deserts he was condemned to be hanged, drawn and quartered, her

---

[1]Baldwin,   Baldwin thought the reference was to the second hanging, of William Hartley, but it probably refers to both the Theatre hangings.

[2]Pollen 2, 306–7.

pleasure was that he should but be hanged."[1] Then he presumably went on the to theatre with Hartley. Although there is no note of his presence at the first hangings of 28 August, it is most unlikely that he would not have been present to see Deane and Morton die—they had both been his prisoners.

According to Fr. Southwell, in London the executions drew large, hostile crowds, and the scale of the spectacle suggests that in the wake of the Armada victory the Council was confident of the support of the London mob. If Fr. Southwell's information was correct, anyone showing sympathy for the victims risked arrest and imprisonment on the spot. It is hard for us to gauge the state of mind of the average, decent London citizen in that atmosphere. Many of them were still Catholic in sympathy if not in open confession.

The Catholics thought Leicester was responsible for the executions. Fr. John Curry, S.J., newly arrived in England, was in York about a month after the execution of Edward Burden there, 31 October. He then left for London, and as he wrote to Fr. Persons, he "found the whole city black with gibbets, on which many Catholics had been hanged in the storm which the Earl of Leicester had raised not long before." Leicester, however, had died unexpectedly a week to the day after the first executions began, and Fr. Southwell, writing to Claudio Aquaviva, 7 September, with the news of his death, also thought that Leicester had been "the chief author of this great cruelty." The author of the Penkevel manuscript, too, ascribed the executions to Leicester, and thought that there would have been many more, had Leicester's surprising death not put a sudden stop to the proceedings.[2]

Were the Catholics right? Leicester was an important member of the Council, but he did not have that kind of personal power, and he was not present at the session of the Council that commissioned Topcliffe and the rest to report on the recusants available for hanging in the London prisons. What Leicester had was fame, visibility, and a remarkable degree of unpopularity.[3] He had also been the commander in charge of

---

[1]Burton-Pollen, 520.

[2]Pollen 2, 313–4, 287; Southwell 1, No.IX. John Gerard, *en route* for England, was told by the fathers at the English college, Eu, that "The Earl of Leicester, then at the height of his power, had sworn that by the end of the year there would be no Catholic left in the country" (Gerard, 8).

[3]Leicester was not only unpopular with Catholics. The impeccably Protestant William Harrison wrote that Leicester was so despised that "all men, so far as they durst, rejoiced no less outwardly at this death, than for the victory obtained of late against the Spanish navy" (Harrison, 272).

the English response to the Spanish challenge. Leicester made an excellent scapegoat, but the actual documents send us back to the Queen and Council, especially the Queen. The Council's commissioning letter leaves no doubt that it was the Queen's pleasure that the recusants "should be proceeded with according to the law and as the quality of their offenses shall have deserved." Then, when the last two priests, Hewitt and Hartley, came to be hanged in London, the Queen personally reduced their sentences to hanging; and if Fr. Walpole's account is correct, Topcliffe communicated the remissions at the scene on her behalf.

This was a characteristic pattern in Elizabeth I's behavior. Her reputation for fearlessness in the face of danger was part of her well-cultivated public image, but those who knew her closely knew better. She did not react well to what she considered threats against her person. After the northern rebellion she wanted 700 executions under martial law, which her provost-marshal, fortunately, failed to deliver.[1] Whatever the real nature of the Babington Plot, she thought it was genuine enough, and when she asked that special punishments might be devised for the plotters "for more terror," Burghley had to assure her that the ordinary punishment, properly carried out, could be just as terrible as she could wish.[2] Equally, she knew that the Armada was a mortal threat to her, emanating not only from Spain but from some of her own exiled subjects.[3] Naturally enough, she had one of her experiences of fear,[4] and when the danger had passed she took vindictive action where she could, this time upon the Catholics she already had in custody. But then, just as the London crowd was revolted by the cruelties of the first Babington executions, so they sickened of the 1588 hangings, and if there was one thing Elizabeth I disliked as much as danger, it was unpopularity. Just as she gave well-publicized orders for a more humane treatment of the second group of Babington executions, so she now took

[1]Fletcher, 102.

[2]Bardon, 45.

[3]*An Admonition to the Nobility and People of England,* published under Willliam Allen's name at Antwerp for distribution in England in the event of Spanish victory, came into the hands of the Council, "confirming the worst they had ever said of Allen and his priests" (Hughes, 3.380). The Council did not allow the *Admonition* to be generally publicized, presumably because they could not be sure of its reception by the population at large.

[4]Sir John Perrot, who knew her well, was in Dublin, but had a good idea of the real mood in the privy chamber: "Lo, now she is ready to bepiss herself for fear of the Spaniards, I am again one of her white boys" (Naunton, 91).

credit for an act of mercy to the last London victims of the Armada revenge. As we shall see, something similar was to happen in the case of Fr. Southwell in 1595. In all these cases, she made sure that the public knew about her act of mercy, equally sure that they did not know that she had been the author of the original cruelty.

When the executions of those last prisoners taken from the London prisons had been dealt with, nearly six months passed before the next Catholic executions, when two priests were hanged, drawn, and quartered in York, 16 March 1589.[1] Then on 18 May, the Oxford University authorities caught two priests, George Nichols and Richard Yaxley alias Tankerd, at an inn called The Catherine Wheel, run by a widow. They arrested the widow, a lay gentleman called Thomas Belson, and a Welsh servant of the inn, Humphrey Pritchard. After a few days, the four men were sent up to London. The priests were put in Bridewell where they were tortured by the manacles; then the Council ordered Yaxley to be sent to the Tower, where only Topcliffe was allowed access to him. According to an account of this case sent to Sir Francis Englefield in Spain, Yaxley was threatened with the rack. The Council ordered all four of them back to Oxford for trial, 30 June, where they were tried and convicted, then executed, 5 July.[2]

Two more executions in York, 24 September, of a priest, William Spencer, and Robert Hardesty, the layman who had harbored and relieved him, close the book on 1589.

This slight remission in the intensity of the persecution was short-lived. There was no change in the policy of the Queen and her Council, who were as determined as ever in their attempt to eradicate Catholicism from the country, especially since it had become very obvious to them that a significant number of people were equally determined to preserve it, even at the expense of life and property. Meanwhile, the war with Spain continued, and there was the threat of another invasion attempt. Even more alarming, even terrifying, to older members of the Council like Burghley, Knollys, and Walsingham, the aging Queen could die at any moment, leaving no heir and no clear succession. They knew that after more than thirty years of being treated as aliens and enemies in

[1] Anstruther, 7–8, 96.

[2] Challoner, 153–8; Anstruther, 250–2, 389–90; Pollen 1, 168; *APC*, 17. 205, 329. Anstruther is mistaken in thinking that Nichols, too, was put in the Tower. Challoner's sources say that Yaxley was racked daily, but this seems unlikely. Sir Francis Knollys was present at the trial, and sent a brief account to Burghley in which he makes the common error of calling the priests Jesuits (Strype 2, 1.605).

their own country, the Catholics would be in no mood to forgive and forget. Burghley candidly told the Queen as much in a memorandum on the dangers of being nice to the Catholics, and the necessity of continued intolerance:

> To suffer [the Catholics] to be strong with hope that with reasons they will be contented carried with it in my opinion but a fair enameling of a terrible danger. For first man's nature is not only to strive against a person's smart but to revenge a by-past injury...when opportunity shall flatter them they will remember not the after-slacking but the former binding, and so much the more when they shall imagine this relenting to proceed from fear rather than favor, which is the poison of all government when the subject thinks the prince doth anything more out of fear than favor.[1]

The government therefore intensified the suppression, with Topcliffe as the chief agent of their purpose.

Beginning in late 1589 with the examination under torture of two priests, Francis Dickenson and Miles Gerard, Topcliffe's appointment book began to fill up, and over the next four to five years there are periods when one can keep an almost daily record of his doings. It becomes clear, too, that for much of the time he was acting autonomously, and did whatever he liked. For instance, in one case he encountered a prisoner being transferred to Bridewell, and asked the man who was escorting him, "Whither are you bound with this fellow?" The escort answered, "To Bridewell," whereupon Topcliffe asked for the warrant:

> and perusing it he went to the next merchant's shop, and borrowing a pen and ink he set down in the warrant what was not before in, that he should have forty stripes; which he had.[2]

A priest, Montford Scott, was to be banished by order of the Council, but when the date of his banishment arrived, Topcliffe committed him to prison again, and saw him tried, convicted, and executed.[3]

Nor were Topcliffe's activities limited to London and the nearby counties. He was in York at least three times, and in Derbyshire,

---

[1]*An Antidote against Jesuitism Written by the Lord Treasurer Burghley*, quoted in Edwards 1, 120. Notice that in Burghley's mind the English people are a mob that he needs to manipulate and control.

[2]Foley, 3.757. This was a "yeoman formerly of Westminster" called Edward Chester, indicted for "not going to church, chapel, or any place of Common Prayer," 1 May 1594 (Jeaffreson, 221).

[3]Pollen 2, 291, with a second account on 304.

Northamptonshire, and his own Lincolnshire. He "put up" policy papers for the Council, in one of them arguing in favor of internment for Catholics of all ranks and degrees of conformity, including women, and in another arguing against the policy of banishing priests.[1] Most of all, he acted as a kind of one-man enforcement squad.

Drawing on information supplied by his personal inquiries, and by his own rough-and-ready intelligence service, he hunted, found, caught, and arrested people. He committed them to prison and interrogated them, often with torture. He then attended the trials, and in a surprising number of cases presided over the executions that followed, in most cases attaching a *titulus* or title to the gallows, identifying the victim and his crime.

It must have been some time about 1589–90, too, that he began to interrogate captives with torture in his own house in Westminster. One sometimes finds it said that he was allowed to do this because the more public torturing in Bridewell and the Tower was causing popular scandal.[2] But there is little evidence for this inference. What we know from his own letter to the Queen is that she—and presumably the Council—allowed him to do it. One imagines that it was convenient, and relieved him of a lot of tramping about London, not to mention Elizabethan red tape. It does not seem to have been a secret.[3]

No-one, moreover, in high position in government objected either to

[1]Lansdowne 72. No. 48, f.133 (Internment); NA/SP12/235/8 (banishment). The government had interned Catholics at the time of the Armada, but had limited the policy to gentlemen they considered influential. Topcliffe wanted to intern much larger numbers, and was really thinking of what we would call concentration camps. Imprisonment on that scale was not possible in Elizabethan England, but thinking very like Topcliffe's produced the act of 35 Eliz. c.2 (1593) that ordered all recusants to return home, and that restricted their movements to a five-mile radius.

[2]Devlin 2, 68: "....the public scenes in Bridewell caused such scandal that, from 1592 onwards, they were confined exclusively to Topcliffe's private house." Devlin's source is presumably a sentence in a letter from Verstegan to Roger Baynes, 1 August 1592: "The frequent use of torture being greatly disliked by all the people, Topcliffe has authority to torture priests in his house as he sees fit..." (Verstegan, 52). Incidentally, there are a couple of inaccuracies in Devlin's sentence. (1) Topcliffe was already torturing in his house in 1589–90, perhaps earlier. (2) Public torturing by Topcliffe and others continued in the Tower and Bridewell.

[3]In December 1591, Robert Southwell wrote Verstegan, telling him all about it: "the manner of imprisonment of priests is that first they are kept in Topcliffe's house, or some other catchpoll's. Topcliffe ever useth to torture them by his private authority before they part out of his doors, and keepeth their taking so secret, that sometimes it is long ere it be known where the party apprehended is, lest the rumor of his torturing should be spread abroad" (Verstegan, 8).

Topcliffe's activities or his methods. Why would they? He was carrying out their policies. The difference between Topcliffe and men like Walsingham, Knollys, Paulet, Mildmay, the Dudley brothers, and Burghley is that they had other matters to attend to, whereas Topcliffe was a specialist, "a primeval common ancestor," in Heath's words, "of Pinkerton's and the FBI," operating under the Queen's and her Council's instructions.[1] He was the Elizabethan régime in battle dress or, as he described himself in the preamble to a bill of complaint in a Court of Requests suit of 1590:

> Your said servant is and hath been for divers years passed continually employed as well by your Majesty's especial direction...as by continual commission and assignment from the Lords and others of your Majesty's Privy Council...in and about the apprehension, examination, and discovery of traitors, conspirators, fugitives, and practicers of mischief against your Majesty.[2]

There was certainly no disagreement at all between him and those he served, whether about the ends aimed at or the means employed. The idea that Walsingham, for instance, kept Topcliffe in check as long as he lived, and that Topcliffe only "really flourished" after Walsingham died in 1590, is a fantasy, one of those apologetic maneuvers that historians of this period deploy to keep up appearances. Walsingham, who worked happily enough with Topcliffe, was alive and, with his fellow-councilors, fully consenting to the policies that produced the Armada hangings in 1588 and, presumably, to Topcliffe's role in them. Walsingham was capable, too, of Topcliffian behavior on occasion. In 1583, examining a priest called John Munden, he fell into a rage about the Rheims New Testament, and then began to put the "bloody questions" to him, finally asking him whether he considered Elizabeth to be the true Queen of England. When Munden answered "Yes," Walsingham refined the question, asking whether he held her to be true Queen *de jure* and *de facto*, and when Munden said he did not understand those terms, Walsingham exploded:

> "How now, traitor!" said Walsingham, "do you boggle at answering this?" And therewithal gave such a blow on one side of the head as perfectly stunned him and made him reel, so that for some days after he complained of a difficulty of hearing on that side."[3]

[1]Heath, 139.

[2]NA/REQ2/276/52 (1590).

Incidents like this will not have been rare, given the Elizabethan propensity for losing tempers. Even the reputedly benign Burghley had his moments. Another priest, John Pibush, arrested in 1593 in Gloucestershire, was sent up to London to the Council, where Burghley questioned him. He told Pibush to show him his crown (i.e., tonsure), whereupon he "bowed down his head, and told him that he had none, and that his Lordship could easily guess at the reason." Burghley, whom one suspects of not enjoying even the mildest joke, promptly lost his temper:

> "O," said my lord, "you think yourself wiser than all the world. Will you stand to the law?"
> "I must, whether I will or no," said the priest.
> "Then have him to Topcliffe," quoth my Lord Treasurer, showing all this while great anger.[2]

Topcliffe, for once (his mind on other things at the time), merely committed the priest close prisoner to the Gatehouse, and left him there until the end of the year, when he sent him back to Gloucester to be tried.

Even Topcliffe's cruelty and word-breaking did not distinguish him from his contemporaries. To give one notorious example: in 1580 during the second Desmond rebellion, a small Papal force of about 600 Italians and Spaniards landed at Smerwick, now Ard na Caithne, in the west of Ireland. Unable to link up with the main Irish groups, they retreated to the fort at Dún an Óir, where the English under the Lord Deputy, Lord Grey de Wilton, backed up by a naval force, besieged them. According to Grey's own account, he insisted upon unconditional surrender, but the Irish accounts say that he agreed upon a surrender conditional upon sparing the garrison's lives. Having taken hostages to secure his terms, Grey then broke his word (an action memorialized in the Irish expression, "Grey's faith"), and sent in groups of his men to put the garrison to the sword. The younger Walter Raleigh was a captain in command of the execution squads. Edmund Spenser, Grey's poetical secretary, was present at the massacre.

They killed all but thirteen, whom they held for ransom. The victims included women, some of them pregnant. Three captives, an Irish priest,

---

[3]Challoner, 99. Challoner's source is Gibbons, 140b: *Quid, scelerate proditor (inquit Walsingamius) an ad hoc respondere recusas? Simulque pugnum ei in faciem subito tanta vi impegit, ut hominem, sensibus obstupefactis, plane attonitum reddiderit: ita ut vacillaret, nec quo loco esset, ad tempus resciret, adeoque postea per multos dies quereretur, sese ex altera parte gravius audire quam solitus erat.* Burton-Pollen, 97–8, has a different, less idiomatic translation.

[2]Pollen 2, 335.

Laurence O'Moore, an Irish layman from Drogheda called Oliver Plun-
kett, and an Englishman called Welsh, were singled out for special bru-
tality. A blacksmith broke their legs, they were left in agony a day and
night, then hanged.[1]

Grey's appalling cruelty at Smerwick was by no means a unique event
during Elizabeth's wars in Ireland, and we should not forget that after
the northern rising of 1569 the Queen had asked for savage reprisals
against her own northern subjects. In fact, a taste for rage, violence, and
cruelty was something that Topcliffe shared with a surprising number of
his contemporaries in governing circles. What was unusual about him
was his passionately focused energy. Until the very last years of his life,
the man never stopped. When his serious policing activity began in the
early 1580s, he was already fifty, and at the height of his power in early
1595, he was in his sixty-third year. By Elizabethan standards, that
made him an old man. Even Fr. Devlin, who treats him as a grotesque
out of a waxworks show, acknowledges that, "He had the same sort of
demoniac energy and courage as Sir Richard Grenville; and one can
imagine him rivalling Grenville's exploits if his career had lain on the
high seas instead of at court."[2]

Why he expended that energy, as well as most of his own considerable wealth, upon that particular late-blooming court career is not at all
obvious. His Burgh-Parr connections, of which he was proud, will have
disposed him to think well of the Protestant side in religion, but other
connections of family and affinity—with Nevilles, Percies, Talbots,
Willoughbies, Brudenells, and Arundells—should have mitigated ten-
dencies to Protestant militancy. Nor was there any obvious economic
motive. He received no salary or emolument, and his attempts to acquire
Fitzherbert money and property came to nothing. He owed his wealth
neither to court service, like Knollys, Hunsdon, or Heneage, nor to the
dissolution of religious foundations, like the Herberts and Russells. His
entire social position did not depend—like the Cecils'—on forcing the
Tudor religious revolution to a final conclusion in an uniformly Protestant state. In fact, he was proud, as he said more than once, that he was

---

[1]For a thoroughly researched account of events at Smerwick, see O'Rahilly. On
Spenser's activities related to the siege at Smerwick, see Hadfield, 161–7. In *The Faerie
Queene*, Spenser allegorizes Grey admiringly as Artegall, the knight of justice and his
servant, the iron man Talus. Topcliffe's friend-to-be, Anthony Munday, wrote a glowing
account of the English success at Smerwick, *The True Reporte of the Rrosperous
Successe which God Gaue vnto our English Souldiours.*

[2]Devlin 1, 210.

"a simple freeholder." Under Mary, he had been a Catholic, and as far as we know showed no sign at all of militant anti-Catholicism until after the Northern Rising. As a member of Parliament for Beverley he drew on his experience as steward of the Norton estates, sitting on a committee inquiring into fraudulent conveyances of ex-rebel property, and making a speech on the subject; but otherwise his parliamentary work consisted of mundane legal and practical matters. Not until the next parliament, as member for Old Sarum, do we find him taking part in anti-Catholic legislation: in February 1585 he was on a committee to confer with the Lords about the ferociously anti-Catholic bill, 27 Eliz. c.2, that made it high treason to be a Jesuit or a seminary priest in England, and a felony to relieve or harbor a priest.[1]

Even if we allow that Topcliffe was one of nature's police-detectives, it is not at all obvious why he should have applied his talents as he did. The explanation lies in his devotion to the person for whom he applied them, the Queen herself. Topcliffe and she were of an age, he about a year older. By his own account, he entered her service the year before she became Queen, and after the Northern Rising that service mutated into service of the state which she embodied. As for the form his service took, he described himself informally as "a diligent scout or watchman in my country,"[2] but more formally as esquire of the body to the Queen. As such it was his duty to protect her, and it was a duty he took very seriously. That was why he appeared with his thirty armed horsemen during the northern rising and why, as the years passed, he came to consider the mere fact of being a Catholic to be a threat to the Queen's safety. There seems, too, to have been an element of adoration in his devotion to her, as his response to a case involving a man called William Randall reveals.

On 22 August 1594, Randall, an English mariner living in Dunkirk, with interesting connections with the exiled Catholics and Spain, was arrested when storms drove his ship into Plymouth. He was taken to London, and imprisoned in the Gatehouse, where Topcliffe examined him. Topcliffe must have reported the capture immediately to the Queen, because just a few days later, 26 August, instructed by the Queen, he was writing an account of the case to Burghley.[3] Randall, it

---

[1]Hasler, 3.513–15.

[2]Lansdowne 72. No. 48.

[3]Hatfield 27/106. A letter from the spy-priest John Cecil, who was on the ship, to acting secretary Cecil, NA/SP/12/255/22, 30 December 1595, fixes the date of landing in Plymouth.

appeared, was an important person. No sooner had he been captured, but offers were made—by whom Topcliffe does not say—to exchange him for some English prisoners on the other side. The purpose of Topcliffe's letter to Burghley was to head off any such exchange:

> Randall being thus desperate, and mischievous a subject born, and now a traitor in her Majesty's hand, there be ten or twelve prisoners of her Majesty's subjects offered in exchange for him: but if my son were one, I would not sue for that exchange, and for hindering such an exchange I am frowned of.

Events had moved quickly. Threatened by the loss of an important prisoner, Topcliffe had gone straight to the Queen. The Queen told him to write to Burghley, and the result was that Randall stayed in the Gatehouse.

Randall's wife, a Flemish woman, then came to England to sue for her husband's release. Topcliffe was appalled that such a person might have access to the Queen herself with a petition on paper that might be poisoned, and persuaded the Lord Chamberlain to dismiss her from the court. But the woman persisted. She followed the court to Greenwich where Topcliffe caught her again, and brought her to the Lord Chamberlain again, who banished her from the court again, "upon pain of deep punishment." And there for a while the matter rested.

Then on the night of 13 February 1595, Topcliffe decided to search a Dutch woman's house where Randall's wife had been staying, and found that she had moved. To his utter horror he discovered that she had been lodging for two months with Garrett, the Queen's shoemaker. "A fearful thing to my jealous mind in this perilous time," he wrote to Lord Keeper Puckering:

> that the wife of so cunning and dangerous, unnatural traitor as Randall is, should lodge, and have opportunity to come near, or be, where anything is made that doth touch her Majesty's person, or converse with any workmen that make shoe, glove, or any other thing whatsoever should touch her body in any sort.[1]

The thought that such a person had access to things that touched the Queen's "precious body, dear and precious to us all," was intensely distressing to him, and he begged the Lord Keeper to inform the Queen and the Lord Chamberlain immediately, otherwise, "I must for the discharge

---

[1]NA/SP12/251/ 25. Topcliffe's letter to Puckering narrates the story of Randall's wife.

of all my duties, reveal this to her Majesty tomorrow."[1]

This case is fascinating because it shows, first, Topcliffe's power. He has such immediate and ready access to the Queen that he can order the Lord Keeper (the officer with ultimate authority over such cases) to carry a message to her, and threaten to take precedence of him if he does not.[2] The case also shows how emotionally engaged Topcliffe was in the Queen's protection, that there was, in fact, a personal relationship between them.

Christopher Devlin goes so far as to describe Topcliffe as a favorite, and although that description probably exaggerates his status, it is not too far off the mark. He never lost favor with Elizabeth, despite incidents that must have tried her patience and she came to his assistance more than once. She maintained her good opinion of him, which seems to have meant everything to him, to the end. "Right honorable sir," he wrote to Robert Cecil, 11 February 1595:

> I think myself so deeply bound unto her excellent Majesty for her gracious acceptation of my simple services, that I cannot but bend my whole endeavor to deserve the continuance of that her princely conceit.[3]

"Conceit" there means personal opinion, or good opinion, and he used the word again in another letter to Cecil: "Unspeakably hath her blessed Majesty bound me with her Sacred Conceit, and her defense of my own credit (the comfort of a true gentleman)." In other words, she liked him, and she stuck up for him.[4]

Naturally, one wonders what, exactly, she saw in him. Perhaps she felt some obligation to him because his grandfather had served her

---

[1]Randall *was* important. Senior Spanish officers lodged at his house; he conveyed priests secretly into England, and Topcliffe, convinced that he was involved with conspiracies, wanted him tried and executed. On 3 May 1596, Egerton, Master of Rolls, Solicitor General Fleming, and Francis Bacon reported their examination of Randall to the Council, occasioned by "an offer to exchange him for Mr. Otwell Smith" (NA/SP/12/257/66). Nothing came of this offer, largely because of Topcliffe's information and opposition, and Randall remained in the Gatehouse until summer, 1599, when he escaped with a key smuggled to him by Catholic friends, and made his way home to Dunkirk (NA/SP12/272/83 [27 August 1599], 274/5 [3 January 1600]). Otwell or Ottowell Smith was an English merchant, captured by the Dunkirkers, and held for a ransom which he could not afford to pay. See *APC,* 25. 361, 377, 385. He was one of Burghley's informants (Guy, 225).

[2]Puckering had succeeded Sir Christopher Hatton as Lord Keeper in 1591. In Topcliffe's eyes he was a social inferior, and he had little respect for him.

[3]Hatfield, 25/27.

[4]Hatfield 90/2.

mother. When she first knew him, he must have been one of the presentable young men who surrounded the young Queen. By the early 1590s
though, Topcliffe's and the Queen's contemporaries were all dying off.
The Earl of Leicester, Sir Amyas Paulet, and Sir Walter Mildmay went
in 1588; the Earl of Shrewsbury, Sir Francis Walsingham, and the Earl
of Warwick in 1590. When Sir Christopher Hatton died in 1591,
Topcliffe was beginning to enjoy the benefits of survivorship. After all,
he had one quality which, in that court, Elizabeth must have valued:
complete, unquestioning devotion and loyalty. A.L.Rowse was right to
say that Topcliffe acted, "out of an overriding sense of duty," and that
"he spent himself on government service and impoverished his estate."
Where Rowse went wrong was in writing that, "In circumstances of war
and religious conflict his was a necessary, if thankless, task."[1] As
Topcliffe himself has told us, his task was not at all thankless; and as for
necessity, that has always been the butchers' argument, and on at least
one occasion Topcliffe himself used it.

In January 1595, acting upon orders from the Queen, Topcliffe rode to
Northampton to examine a prisoner, Thomas Gravener, whom a pur-
suivant was bringing to London from Berwick. Gravener had taken ill
on the road, and the pursuivant left him at Northampton, notifying the
Cecils of the situation. They and the Queen sent Topcliffe to Northamp-
ton. Gravener, though, defeated them all by dying, leaving a frustrated
Topcliffe with nothing but his death to report, which he did in a letter to
Robert Cecil, 17 January.[2]

Gravener, a Catholic, was a political prisoner from whom the Queen
and Council expected to receive information about the Earl of Tyrone.
When Topcliffe arrived, the coroner had delivered his verdict on
Gravener, and the mayor had buried him, but Topcliffe, "being somewhat acquainted with the malice of his church," wanted him exhumed
and cut open to find out if he had taken poison: "It is a resolution taught
in their church to such as to whom they commit these desperate acts and
practices, I have found often." Failing that, though, they arrested
Gravener's companion, and all that remained now, as Topcliffe wrote to
Cecil, was to "enforce" him to utter Gravener's secrets:

> And it will prove no lost labor: for assuredly (honored Sir), by hearsay you
> cannot believe that disloyalty we simple commissioners do see by their
> fury expressed, being put to trial.

[1]Rowse, 193.

[2]Hatfield, 24/102.

And then comes the argument from necessity: "And that is our grief, and mine especially, that we are often mistaken to be cruel." In Topcliffe's mind, what his critics failed to understand was that because his acts were the necessities of state, by definition they were not cruel, and presumably not illegal either. It is an all too common argument which one still hears today.

To follow Topcliffe's career of devoted service to Elizabeth I is to descend deep into the lower circles of a secular hell, and all one can say, really, in mitigation of his role in it is that he had companions in evil with whom he shared a common purpose, who laid down the pattern for his work, and who thanked him for realizing it.

*****

Nine

A Spider in the Cup

Topcliffe inaugurated the climactic years of his policing career with a run of cases that illustrate the patterns of his ordinary operations. In the first case, a pair of seminary priests, Francis Dickenson and Miles Gerard, had been arrested in Kent after a violent storm drove their ship ashore, 24 November 1589. When the local authorities in Dover first examined them, they gave false names and cover stories. Re-examined, they gave their real names, and confessed that they were priests. One presumes that other people from the ship had betrayed them. Knowing that they were priests, the Dover people informed the Council, who ordered the pair to be sent up to London. There they were put in Bridewell, and turned over to a panel of three interrogators, Nicholas Fuller, James Dalton, and Topcliffe. The surviving accounts agree that they were interrogated with torture by the manacles. The three interrogators signed the copy of their examinations on 3 December, and Fuller and Dalton forwarded them to the Council with a covering letter nine days later, 12 December, an unusually long delay.[1]

Dickenson was a Yorkshireman, 24 years old. Gerard, from Lancashire, was forty. The statements attributed to them in their examinations are peculiar, to say the least. Both are supposed to have used an expression, "the Romish Catholic Church" or "The Catholic Romish religion" that no Catholic would have used, and both of them, asked the notorious "bloody question," said they would not oppose an army sent into England to restore the Catholic Church. Dickenson is even quoted as saying that he would join such an army—an extraordinary thing for a priest to have said. The oddity of these examinations probably explains Fuller's and Dalton's tardiness in forwarding them. The Council seems not to have been impressed by them, but they allowed Topcliffe to commit both men to the Gatehouse prison.[2] There, according to Fr. Curry,

---

[1]Pollen 1, 169–73; Anstruther, 101–3, 130; Pollen 2, 314, 322.

by allowing them to write letters to friends for help, which he then intercepted, Topcliffe hoped to trick them into self-incrimination. When this stratagem failed, the Council decided to charge them with intending "to draw off sailors from England for the service of the Catholic King," and sent to Dover for witnesses.[2]

Under the act of 1585, of course, both men were guilty of treason simply for being priests in England, but Topcliffe and the Council always preferred to hang priests for rather more than that. Brought to trial and found guilty, they were sent to Rochester for execution, which happened 13 April 1590.

Another case to come into Topcliffe's hands in 1589–90 centered upon another seminary priest, Christopher Bales, a Durham man. He was seventeen when he arrived at the Rheims seminary in June 1581. Two years later he was one of a party sent to the Roman College, but then, owing to ill-health, he returned to Rheims. He was ordained at Laon, March 1587, aged only 23, a year under the canonical minimum age for ordination, having been given the dispensation that he requested a year earlier from Fr. Agazario, rector of the English College, Rome. He was sent into England in November 1588, and survived a little less than a year before being arrested at a house in Gray's Inn Lane, London, 15 August, 1589, then imprisoned and tortured in Bridewell.[3]

A pair of draft warrants in the state papers, endorsed, "Remembrance for these warrants to be made forthwith for Mr. Topcliffe. Granted at the Council Table," authorize the imprisonment and torture. The remarkable thing about these drafts is that Topcliffe wrote them out himself. They are in his handwriting, and the strong implication is that he was now issuing his own instructions through the medium of the Council.

The first of the drafts is a warrant to the master and keeper of Bridewell to receive and keep as close prisoners Christopher Bales, his brother John Bales, a taylor, Henry Gurney, haberdasher, Anthony Kay, and John Coxed, yeoman: "and no person to resort to any of them but

---

[2]The evidence is a letter, 15 May 1590 (*APC*, 19. 131) from the Council to the Lord Treasurer asking him to reimburse the keeper of the Gatehouse for diet and other charges incurred by a list of prisoners, including Dickenson and Gerard, whom Topcliffe had committed. (The council, acting on the basis of a request by Topcliffe, asks the Treasurer to pay because, "there hath little benefit grown to her Majesty by their condemnation," i.e., they had no property to speak of.)

[2]Pollen 2, 314–15; Anstruther, 102.

[3]Anstruther, 18–19; Pollen 1, 129–31.

Mr. Richard Topcliffe and Mr. Richard Young." The second warrant is for Topcliffe and Young:

> Another warrant from their Lordships to Richard Topcliffe and Richard Young, Esquires, to examine the said persons...and, if they see further occasion, to commit them or any of them unto such torture upon the wall as is usual for the better understanding of the truth of matters against her Majesty and the State.

The notion that Topcliffe was some kind of freebooter who made his way into the system does not survive a reading of this warrant written up for the Council in his own hand. Its language, authorizing Topcliffe and Young, *if they see further occasion* to put these people to *such torture upon the wall as is usual* shows that the Council was now thoroughly habituated and fully consenting to the use of torture."[1]

What happened to Bales's brother and his other associates we do not know, but Christopher Bales himself was severely tortured "upon the wall" in order to find out where and for whom he had said mass. According to Fr. Southwell's account, sent to Rome 8 March just four days after Bales's execution, he was hung in the manacles for twenty-four hours, "suspended by the hands, just touching the ground with the tips of his toes."[2] He was then moved to the Gatehouse, and shortly after brought up for trial, convicted, and executed on a gallows erected in Fleet Street, next to Fetter Lane. He was 25 years old.

At his trial, when the sentence was to be pronounced, the judge, as usual, asked him whether he had anything to say for himself:

> He desired to ask one thing, which was—Whether St. Augustine, the monk sent by the Pope of Rome to preach the Christian Catholic faith to the English, was guilty of treason in complying with that commission or no? To which, when the court had answered that he was not, "Why then," said the confessor, "do you arraign and condemn me for a traitor, who do the same thing as he did, and to whom nothing can be objected but what might equally be objected to him?" They told him the difference was, that by

---

[1] NA/SP12/230/57, printed in Pollen 1, 178–9 (The Calendar dates these drafts Feb. 1590, but this too late by several months). There is a photograph in Hughes, 3, between 384 and 385 ("Torture I"). The facing photograph of Topcliffe's letter to the queen (BL Ms. Lansdowne 72.39), 22 June 1592, enables a reader to compare the hands. Fr. Hughes did not notice the identity.

[2] Foley 1.325.

their laws his case was now made treason; and without any further arguing proceeded to pronounce the sentence of death in the usual form.[1]

Two layman were hanged the same day as Bales, convicted as felons for having assisted him. The first was Alexander or Sander Blake, described in the Penkeval Ms. as "a poor man that was an hostler in Gray's Inn Lane," where he kept a lodging. They hanged him in front of his own house because Bales had been arrested there.[2] The second victim, similarly hanged in front of his own lodging, was an elderly man, Nicholas Horner, a tailor from York.

Horner had gone to London because of a sore leg needing medical treatment, and had not been long there when he was arrested and sent to Newgate. There he was put in close imprisonment in irons. The irons plus his not being allowed to see a surgeon made his leg so much worse that it had to be amputated in the prison without anesthetic of any kind. With the help of other prisoners and especially of the priest John Hewitt, he survived this ordeal, and after about a year's pain in the healing of his wound, was set free. He found a lodging in Smithfield, and set about earning a living by his trade.

He had not been there long when Topcliffe raided his lodging, took away all his possessions, and committed him to Bridewell. There, in order to find out what priests had visited him, Topcliffe, "besides many railing words and threatenings according to his accustomed tyranny," tortured him severely in the manacles until he was nearly dead. At the next sessions he was arraigned and condemned as a felon on evidence offered by Topcliffe and Young that he had made a jerkin for a priest, the priest being Christopher Bales.

After trial he was sent back to Newgate, but because execution did not immediately follow, the keeper began to doubt whether he would be put to death at all, and allowed him the liberty of the prison with other prisoners. But then the order for his execution came, and he too was hanged on 4 March, in front of his lodging in Smithfield.[3]

---

[1] Challoner, 160. Robert Southwell's letter narrates the same exchange between Bales and the bench.

[2] Pollen2, 191; Morris 1, 3.39.

[3] Pollen 2, 227–31. The account of Nicholas Horner's imprisonment, trial, and execution was written by a fellow-prisoner, who was present when Horner, readmitted to "the Justice Hall" in Newgate, told his fellow-Catholic prisoners about a vision he had had, binding them to secrecy should he not be executed. Horner also told the story (upon the same terms) to a visitor, Mrs. Dorothy White, who told it to Fr. Southwell, who included it in his letter to Aquaviva, 8 March 1590 (Foley 1.326): "Before his death, while he was

Topcliffe was present at all three executions, which followed in sequence, Bales being executed first in Fleet Street; then, as Southwell put it, "the hangman, with hands all bloody with this butchery and quartering, hastened to another street," i.e., to Smithfield to hang Horner, then on to Gray's Inn Lane to hang Alexander Blake.

The third of this cluster of cases concerned another pair of priests, Edward Jones and Anthony Middleton. Jones was a Welshman from the diocese of St. Asaph in North Wales. Early travels had taken him to Spain, Greece, Venice, and Rome, where he had found himself in the Inquisition House for two weeks. While he was there, an Italian friar reconciled him to the Catholic Church, the English Jesuit Simon Hunt serving as interpreter. (Before leaving for Douay and Rome in 1575 and becoming a Jesuit, Hunt had been the schoolmaster at Stratford-upon-Avon, where he may have taught William Shakespeare.) Jones then went to the seminary at Rheims, where he arrived in June 1587. Ordination as a priest followed a year later, and in October 1588 he was sent into England. Some time in 1589 or early 1590 he was captured at a grocer's in Fleet Street by a priest-catcher who pretended to be a Catholic. He was taken first to Topcliffe's house, then to Bridewell; Topcliffe interrogated him under torture in both places.[1] He was then transferred to the Gatehouse.[2]

Anthony Middleton was a Yorkshire man, trained in the seminary at Rheims, ordained in May 1586, and sent into England in July.[3] He was a little man, and slightly built, according to Fr. Curry, but "of an indomitable soul."[4] He survived nearly four years until 3 May 1590 when he was caught "by means of those wicked men" Topcliffe and Young in a

---

sitting with a lighted candle in his filthy and dark dungeon, seeing the form of a crown on the head of his shadow, he put up his hand to feel what could cause such an appearance; but finding nothing, he changed his place, to try whether it came from some peculiar position of his body; but, as he walked, there was the same appearance, which moved when he moved, and stood when he stood, and so remained visible for a whole hour, like a diadem upon his head, to foreshadow his future glory. He told this a little before his martyrdom to a pious woman." The fellow-prisoner's version is substantially the same, except that the light is far brighter than the candle, "even as bright as the light of the sun."

[1] Anstruther, 192–3; Pollen 1, 183; Challoner, 162–3l; Verstegan, 9. Fr. Curry said that the sham Catholic was a woman pretending that she wished to become Catholic (Pollen 2, 316).

[2] *APC*, 19. 131.

[3] Anstruther, 229.

[4] Pollen 2, 317.

house belonging to a Mr. Saunders in Clerkenwell. Young committed him to the Clink prison, and the next day he was brought to trial with Edward Jones, along with the thieves and other common criminals, at the Old Bailey. A detailed eye-witness account of the trial and the execution that followed it survives.[1]

The indictment charged both men with high treason for having been made priests by Papal authority, and coming "contemptuously" into England. Jones, a confident, able speaker who had built up a reputation as a preacher, was a courageous man. At every stage in the proceedings where he had an opportunity to speak, he challenged the justice, even the legality of the trial. He began with the indictment: he had not come "contemptuously" into England, he said, but to save souls:

> And whereas there is a penalty appointed for the not observing of a law (as do this or pay this sum of money, or suffer this punishment), there is no contempt.

This response puzzled Lord Chief Justice Anderson since it implied that Jones was quite willing to suffer the penalty for breaking the law, and so he asked him if that was, indeed, the case. When Jones agreed that it was, "Then," said Anderson, "you were best confess the indictment." But Jones still refused, insisting that there was no contempt in his coming to England, whereupon the two justices and other members of the bench fell into a long attempt to prove contempt. This so exasperated Topcliffe, who was present, that he urged the Recorder—at that time still William Fleetwood—to sentence Jones before he pleaded. Jones eventually pleaded "Not guilty," and the court turned to Middleton.

Like Jones, Middleton objected to the word "contemptuously," but agreed that he was a priest as defined in the indictment, saw no point in arguing, and pleaded guilty. The court then turned to the business of trying Jones, and swore in Topcliffe as a witness. He read out the text of his examination, telling the story of Jones's travels, his reconciliation, education at Rheims, ordination, and arrival in England. There being no other witness, the court asked Jones to tell the jury why he should not be found guilty, thus giving him a second opportunity to expose the proceedings for a legal sham.

He told them that under a statute of Edward VI no-one could be indicted for high treason, petty treason or misprision of treason unless the offense was proved either by two witnesses or voluntary confession,

---

[1]Printed from a manuscript now at Oscott College in Pollen 1, 182–6.

and in this case there was no second witness, and no voluntary confession. "Will you deny that this is your confession?" asked Topcliffe, to which Jones replied, "It was done by torture, for I was hanged by the wall by the arms, and therefore it was not voluntary." Then, when one of the justices asked "Will you deny yourself to be a priest," Jones replied, "I am to be tried by law, and therefore I pray you, My Lord Chief Justice, let me have the law." To that Lord Chief Justice Anderson could only say that Jones's statute was irrelevant because he was being tried under a later law. "It was never repealed, and therefore in force," replied Jones. The only reply to that came from Recorder Fleetwood, who said, "You are in a wrong box."[1] The court then swore in the jury, who "stayed not a *Pater noster* time, but returned with a verdict grateful to Mr. Topcliffe, which was that Mr. Jones was guilty."

As was customary, the court then asked Jones what he could say why judgment should not be passed upon him, and he took his third opportunity to expose the proceedings, telling them that like St. Maurice, he would die rather than deny his faith; but, nonetheless, he had seen it published in pamphlets both English and Latin that the Queen herself had said that none of her subjects should be put to death for their consciences. Therefore since no treason had been proved against him except his priesthood, which was a matter of conscience, he craved the favor of a subject and the Queen's mercy.

Again, there was no response: just the Recorder saying, "There is treason enough proved against thee in that thou art a priest." Jones, though, was not done with them. He told them that there was no charity in their religion which was, in any case, not a real religion but "a fond new devised opinion." What was more, in Queen Mary's time the heretics had not been burned under some peculiar law made for the purpose:

> But what may be said after in the reign of Queen Elizabeth when so many priests and Catholics are butchered by a peculiar law made by herself and never heard of before, without all charity, except it be charity to carry them to Bridewell or to the Tower to be racked, or hanged against a wall by the

---

[1]William Fleetwood, client of Leicester and Recorder of London 1571–92, was another angry Elizabethan. Examining George Haydock at the Guildhall (1584), he "received him in his customary froward manner with torrents of abuse." When Haydock shrugged this off, Fleetwood, taking his response as an insult, "became white-hot with rage, and raised his fist to strike the prisoner" (Harris, 115, quoting Burton-Pollen, 44). Fleetwood, incidentally, was a good example of vested interest in the Protestant settlement. His own dwelling had been a house of Augustinian Canons; his Protestant cousin Edward, parson of Wigan (a rich benefice), "seized Rossall Grange from the Allens," and his uncle John gained possession of Penwortham Priory.

arms, or some other torture, & without any conference of religion, except it be religion to examine him where he hath said Mass, who gave him any maintenance, who relieved him, or what money he hath in his purse, as you, Mr. Topcliffe, did by me.

This time the response was to shout him down, and ask that he be put to silence or gagged. The court then turned to Middleton, who again said very little: that he had no intention of denying his faith, did not really care what sentence they imposed, and thanked God for calling him to this suffering, although he was unworthy.

The Recorder pronounced sentence, and even then Jones wanted to speak, but this was not permitted. They were taken to Newgate, and then the next day, Tuesday, they were required, so our witness heard, to take part in a disputation with "the Doctors" in St. Sepulchre's church; but since our witness was not present he cannot tell us anything about it. On the Wednesday they were laid on hurdles at Newgate and drawn, first, to Fleet Street, where Jones was dealt with on a gibbet erected near the Conduit. There he was told he could save his life if he conformed to the state church, and as an additional argument Topcliffe showed him the fire in which his heart and bowels would be burned. But of course, he refused, was put off the ladder, cut down alive, and quartered.

They then took Middleton to be executed outside the place of his arrest, Clerkenwell. There, as he stood on the ladder with the halter round his neck, he finally asked if he could speak:

"No," quoth Topcliffe, "except thou speak to the glory of God, the honor of thy prince and country. If thou wilt speak," quoth Topcliffe, "as I have told thee I will entreat Mr. Sheriff thou shalt speak this hour, otherwise thou shalt not preach that doctrine which thou hast taught in yonder place" (which was the house where he was taken), "and in other places, as in Gray's Inn Lane, Shoe Lane, and other places you know," quoth Topcliffe, "I know where."

Middleton's response, like Jones's, was a refusal, saying that he was suffering for his faith, and that he hoped his death would confirm many Catholics in their faith, too. Topcliffe told him to hold his peace, "and make himself meek to God," to which Middleton replied merely that he hoped he *was* meek to God, and with that, not allowing him time for his prayers, Bull, the hangman, threw him beside the ladder, cut him down like Jones, alive, and proceeded with the rest of the sentence.

*****

These cases are characteristic of Topcliffe's operation. First, he liked to catch and arrest prisoners himself or through his agents or "satellites" as one account calls them.[1] He personally arrested Horner, and it seems probable, given the linkage between Horner and Bales, that he arrested Bales too. He and Justice Young were responsible for Middleton's arrest. Once arrested, a prisoner would be committed to prison, and examined. The local authorities in Dover arrested Dickenson and Gerard, but once brought to London they were committed to Bridewell, and turned over for examination to a committee of which Topcliffe was the senior member. They used torture. Bales, Horner, and Jones were similarly committed to Bridewell, where Topcliffe examined them with torture.

The accounts agree that the torture was severe, alleging that Christopher Bales was in the manacles for 24 hours, and that old Horner, the tailor, nearly died. In three cases the accounts allege that the torture was obscene. According to two different accounts, Fr. Gerard's catalogue, and a letter by Fr. Southwell, Topcliffe tortured Edward Jones "in the privy parts." Peter Penkevel's manuscript says the same of Topcliffe's torture of Christopher Bales. Fr. Pollen omits the passage from his copy of the manuscript, saying only in a footnote, "The outrages here recounted cannot in decency be specified." Thomas Fitzherbert, writing in his *Apology* about twelve years later, gives a hair-raisingly detailed account of the same kind of torture being practiced on Francis Dickenson, and we know that Topcliffe was Dickenson's torturer-interrogator.[2] In all five cases, too, no formal warrant for the torture survives; there is no evidence that Topcliffe's own draft warrants for Bales and his associates found in the State Papers were ever formally issued.

The examination completed, a prisoner would often be moved from Bridewell to another prison. Topcliffe transferred the four priest-prisoners—Dickenson, Gerard, Bales, Jones—to the Gatehouse in Westminster, next door to his own house. There, as in the case of Dickenson and Gerard, he would sometimes continue his attempts to incriminate a prisoner. Then, if a prisoner was brought up for trial in London, as were Bales, Blake, Horner, Jones, and Middleton, Topcliffe would attend as

[1]Fr. Curry, in Pollen 2, 316.

[2]Fitzherbert, 6–6b; Challoner, 160; Pollen 1, 291; Pollen 2, 289–90; Verstegan, 9. This Fitzherbert was Thomas, William Fitzherbert of Swynnerton's son and heir. He and his wife went to France, and after her death he moved to Spain. In 1602 he was ordained, and in 1615 became a Jesuit (*ODNB*).

witness, spectator, and—as Jones's trial illustrates—as a kind of free-lance prosecutor.

The outcome of such trials was a foregone conclusion, and execution usually followed the next day after sentencing. The legal responsibility for carrying out executions lay with the sheriffs, and the actual implementation of the sentence was the business of the hangman. In 1590s London this was a man called Bull, who had a number of assistants. Topcliffe, therefore, had no formal or official role to play in executions. Nonetheless, he was a constant attendant at them, acting as a kind of master of the ceremonies. He would engage in conversation with victims, and he would usually attach a notice or title to the gallows, naming the crime for which the victim was suffering. In all five of the present cases, he attached a title reading, "For treason and favoring foreign invasions," which in all five cases was simply a lie. When Edward Jones saw it written over his gallows, he shouted out that it was false.[1]

A few years later, when Topcliffe's behavior at executions had become notorious, it attracted—in private at least, because attacking Topcliffe publicly would have been a very risky business—satirical comment. Someone in the Bacon brothers' circle wrote a funny sonnet on the subject, which remains in the papers of Anthony Bacon preserved in the Lambeth library:

> Topcliffe and Bull contended for to have
> The silken garments of a Priest put down,
> No less than for Achilles' armor strove
> Two noble Greeks for honor and renown.
> Bull did prefer the service of his hands
> Before the practice of the other's wit;
> Topcliffe then straight upon the ladder stands
> To show himself for th'one and th'other fit.
> The whole assembly gave to him the prize,
> Allowing him as officer in chief,
> And Bull to wait at session and at 'size:
> For him the spoils of every common thief.
> Thus well he keeps that happily he sowed;
> Would every office were no worse bestowed.

The manuscript sheet is endorsed, "Topcliffe and Bull's Contention for the priest's apparel the month of March made 1596." If this means what it apparently says, that the sonnet was made in 1596, and that the altercation between Topcliffe and the hangman took place in March, then the

---

[1]Morris, 3.45–46; Pollen 2, 316.

priest can only have been Christopher Bales, killed 4 March 1590. No other priest was killed in March, and no priests were killed in 1596.[1]

This is a rather clever sonnet. To understand its full force, one needs to know that in Topcliffe's time to be a hangman was to be lowest of the low. That understood, the basis of the joke was the Elizabethan custom of considering the clothes of executed criminals as perquisites that went with the hangman's job. The implication is that Topcliffe was in competition with Bull not only for his perquisites, but for his job or office of hangman as well: that in bringing priests to the gallows by his wit (or intelligence) Topcliffe, despite his sixteen quarterings and court connections, was as much a hangman as Bull. And, of course, there's a further implication. The antitype of these two killers quarreling over a priest's clothes is the scene of the Roman soldiers gambling for Christ's garment at Golgotha.

A few years ago, an essay published in *English Literary Renaissance* argued convincingly that in the character of Falstaff Shakespeare was poking quiet fun at the aging roués of Elizabeth I's court, Leicester in particular; but any reader of the Bacon papers sonnet who remembers Prince Hal's jokes about making Falstaff his hangman in *Henry IV, Part I*, will be tempted to suspect that Shakespeare had Topcliffe in mind as one of the moon's minions as well as his friend Leicester.[2]

Young John Donne made a similar joke about Topcliffe. In *The Courtier's Library, or Catalogus Librorum Aulicorum,* a jokey little catalogue of imaginary books by real authors that circulated in manuscript among Donne's friends in the early years of the seventeenth century, one of the imaginary books is by Topcliffe:

> *A Rival of Moses: the Art of Preserving Clothes beyond Forty Years,* by Topcliffe, an Englishman: with an English commentary by James Stonehouse, who has published a treatise *To Keep Clothes near the Fashion* in the same peculiar language.

No-one has explained this joke. Its point, though, seems to be that Topcliffe is in the old clothes business, and it must refer to the same

---

[1]The sonnet (written, one notices, after Topcliffe lost his power along with his commission) is in Lambeth Palace Library, Ms 656, f.199. I owe this reference to Roy Kendall.

[2]See Jacqueline Vanhoutte, "'Age in Love': Falstaff Among the Minions of the Moon," *ELR* 43 (2013): 86–127. One is bound to wonder, too, about the implications of the Doll Tearsheet scenes. When Shakespeare wrote *Henry IV, Part II,* Leicester had been dead some eight years, but Topcliffe was alive, and notorious among the informed for bragging about his intimacies with the old Queen.

kind of behavior that produced the sonnet. Evelyn Simpson, editor of
The Courtier's Library, dates the little book and its contents sometime
after about 1603, but this joke must be a good deal earlier than that.[1]
Donne as a young Catholic knew all about Topcliffe in the 1590s, and
was afraid of him, with good reason. His presence haunts Donne's "Satire IV."[2]

*****

The Council employed Topcliffe in other tasks, too. In April 1590 the
port authorities at Dover apprehended a young boy, Henry Brettam,
about to sail to Calais on his way to the seminary at Rheims. The Council wrote telling the boy's father, George Brettam, that they were placing
the boy with Mr. Leech, "a very discreet and learned schoolmaster" in
Hornchurch, Essex; that he was to contribute £15 a year to his son's
maintenance with Leech, and that he was "to repair to Mr. Richard
Topcliffe, esquire, one of her Majesty's servants, who shall from time to
time take order with you for the accomplishing of the premises."

The irony of this case was that Leech was a thorn in the flesh of the
local ecclesiastical authorities, an excommunicated puritan who refused
to attend his local church or take communion, and who insisted on doing
his own preaching and catechizing. He had even performed an amateur
burial. So the Council—one assumes unknowingly—had removed
young Henry Brettam from one form of recusancy to another.[3] Was
Topcliffe responsible for recommending Leech? Very probably. If he
did, it is equally probable that he took a cut of the £15 yearly to maintain
the boy.

Topcliffe went north a good deal, too, usually on some specific
assignment for the Queen or Council. Fr. Holtby's narrative of events in
the north places him in York on just such an assignment in May 1590,
sitting with a commission of inquiry into a case involving three young

---

[1]John Donne, *The Courtier's Library, or Catalogus Librorum Aulicorum*. Edited by
Evelyn Simpson (London: The Nonesuch Press, 1930), 43-44. A James Stonehouse "of
London, gent." matriculated at Magdalen College, Oxford, aged 15, in 1581, and became
a student of Lincoln's Inn in 1585. He seems to have been knighted 23 July, 1603 (Foster, 4.1429). Why Donne found him funny is not known...

[2]As the speaker of the Satire IV talks to someone who is probably a spy, he imagines
that he sees, "One of our giant statutes ope his jaw / To suck me in" (132–3). At line 216,
the earliest Ms. reads "Topcliffe" instead of "pursevant." One understands the change. It
would have been very dangerous to mention Topcliffe publicly.

[3]*APC*, 19. 87–88 (28 April 1590). On Leech, see McIntosh, 205–11.

men, Oliver Cottam, Robert Musgrave, and Roger Ashton, arrested trying to leave the country from South Shields, Durham.

Roger Ashton was the reason for Topcliffe's presence. He had originally been arrested at Dover in January 1588, "coming in secret manner into the realm with a bill of the Pope's about him to dispense with him for the marrying of a gentlewoman, being near of kindred unto him." When the authorities found that he had served under Leicester in the Low Countries in Sir William Stanley's regiment at the time of Stanley's surrender of Deventer to the Spanish, they became very interested in him. He and Stanley were friends, and Stanley, it emerged, had commissioned him to go to Rome and ask Cardinal Allen to write a defense of the surrender, which duly appeared under the title, *The copy of a Letter written by M. Doctor Allen concerning the yielding up of the City of Deventer* (1587), with a preface by Ashton.[1]

Roger Ashton, therefore, found himself in the Tower, where he was put to examination under torture, 14 January 1588. He remained there until September, when they moved him to the Marshalsea.[2] He escaped from the Marshalsea, and made his way home to Croston in Lancashire where his brothers and a brother-in-law assisted him, even though they knew he was an escaped prisoner. He then traveled to the Durham coast with Cottam and Musgrave, intending to escape overseas; but as they waited for a favorable wind, they were all three arrested, and after a preliminary examination by the dean of Durham, were sent to York.

The Council wished Ashton to be prosecuted in York, but when the lawyers told them that he had to be tried in the county where he was first arrested, they brought him to London.[3] There he was tried on the original treason charge for bringing a papal dispensation into the country, and found guilty. He was hanged, drawn, and quartered at Tyburn, 23 June 1592.

Topcliffe was present at the execution. On the scaffold he charged Ashton with having been a principal in the yielding of Deventer; that he had been a pensioner of the king of Spain, and had had dealings with traitorous fugitives beyond seas. In reply Ashton said that he was not

---

[1]Morris 1, 3.173; *APC*, 20. 356; Gillow, 1.73–4; Verstegan, 56.

[2]CRS 3.26, 27 ("Tower Bills"); *APC*, 15. 334–5. The torturers were the lieutenant of the Tower (Owen Hopton), Sir Edward Waterhouse, William Waad, Thomas Owen, and Richard Young.

[3]*APC*, 22. 524. The Council issued a warrant on 11 June 1592, paying the messenger who brought him £18. 6s.

"any principal actor" in the yielding of Deventer, that he had never practiced treason with any fugitives, and that he'd never even heard any of them talk treason. He was, however, a pensioner of the king of Spain:

> For I, being a younger brother, had only £5 annuity by year, and it pleased the king to give me 25 crowns the month.

He then prayed for the Queen, took leave of his friends, and died, having refused the ministrations of Richard Fletcher, bishop of Bristol. If Verstegan's informant was correct, Ashton made a good impression on the onlookers, so that, "he was not exclaimed on, but rather pitied of the people, in such sort as the like in this time hath not been seen."[1] Topcliffe's effort at blackening his character, it seems, had fallen flat. After all, Ashton had not been convicted of yielding Deventer or practicing treason abroad or being a pensioner of the king of Spain. He was dying a horrible death because he had brought home a dispensation to marry his cousin, and the people knew that.

After the deaths of Jones and Middleton there were no priestly executions in London for over a year. Topcliffe had to wait until May 1591 to attend another one, and he had to go all the way to York for it. Meanwhile his chief business north of London was in Derbyshire, where his campaign against the Fitzherberts remained unfinished, his £3,000 unearned.

*****

In the spring of 1590 two of the Fitzherbert brothers were in prison: Sir Thomas Fitzherbert was still interned with fifteen other Catholic gentlemen at Broughton Castle near Banbury in Oxfordshire, home of the Fiennes family, and John Fitzherbert was still in Derby gaol. The third brother, Richard, had lost the family's property, Hartsmere in Staffordshire, to Edward Thorne, and was now living at Norbury. Topcliffe decided to focus his attention on Richard, once again using Thorne as his agent, and working, as usual through the Privy Council.

Acting "upon certain notice given us of sundry dangerous and suspected persons as priests, seminaries, and such like, that lay lurking in the manor house of Sir Thomas Fitzherbert called Norbury," the Council gave Thorne a warrant to search Norbury and arrest Richard Fitzherbert and anyone else of interest.[2] Off Thorne went to Norbury with his

---

[1]Verstegan, 57.

[2]*APC*, 19. 141–142.

warrant, but he failed to arrest Richard Fitzherbert because he tried to be too clever.

Knowing that there was a regular distribution of alms at Norbury, Thorne sent three bogus lame beggars there, a man and two women, to ask for alms. When the alms had been distributed as usual, these three stayed, calling out for more so effectively that Mr. Fitzherbert himself came out to give them more money. The male member of the party then seized hold of him, and threw him down on the ground. The people in the house, hearing the noise of the scuffle, came out to the rescue, whereupon the supposed beggar, having a pistol ready charged, pointed it at Mr. Fitzherbert's chest, but fortunately—being an Elizabethan pistol—it did not go off. With that, the "beggar" dropped his pistol and ran away. When one of the household picked the pistol up, it went off, but hit no-one.[1]

Topcliffe, outraged, reported a highly-colored version of this incident to the Council. In his version, the bogus beggar (whose name was Thomas Elkin) had actually arrested Richard Fitzherbert when "divers like evil-disposed persons inhabiting the house" rescued him and took him away "with strong hand," in the process wounding Elkin and others, "whereof they are at this present in great peril of life."

The Council's response was a letter to the Earl of Shrewsbury, first giving him Topcliffe's version of the Norbury incident, and then instructing him to help Topcliffe carry out the search and arrest properly:

> Forasmuch as this notable outrage ought speedily to be redressed, and that your Lordship by reason of other your occasions and indispositions of body cannot so conveniently travail[2] yourself, we have therefore thought it expedient to pray your Lordship to appoint your son, the Lord Talbot, or some of your Lordship's -----------,[3] calling to him the bearer hereof, Mr. Richard Topcliffe, purposely sent down to attend your Lordship about this matter, and such others as his Lordship shall think fit, to make his present repair unto Norbury abovesaid, or any such place or places where it may be any ways suspected that Richard Fitzherbert or any other abovesaid delinquents to be lurking and remaining, and by virtue hereof to search all houses, apprehend and send up hither the principal and chief of the men so offending under safe custody, to be proceeded with here according to the law and as the quality of their several offenses shall require.[4]

---

[1]Morris 1, 3.15–16.

[2]This word in the original can be modernized as either "travel" or "travail."

[3]Similarly left blank in the original, now in the Talbot papers at Lambeth (Vol. I [Lambeth Ms 3200], f. 71), but beginning "depute."

Having written their letter, the Council gave it to Topcliffe to deliver.

Topcliffe, though, did not deliver it. Instead he sat on it for about six weeks, and then, instead of taking it himself, sent Thorne, carrying both the Council's letter, and a long, rambling letter of his own dated 30 June, attempting to explain to Shrewsbury why it had taken him so long to deliver the Council's letter.[2]

He came up with three reasons. First, Shrewsbury had been unwell, and there was no point in delivering the letter until he was better. Second, "the offenders were fled and gone from the place," fearing Shrewsbury's authority, and it was decided "by the deepest judgment of my Lords," that it was best to wait until they had regrouped. Thirdly, Topcliffe himself had been kept at court until 15 June "about some service specially appointed me."

This was all nonsense and fabling. As long as the Council's letter remained undelivered, the Norbury people had no reason to fear Shrewsbury. Equally obviously, the Council knew nothing about the delay. Had it been their decision, they would have timed their letter accordingly, and Topcliffe would not have had to write such a peculiar letter on his own initiative.

Truth begins to emerge when he tells Shrewsbury that he had sent Thorne to scout out the neighborhood, with instructions to report to him at his Lincolnshire house. Thorne had done that, and was now on his way to Lord Shrewsbury, carrying Topcliffe's letter and the Council's. And why is Topcliffe, even now, not bringing the letter himself? His reason is that his mere presence in the neighborhood would alert the prey:

> I am among such malefactors reputed a bug or like a scarecrow when I come into an unwonted place, country, or unto a man of your honor's estate, so would my waiting upon your Lordship now for the delivery of this letter and to know your pleasure procure every traitorous priest and their patrons to examine their own estates, and danger, and to fly their dens and haunts, and my experience teacheth me, that such men hath strange espial and intelligence in court, in country, and about the greatest persons whosoever.

That may or may not have been true, but more truth emerges at the end of the letter when Topcliffe tells Shrewsbury that it would be better, all things considered, if Shrewsbury did nothing about the matter him-

---

[4]*APC*, 19. 141–142 (20 May 1590).

[2]Talbot papers (Lambeth), Vol. 1, Ms. 701, f. 29.

self, but left the job to Thorne, a "discreet wise secret person...(a man of as good experience and foresight as ever I did meet withal) [who] will serve for this enterprise, being well, wisely, and surely assisted."

So Topcliffe not only delayed the Council's letter; he did his best to rewrite it. He makes no mention of Shrewsbury's son, whom the Council had instructed to make the arrest, and the last part of the letter (damaged, unfortunately) makes the real reasons for Topcliffe's behavior insultingly clear. Lords Lieutenant, wrote Topcliffe, are wise, secret, and sufficient; but the same cannot be said for their servants and followers who, as soon as they see preparations made for a search and arrest, put out a general warning to the friends and kin of the quarry; and that warning:

> will fly from one man and place to another as swiftly through a shire, and so from shire to shire, as posts from place to place, and papist to papist, can ride. Nevertheless I submit myself and my opinion to your Lordship's judgment, and direction....

Since Shrewsbury himself was the only Lord Lieutenant for miles around, one can imagine his reaction to these remarks and their implications. Topcliffe trusted neither him nor anyone in his household, including his son, and that is why he wanted to substitute Thorne for Gilbert Talbot. His clumsy attempts to offset insult with flattery will have cut no ice at all with Shrewsbury:

> But when I think how your Lordship did overreach them at Padley, I then [doubt] no other place, which service unto her Majesty and the state at Padley, done by you, I have heard her Majesty highly esteem in some private discourse it hath pleased her Majesty to have with me of like places, and persons.

The back story to this letter must be that Topcliffe, having grown used to writing his own instructions through the medium of the Council, had not been prepared for their insistence on deferring to their fellow-councilor's authority in his own territory. In Topcliffe's mind, the eradication of the Fitzherberts and their Catholicism took precedence over all other considerations, and so, amazingly, he took it on himself to exclude Shrewsbury, if possible, from the operation. For Shrewsbury, this performance proved to be the last straw where Topcliffe was concerned.

The private business that kept Topcliffe in London until mid-June almost certainly involved one of Thomas Fitzherbert's strategies to forestall his uncle's attempts to disinherit him. In May–June 1590, Fitzherbert "levied a fine," i.e., conveyed Padley and its associated properties to Topcliffe in trust:

> The deforciant, Thomas Fitzherbert, Esquire, grants to the plaintiff, Richard Topcliffe, Esquire, and to his heirs forever, the manors of Over Padley and Nether Padley, on the Derwent, with six messuages, two cottages, ten gardens, ten orchards, a thousand acres of land, five hundred acres of meadow land, six hundred acres of pasture, three hundred acres of wood, a thousand acres of furze and heath, etc., in Padley, Grindelford, and Lyham, in the parish of Hathersage, in consideration of eight hundred marks of silver.[1]

Fitzherbert thought he was protecting his inheritance, but Topcliffe, who treated the transaction as an outright conveyance of the property, considered his eight hundred marks well spent.

Despite Topcliffe's maneuvering over the Norbury arrest, Shrewsbury, who always knew what he had to do, wrote to the Council, 21 July, announcing that he had made the arrests, and asking for further instructions. In their reply, 9 August, the Council, after thanking him, turned to the subject of John Fitzherbert, still in Derby gaol and doing "great hurt by his lewd[2] disposition," and asked Shrewsbury to send him up to London. They ended their letter with an order that Richard Fitzherbert, who was in poor health, "be brought up hither so soon as might be without endangering of his life in respect of his infirmity."[3] It also appears from the Council's letter that Sir Thomas's nephew, William Bassett of Blore, had taken the precaution of searching Norbury House (presumably for essential deeds and other papers that it was necessary should be kept out of the hands of people like Thorne).

That same day, the Council wrote to Topcliffe, along with four other people, instructing them to examine Richard Fitzherbert, Martin Audley, and Richard Twyford "severely and strictly...upon such articles as they should conceive and think fit...to be ministered unto them upon such information as Mr. Topcliffe, being already made acquainted with their lewd behavior, shall be able to give knowledge of."[4] Nothing more is heard of Richard Fitzherbert, and one has to presume that he died in

---

[1]Camm 2, 37–8. 800 marks was £533.6s.8d.

[2]Used like this of people and their actions, "lewd" meant "Bad, vile, evil, wicked, base; unprincipled, ill-conditioned; good-for-nothing, worthless, 'naughty'." (*OED*). It was a favorite word with Topcliffe and his Council friends.

[3]*APC,* 19. 368.

[4]*APC,* 19. 370. Heath does not include this case in his book on torture, but "severely and strictly" in that context can only imply torture or the threat of it.

prison, probably from the effects of Topcliffe's "severe and strict" examination.

It becomes apparent that Topcliffe was still calling the tune in the matter of the Fitzherberts when, probably as a result of these interrogations, the Council wrote to Shrewsbury again, 21 September, saying that they had been "thoroughly made acquainted [no doubt by Topcliffe] with the great care and diligence your Lordship hath used in the apprehending of Richard Fitzherbert, Martin Audley, and Richard Twyford, and the rest." They then ordered him as Lieutenant to authorize Thorne to arrest Alice Royston, the housekeeper at Norbury, and Thomas Coxon, keeper of the park at Hamstall Ridware.

Shrewsbury cannot have liked this, and he would have liked even less to be told to dispose of these prisoners as Thorne would instruct him on the Council's behalf.[1] Meanwhile, Shrewsbury had sent John Fitzherbert, in very poor health after his experience in Derby gaol, to prison in London. His son-in-law, Thomas Eyre of Holme Hall, had raised the huge sum of £10,000 as a bribe to the Council to secure a reprieve of the death sentence, and to procure John's liberty; but as Camm says, since this was a secret transaction, the recipients of the money could not be brought to task, and so John Fitzherbert died in prison, 9 November 1590, "in great destitution."[2]

*****

As for Sir Thomas Fitzherbert, imprisoned at Broughton, in early October the Council released the Catholic gentlemen in custody there to Archbishop Whitgift of Canterbury, on bond either to return to the places from which they were committed or to any other places that the archbishop should think "most convenient and may least hurt and infect others." The Council also wrote, telling Fiennes, the owner of Broughton, to release his prisoners, though not before they had reimbursed him for their upkeep plus "a reasonable allowance" towards "the use and spoil of his linen and other his household stuff used and employed in their service"—which their Lordships don't think they'll refuse, "being all persons of quality and behavior," who will understand "what appertaineth thereunto."[3]

---

[1] *APC*, 19. 451.

[2] Camm, 44.

[3] *APC*, 20. 16, 18 (5 October 1590).

The Catholic gentlemen balked at these new conditions. Nonetheless, they were all released—all except Sir Thomas Fitzherbert. Topcliffe was not about to let him go free under any conditions, and so the Council instructed the Archbishop to keep him in his house "until her Majesty's pleasure be known, and his Lordship receive further order for him."[1]

"Further order" came soon enough. A month later the Council wrote to Robert Beale and four others, saying that because Sir Thomas "stood charged with certain matters of great importance that concerned her Majesty and the state," they had committed him to the house of Sir John Hart, late Lord Mayor of London, and that it was her Majesty's pleasure that they should examine him there upon "certain interrogatories" that Mr. Topcliffe "should exhibit unto him under the hand of Mr. Attorney-General:"

> And because the said matters did concern her Majesty they were required by their Lordships to repair to the house of the said Sir John Hart and use that discretion and care in the taking of the examinations as well of Sir Thomas Fitzherbert, as of such others as Mr. Topcliffe should give them notice of that were privy or able to disclose any of his dealing, which was requisite to be used in matters of that weight, and were to certify unto their Lordships with convenient speed the examinations taken by them in that behalf.[2]

So Topcliffe finally had his way: the Queen had allowed him to put his questions to Sir Thomas, connecting him retrospectively with the northern rising and the Babington Plot as well as with the harboring of priests in his house, and the Council's letter made it clear that Topcliffe was in charge of the interrogation. The object, of course, had not changed. It was still to have Sir Thomas charged with treason, condemned, and executed.

This proceeding was extraordinary enough, but the next step was even more surprising. The Council instructed the Attorney-General (at this time Sir John Popham, later to be Lord Chief Justice) to confer with Topcliffe about the examinations of Sir Thomas, "his brethren, servants, tenants, and others," and to decide upon the next legal move:

> we have thought good to require you with expedition to call unto you the said Mr. Topcliffe, who will impart and deliver unto you the said examinations and confessions which you shall carefully and diligently peruse, and after you shall have with good deliberation considered thereupon, to cer-

[1]*APC*, 20. 62 (28 October).

[2]*APC*, 20. 100 (30 November).

tify us with speed your opinion what the danger of Sir Thomas Fitzherbert's offense may appear to be, and how far he may be charged therewith by law, that we may take such further order for the preventing of such inconveniences as might thereby ensue and for his restraint as shall be judged most expedient. Whereof praying you there may be no delay nor default.[1]

The text of the examinations does not survive, but Mr. Attorney, as commanded, consulted Topcliffe promptly. The upshot of his study of the examinations was a warrant from the Council issued twelve days later to the Lieutenant of the tower (Sir Michael Blount), ordering him to receive into custody Sir Thomas Fitzherbert and John Gage, "to be kept close prisoners in such strict sort as no manner person be suffered to have access unto either of them without special direction from us." And they were both to pay their own expenses.[2]

Sir Thomas was now seventy-three years old, and in no state to survive close imprisonment in the Tower. Cox thought he was interrogated there under torture. That is possible, but unlikely: no such warrant survives. By June the Lieutenant, showing a degree of responsibility for his prisoner, had informed the Council that through lack of exercise, Sir Thomas was likely to lose the use of his legs. They therefore ordered him to allow the old man to walk in the Tower, either accompanying him himself, or appointing some other trusty person to do so, always making sure that no-one could have access to him.[3]

Sir Thomas died in the Tower, 3 October, 1591. Before his death he made a will disinheriting his nephew, but Topcliffe acquired possession of it, took it to the Archbishop of Canterbury, and with his sanction destroyed it.[4] By an act of the probate court of Lichfield, Thomas Fitzherbert as next-of-kin administered the goods of his uncle, considered intestate, and thus inherited the family's properties. Topcliffe, therefore, had successfully removed his father and his uncle, but as long as cousin Bassett of Blore was still alive he had not earned his £3,000.

---

[1] *APC*, 20. 175 (29 December).

[2] *APC*, 20. 207 (10 January 1591). Thomas Phelippes writing to Thomas Barnes, 22 March 1591, mentions Topcliffe's expertise in Catholic matters: "Topcliffe is the man that follows these things as against Sir Thomas Fitzherbert, John Gage, and others" (NA/SP12/238/82). John Gage and his wife, Margaret, were condemned as felons for harboring a priest, but were reprieved on the way to the scaffold (Foley 1, 188).

[3] *APC*, 21. 187–8.

[4] Cox 1, 248.

With his uncle dead, and his inheritance of the family's property assured, Thomas Fitzherbert regretted his over-hasty transaction with Topcliffe to preserve Padley from sequestration, and asked for the return of the property. Topcliffe, of course, refused. Fitzherbert sued him for the property in Chancery, and the court confirmed Topcliffe in possession. It seems that his friend the Queen took a hand in the matter. As Topcliffe later wrote to Gilbert, Earl of Shrewsbury about the earl's intention to "heave" him out of Padley, "I can prove good Queen Elizabeth entreated your Lordship's favor and assistance, under nine of her councillors' hands in the defense of my right unto Padley, when you were first earl."[1]

In the long run, Topcliffe's attempt to destroy the Fitzherberts failed, but at the time it caused great suffering to the family, their tenants, and dependants. Just one moment of grotesque comedy with aptly symbolic overtones occurred to lighten the atmosphere a little. At some time between Richard Fitzherbert's arrest and the interrogation of Sir Thomas in London, Topcliffe went to Norbury to search the house. He knew that William Bassett had been there before him, but he hoped, nonetheless, to find something incriminating. He stayed overnight, and the servants prepared breakfast for him.

William Bassett was there, too. He was walking up and down by the table when Topcliffe found "a foul spider" in his milk, and being Topcliffe, immediately suspected that the women ("whose husbands, father, and friends had been lately committed to prison in London for Sir Thomas's and their own treason") had put it there to poison him.

Everyone believed that spiders were venemous, but as we learn from Shakespeare's Leontes in *The Winter's Tale* (2.1.39–45), for the poison to work one had to *see* the spider in the cup:

> There may be in the cup
> A spider steep'd, and one may drink, depart,
> And yet partake no venom (for his knowledge
> Is not infected), but if one present
> Th' abhorr'd ingredient to his eye, make known
> How he hath drunk, he cracks his gorge, his sides,
> With violent hefts. I have drunk, and seen the spider.

One can imagine the earnestness with which Mr. Bassett tried to persuade Topcliffe that it was a bumble-bee and not a spider that he had

---

[1]Chancery, 320 (F.f.9, No.63); Talbot Papers, Vol. M (Lambeth MS 3203), f. 184.

seen, but Topcliffe was having none of that. He told Bassett that he had found the legs, and if Bassett could find the wings, then perhaps he would believe it was a bumble-bee.[1]

As Topcliffe knew, by now quite a lot of people in England would have rejoiced at his death. Not only would they have been happy to hear of spiders in his milk; they would have cheerfully put one there themselves, on the principle that a spider in the cup was a satisfactorily accurate symbol of Topcliffe himself, considered as a feature of English life.

*****

[1]BL Ms Harleian 6998, ff.249–51. This document is an undated set of articles against William Bassett that Topcliffe wrote out for Thomas Fitzherbert to exhibit to the queen, ca. 1592–3. The account of the spider is Topcliffe's own.

Ten

"Nowhere Left to Hide"[1]

On 18 November 1590, George, Earl of Shrewsbury died aged 68, and Topcliffe, faced with Gilbert Talbot's succession as the seventh earl, found himself having to write another tricky letter. Ostensibly a letter of congratulation, offering the new earl his allegiance and service, it came out as a peculiar series of thinly veiled warnings.

As a young man, Gilbert Talbot, twenty years younger than Topcliffe, had had great respect for him. But that was before Topcliffe's career in law-enforcement had made him notorious and, from the Talbot point of view, an officious nuisance. As we have seen, Topcliffe did not trust either Gilbert or his father to carry out the arrest of Richard Fitzherbert. Gilbert's intervention on behalf of two of Thorne's victims[2] will not have pleased Topcliffe, either, and to make things worse, the new Countess of Shrewsbury was a known Catholic sympathizer if not already a convert. Not surprisingly, therefore, it took a little time for Topcliffe to write his congratulatory letter.

On 8 December he eventually picked up his pen, and began by admitting that he was not among the first to congratulate Earl Gilbert:

> Although I be not one of the first of those who have acknowledged gladness that it hath pleased God to set you in the seat of your noble ancestors (which I have long expected you should win by degrees of time), yet am I in heart with the foremost of your Lordship's plain friends joyfuller thereof, for the service of God, of my Queen, and of my country good: for I do not doubt but your virtues, and your zeal have been equal heretofore with the best of your degree. Then is there expectation that the same will swell, as degrees rise upon you, and Authority shall increase.

Topcliffe always liked to assure his correspondents that he was a plain-

---

[1]Devlin 1, 256.

[2]See above, 156–7.

spoken, simple fellow, but one suspects that what he really wanted to say in this first paragraph was that something long expected had finally come to pass, and that the only thing a man in his position could do was to make the best of it, hoping that as time passed the new earl would rise to the demands of his position. The letter's ambiguous tone then continues into the second paragraph, with an offer of service:

> For my part, if you will license me to honor you and love you still in that plain manner I have done, I shall not leave any faithful part or duty unperformed that shall become one of my profession to one of your state; and I was never so fit to offer and perform so much as now I am, for I that was entangled by many obligations (not long since) unto Leicester and Warwick (never for that lucre which was the lure to many followers) now am a freeman, and all bonds be canceled by their deaths, and I at liberty to love whom, and where, I list, owing no man so much as your Lordship's self if it please you so to esteem of me, so as you give me leave and freedom never to dissemble with your Lordship. And fit it is that some of plain disposition should be entertained among many smilers that this world will afford unto princes.

That is a decidedly conditional, even confrontational, offer of service. Set free of obligation by the deaths of the Dudley brothers, our plain man who is no "smiler," no yes-man of the kind that tends to cluster around great men, offers loyalty and love on condition that he be allowed to speak his mind and never dissemble. And he promptly gives an example of what he means:

> Let me remember your Lordship that you are a prince alone (in effect) in two countries in the heart of England more dangerously infected than the worst of England, of my knowledge. There and everywhere else, bad weeds will seek to shroud themselves under great oaks, whose policies (I trust) your Lordship will discern now, when God hath so abundantly blessed you, whom I knew so virtuous, honorable, and circumspect when you were lower.

The dangerous disease infecting Earl Gilbert's territories, of course, was Catholicism, and Topcliffe proceeds to name the Fitzherberts in particular, "in whose three houses hath been molded and tempered the most dangerous and loathsomest treasons that this age hath heard of." What is more they, their kindred and friends:

> have corrupted and crept under the shadow and shelter of your noble father, whom they had no power to enchant, which turneth greatly to his honor. Yea, it appeareth they devised to have cunning dissembling papists preferred to his service to serve their turns, who might have betrayed a man of the deepest watch.

And there it is. As Topcliffe had told the sixth earl only six months earlier, his household was riddled with Catholics and Catholic sympathiz-
ers, and not to be trusted. He therefore warns Earl Gilbert:

> Of such, my dear Lord, for the particular love I carry to you, and for the
> old honor my foregone friends have born to your house, which died not in
> me when your father used me most unkindly. Suffer me to wish your
> Lordship to take heed, and beware that they come not in fair skins, and
> prove adders, with some good outward quality (and therefore may allow
> liking), and have an inward infection that (in time) shall poison a house-
> hold. God keep your Lordship from such serpents. And such as knows you
> throughly doubts not of your Lordship's constancy. You are able to dis-
> cern colors, good from bad, and not unable to stand by yourself.

The letter then ends abruptly with a renewal, still conditional, of this
bizarre offer of service: "I will never leave to honor your Lordship, if
you will license me in this sort to love you."

It is hardly surprising that Gilbert's father, towards the end of his life,
had used Topcliffe "most unkindly." One has to wonder, too, what the
new earl and countess made of Topcliffe's offer. They probably decided
that for the time being he was a useful ally to have because, with his
family's long connection with the Talbots, they could probably count on
his loyalty, whatever his personal opinons.

They certainly needed allies. The seventh earl has a reputation for
quarrelsomeness, but he inherited most of his quarrels from the divisions
brought into the Talbot family by his father's second marriage to Elizabeth Cavendish, the famous Bess of Hardwick. Those divisions, added
to the religious divisions in his family, its territory, and the country at
large, brought the earl more than once into some danger, and in at least
one case there is evidence that Topcliffe—as he promised—was willing
to take his part, and look after him.

One of the earl's inherited quarrels involved him with an equally
quarrelsome neighbor. Sir Thomas Stanhope, some years earlier, had
built a weir across the river Trent. On the death of Earl George, Sir
Thomas—with Cecil backing—moved to diminish Earl Gilbert's influence in Nottinghamshire, and in particular to keep him out of his father's
lord-lieutenancy of the county. The resulting quarrel flared into a feud,
and came to a climax when Earl Gilbert's men, just before Easter 1593,
destroyed Sir Thomas's weir. Sir Thomas then saw to it that this operation was prosecuted as a riot in Star Chamber, and although the Queen
would not allow him to prosecute Earl Gilbert, a number of Gilbert's
men were fined.[3]

One of them was a Catholic bailiff or steward called Nicholas Williamson, whose wife had a little dog that a priest kicked down stairs and killed because it barked during mass.[2] Finding himself heavily fined and abandoned by the Shrewsburys, Williamson went overseas where he met the Scottish Jesuit, William Creighton, and other exiles. Returning to England *en route* to Scotland, he was arrested at Carlisle in early March 1595 in company with a young Scot called Law, who later turned out to be a priest. Williamson was then sent under guard to London, and committed to the Gatehouse, where Secretary Cecil and Attorney-General Coke went to work on him, convinced that he had been up to something that might add up to an indictment for treason, though Cecil—to judge by the documents—was more interested in finding out exactly what had happened to Sir Thomas's weir.

When Williamson did not respond to their questions as readily as they would have liked, they decided—acting on the Queen's advice—to frighten him into speaking more freely by putting him in the Tower.[3]

The Earl of Shrewsbury's reaction to Williamson's arrest had been immediately to send some of his people to secure the Talbot deeds and other business documents that had been in Williamson's possession, including letters from the earl and countess. This action struck a number of people, including Robert Cecil, as suspicious, and the rumors started. An ex-mayor of Nottingham called Bonner was reported as saying that Williamson, the earl's man, was arrested for treason, and this would hurt the earl greatly, "for that he had often given his word that he was a good subject—such things as that brought the Duke of Norfolk to his death."[4] A couple of years earlier, a man from Derby called Bainbridge had sent a list of "notorious papists and dangerous recusants" in Lord Shrewsbury's household, including Williamson, to Lord

---

[3]For an account of this affair, see MacCaffrey.

[2]NA/SP12/252/13,14 (1595). "Mr. Williamson dwelleth at Sawley five miles from Mr. Palmer's, & there kept a priest called John Redford alias Tanfield until a certain time that Mrs. Williamson having a little dog which barked & made a great noise at mass-time, the said Tanfield spurned him down the stairs with his foot & killed him, for which cause she fell out with the priest; and that house is seldom without another." [Marginal note: "Mr. Williamson is fled beyond sea & was a chief man with the Earl of Shrewsbury."] Although John Redford is described as a seminary priest in a report of Newall the pursuivant (Strype 1, 4.307), he is not listed in Anstruther. He was probably a Marian priest.

[3]The story of Williamson's arrest, imprisonment, and interrogation can be read in *Hat. Cal.* 5 passim.

[4]*Hat. Cal.* 5.135 (8 March).

Burghley.[1] Since Stanhope was a keen Protestant as well as a Cecil client, and since the Cecils never missed an opportunity to take a member of the old aristocracy down a peg, the Williamson affair began to look potentially ominous for the Shrewsburys.[2] Fortunately for them, the Queen, who had always been rather fond of Gilbert Talbot, let it be known she had no interest at all in harassing him.

Meanwhile, Mr. Topcliffe—as Williamson told Robert Cecil in some panic in a letter of 6 June 1595—had encountered Williamson three months before on the day of his commitment to the Gatehouse, and said to him, "Williamson I am sorry for thee. Thou hast been beyond sea amongst traitors, for the which I will now think as evil of thee as I thought well before, and thy Lord will abhor thee." But now, said Williamson, Topcliffe was telling Williamson's keeper, Stanwardine Passy, that what he had actually said was something quite different, and altogether more sinister: "Williamson, thou hast been amongst traitors, and hast there played the traitor, and art now come over to accuse thy Lord and Master."

Even worse, the very next day, Topcliffe had given Passy a message for Williamson, telling Passy "to charge and command me from him, not to spare to touch or accuse any whomsoever with any matter I could of state, and if I did, he would help to hang me." Topcliffe also told Passy that if he saw any of Williamson's friends pass his window, and raise their hats to him, he should arrest them on the spot and bring them to him.[3]

The reason for Williamson's panic was that Topcliffe, well-informed as always, was right. Just a few days earlier, Williamson had agreed to give damaging evidence against the earl in the matter of the weir, and Topcliffe was letting him know there would be a very high price to pay for that. What seems not to have occurred to Williamson was that

---

[1]NA/SP12/241/25 (25 January 1592).

[2]As indeed it was. On 21 June, Robert Cecil wrote personally to Williamson in the Tower, inviting him to tell everything he knew, and covering his tracks by instructing Williamson to return his letter with his reply (*Hat. Cal.* 5.251). An undated, unsigned memorandum from this period in the Hatfield papers, "The Earl of Shrewsbury's Causes" (*Hat. Cal.* 5.526–28) sets out the earl's guilt or otherwise in a list of propositions, pro & con, centering on the earl's tolerating papists in his entourage, on the business of the Stanhopes and the weir, and on the earl's move to retrieve documents after Williamson's arrest. It is a hostile document, leading one to think that the whole Williamson business was really a characteristic Cecil operation aimed at incriminating the Shrewsburys. Why else is this document at Hatfield?

[3]Hatfield 33/81 (*Hat. Cal.* 5.233: 6 June 95.).

Topcliffe was using him as a means of alerting the people who were manipulating him against the earl to the fact that the earl had friends who knew exactly what his enemies were up to.

Sure enough, after a few weeks Robert Cecil lost all interest in interrogating Williamson, either about the weir or about possible treasons, and he let it be known that there was no intention of prosecuting the earl. By 9 July, his brother, Sir Thomas Cecil, was saying, "I am very glad to hear by your letters that the earl is not to be touched *in capite*, whereas here it was in common report doubted, by reason of Williamson's committing to the Tower."[1]

Williamson, who had thought he was going to talk himself into freedom by accusing others, the earl and countess among them, was now told that he had confessed to nothing but "toys and trifles,"[2] and found himself forgotten and abandoned in the Tower. There he stayed until he was released sometime in 1598.[3]

It looks very much as if the Queen, after one of her conversations with Mr. Topcliffe, had told Cecil to back off.[4]

*****

To return now to 1590–91, when Topcliffe interrogated Oliver Cottam at York in May 1590, one of the things he wanted to know was whether Cottam knew a priest called George Beesley. Beesley was another Lancashire man, born 1562 at Goosenargh. He was educated at the Rheims seminary, ordained in March 1587, and sent to England, 2 November 1588. In May 1590, therefore, Topcliffe was on his trail, and in December, just about the time that he was writing his peculiar letter to the new Earl of Shrewsbury, he captured him.

The exact date of the capture is not known, but it was before 21 December when the Council issued a warrant to the Lieutenant of the Tower instructing him to receive George Beesley into custody from the bearer of the warrant, and to commit him close prisoner "in such sort that he may not have conference with any, and that no person whatsoever may be permitted to have access unto him." It is a reasonable

---

[1] *Hat. Cal.* 5.273.

[2] *Hat. Cal.* 5.302.

[3] *Hat. Cal.* 8.430.

[4] All this happened, too, as we shall see, at a time when Topcliffe was himself recently out of prison, and supposed to be out of favor. See below, 302ff.

assumption that Topcliffe was the bearer of the warrant—one of the news reports asserts that Topcliffe committed him.[1] He remained in the Tower until 19 June, when he was moved to Newgate to be tried.[2] As usual, having caught him, Topcliffe was at the trial and at the following execution in Fleet Street, 1 July 1591.

The accounts of Beesley's death sent out of England agree that he was severely tortured in the Tower. On 10 January 1591, the Council had issued a warrant to the Lieutenant, to Sir Henry Killigrew, Robert Beale, Topcliffe, and Dr. Fletcher[3] to examine Beesley and a companion, Robert Humberson, "diligently" about "such matters as Mr. Topcliffe, the bearer hereof, shall inform you:"

> And if you shall see good cause by their obstinate refusal to declare the truth of such things as shall be laid to their charge in her Majesty's behalf, then shall you by authority hereof commit them to the prison called Little Ease, or to such other ordinary place of punishment as hath been accustomed to be used.[4]

Once again, Topcliffe is the bearer of the warrant, and the man in charge of the questioning; and although the warrant seems to allow only the use of punishment cells, the clause "such ordinary place of punishment as hath been accustomed to be used" was easily stretched to include the rooms housing the rack and the manacles, and no-one on the Council would have objected.

Some of the interest of this case, though, hinges upon events between Beesley's arrest and his committal to the Tower. A newsletter of 21 April 1591 says that, "Mr. Beesley was kept in Topcliffe's house, tied by the neck with a chain and in a cellar, to make him confess where he had been harbored."[5] This incarceration in Topcliffe's house could only have happened during the period between his arrest and committal to the Tower. That being so, George Beesley has the distinction of being,

---

[1] *APC*, 20. 148–9; Pollen 2, 291.

[2] Anstruther, 28.

[3] This was Giles Fletcher the elder, described by *ODNB* as diplomat and author. He was a civil lawyer as well as a writer, and as such took part in interrogations with Topcliffe at least three times, twice with torture, activities not mentioned in *ODNB*. Richard Fletcher, bishop of London, who presided at the execution of Mary, Queen of Scots, was his older brother.

[4] *APC*, 20. 204.

[5] Pollen 2, 303.

along with Edward Jones, Thomas Pormort, and Robert Southwell, one of the prisoners known to have been mistreated in Topcliffe's house.

Beesley was about twenty-eight at his death. He was known as a strong, robust young man, but the effect of his six months' imprisonment with torture, says Challoner's source, was that he "was reduced to a mere skeleton." The people who had known him previously hardly recognized him when they saw him being drawn to execution.[1]

Beesley's companion in arraignment and death was another seminary priest, Montford Scott, whose banishment Topcliffe had forestalled. Scott, who had been in England as a priest since 1577, had led something of a charmed life until his arrest, December 1590, in his native village, Hawstead, Suffolk. Topcliffe was present at the trials, where his examinations of the defendants were read out, and he appeared as a witness. He said of Scott that, "He thought no ten priests in England did so much hurt as he," to which Scott replied , "I thank God I never did hurt in all my life, neither do I care, though you and all the Bench be privy to my doings." Topcliffe attended the executions, which took place early on 1 July, and—as usual—put a *titulus* or title over each of them on the gallows.[2]

Among the Catholics, Scott was known for his devout life, and one of the witnesses says that when the hangman displayed Scott's quarters, the people saw that his knees "were hardened as horn by much prayer." This led one of the spectators to say, "Is this treason? I came to see traitors and have seen saints," with the result that he was arrested on the spot.[3] Back at court, Topcliffe is reported to have bragged that:

> He had done the Queen a better service that morning than he had for many a day before, for he had ridded the Queen of a Papist hypocrite, one who fasted more and prayed longer than any other in Europe.[4]

Between the arrest and execution of Beesley and Scott, Topcliffe attended to two other cases. In the first, a priest called Roger Dickenson, alias Richard Johnson, and the layman who had assisted him, a poor farmer called Ralph Milner, having been arrested in Hampshire, were

---

[1]Challoner, 167–8.

[2]Anstruther, 303–4; Pollen 2, 300, 291–2.

[3]Pollen 2, 303.

[4]Pollen 1, 203. At Scott's trial, Topcliffe said that it was good policy to put him to death because his austere life was a way to draw people to him, that he was accounted to be a saint (Pollen 2, 291).

sent up to London, January 1591, for interrogation. According to Fr. Thomas Stanney, S.J., who knew them both well, while in London they "were subjected to divers tortures," and while it is not certain, it is very probable that at this period Topcliffe was responsible. After six months in London, Dickenson and Milner were sent back to Winchester for trial. As usual, they were found guilty, and executed 7 July 1591.[1]

There is no doubt about Topcliffe's role in the second pair of cases. In Yorkshire, March 1591, a priest called Robert Thorpe was arrested early on Palm Sunday morning in the house of a well-to-do elderly yeoman, Thomas Watkinson. After brief imprisonment in York, Thorpe and Watkinson were sent up to London. There they were interrogated under torture by Topcliffe, and when they were sent back to York for trial, Topcliffe went with them, for we find him in York sitting with the Council there, 21 and 24 May, interrogating prisoners, Thorpe among them. The trials of Thorpe and Watkinson followed, and they were executed in York, 31 May, Topcliffe present.[2]

*****

The next case is one of the most important in the Topcliffe dossier. Thomas Pormort was a north-country man, probably from Little Limber in Lincolnshire. He was educated at Trinity college, Cambridge, and John Whitgift, archbishop of Canterbury, was his godfather—hence, presumably, his later adoption of Whitgift as an alias. Despite all that, he left England for Rheims, arriving there in January 1581, going on to Rome in March, where he entered the English College. He was ordained priest in the Lateran, August 1587, and after leaving the college in March 1588 served bishop Owen Lewis for a short time in Cassano. He came into England in late 1590. Fr. Robert Southwell took care of him, and established him in what seemed to be a safe position, but in July 1591 he was captured through the information of William Tedder, an apostate priest. He managed to escape, only to be captured again in late September, when he was taken, first to Bridewell, then to Topcliffe's house in Westminster. When news of his imprisonment with Topcliffe spread, "Men stood in fear of his confession."[3]

Topcliffe tortured him by hanging in the manacles or gauntlets for the usual reasons, to find out whom he knew and where he had been.

[1] Anstruther, 103; Pollen 2, 90.

[2] Foley 3.748–50; Morris 1, 1.240; Pollen 1, 200, 202–3..

[3] Challoner, 186; Anstruther, 280–1; Pollen 1, 200.

Pormort was not a strong man. While overseas, he had been dogged by ill-health. Nonetheless, he seems to have told Topcliffe nothing, even though the torture was severe enough to cause a rupture (When he was back in prison, "an ancient prisoner in the house with him, got him a truss made"[1]).

At some point in these proceedings, probably before the torture, Topcliffe decided that it was time to let Thomas Pormort know just how powerful the man in whose hands he found himself was, and he started talking.

Later, having succeeded in getting pen and paper, Pormort wrote out notes of Topcliffe's talk. The original, in fragile condition, is now at Stonyhurst College. James Younger knew the contents when he wrote up his account of Pormort's martyrdom a few years later in Douay, and according to a note on the manuscript, a copy was sent to William Waad, clerk to the Council. Pormort himself brought up some of Topcliffe's remarks at his trial, 8 February 1592. Here follows the substance of Topcliffe's conversation as Pormort recorded it:

> That Topcliffe said that all the Stanleys in England are to [be] suspected to be traitors.
> Item Topclifffe offered this priest his liberty if he would say that he was a bastard of the Archbishop's of Canterbury, and that the Archbishop had maintained him beyond the seas. [*Marginal note:* Whitgift of Canterbury was godfather unto the said Mr. Pormort.]
> Item, Topcliffe told (unto the said priest) that he was so great and familiar with her Majesty that he many times putteth his hands between her breasts and paps, and in her neck.
> That he hath not only seen her legs and knees, but feeleth them with his hands above her knees.
> That he hath felt her belly, and said unto her Majesty that she had the softest belly of any woman kind.
> That she said unto him, be not these the arms, legs and body of King Henry, to which he answered, "Yea."
> That she gave him (for a favor) a white linen hose wrought with white silk, etc.
> That he is so familiar with her that when he pleaseth to speak with her, he may take her away from any company; and that she is as pleasant with everyone that she doth love.
> That he did not care for the Council, for that he had his authority from her Majesty.
> That the Archbishop of Canterbury was a fitter councilor in a kitchen among wenches, than in a Prince's court.

[1]Pollen 2, 292 (Fr. Gerard's catalogue).

> And to Justice Young the said Topcliffe said that he would hang the archbishop and 500 more if they were in his hands.[1]

The few people who have commented on this document have focused their attention on Topcliffe's claim to intimacy with the Queen, and they either dismiss it as fantasy or as bragging lies.[2] But this document, like any other, has to be seen as a whole. It has eleven clauses, and only three of them boast of familiarity with the Queen's person. Three boast of his close personal friendship with her. Three communicate a low opinion of Pormort's godfather, the archbishop of Canterbury. One slanders the Stanleys, and one declares his independence of the Council.

Topcliffe's reason for making these statements was to impress Pormort with the fact that his power was real, and came from the very center, from the Queen herself. Since he and Pormort both knew that once Pormort went to trial his death was inevitable, Topcliffe's only reason for talking to Pormort like this will have been a wish to "turn" him, and so forestall the trial and its consequences.

Something about Pormort evidently led Topcliffe to think that he was not only vulnerable, but potentially a valuable asset. In fact, he was making Pormort the same kind of offer that he had made to Thomas Fitzherbert in Derby gaol. Pormort, though, finding a bedrock of courage in himself that no doubt surprised him as much as it surprised Topcliffe, refused. His refusal no doubt brought on the tortures that gave him his rupture.[3]

Yet Topcliffe's experience had not entirely misled him. Pormort was in no hurry to be a martyr. At his trial he asked if he might be banished; then after his conviction, he told the court that he was ready to admit conference, i.e., discuss religion with Protestant clergy. Chief Justice

---

[1] Verstegan 97, checked with the original, Stonyhurst MS. *Anglia* I, no. 68, f. 119. Also printed in Pollen 1, 210–11.

[2] E.g., Levin, 141–3: "A bizarre fantasy...We will never know who invented this story—Topcliffe or Pormort—though it is undoubtedly an invented story, and it was taken for one at the time." Also Montrose, 200: "Even if Younger's version of Pormort's trial was substantially accurate and Pormort's claim was true—if Topcliffe really did say such things, and did so for the tactical reasons claimed—this would not begin to explain why the fantasies purveyed by Topcliffe should have taken the specific form that they did..." John Guy (Guy, 172) also thinks Topcliffe was fantasizing, even though his account of Topcliffe's words is more explicitly sexual than Topcliffe's original.

[3] James Younger's account attributes a similar motive to Topcliffe: "This Topcliffe spoke to Mr. Pormort when he thought to have persuaded him to recant, in hope to come to preferment by Topcliffe's means, being as it might seem by that action in great favour with her Majesty" (Pollen 1, 209).

Anderson told him it was too late for that, but Pormort's godfather the archbishop intervened, sending his chaplains to him, and commanding the sheriff not to carry out the execution until he had authority from himself.

Topcliffe, stung by Pormort's revelations about their conversation, "withstood" the request for banishment, and put the archbishop in his place by going straight to Burghley for a *mandamus* to the sheriff to have Pormort executed according to his sentence.[1]

Meanwhile, Topcliffe's remarks, some of them at least, had become public. According to James Younger, at his trial Pormort produced both Topcliffe's remarks about the Queen and the slander against the Stanleys. Ferdinando Stanley, Lord Strange, and the Earl of Essex were both on the bench at Pormort's trial, and the Earl of Essex, as one would expect, said that, "if Topcliffe had said so much of a Devereux, he would have stabbed him." Lord Strange responded more calmly:

> "Topcliffe, I trust you know to use noblemen with honor, otherwise you shall understand of it."
> "My lord," quoth Topcliffe, "believe not a traitor priest, who doth belie me."

Pormort, nonetheless, would not retract his words. He was executed 21 February 1592 on a gibbet erected in St. Paul's churchyard, near to the house of a haberdasher, John Barwys, who had harbored him.[2] It was a cold day. Topcliffe, of course, was present, and kept Pormort standing in his shirt on the ladder for two hours, trying to persuade him to retract his allegations. Pormort refused, and finally, "the ladder was turned, and the priest was quartered after their manner."

What, then, do we make of Thomas Pormort's record of Topcliffe's conversation? Recently a couple of writers have raised the possibility that Thomas Pormort was lying, but this proposition can be ruled out immediately as absurd.[3] A Catholic priest, on the verge of martyrdom, had no reason to go to his death with a lie on his conscience. So we come back to Topcliffe. Was he lying? Was he fantasizing?

His statements do not look like lies or fantasies. We can be sure that the Queen really did give him a gift of fine linen hose, equally sure that

---

[1] Pollen 2, 118–20 (James Younger's account of the trial).

[2] Barwys had been condemned for harboring Pormort, but recanted on the scaffold (Pollen 2, 120).

[3] Levin, 142; Montrose, 200.

one day—perhaps lifting her skirts—or even in a more intimate moment—she asked him, "Be not these the arms, legs and body of King Henry?" Topcliffe can hardly have made up so bizarre a question himself. What one would really like to know is the context in which the Queen asked it, and the sense in which she meant it, especially if she was anywhere near the famous Holbein portrait of her terrifying father at the time.

As for the other statements, in Topcliffe's mind they were enormously complimentary to a woman whom he seems to have adored, and in one case he claims to have paid her the compliment personally, on the spot, so to speak. Indeed, that may have been the occasion when she asked him the question about her father.

No-one can know for certain whether these statements are true, but there is no ground at all for ruling them out *a priori*. The Queen was a good deal less self-protective in these matters than contemporary American scholars think. Two famous examples come to mind, the first described by the French ambassador, Monsieur de Maisse, in his memoirs.

The date is 8 December 1597, and the ambassador is having his first audience with the Queen in the Privy Chamber. Others are present, but he and the Queen are together, separated from others in the room:

> She was strangely attired in a dress of silver cloth, white and crimson, or silver 'gauze', as they call it. This dress had slashed sleeves lined with red taffeta, and was girt about with other little sleeves that hung down to the ground, which she was for ever twisting and untwisting. She kept the front of her dress open, and one could see the whole of her bosom, and passing low, and often she would open the front of this robe with her hands as if she was too hot. The collar of the robe was very high, and the lining of the inner part all adorned with little pendants of rubies and pearls, very many, but quite small. She had also a chain of rubies and pearls about her neck. On her head she wore a garland of the same material and beneath it a great reddish-colored wig, with a great number of spangles of gold and silver, and hanging down over her forehead some pearls, but of no great worth. On either side of her ears hung two great curls of hair, almost down to her shoulders and within the collar of her robe, spangled at the top of her head. Her bosom is somewhat wrinkled as well as [one can see for] the collar that she wears round her neck, but lower down her flesh is exceeding white and delicate, as far as one could see.[1]

On 15 December, he had another audience. Mildmay met his coach, and took him to the Presence Chamber. There the Lord Chamberlain met

[1]Maisse, 25.

him, and took him to the Privy Chamber, "where the Queen was standing by a window:"

> She looked in better health than before. She was clad in a dress of black taffeta. She had a petticoat of white damask, girdled, and open in front, as was also her chemise, in such a manner that she often opened this dress and one could see all her belly, and even to her navel. Her head tire was the same as before. She had bracelets of pearl on her hands, six or seven rows of them...When she raises her head she has a trick of putting both hands on her gown and opening it insomuch that all her belly can be seen.[1]

What is interesting about this account is that although the Queen is off apart with the ambassador on both occasions when the dress-opening happens, there are other people in the chamber. If the Queen was as easy-going as this about exposing herself, then the men who were close to her—Leicester and Hatton, for instance—no doubt caressed her as intimately as Topcliffe claims to have done. We should remember, too, that Elizabethan women's clothing could be extremely constricting and uncomfortable. Opening it must have been a great relief.

The second example is provided by a famous, much-quoted reminiscence of Sir John Harington, the Queen's godson. Apparently, he asked Sir Christopher Hatton outright whether he had ever gone the distance with the Queen, and Hatton's response bears thinking about:

> The man lives yet to whom Sir Christopher Hatton, the goodliest man of person of all the favorites her Highness hath had, did swear voluntarily, deeply, and with vehement asseveration, that he never had any carnal knowledge of her body, and this was also my mother's opinion, who was till the twentieth year of her Majesty's reign of her Privy Chamber, and had been sometime her bedfellow.[2]

Sir John's mother's opinion is neither here nor there, but Sir Christopher's answer sounds—to a twenty-first-century reader—very much like a nuanced denial. "Carnal knowledge of her body" meant what today would be described as having sex. Hatton's denial of that by no means rules out other intimacies.[3]

---

[1]Maisse, 36–7. Martin has a good account of the ambassador's experience, and gives much of the original French.

[2]Harington 4, 40–1. "The man [who] lives yet" was Harington himself.

[3]In October 1572, Edward Dyer wrote to Hatton on the subject of Hatton's worry about a rival for the Queen's affections, and what if anything he should do about it. Dyer's advice was to act as though nothing were happening. "For though in the beginning when

The real interest of Pormort's notes is Topcliffe's revelation that he worked for the Queen and derived his authority directly from her, only secondarily from the Council. In making his notes, and bringing them up at his trial Pormort, like Edward Jones, was trying to discredit the whole legal process, and like Jones, he failed. His revelations produced no consequences for Topcliffe, although one suspects that some members of the Council remembered his insult to them.

One reason why Topcliffe enjoyed a kind of immunity at the time of Pormort's trial may have been that he had recently enjoyed a major triumph when he attended seven executions in one day. On 10 December, three priests (Edmund Gennings, Polydore Plasden, Eustace White) and four laymen (Swithin Wells, Brian Lacey, Sydney Hodgson, John Mason) were executed in London with Topcliffe present and presiding at all the executions.

Eustace White, a Lincolnshire man, had been sent to England from Rome via Rheims in November 1588. He survived until late summer 1591 when, traveling westwards from London, he fell in company with a lawyer whom he mistakenly took to be a Catholic. The lawyer reported him to be a seminary priest, and he was captured at Blandford, Dorsetshire. He was then sent up to London, and committed to Bridewell, 18 September. On 10 October, the Council first instructed Justice Young, Giles Fletcher, Mr. Braithwait, and Topcliffe to interrogate him; they followed up this warrant with another, 25 October, ordering torture by the manacles. The torture followed, 29 October, when Topcliffe kept him in the manacles for eight hours.[1]

On 23 November, White managed to get a letter out of the prison, asking Fr. Henry Garnet, S.J. for help. Like so many prisoners he had been robbed by the crown's "officers" of everything he had—his horse, his

---

her Majesty sought you (after her good manner), she did bear with rugged dealing of yours, until she had what she fancied, yet now, after satiety and fullness, it will rather hurt than help you; whereas, behaving yourself as I said before, your place shall keep you in worship, your presence in favour...." Had Cardinal Allen ever seen that letter it would have convinced him that the rumors about the Queen's sexual activities were true. More interesting is the glimpse into Hatton's attractiveness to Elizabeth. He had treated her roughly, and she liked that. But as Dyer wisely points out, without the sexual interest, roughness will have no appeal, so if Hatton has any sense he won't even think of trying it on. The letter certainly implies that these otherwise Petrarchan relationships had a real sexual element to them (Nicholas, 18–19). Francis Tregian, the Cornish recusant gentleman who spent 28 years in prison for his religion, was famous among Catholics because, according to his grandson's biography, as a younger man at court he offended the queen by refusing her advances (Morris 1, 1.163).

[1]Challoner, 182–4; Anstruther, 377–8; *APC*, 22. 15–16, 39–40.

clothes, £4 in money plus change, and a silver flute worth twenty shillings. He had been lying manacled in his boots on straw, wearing only his light summer clothes, for forty-six days, He hoped that Fr. Garnet would be able to collect a small debt of £2 for him, and he knew that his west-country friends would help him if they knew of his condition. One hopes Fr. Garnet was able to help him.[1]

He was moved to Newgate, arraigned and condemned, 6 December.

Eustace White's lay companion in the Council's torture warrant was Brian Lacey. He was Montford Scott's cousin. The Council's warrant describes him as "a disperser and distributor of letters to papists and other evil-affected subjects," and like White he was committed to Bridewell and tortured there by Topcliffe, presumably to find out whose letters he had been carrying and what masses he had attended.

The other five victims were all arrested together, 28 November, at a house in Gray's Inn Fields, Holborn, belonging to Mr. Swithin Wells, an elderly schoolmaster with connections to the Earls of Southampton. Two seminary priests, Edmund Gennings and Polidore Plasden were celebrating Mass there when Topcliffe, who must have been tracking them, burst in with his helpers. Running up the stairs, he was met by a young man, John Mason, who grappled with him, and knocked him down the stairs, but this did no more than delay the arrests a little.

Topcliffe arrested Mrs. Wells, the two priests, and two servants, John Mason and Sydney Hodgson. When Mr. Wells came home and found his house ransacked and empty, and heard from his neighbors what had happened, he went to demand the return of his keys and his wife, and was himself arrested.[2]

The same day the Council wrote instructing Topcliffe, Young, and Waad to examine the prisoners.[3] Swithin Wells himself, of course, had not been present at the Mass. Nonetheless, he told Justice Young that although he had missed the Mass, he thought his house the better for it,

---

[1]The letter is printed in Pollen 2, 123–6, and Camm 2, 57.

[2]There are two accounts of this case. The first, printed in Pollen 2, 100–115, is an eyewitness account by James Younger, a seminary priest. A few months later he was arrested himself, and saved himself by informing on his fellow priests and Catholics (Anstruther, 391–3). He wrote his account in February 1595, after he had returned to Douay. The second is in the *Life* of Edmund Gennings written some years later by his brother John, who was converted by his brother's death, and became a Franciscan. There are differences of detail between the two accounts. I have followed James Younger's account of the executions, both their order and the things said..

[3]*APC*, 22. 92. (28 November 1591).

and Young is reported to have replied that, "he came time enough to taste of the sauce, although he were ignorant how the meat savored," and left him in prison.[1]

The arraignments and trials followed quickly on 4 December. They were all sentenced to death, the priests as traitors guilty of treason, the others as felons guilty of being present at a Mass.

James Younger, who was present at the trials and the executions that followed, gives some interesting details. As usual, after the verdict, the prisoners were asked why the judge should not pronounce sentence upon them. Plasden said they had not offended any just law, but merely exercised their priestly function, "which was in all ages an honorable calling." Fleetwood, no longer Recorder, but a Sergeant at Law, knew that Plasden was a Londoner, and called out a reply:

> What, dost thou talk so, Plasden? Methinks thou wouldst better wind a horn; for I think thy father is an horner dwelling at Fleet Bridge.

They all laughed at that. Younger also tells us that as soon as sentence was pronounced, the "catchpolls" who were guarding the prisoners at the bar, began immediately to grab their clothes—hats, cloaks, ruff, handkerchiefs, even the points from their hose. When one of the priests protested, Mr. Justice Wray ordered their belongings returned to them.

The executions, on 10 December, began in Gray's Inn Fields with Mr. Wells, even though he had not been present at the time of the mass (Mrs. Wells had been sentenced to death, too, but her sentence was commuted to imprisonment during the Queen's pleasure. She died in Newgate prison, over 10 years later, in 1602). Topcliffe told Mr. Wells to look at Mr. Gennings, lying upon his hurdle, and when Mr. Wells asked the priest for his blessing, Topcliffe told him that he ought rather to blame him for bringing him to a shameful end. "I count it honorable," said Mr. Wells:

> "Dog-bolt Papists!" said Topcliffe. "you follow the Pope and his Bulls; believe me, I think some bulls begot you all." Herewith Mr. Wells was somewhat moved, and replied, "If we have bulls to our fathers, thou hast a cow to thy mother."

Mr. Wells immediately regretted saying that, and reproved Topcliffe for goading him to impatience. He asked Catholics present to pray for him, and told Topcliffe that he hoped God would pardon him, and make of

---

[1]Gennings, 70.

him a Saul a Paul, "of a bloody persecutor one of the Catholic Church's children."

The executioners then turned to Edmund Gennings, a very young priest. He had been ordained at twenty-three by a dispensation, and at the time of his death was twenty-four. As Younger says, the people standing near him in the crowd pitied him. Topcliffe would not allow him to speak unless he first confessed his guilt. While all this was happening, the second sheriff took the other five prisoners to Tyburn. Once Gennings had been killed, very cruelly, Topcliffe hurried off to Tyburn, and James Younger followed him.

There Brian Lacey, John Mason, and Sydney Hodgson were hanged James Younger records an exchange upon the scaffold between Lacey and Topcliffe, who urged Lacey, the rope around his neck, to confess his treasons, "For there are none but traitors who are of your religion." "Then," said Lacey, "answer me. You yourself in Queen Mary's days were a papist, at least in show. Tell me, were you also a traitor?" When the people laughed at this, Topcliffe said, 'I came not here to answer thy arguments. Thou art to answer me." "I have said," replied Lacey, "as merry," writes Younger, "as though he had been far from death."[1],

When the executioners turned to the two priests, Polidore Plasden was put into the cart first. Sir Walter Raleigh was present, and when he heard Plasden pray for the Queen and the whole realm, he interrupted the proceedings, asking him if he really believed what he was saying. When Plasden told him that he did, Raleigh went on to ask him whether he acknowledged the Queen to be his lawful sovereign, and whether he would defend her against all enemies, domestic and foreign, to the best of his ability. Again Plasden said that he would. The people, knowing that he would not die with a lie in his heart, began to wonder why he was being put to death, and Raleigh asked him why he had not said as much before the judges:

> "I know, good people," said Raleigh, turning himself, "her Majesty desireth no more at these men's hands, than that which this man hath now confessed. Mr. Sheriff," said he, "I will presently go to the Court, let him be stayed."

This was not what Topcliffe wanted to hear. First asking Raleigh's permission, he proceeded to ask Plasden the notorious "bloody questions." If the king of Spain or the Pope were to come into England solely to re-

---

[1]Pollen 2, 120. Six years earlier, Brian Lacey had been betrayed by his own brother (Pollen 1, 71–4).

establish the Catholic faith, would Plasden resist them? To this Plasden replied that he was a priest, and so not allowed to fight. Would he advise others to fight? To this Plasden replied that he would advise everyone "to maintain the right of their prince." This reply pleased Raleigh immensely. Again he said he would go to the Queen, and again Topcliffe asked to be allowed to put another question. Although Plasden would advise everyone to defend the Queen's right, he asked, did he think she had a right to establish her religion and forbid his? To that Plasden could only answer, "No." So, said Topcliffe, how could you defend the Queen against the Pope if he came to establish your religion?

To that Plasden could only say, "I am a Catholic priest, therefore I would never fight, nor counsel others to fight against my religion, for that were to deny my faith." With that the execution proceeded. Nonetheless, it is remarkable that Raleigh almost saved him, and then insisted that he be allowed to hang until he was dead.

That done, they turned to Eustace White, and carried out the full, unmitigated sentence upon him, and with his death Topcliffe had seen seven men to their deaths in one day.

*****

Topcliffe's big day in early December coincided with the onset of an extended period of intensified anti-Catholic activity inaugurated by the publication, in late November, of a remarkable Proclamation issued in the Queen's name, *A declaration of great troubles pretended against the realm by a number of seminary priests and Jesuits, sent, and very secretly dispersed in the same, to work great treasons under a false pretense of religion.*[1] The ostensible occasion of the proclamation was Spanish belligerence, but its real purpose was to reinforce the government's domestic Catholic policy. It described the missionary priests as "a multitude of dissolute young men, who have partly for lack of living, partly for crimes committed, become fugitives, rebels, and traitors." They had been trained as an underground fifth-column of "seedmen" for the subversion of the realm in "dens and receptacles, which are by the traitors called seminaries and colleges of Jesuits."

The Proclamation concluded by setting up commissions in each county charged with taking and keeping a census of Catholics. It also instructed every householder "to make a present due and particular inquisition of all manner of persons that have been admitted, or suffered

---

[1]Printed in H & L, 3.88.

to have usual resort, diet, lodging, residence in their houses" during the past year, and it charged everyone who knew anything about suspicious people come from overseas to report them to the commissioners on pain of being charged as an accessory.

This proclamation was one in an escalating series of enactments against the English Catholics. The one really new thing about it was its vulgar style and its vituperative, scurrilous content. Insofar as it made statements about the priests and the people who supported them, everyone, including the man who wrote it—probably William, Lord Burghley himself—knew that it told obvious lies. As a document laying out a set of administrative requirements, its effect, and presumably its intention, was to recruit as many of the population as possible as spies on their Catholic friends, relations, and neighbors. The proclamation's style and content, taken together, constituted a license for the worst kinds of authorized hooliganism, and its effects began to be felt very quickly.

The consequence in the north under the Earl of Huntingdon, President of the Council there, as narrated by Fr. Richard Holtby in a report he drew up for Fr. Garnet in about 1594, was a state of government by ruffians that lasted until Huntingdon's death in late 1595. Spies and informants were everywhere, and Huntingdon's pursuivants did not merely search for evidence of Catholicism; they plundered people of everything they owned.[1]

---

[1] Fr. Holtby's narrative is printed in Morris 1, 3.118–213. Like all these people, the Earl of Huntingdon, Lord President of the North, has his defenders, most notably Claire Cross, who argued in an article in *Recusant History,* "The Third Earl of Huntington and trials of Catholics in the North, 1581–1595," that Huntingdon was an effective servant of the crown who faithfully carried out policies not of his own devising. Although she quotes Fr. Holtby's descriptive phrase about him, "his bloody and cruel mind," she produces Holtby as a witness in favor of her assessment of his motivation, that he was merely the agent of others' policies. The passage quoted, though, says that Huntington did *not* merely take instructions from London:

> What helps he hath herein, you may consider; for he wanteth not his special authority and commissions, granted him from the higher magistrates of purpose. He is not to seek his directions and instructions, and especially from the old practising Treasurer. He hath his council of chosen men for the turn, his espials, his informers, his executioners, of picked companions, so ready to run, to seek, to take, to spoil and to execute whatsoever he biddeth them, with such expedition, such insolency, such cruelty, that neither fear of God, respect of law or equity, nor regard of civil honesty, taketh any place amongst them: and although himself be of a weak constitution of body yet it is incredible what pains he taketh, both day and night, in watching, in writing, in traveling, without respect of frost, snow and other importunate weather, that a man may well perceive that his malice goeth far beyond his might, yet is his might more than enough, seeing unjustly it oppresseth many (Cross 2, 138, quoting Morris 1, 3.132–3).

Things were no better in the south. "So desperate has our state become," wrote Fr. Garnet, 11 February 1592, "and so close, unless God intervenes, to utter ruin; for more often than not there is simply nowhere left to hide."[1]

This was the atmosphere in which Topcliffe was able to act so arbitrarily, and so lawlessly that eventually even the Privy Council seems to have realized that his wings had to be clipped.

*****

[1]Devlin 1, 255–6.

Eleven

"Very Vile Rumors"[1]

For Topcliffe, 1592 began with the promise of more executions. On 12 December 1591, a party of church wardens caught William Pattenson, a north-country priest, in Clerkenwell at the house of a Catholic gentleman called Laurence Mompesson. Mompesson was indicted of felony, and lost all his goods. He and his wife succeeded in escaping from England, and went to Brussels. The priest, meanwhile, was tried, convicted, condemned, and executed, very cruelly, 22 January 1592.

After his trial Pattenson had been imprisoned as usual in Newgate, where he found himself in a dungeon with seven prisoners convicted of felony. He reconciled six of them to the Church, and gave them the sacrament. The unconverted seventh prisoner informed on him, and according to the account that Richard Verstegan sent to Fr. Persons, anger over the conversions motivated his executioners' cruelty.

It was in connection with this case that Verstegan's informant wrote that although the priests were not allowed to speak at their deaths, Topcliffe would make a speech accusing them of intending to assist an invasion of the realm: "And to that end he fixeth also papers upon the gallows or gibbet." The implication of this detail is that Topcliffe was, as usual, present at Pattenson's death. We can be sure that he would have done nothing to discourage the cruelty.[2]

Another impending execution was Thomas Pormort's. He was tried and convicted on 8 February. Legal maneuverings in hope that he would apostatize delayed his execution until 21 February, when Topcliffe tried in vain for two hours to persuade him to withdraw his report of Topcliffe's remarks about the Queen, the Stanleys, Archbishop Whitgift, and the Privy Council.

Between these two executions, the Council issued a long, detailed

---

[1]BL Ms. Lansdowne 73, No. 47.

[2]There are accounts of Pattenson's capture and execution in Challoner, 185–6; Morris 1, 3. 49; Verstegan, 39–40.

instruction to Topcliffe and eleven other people to make a census of Catholic prisoners in London.[1] But on that very same day, 26 January, the ordinary routine of Topcliffe's police work was interrupted when John Aylmer, Bishop of London, arrested a woman called Anne Bellamy, and imprisoned her in the Gatehouse prison, next door to Topcliffe's own Westminster house. She was the eldest daughter of Richard Bellamy of Uxendon, and her arrest and its consequences would preoccupy Topcliffe for the rest of the year.

*****

The Bellamys owned the manor of Uxendon in Harrow parish, a property of about a thousand acres some nine miles north of London. The manor had come to them in 1516 when Mabel, Richard Bellamy's wife, inherited it from her father, Thomas Boys. There they lived, peaceably enough, until the missionary priests started arriving. Richard's son William and his wife Katherine entertained Edmund Campion in 1581. Robert Persons stayed with them while he was in England, and Richard Bristow, one of the translators of the Douay-Rheims Bible, found a refuge with them when he returned to England in poor health in 1581.

Katherine Bellamy and two of her sons, Richard and Jerome, were indicted for recusancy in 1583,[2] but their real troubles began in the summer of 1586 with the Babington Plot. Five of the conspirators, including Anthony Babington,[3] having taken refuge in the woods north of London, made their way to Uxendon, where they begged the Bellamys for food. By then William was dead. Katherine Bellamy allowed her sons Jeremy and Bartholomew to carry food to them, with the result that she and they were arrested in the general round-up, and imprisoned in the Tower. Bartholomew and his mother died there. Bartholomew was "tortured with such cruelty that he sank under it and died," though the government put it out that he hanged himself.[4] According to a note in

[1] *APC* 22. 213–15.

[2] *VCH, Middlesex*, 4 (1971). 260; Jeaffreson, 140.

[3] The others were John Charnock, Robert Gage, Henry Dunne, and Robert Barnewell (Pollen 3, clxxii, & n.

[4] The words are Fr. Weston's in his autobiography (Morris 1, 2.187; Weston, 104). The son's name is not given in the Morris translation; Morris suggests it must have been Bartholomew who died in the Tower. The Caraman translation gives the name as Thomas, but this is definitely wrong. A letter from George Stoker, writing to Mr. Sebright, chaplain to the lord cardinal "at Bullonia," in favor of Robert Bellamy, 19 June 1589, confirms Bartholomew's death by torture (*CSPF*, 23. 367).

Walsingham's hand, if Katherine Bellamy had not died in the Tower, she would have been arraigned and condemned.[1] Her son Jeremy was condemned and executed with Babington, Ballard, and the rest, his offense having been that he "relieved" Dunne and Barnewell.[2]

William and Katherine Bellamy had three other sons, Thomas, Robert, and Richard. Thomas married well, and moved into Buckingham-shire. On 30 January 1586, Robert was arrested and committed to Newgate for having a Mass said at his house in Holborn by a seminary priest, William Thomson. On 18 April he went to trial, and was convicted of hearing Mass, "and had judgment accordingly." Thomson was tried and convicted the same day, and executed at Tyburn the day after.[3]

Robert was still in prison in September 1588. In the following February, along with two fellow-prisoners, George Stoker and Thomas Heythe, he made a dramatic escape from Newgate, and made his way via Scotland into Germany, where the Calvinist Pfalzgraf Johann Casimir of Kurpfalz-Lautern, known as "the hunter of Kurpfalz" arrested him and sent him back to England. There Walsingham committed him to the Poultry. He was in and out of prison until April 1593, when a commission of which Topcliffe was an occasional member examined him in the Marshalsea. He told the commissioners that he was loyal to the Queen, but that he would not attend the state church. He is not heard of after that.[4]

The fourth brother, Richard, with his wife Katherine, lived at Uxendon after his mother's death. They had five children: Frith, Thomas, Anne, Audrey, and Mary.

Anne seems to have been the oldest daughter. Why Aylmer, Bishop of London, arrested her, and why she was imprisoned in the Gatehouse is not known. The information about Topcliffe's subsequent dealings with her comes from two sources. The first is a petition, preserved among the Lansdowne manuscripts, that Richard Bellamy's brother Thomas presented to the Council on his brother's behalf sometime in late April or early May 1595.[5] The second is Robert Barnes's speech in his own defense at his trial, July 1598.[2]

[1]Morris 1, 2.48–9.

[2]Morris 1, 2.49.

[3]CRS 2. 248; Morris 1, 2. 49–51; Anstruther, 351.

[4]*CSPF*, 23.364ff. (John Casimir to Walsingham. Heidelberg. 4 July 1589); Ellesmere, 66–7.

Robert Barnes was a gentleman-retainer or servant of Anthony Browne, 1st Viscount Montagu and his family. He had a number of aliases, and is consequently a rather elusive character, but he was one of an elite group of Catholic gentlemen who acted as couriers and guides for the seminary priests and the Jesuits as they came into England. Anne Bellamy accused him of traveling abroad with George Birket, afterwards archpriest in succession to George Blackwell. He may have been the Mr. Barnes who was with Fr. Persons in Tuttlefields when a search-party arrived, and Persons escaped by running to the haymow. He comes into this story because Anne Bellamy accused him of receiving priests at his house, a felony for which Topcliffe hoped to secure his conviction, and so acquire his property. He arrested him, 5 June 1594.[3]

Let Mr Barnes begin the story:

> The first original of all my troubles proceeded from Anne Bellamy, the daughter of Richard Bellamy, of Uxenden, in the county of Middlesex, who, about the twenty-sixth of January last past was six years, was committed to the Gatehouse prisoner by my late lord of London; where she lay not the space of six weeks, but was found in most dishonest order; and before six weeks more, being with child, was delivered by Mr. Topcliffe's means, upon bail, not to depart above one mile from the city.

The bare outline of events is plain enough. Having been arrested and imprisoned in the Gatehouse, within six weeks Anne Bellamy was enjoying sexual relations with one or more people. That is the meaning of "found in most dishonest order." Six weeks later, she was visibly pregnant, and on Topcliffe's orders was released on a bond of £200 not to go more than a mile out of the city (She could not, therefore, go home). Until some time in late June she lived in Holborn with one Mr. Bashford, and during that time she collaborated with Topcliffe and his man Nicholas Jones (an under-keeper at the Gatehouse) in a scheme to entrap and arrest Fr. Robert Southwell, S.J. The scheme was successful, and, as we have seen, Southwell was captured at Anne Bellamy's parents' home, Uxendon Manor, 26 June.

---

[5]BL Ms. Lansdowne 73.47. Thomas Bellamy's letter to the Council, 11 June 1595, dates the presentation of the petition. A note by Richard Bellamy at the end of the petition mentioning his family's arrest was written after July 1594. The body of the petition could have been written somewhat earlier.

[2]Printed in Dodd, 3.cxci-ccxii, Appendix, No. xxxvii. The original is in Stonyhurst Ms. Anglia A.ii.41.

[3]CRS 5, 242.

Inconsistencies of date and detail make it difficult to reconstruct the whole scheme, but its general outline is clear. Topcliffe primed Anne Bellamy with information about Southwell. When her sisters, and then her brother Thomas, visited her, she passed this information on to them. He was living, she said, in Holborn, and she asked them to let her know should he ever arrange to visit their home, because she would break her bond to see him there. She even tried to persuade her brother to visit Southwell with her, but he (very wisely) refused. Nonetheless, a meeting somehow took place between Thomas Bellamy and Robert Southwell, and they arranged that Southwell, who was leaving for Warwickshire, would ride to Uxendon with Thomas on the first stage of his journey to Warwickshire.

In all innocence, Thomas then told his sister about this plan. She notified Topcliffe, who had men and horses in readiness at Greenwich. He captured Southwell at Uxendon on the night of 25–26 June within twelve hours of his arrival at the house.

There is more here than meets the eye. If Topcliffe knew so much about Southwell's whereabouts, why did he not simply pick him up? Christopher Devlin suggests that if Southwell was living in Holborn, he was probably staying at Southampton House, a place which even Topcliffe could not raid. Hence the elaborate scheme.[1]

The standard interpretation of this story used to be that either Topcliffe or Jones seduced, perhaps raped, Anne Bellamy, then blackmailed her into betraying Southwell and her family.[2] Before jumping to conclusions, though, one would like to know how she came to be arrested in the first place, because the fact of her arrest implies that she was already living apart from her family, who were in continual danger of search and arrest at Uxendon. Is that why she was away from home? She was an unmarried woman of twenty-nine whose behavior does not suggest that she was altogether a victim.

The well-informed Barnes did not think so. At his trial, he told the court that she provided Topcliffe with a letter, "giving him the way to the house, giving him marks to know the house by, and directing him right unto a secret place within the house." Even her own family, once they had put together the story, and her part in it, suspected that she had intended to "entrap" her father into giving her "a good child's portion."[3] In fact, it is possible, even probable, that the plan to arrest

---

[1]Devlin 1, 277.

[2]For example, Morris 1, 2.51–2, Devlin 1, 275–6, and Swärdh, 57ff.

Southwell partly originated with Anne Bellamy, that like Thomas Fitzherbert, finding herself in a difficult position, she decided to preserve herself by betraying her family.

The advantage of the scheme for Topcliffe was that besides capturing Southwell, he would have the Catholic Bellamys in his grip, either to be used or destroyed. Meanwhile, he had a pregnant woman on his hands to be provided for. Legally speaking, she was the Queen's prisoner, and therefore under her protection. With Southwell caught and imprisoned, Topcliffe immediately set about solving the problem set by Anne Bellamy and her condition.

Because Anne had arranged Southwell's visit to Uxendon—an action that brought her within reach of the law—Topcliffe arrested her again, "to color this foul fact," as Barnes put it. Then he wrote to Anne's mother from his Westminster house, 30 June, assuring her that he had spoken favorably of her to the Queen that very day, and that despite recent events neither she nor her children had anything to fear:

> Mistress Bellamy, it may be that I did leave you in fear the other night for the cause that fell out in your house, better known to yourself than to any of us that went there; but because I myself found you carried a duty and reverence to the name of my sovereign Queen and yours, and showed the fruit of obedience, you know wherein I presumed to adventure to show you more favor than like offenders unto you have had showed in like cause, and your sons and your household for your sake. For I know her Majesty's pleasure is, and so hath always been my disposition, to make a difference of offenders and offenses, and between those that owe duty and perform duty to her Majesty, and such as show malice unto her in word and deed. This day I have made her privy of your faithful doings (which traitorous Papists will say is faithless). Your seeming to bear by this your doing a good heart scented with a little crapulousness, her Majesty is disposed to take better than you have deserved, and I trust will be your gracious lady at my humble suit, which you shall not want, without bribe and with a good conscience of my part. And therefore take no care for yourself and for your husband, so as he come to me to say somewhat to him for his good. Your children are like to receive more favor so as from henceforth they continue dutiful in heart and show; and although your daughter Anne have again fallen in some folly, there is no time past but she may win favor. And knowing so much of her Majesty's mercy towards you as I would wish you to deserve more and more, and no way to give cause to her Majesty to cool

---

[3]Lansdowne 73.47. At first, the family knew nothing about Anne's role in the raid and arrest. Topcliffe told Anne's sisters that Richard Davies (a priest who led an extraordinarily charmed life), who had been at the house that day, betrayed Southwell (Ms. Harleian 6998, f. 23).

her mercy. And so I end at my lodging in Westminster Churchyard, the 30th day of June, 1592.[1]

Katherine Bellamy had already been indicted for receiving, comforting, aiding, and maintaining Southwell when Topcliffe wrote his letter to her indicating that he had decided to treat the family leniently.[2] His letter hints that Mrs. Bellamy might be open to conforming to the Church of England, but the reference to her husband Richard suggests that a more important motive for Topcliffe's lenience is a hope that Richard Bellamy will provide for Anne's support. The letter also reveals that Topcliffe has discussed his treatment of the family with the Queen, and that she has approved of his approach.

As we learn from Richard Bellamy's petition, the result was that for two years after the capture of Fr. Southwell at their house, "Mr Topcliffe stood very good friend unto Richard Bellamy," and the family did indeed remain unmolested.

Meanwhile, towards the end of July, Topcliffe instructed Nicholas Jones to tell the Gatehouse keeper, Pickering, that he had to take Anne out of the prison to be examined by the commissioners. Instead of doing that, though, he and Topcliffe took her to Greenwich, where Nicholas Jones, Topcliffe's "boy," married her.[3]

On 16 August, Topcliffe wrote a letter announcing his plans for Anne that Richard Bellamy summarized in his petition:

He meaneth from the Gatehouse to send his daughter Anne to his sister Brudenell's,[4] and if his Sister and she can agree, there to continue; or else to send her to his own house to Somerby. He confesseth that he hath undertaken to her Majesty for her forthcoming. And that he will answer his behavior towards her to her Majesty. And that he will defend her from wrong against all creatures. He will not regard the speeches of venomous tongues more than stones cast against the wall. He writeth he shall continue 5 or 6 or 7 months to see how God will work with her.

[1] Ms. Harleian 6998, f.21.

[2] Jeaffreson, 1.207. She was also indicted for receiving, &c., Richard Davies, alias Wingfield.

[3] We learn this from Barnes's speech.

[4] According to Maddison's *Lincolnshire Pedigrees*, Topcliffe's sister Agnes married Thomas Brudenell of Glapthorne, Northamptonshire, 2nd son of Sir Thomas Brudenell, of Deene (Maddison, 1000–01. Godfrey Anstruther, though, citing the Brudenell Manuscripts, marries Agnes to William Brudenell of Stanion, Northamptonshire. There was little love lost between Topcliffe and the Catholic or Catholic-favoring Brudenells Sir Edmund Brudenell of Deene threatened "to entertain [Topcliffe] with a case of pistols fixed in his bosom" if he came to Deene (Anstruther 2, 142).

Topcliffe, then, understood that he had to see Anne Bellamy through her pregnancy, but he was not sure of the timetable—and that fact alone suggests that she had been enjoying continual sexual relations with whoever fathered her child. Just three days later, he sent Richard Bellamy a bill for £5/8s/ due to keeper Pickering for her upkeep in the prison, and included a trunk in which Bellamy could send her clothes to Topcliffe's sister. The move, therefore, was definitely under way.

The arrangement with sister Brudenell did not last long. Another letter to the Bellamys, 6 September, announced that "by his appointment and her consent" he had moved her to his own house at Somerby. There he proposed to visit her by the end of the month, "to see how she doth housewife it." Topcliffe added that he had no doubt that after he had gone to Anne at Somerby, her parents would hear:

> very vile rumors of matters that may offend them, and confesseth that in the Gatehouse already where she was prisoner malicious papists have shot their venomous arrows and stinking breath at him, and glanced at their daughter. But he sayeth that he will answer his doings and knoweth that she feareth God.

Other prisoners in the Gatehouse, it seems, knew that Topcliffe was involved with Anne, and the last phrase means that she had become a Protestant. This must have been distressing news to her parents who, at this stage knew nothing about the marriage; but they must have heard plenty of gossip about Anne's condition and the way she arrived at it. Jones himself wrote to Mrs. Bellamy, 21 December, "[musing] that such unseemly speeches should be used of Mrs. Anne Bellamy," but still not admitting that she was now his wife.[1] Topcliffe followed up with at least two more letters to the Bellamys, 12 January and 19 February, telling them that after leaving his sister's, Anne had been living openly at his house. He added that he would "maintain her because he took her into his protection, not without warrant sufficient and upon a good ground"—language indicating that as he had already told the Bellamys he was operating as usual with the Queen's backing and approval. In a postscript he denied that Anne was with child—which was, literally speaking, true since, as Barnes tells us, Anne's child had been delivered at Christmas time.

All these posturing denials came to an end on 12 March when Anne wrote to her mother from Somerby, announcing her marriage, and confessing that she had been delivered of a child "before her time." It seems

---

[1] Since Jones was illiterate, someone (probably Topcliffe) wrote the letter for him.

that one of Topcliffe's Burgh kinswomen had taken care of her and the child.

Who, then, fathered Anne Bellamy's child? As the Bellamys said in their petition, no-one knew for certain. Henry More's history of the English Jesuit Mission, written sixty years later, put the blame squarely on Anne herself and Nicholas Jones, though without naming him;[1] and Topcliffe's letter to the Queen gave Jones the credit for Southwell's capture: "Nicholas being the man that caused me to take him, by setting of him into my hands, ten miles from him."[2] The implication of this statement is that Anne gave the information about Southwell's movements to Jones, not Topcliffe. The Bellamys, too, responding to Topcliffe's objections to their petition, named Jones the culprit.

In their original petition, though, the Bellamys ruled Jones out in favor of Topcliffe:

> For as for Jones, no man suspected him with her until herself writ that she was married unto him. But all the rumors of suspicion of her lewd behavior both at the Gatehouse and at Somerby, were of rumors of unseemly dealings between Mr. Topcliffe and her, which he endeavoreth in all his letters to purge himself and her of, which hath been and is a most grievous corsie to the hearts of her parents, who hoped that she should have been kept undefiled being the Queen's prisoner. And they greatly marvel, if Mr. Topcliffe were clear, why he conveyed her so carefully from the Gatehouse being the Queen's prisoner, first to his sister's, then to his own house, and there kept her with great infamy until she was delivered with child, her friends not knowing any such matter, and he so manifoldly defending her honesty and denying her to be with child until she was delivered, and that it could be kept close no longer.

Topcliffe himself said that he and Anne were the subject of Gatehouse gossip. Her removal to Topcliffe's house in Lincolnshire, and her protracted stay there after she became Jones's wife certainly imply that Topcliffe was the guilty party.

Robert Barnes thought so, too. After he and Mrs. Wiseman had been found guilty at their trial in July 1598, he indignantly refused Topcliffe's offer to intercede for him with the Queen. and told the judge straight that he had proved directly that Topcliffe wanted his property "for his woman Jones's wife," revealing in that phrase "his woman, Jones's wife" a world of contempt and disgust. It looks very much as if Topcliffe entered upon an affair with Anne Bellamy, and when she

[1]Edwards 2, 241–2.

[2]BL Ms. Lansdowne 72.39.

became pregnant, married her off to Jones. It is even possible that she was involved with both of them.

As for the Queen's opinion of these sleazy goings-on, Topcliffe only told the family that "he hath undertaken to her Majesty for her forthcoming. And that he will answer his behavior towards her to her Majesty." He made it clear that he had the Queen's authorization for taking her to his house. In fact, although some writers (Southwell's biographer Christopher Devlin, for instance) assume that the Queen disapproved strongly of Topcliffe's behavior,[1] there is no sign whatever in the evidence of any such disapproval. The Queen merely required that Topcliffe produce Anne if she were needed in court—that is what "her forthcoming" refers to.

The Queen, as usual, had accepted Topcliffe's version of a story, and authorized Anne's removal to Somerby. At no point did she show any interest at all in protecting her former prisoner, whatever the Bellamys might say or expect.

*****

Managing the Anne Bellamy affair, capturing Robert Southwell, and keeping the Bellamys quiet occupied Topcliffe for most of 1592 and well into 1593. Except for attending Roger Ashton's execution, 23 June 1592, he was inactive until September, when we find him working on two ordinary police cases. One of them, as he told Lord Keeper Puckering, concerned coiners. The other was a murder case. The victim was one of the Queen's guard, a man called Crow. If Topcliffe's inferences were correct, he had been "murdered with a pistol in the highway as he went" by James Douglas, servant and nephew of the Scots ambassador. Not wanting to commit the ambassador's servant to prison, Topcliffe took him into his own custody, undertaking to examine him, to treat him "like a gentleman," and to bring him before the Lord Keeper.

We learn this because the mayor of the town where the murder occurred wrote in some anguish about his difficulties with the ambassador. He must have written to the Lord Keeper, though there is no superscription in the document:

> Now Mr Douglas [the ambassador] hath been twice with me about the delivery of his servant, at the first of which times he threatened that some of the people of this realm should be imprisoned in Scotland for his ser-

---

[1]"Robbery, extortion, perjury, even murder she might countenance in her favorites, but against rape she set her face sternly" (Devlin 1, 275).

vant's cause, and at the second time he said that cannibals would not use any as his servant was used. Whereat I was somewhat offended, and said he did greatly abuse himself.[1]

Meanwhile, Topcliffe had also written in some haste to the Lord Keeper:

> My duty done, if ever there were a murdering devil in England, lurking for an evil purpose, and for an evil hour, I think it was this John Douglas that murdered Crow, and so doth his look almost bewray.[2]

Topcliffe's conclusion, after talking to Douglas's "boy," whom he was keeping "in store," was that quite apart from the murder, Douglas and his master meant no good to their king, James VI, and he thought Puckering should be in touch with the Queen and Lord Chamberlain Hunsdon about it. How the case was finally resolved is not known, but it is interesting to see Topcliffe acting, as he sometimes did, as an ordinary policeman.

He carried out only one more official duty in 1592. Lord Keeper Puckering instructed him to find and apprehend a man called Ralph Marshall who lived in South Muskham, Nottinghamshire, fairly close to Topcliffe's house at Somerby.[3] Detained in London by his inquiries about the coiners and the murder of Crow, he sent Anthony Munday ("a man that wants no wit") as assistant in his place. Topcliffe himself left for his Lincolnshire house at Somerby (where he had just moved Anne Bellamy) about a week later.

Marshall turned out to be a man in his thirties, son and heir of Henry Marshall, a merchant of the staple. As instructed, Munday arrested him, took bond for his appearance, and returned to London. As soon as Marshall heard that Topcliffe was at Somerby, he presented himself to him, anxious to show himself as a loyal, conforming member of the state church. Topcliffe, not entirely convinced, questioned him, and wrote out his replies as "The Declaration of Ralph Marshall of South Carleton in the parish of South Muskham, gentleman." He then sent Marshall and his Declaration off to Puckering in London.

The interest of this case is that Marshall's "Declaration" is a striking piece of autobiography. His father, having decided to take himself and his business to France, brought the boy up Catholic, sending him for his

---

[1] BL Ms Lansdowne 71, No. 21, f. 40 (12 September 1592).

[2] NA/SP12/243/8 (11 September 1592).

[3] Ms Harleian 6998, ff. 31–33v.

education to the university at Douay. Then, caught between fear of the consequences of being Catholic and affection for his father (who had been generous to him), young Ralph married into a Protestant family, and conformed to the Church of England. He then tried to persuade his sister to follow his example, but she proved resistant.

One sees why Topcliffe was skeptical of some aspects of Marshal's story. Yet the man was so obviously terrified of the power vested in the name "Topcliffe," both as it might affect himself and his family's property, that it was extremely unlikely that he would renege on his new-found Protestantism.

A major outbreak of the plague in the summer of 1592 prolonged Topcliffe's long period of inactivity. The plague continued into the spring of 1594,[1] and Topcliffe's consequent absence from the London scene no doubt explains a rumor that Verstegan circulated in January 1593: "Topcliffe is either dead or dying in the north."[2]

That was by no means the case, and by April 1593 he was back in London. On 1 April, the Council wrote congratulating three men for their pains in watching and searching Laughton Park, Warwickshire, the home of Thomas Throgmorton, where Mary Arden, née Throgmorton, Edward Arden's widow, was living. They had found "divers superstitious things" and "furniture for Mass," and so the Council instructed them to commit Mrs. Arden and her servants to prison. There is no sign of Topcliffe himself in this operation, but the searchers reported to him, and he reported their activities to the Council, so he must have planned the search.[3] Then, between 10 and 21 April he was busy examining Catholic prisoners with Justice Young, Dean Goodman of Westminster, and others.[4] But there is still no sign that Topcliffe himself was back in action.

*****

Having seen Anne Bellamy married off to Jones and through the delivery of her child, Topcliffe next put his mind on securing an income for the newly-married couple. His first target was the Bellamy family's

---

[1] Verstegan wrote to Fr. Persons, early December 1593, "This time of the plague hath given the Catholics some little liberty to breathe them" (Verstegan, 193).

[2] Verstegan, 99.

[3] *APC*, 24. 148 (1 April 1593). In July 1593, Thomas Throgmorton, too, was in prison, and ailing (*APC*, 24. 399).

[4] Ellesmere, 68,

estate. On 6 April 1593, Robert Southwell, a prisoner in the Tower, knowing by then that further concealment was futile, wrote to Robert Cecil, owning to his priesthood, and asking that his situation be resolved one way or another.[1] Once the authorities knew by Southwell's own admission that he was a priest, his capture at the Bellamys' house exposed them to prosecution as felons with consequent loss of life and property. Topcliffe, therefore, thought that an eighty-acre farm called Preston, part of their manor at Uxendon, would be a suitable price to pay for his continuing protection, and so he asked Richard Bellamy to make Preston over to the Joneses.

Bellamy refused. Instead, he petitioned the Council to punish Topcliffe's behavior:

> in respect that she [Anne Bellamy] being born a gentlewoman of an ancient house, and the Queen's prisoner was by Mr. Topcliffe's means without the privity of her parents married to Jones a weaver's son and base fellow to her great disparagement and the continual discomfort of her friends.

That language, especially "her great disparagement" and "continual discomfort of her friends" (i.e., relations), reflects the wording of Tudor statutes against abduction and rape,[2] and there is no question that in normal circumstances under a law-abiding government Richard Bellamy would have prevailed in law. Instead, Topcliffe invoked the laws against receiving and comforting priests, and by July 1594 the whole Bellamy family except Richard found themselves in prison.

The Bellamys' refusal and its consequence explains an otherwise puzzling development. Topcliffe's period of inactivity ended on 24 June when the Council, acting on information that Topcliffe provided to them, instructed him to search all the houses belonging to "the old Lady Montagu" in order to find some priests alleged to be living there. This instruction represented a major, if temporary, change in Elizabeth I's toleration of the Montagu family's Catholicism.[3]

Magdalen Browne, née Dacre, Viscountess Montagu, was the widow of Sir Anthony Browne, 1st Viscount Montagu, who had died eight

---

[1] Brown, 85. Devlin 1, 299, writing before the manuscript was known, dates the letter to the winter of 1594.

[2] See Swärdh, 70ff.

[3] *APC*, 24. 328. This letter went to Topcliffe and three local JPs. A second, virtually identical instruction went out on 16 July, addressed only to Topcliffe (*APC*, 24.399–400).

months earlier, 19 October 1592. The family, which was immensely wealthy, had shown a remarkable ability, beginning with the first viscount's father, to navigate the political dangers inaugurated by Henry VIII's break with Rome. They remained Catholic. Elizabeth I trusted Lord Montagu despite his opposition to the acts of uniformity and supremacy, and she seems to have been genuinely fond of Lady Montagu, whom she admired. "The Queen commanded me," Lady Scudamore wrote to Lady Montagu, "to signify to your ladyship that she is persuaded she fareth much the better for your prayers, and therefore desireth you ever hereafter to be mindful of her in your prayers."[1]

To understand why the Queen should have suspended her protection of Lady Montagu to allow the Council to send Topcliffe off searching her Sussex properties (something they would never have done on their own initiative) one needs to know just what it was that Topcliffe wanted out of the Montagus.

In mid-1593, he still had two personal problems on his mind. He had not yet earned his £3,000 from Thomas Fitzherbert because although Sir Thomas and John Fitzherbert were dead, their nephew William Bassett was alive and well. Bassett, moreover, must have known what his cousin was up to because, in the spring of 1593, acting in his capacity as sheriff of Derbyshire, he had arrested Thomas Fitzherbert. By then Fitzherbert was in so much trouble of his own making that he had procured for himself a seat in Parliament (as member for Newcastle-under-Lyme), hoping to be protected from the law by parliamentary privilege. Parliament applied for a writ of *habeas corpus*, and had Fitzherbert transferred from Derbyshire to the Fleet prison; but Bassett was able to prove that he arrested Fitzherbert three hours before his election, and so he was denied privilege.[2]

At the time of these proceedings, Topcliffe, although no longer an M.P. himself, caused "much stir" in the House of Commons by accusing Bassett of harboring priests and being in communication with exiles. Nothing much came of these accusations, except that Bassett was temporarily removed from the Staffordshire commission of the peace. Topcliffe was left still looking for ways of incriminating him.[3]

Topcliffe's second problem was that he had still not found a property for Anne Bellamy and Nicholas Jones. By mid-1593, they all knew that

[1]Southern, 67.

[2]Hasler 1.404, 2.125–6.

[3]*CSPD*, 1591–94, pp. 342–2 (Vol. 244, No. 124, 7 April? 1593).

the Bellamys were not going to part with any of their land, but Anne Bellamy had told Topcliffe that Robert Barnes, a well-to-do gentleman-servant of the Montagus, was not only a friend of her family, but himself a receiver and helper of priests. If Topcliffe could incriminate Barnes and have him convicted as a felon, his property would be forfeit to the Crown, and the Queen could give it to Topcliffe for Anne Bellamy and her husband.

Topcliffe's interest in Basset and Barnes explains the raid on Lady Montagu's houses. Her deceased husband, the first Lord Montagu, would have no dealings with either the Jesuits or the seminary priests, but he kept a number of aging Marian priests as chaplains.[1] At least two of the Montagus' priests had connections with recusant families in Staffordshire and Derbyshire, the Bassetts and Fitzherberts among them. Topcliffe thought that by interrogating these old priests, and searching their belongings for letters or papers, he would acquire evidence that would incriminate William Bassett. As for Barnes, according to Anne Bellamy he had been a frequent guest at her family's house, where he had paid for the keep of George Birket, an important priest who would later become archpriest, and so the same old priests might incriminate him, too.

Topcliffe's friend the Queen evidently thought these leads were worth pursuing, and so the Council issued their letter of instruction, narrowly focusing the search upon the old priests and a couple of laymen, and reminding Topcliffe to conduct his search "with all due moderation...with regard to the quality of the lady." He was also instructed to notify the council of his findings.[2]

There was no intention of incriminating Lady Montagu herself, and for once, even though Topcliffe had initiated the action, the Council told him to behave himself and to keep within the terms of his commission. They addressed their first letter to Topcliffe and some local Justices; three weeks later they issued a second letter to him alone. It was similar to the first except that it included specific instructions to search the priests' "studies, desks, and chests...for such writings as may any way concern her Majesty or the state."[3] This second letter had nothing to say about the importance of using moderation or respecting the quality of the lady, and Topcliffe probably wrote it himself.

[1]Questier, 184ff.

[2]*APC*, 24. 328 (24 June 1593).

[3]*APC*, 24. 399-400 (16 July 1593).

An inescapable conclusion from this operation is that the Queen, just as in the case of Anne Bellamy and her family, knew exactly what Topcliffe was up to, and backed him to the extent of turning him loose on a woman whom she had asked to pray for her, and whom she considered a friend.

*****

Sure enough, when Topcliffe went to work on the Montagu properties the only people he showed any interest in were a pair of the priests and, through one of them, Robert Barnes.

First, he arrested an old Marian priest, Robert Gray. Gray was at least over seventy (Barnes says he was over eighty).[1] He had been William Bassett's schoolmaster, and was still in touch with him. Hence Topcliffe's interest. Topcliffe's second target, another Marian priest with Basset-Fitzherbert connections, whom he calls Francis Ridcall, served as a steward to the 1st viscount. He was away at another property when he heard of Gray's arrest, and immediately fled north to Buxton to be out of the way.

We know this because Topcliffe wrote to Burghley describing Ridcall's movements in detail, including the names of the people he visited.[2] The letter is a tribute to Topcliffe's intelligence-gathering system, and reminds one of a line from *Macbeth*, "There's not a one of them but in his house / I keep a servant fee'd." Yet despite very good intelligence, Topcliffe never caught Ridcall.

Instead, he set about interrogating Gray. There were three interrogations in August.[3] The first and second, beginning 6 August, produced nothing of any use against Bassett or anyone else, since Gray stuck to the Montagu line that they had no dealings with Jesuits or seminary priests. But by the time of the third interrogation, 29 August, Topcliffe knew that at least one Jesuit, Fr. Curry, had been in touch with the Brownes. So he told Gray that he had not told the whole truth, and badgered him into confessing that three years previously his master Sir George Browne (the 1st viscount's son by Lady Magdalen) had taken him to see a man who, someone told him, was Fr. Curry, S.J.

---

[1]Anstruther, 135–6, confuses the Montagus' Robert Gray with a much younger seminary priest of the same name.

[2]NA/SP12/245/98 (19 September 1593). This priest's name is variously spelled as Rydell, Rither, or (Topcliffe's choice) Ridcall.

[3]NA/SP12/245/138 (After 29 October 1593). This document contains all the interrogations.

A sinister feature of these interrogations is that Nicholas Jones, for whose benefit Topcliffe had mounted the operation against Barnes and the Montagus, was one of the examiners. Since he was illiterate, the clerk had to subscribe his name for him.

Topcliffe now redirected his inquiries. He went into Hampshire, probably in mid-August, and arrested another old Montagu priest, Anthony Garnet, along with his servant, James Atkinson, whom he imprisoned at Windsor.[1] Garnet had briefly been the master of Balliol College, Oxford until 1560 when the Elizabethan religious changes forced him out. He then attached himself to the 1st Viscount, becoming his steward of the household.[2] He too was a septuagenarian and, according to Barnes, blind.

The person Topcliffe really wanted was Garnet's servant, Atkinson, because Robert Barnes was his neighbor. Barnes owned a property in the village of Mapledurham, Hampshire, and if Topcliffe and Jones could prove that, as Anne Bellamy alleged, Barnes entertained priests there, he could be tried, found guilty, and hanged. His property would then revert to the crown, and the Queen could give it to Topcliffe for Jones and his bride. So Topcliffe and Jones now set about forcing the evidence they needed out of Atkinson.

Atkinson was in prison at Windsor for two months.[3] Jones began by pretending friendship towards him, and then proceeded to start asking questions about Barnes. Finally, he told Atkinson that if he would accuse Barnes of entertaining priests he would be his friend; if not, he would be his enemy and see to it that he died. He even told Atkinson that Topcliffe had asked the Queen for Barnes's property, and that the lords of the Council had given Topcliffe a warrant to search Barnes's house, and arrest him.

Atkinson's response was to write a warning letter to another Montagu retainer, Anthony Fletcher. Unfortunately, the man to whom he entrusted the letter gave it to Topcliffe. After reading the letter, Topcliffe ordered Jones to bring Atkinson to him.

As Barnes tells the story, it was ten o'clock at night, and Topcliffe was lying in bed with a drawn sword. Jones told Atkinson to kneel; he put pen and paper in front of him, and told him to write out what he could about priests going to Barnes's house at Mapledurham. When

[1] CRS 5.287, 362.

[2] Questier, 157, 184–5.

[3] CRS 5.287.

Atkinson protested that he could do nothing of the kind, Jones told him that unless he changed his tune he would dash his brains out, and Topcliffe told him that unless he accused Barnes, he would chop off his legs with his sword, break his thighs, and send him to London, where either the plague would get him or the rats would eat the flesh off his bones.

Not surprisingly, Atkinson, shaking with terror, wrote out the confession. Topcliffe then proceeded to commit him to Bridewell.[1]

In the meantime, someone—Lady Magdalen?—had been trying to alleviate the situation of the two old priests. On 19 August, the Council wrote to both the dean of Windsor and Topcliffe requiring them to place them, "in respect of their age," with some of the prebendaries there or "other sufficient and learned preachers to persuade them...to conformity...and further to examine them also upon such interrogatories touching other matters as Mr. Topcliffe, whom we have appointed to join with you in this service, shall acquaint you with."[2]

Evidently the Dean of Windsor found a way to excuse himself from the task, for a week later the Council sent an identical letter to the Dean of York.[3] There is no sign that he did anything about the old men either. In any case, as we have seen, Topcliffe paid no attention to either letter, no doubt by tacit consent of the Council, and continued to interrogate Gray. On 29 October, fortified by his dealings with Atkinson, he submitted Gray to further questioning. This time Gray wrote out his confession himself. It was far more detailed, and ended by implicating Barnes in the meeting with Fr. Curry:

> But the same day after Sir George [Browne], Fr Curry, and this examinate had been together in conference, Sir George told this examinate his name was Curry the Jesuit with whom we had been in conference at Todham in Dennis his house; and this examinate remembreth that Robert Barnes dwelt in that house, which Barnes hath lands in Cambridgeshire in Granchester a mile and a half from Cambridge; and he remembereth that the same Robert Barnes was in Todham house at that time of their conference.[4]

That was what Topcliffe wanted, and one suspects he used the threat of

---

[1]Although Atkinson's fate is known from other sources, Barnes's speech is the source of these details.

[2]*APC*, 24. 475.

[3]*APC*, 24. 487.

[4]NA/SP12/245/138.

torture to get it. It was on this occasion or a later one that, according to Barnes:

> Mr Topcliffe threatened one Mr. Gray, an old priest of the age of four-score, to put irons on his hands, laying the irons before his face, and threatened to lay him upon the bare boards if he would not accuse me of that [which] Mr. Topcliffe charged me withal.

Topcliffe now committed both the old priests to prison, Gray to the Marshalsea, Garnet to the Gatehouse, where they remained until Christmas Eve, 1594 when the Council ordered Archbishop Whitgift to release them.[1]

Young James Atkinson remained incommunicado in Bridewell until June 1594. On 5 June, Robert Barnes was arrested, and turned over to Topcliffe, who committed him to the Gatehouse, and nailed up his window so that he could not see into Topcliffe's yard. Later that month Topcliffe brought Atkinson's forced statement to Barnes, and asked him to confess to it; but Barnes refused to confess an untruth against himself, because, he said, self-incrimination would be a kind of suicide: "for so I should be the author of the shedding my guiltless blood." Topcliffe then had the under-keeper, Passy, put him in irons for ten days. After that, he tried to bully Barnes into submission, threatening to bring him before a picked jury that would hang him, to send him either to the Tower for racking or to Bridewell and the tortures there. He even threatened to hang him as high as the trees outside Lord Burgh's house, "so as to make his head and his feet meet together."

When, finally, he arranged a meeting between Atkinson and Barnes, Barnes challenged Atkinson:

> as he would answer, at the dreadful day of judgment, for the shedding of my innocent blood...whether ever he saw Mr. Curry, the Jesuit, to say mass, or he ever heard mass, or I served at any altar, in my house, in his life: and he, before Mr. Attorney, denied the same.[2]

Atkinson having denied his confession, Topcliffe transferred him from Bridewell to the Gatehouse where both he and Jones had continual access to him. Eventually, on 8 October, they brought him before a panel of lawyers—the attorney-general, the solicitor-general, sergeants Drew and Daniel, and Justice Young—to own to his confession, but

---

[1] Questier, 249, whose source is Lambeth Ms. 3470, f.150r.

[2] Edward Coke had been attorney-general since April 1594.

instead Atkinson, on his knees, not only denied it, but told his whole story to the lawyers. The law-officers sent Atkinson back to the Gatehouse, but to be revenged on him Topcliffe found a way, says Barnes, to commit him again to Bridewell, "where he lived not the space of five weeks, but was dead and buried."

Barnes's dramatic account of Atkinson's death is verified and filled out from two other sources. On the very day of his commitment to Bridewell, 25 January 1595, an English Jesuit, William Baldwin, was captured at sea by English pirates, taken into England, and committed to Bridewell. Being a fluent Italian speaker, he passed himself off as a Neapolitan merchant, Ottavio Fuscinelli, who could speak no English. As he later told the story himself, he found in prison with him a young Catholic in acute distress between remorse for false accusations against others which had been wrung from him by torture, and fear that he might be tortured to death if he retracted. Baldwin could not speak to him or even show that he understood him without endangering his own incognito. But he managed to absolve and comfort him at night when the other prisoners were asleep. As the young man feared, the tortures were renewed. Fr. Baldwin tells us that, as the young man expected, he died under the torture, but without giving in to his tormentors.[1] Although Fr. Baldwin does not give the victim's name, he can only be James Atkinson. Baldwin was released on 20 February. Topcliffe and Jones killed Atkinson, therefore, some time before then.[2]

The third source is a letter by Henry Garnet, S.J., 23 October 1595, about the torture and martyrdom of Henry Walpole. In it Garnet refers to Atkinson's death:

> It is a common thing to hang them up in the air six or seven hours by the hands, and, by means of certain irons, which hold their hands fast and cut them, they shed much blood in the torture. The force of this torment may be gathered from what happened last Lent to a laic called James Atkinson, whom they most cruelly tortured in this manner to oblige him to accuse his own master and other Catholics and priests, and kept him so long in the torture that he was at length taken away for dead after many hours suffering, and, in effect, died within two hours.[3]

[1] More, *Historia*, 375, quoted by Pollen 1, 287.

[2] Henry Garnet, SJ, anxious that Baldwin should be out of Bridewell before his cover was broken, succeeded in raising a ransom (or bribe) of two hundred gold crowns for his release (Caraman 2, 202–3). He went on to have a distinguished, at times adventurous, career, and died of natural causes, 28 September 1632 (Foley 3. 511).

[3] Challoner, 224.

There is no doubt, then, that Topcliffe and Jones killed Atkinson.

With Atkinson denying his confession, and then dying as a result of his torture, one would have expected Topcliffe to abandon his plan to incriminate Barnes by his servants' evidence. Instead, he decided to tackle another servant, Michael Thompson. He had him arrested by writing to a Hampshire justice and telling him that Thompson was the servant of a man in the Tower on charges of high treason. So Thompson was arrested, and brought to Topcliffe under a guard of three men and a constable.

Topcliffe put to him the same questions he had asked Atkinson. Did he know Parker alias Stanny; did he know Jetter; did he know Curry? When Thompson denied knowing any of them, Topcliffe told him he was a liar, that he knew them perfectly well, that he knew they were seminary priests, and that they all used his master's house. If he would not admit as much, he would go to prison and stay there until he rotted. Thompson, though seriously frightened, was an older, more experienced man than Atkinson, and stayed firm.

With Atkinson dead, Topcliffe wanted Thompson to copy out his confession in his own hand-writing. Thompson still refused, and Topcliffe sent him home, a very worried man. As Barnes told the court, after his encounters with Topcliffe, Thompson "was never quiet in mind, but said he thought he should have run out of his wits." He therefore wrote to the lords of the Council, and arranged to go before them in the fall of 1595.

Topcliffe, of course, heard all about this move, saw to it that a King's Bench attorney and a minister arrested Thompson as a Catholic, and procured a warrant to send him to the Clink prison. He was still in the Clink three years later at the time of Barnes's trial. In the meanwhile, Topcliffe had to think of another way of acquiring Barnes's property.

*****

In June 1594, at about the same time that Topcliffe arrested Robert Barnes, he moved against the Bellamy family. He wrote to Lord Keeper Puckering, suggesting how the family should be placed in the London prisons:

> It may please your Lordship, at my return out of the country this night, I did hear of Mrs. Bellamy's two daughters committed to the Gatehouse, but the old hen that hatched those chickens (the worst that ever was) is yet at a lodging: let her be sent to the prison there, at the Gatehouse, and severed from her daughters, and her son Thomas Bellamy committed to St. Catherine's, and you shall hear proof cause enough, and see it work a strange example thereabouts.

But Mr. Young nor other commissioner must know that I do know thereof, or am a doer in this device: nor by my will other than his Lordship that was with you when you did conclude what should be done at Greenwich last.

Let them feel a day or two imprisonment, and then your Lordship shall see me play the part of a true man, with charity in the end, to the honor of the State: and so in haste at midnight this Friday.[1]

The letter is undated, but must have been written some time in June. The order for the arrest, also undated, probably preceded the Puckering letter, though one cannot be sure:

Mr. Justice Young, or some other like commissioner, do apprehend Richard Bellamy of Oxenden, in the parish of Harrow-on-the-Hill, and his wife, and the two sons and their two daughters, in whose house Father Southwell, alias Mr. Cotton, was taken by Mr. Topcliffe a commissioner, and where a number of other priests have been received and harbored, as well when Southwell hath been there, as when Mr. Barnes *alias* Strange *alias* Hynd *alias*Wingfield, hath been a sojourner in Bellamy's house. And they to be committed to several prisons: Bellamy and his wife to the Gatehouse, and their two daughters to the Clink, and their two sons to St. Catherine's, and to be examined straitly for the weighty service of the Queen's Majesty.[2]

Sure enough, by July Mrs. Bellamy, her daughters Mary and Audrey and her son Thomas were imprisoned. When Justice Young examined them on 18 July, Mrs. Bellamy said that she and her two sons, Frith and Thomas, went to church but did not receive communion. Thomas said that he went to church, and that although he had not received communion, he was now willing to conform completely; but the two daughters, both living with their mother, said that they could not in conscience go to the state church. Audrey had never gone; Mary had not been there for fourteen years, and neither of them would "admit any conference."[3] A later report indicates that, like Thomas, Mrs. Bellamy did, in fact, conform; but although Thomas was released, she remained in the Gatehouse with her daughters, "close" prisoners.

---

[1]SP12/243/26. This letter is misdated in *CSPD*. Why the secrecy? No doubt Topcliffe did not want news of his role in the arrest to reach the Bellamys.

[2]SP12/246/81. This undated order is misdated in *CSPD 1591–94*, 403–4. Morris 1, 2.62–3, printing the original, thought Topcliffe had written it, though the spelling of his name in the original, "Toplay," rules that out—unless a clerk copied Topcliffe's original draft.

[3]NA/SP12/249/31.

Topcliffe was furious with the Bellamys for refusing to turn over Preston. According to Barnes in his speech at his trial, Topcliffe's first retaliatory move was to have Anne Bellamy accuse other people, among them Barnes; and then, since she was his only witness, he "caused her further to accuse her father, mother, uncle, brothers, sisters, friends, and acquaintance, to the number of twenty-six persons." Topcliffe examined them all, imprisoned fourteen of them, and set about trying to force out of them the evidence he needed, starting with her mother. He bullied Mrs. Bellamy into confirming her daughter's accusations by threatening to bring her before a picked Middlesex jury that would condemn and hang her.

Barnes, who was in prison with Mrs. Bellamy, and had the account from her own mouth, says that Topcliffe raged at her, calling her "old bawd, old witch; dishonesting her that she had lain with twenty priests." When Mrs. Bellamy withdrew her corroboration, he determined upon her destruction, first making sure that she was indicted and condemned as a felon.

A report on prisoners prepared for Lord Keeper Puckering sometime in early 1595 by "learned counsel," describes Mrs. Bellamy as "close prisoner indicted of felony for relieving Southwell the Jesuit at Newgate, but the indictment insufficient...This gentlewoman is very dangerous and her house a receptacle of popish priests." A further note adds the information that, "She hath conformed herself, and proffereth willingness to take the oath of obedience and supremacy." Even so, she was by no means out of danger, as another note indicates:

> If the Lords shall direct that there should be (after her conformity) a proceeding against her for this cause, it were meet the witnesses were examined (which we have had no time to do), and that the judges' opinions were had...In the meantime she is bailable by law, the offense wherewith she is charged being but felony.[1]

Of course, she was not bailed, and the Lords of the Council, prompted as usual by Topcliffe, proceeded against her. At the trial, Topcliffe gave "sharp" evidence,[2] against her, and in another survey of prisoners dated at the end of 1595, she is listed as "convicted of felony." The same document has another note on her: "Her Majesty to be moved." The sentence, therefore, was not immediately carried out,[3] but Topcliffe was

---

[1] BL. Harleian 6998, f.230.

[2] Ms. Harleian 6998, f.185.

unrelenting. As Barnes puts it:

> To be revenged, he brought her to that pass, that, if God had not prevented
> her by death, she had now stood at her Majesty's mercy, notwithstanding
> her most merciful commandment to the contrary.

Mrs. Bellamy, then, died in prison.[2] It looks as if the Queen, although
she allowed Topcliffe to proceed against the family, drew the line at killing Mrs. Bellamy. No more is heard of her daughters or her two sons.
As we shall see, when the under-sheriff of Middlesex attempted, in the
spring of 1595, to attack Topcliffe by arresting his son Charles, his
motive was to revenge his friends the Bellamys. Not only had he "sore
persecuted and plagued" the family, but several of them had been hanged
by Topcliffe's agency, and that was why he and his friends would never
give up until "they had hanged the young dog for the old cur's sake."[3]

The reason that Richard Bellamy's name does not appear in these
prison reports is that he seems to have conformed, if only occasionally,
and in any case he was not at his house when Topcliffe captured
Southwell there. Even so, he lost his property, though neither to
Topcliffe nor the Crown, but to a kinsman, Richard Page. Preston, the
farm that Topcliffe wanted for the Joneses, went initially to Stanwardine
Passy, an under-keeper at the Gatehouse, but in 1609 Richard Page
acquired Preston, too.[4] It is likely that crippling fines ruined Richard
Bellamy. He left England for Flanders where Henry More, S.J., claimed
to have seen him in old age:

> "We saw in Flanders subsequently the old man Bellamy, fallen from what
> was a tidy fortune, and become an exile dragging out the little of life that
> would remain to him in a manner poor enough.[5]

---

[3]CRS 2.284, 287.

[2]*VCH*, Middlesex, 4.260, does not think she died: "Although there is a tradition that his
wife died in prison, 'Catherine Bellamy of London, widow, late wife of Richard
Bellamy', figured in a mortgage of Preston manor-house in 1609." Barnes is not a "tradition." He was in prison with her, and knew the whole story and its outcome. Mrs.
Bellamy figured in the mortgage posthumously.

[3]See below, 308–9.

[4]*VCH*, Middlesex, 4.203–11. The Pages owned Uxendon until 1825.

[5]Edwards 2, 242.

Twelve

"Merciless Mr. Topcliffe"[1]

Despite his obsession with private business, Topcliffe did not entirely neglect the Queen's business during late 1593 and 1594. Between October 1593 and June 1594 he interrogated three priests with torture. All three had been captured in the north under Huntington's presidency and sent south for interrogation and torture. They were then sent back north for trial and execution. They proved to be the last priests Topcliffe would torture.

The first was John Boste, a successful and popular seminary priest who had been active in the north for twelve years. In early September 1593, the Earl of Huntington succeeded in catching him. He promptly notified the Queen and Council, who ordered him to send Boste to London under close guard. Boste was at Windsor by 9 October when Topcliffe wrote Lord Keeper Puckering to tell him that he, Sir Robert Cecil, and Sir John Woolley had examined him.

Boste, a high-spirited man, told his examiners straight that for every priest in England he wished there were twenty, and that for every soul he had won for the Church, he similarly wished he had won twenty. When they asked him the notorious "bloody question," he said he loved the Queen, and would take her part even if the Pope himself sent an army into England. But then he spoiled the effect of that declaration by going on to say that if the Pope "by his Catholic authority" proceeded against the Queen to deprive her as an heretic, the Catholics would have to obey him, since neither he nor the Church can err.

"Since their honors knew the world," wrote Topcliffe to Puckering, "they never heard a more resolute traitor...[as] full of treason as ever wretch was." Topcliffe was in his element, and feeling very pleased

---

[1]BL Ms. Lansdowne 79, No. 93.

with himself:

> I dare say they learned to know more of a Traitor's disposition than ever
> they knew before, and never heard a traitor lead to his haunts better on the
> borders, than I lead him.

And then came the menacing conclusion: "He must to the Tower."

Sure enough, to the Tower Boste went, as Topcliffe recommended. He was there until July 1594 when he was sent back to Durham for trial and execution.[1] During that time, according to Fr. Holtby (who had his information from Boste's letters) he was examined fifteen times, four times on the rack, and once by hanging in the manacles.[2] The manacles, he said, was the worst kind of torture, even though the racking crippled him so badly that "he was afterwards forced to go crooked upon a staff."[3] As usual, the torturers' object was not to incriminate him, but to extract from him the names of his hosts and communicants.

It is a reasonable inference that since Topcliffe began Boste's interrogation at Windsor, and recommended his removal to the Tower, he was the chief agent in the inquiries, and responsible for the torture.

When John Boste was sent back north for trial, the second of these three priests was sent with him. He was John Ingram, a Herefordshire man, sent as a boy to be educated at Douay. He was eventually ordained in the Lateran, December 1589. In September 1592, he left Rome, presumably for England, going first to Brussels and Antwerp. But then, instead of going to England, he landed in Scotland, and became chaplain to Sir Walter Lindsay of Balgavies Castle near Forfar. When the mutual hostility of the Scottish Catholic earls and the ruling Protestant party broke into violence in the fall of 1593, Ingram left for England, crossing the Tweed at Berwick.[4]

---

[1] He was of course found guilty and the sentence was carried out the same day, 24 July 1594, at Durham. According to the account of John Cecil, the spy-priest, "When they took off the good father to the place of execution, more than 300 ladies and women of good position (all with black hoods, which with us is a sign of gentlewomen) set out to follow him. Of this spectacle the heretics asked them whither they were going. They answered, 'To accompany that servant of God to his death, as the Maries did Christ.' A minister offered to dispute with him by the way, and a horseman came and pushed him away, and said, 'Begone, knave, Mr. Boste has shown himself a true gentleman and a true man'" (Pollen 1, 286).

[2] For Fr. Holtby's account, see Morris 1, 3. 196.

[3] Challoner, 203. Since the Council records are missing from August 1593 to October 1595, no warrants for torture in the Tower survive. Boste told his tormentors nothing of importance.

On 25 November, after only 10 hours at Berwick, Ingram decided to return to Scotland, but was stopped by the keepers of Norham Castle on board a boat about to cross the Tweed. They sent him to the governor of Berwick. This was John Carey, the son of Lord Hunsdon. Letters from Carey to Burghley about his catch survive. Although Ingram gave nothing away, requests from Scotland that he be used well tipped Carey off to the possibility that he might be important. Carey, though, was mostly worried about the expense of keeping him, and the value of his possessions: "his trash of papistry which was in a cloak bag with him—viz. his mass books, his little God Almighty's oil boxes, vestment, stole, and all the appurtenances to say Mass withall. The worst is, his chalice was but pewter."[2].

Dressed like a Scot, and talking like one, Ingram presented himself as a Scot called Ogleby. Eventually Carey sent him to Durham under heavy guard (for fear of a Scots rescue), then on to Huntington at York, who kept him close prisoner. Ingram refused to tell them anything, even his own name and nationality, but he was eventually recognized and identified. Huntington then wrote to Burghley, 23 February 94:

> Whatsoever he be for his birth in gentry, he is English and not Scottish born. This I may affirm, for so he confesseth, and I think he will not say much more that is fit her Majesty should know by him until he see or feel the rack.[3]

So Huntington sent him to London "to feel the rack," and he was imprisoned in the Tower.

In the Tower, Topcliffe interrogated him with torture, no doubt to extract information about events in Scotland and his reasons for going there. In a letter that Ingram wrote to his fellow prisoners, he assured them that contrary to anything they might hear, he had remained silent:

> I take God to record that I neither named house, man, wife, or child in time of or before my torments. Therefore if any report the contrary they Machiavillianly belie me, for my bloody Saul Topcliffe said I was a monster amongst all other for my strange taciturnity.[4]

---

[4] For Ingram, see Cashman. This is the best account of this priest.

[2] Cashman, 125.

[3] Pollen 1, 241.

[4] Pollen 1, 283. Ingram's letter, incidentally, is evidence that, as in Campion's case, the government continued to put out false reports of confession under torture.

William Hutton, a Catholic prisoner in York who met Ingram after he had been sent back north for trial, is another witness to Ingram's torture:

> They sent him to London to the torturers, where he hung by the joints of his fingers and arms in extreme pain so long that the feeling of his senses were clean taken from him.[1]

So Topcliffe used the manacles on him, not the rack.

John Ingram was a good Latinist, and comforted himself in the Tower by writing Latin epigrams (His holograph manuscript survives at Stonyhurst).[2] These touching epigrams, conveying with wry humor and resignation the state of mind of a man waiting in acute discomfort for death, should be better known. There are even some lines on the mice nesting in his bedstraw. Number 17 implies that he entered the Tower on Good Friday 1594.

In July he was sent back to York with John Boste, and we learn from William Hutton that they put him in Ousebridge prison, "in a low stinking vault, locked in a jakeshouse the space of four days, without either bed to lie on or stool to sit on." He was then taken pinioned to Durham for trial. At his trial, he told the court that he had come into England in fear for his life, but had stayed only ten hours. He had been captured on the River Tweed before he had performed any priestly function in England. When he argued that he was therefore not guilty by force of any law or statute in England, "considering that I was forced for safety of my life to come in, and made no stay," Huntington merely told him he had a witness to prove he had stayed longer.

Ingram told Huntington that in Roman Law the accused in a case of life or death has the right to confront a witness, and he denied having been in any house except the ale-house where he ate and drank. This argument proved irrelevant when Mr. Justice Beaumont ruled that since Ingram admitted to being a priest and being in England, he was guilty under the statute of 1585. The case then went to the jury, and John Ingram was condemned for treason for being in England for 10 hours.[3] The conduct of Ingram's trial indicates that these people *enjoyed* killing priests.

For some reason the authorities took him for execution to Gateshead, across the Tyne from Newcastle, where he died on 26 July. Since the

---

[1]Morris 1, 3.314.

[2]Ms Anglia vii.8, printed in Pollen 1, 270–82.

[3]Fr. Holtby describes Ingram's trial. see Morris 1, 3.200–3.

town of Newcastle was to receive his quarters, the record of the expenses of his execution is preserved there:

> Paid for charges at the execution of the seminary priest in Gateshead, John Ingram 2s. 6d. Paid for bringing his quarters off the gibbets, 18d., and for a pannier which brought his quarters to the town, 4d.—22d.[1]

*****

The third of Topcliffe's last cases, and a fitting climax to his active career, was Fr. Henry Walpole, S.J. He was the eldest of six sons of Christopher Walpole of Docking and Amner in Norfolk, and so born into a family whose combined estates covered upwards of 60 square miles. Insofar as the men of the family followed a profession, it was the law, and Henry Walpole was already embarked upon a legal career that would no doubt have proved successful and profitable when, aged 23, he attended the execution of Edmund Campion. As he stood under the scaffold some of Campion's blood spattered upon him, and in that moment his life's course changed completely.

His first response was to compose a 30-stanza "epitaph" or elegy upon Campion, beginning "Why do I use my paper, ink, and pen." This very effective poem, which began almost immediately to circulate in manuscript, was published with other poems as part of Thomas Alfield's account of the executions, *A true report of the death and martyrdom of Mr Campion, Jesuit and priest.*[2] William Byrd, himself Catholic, set some of Walpole's stanzas to music.

As we have seen, the government immediately began trying to find out who wrote the book and the poems, and Fr. Persons believed that it was because Walpole was in danger of capture that he left the country in the summer of 1582.

He arrived at the seminary in Rheims, 7 July. The next March he left for Rome, where he was received as a student of the English College. By the fall of 1583 he was in minor orders. Early in 1584 the Jesuits received him as a probationer, but it seems that the Roman climate did not agree with him, and so the Jesuits sent him back to France to complete his probation. His probation completed, he was ordained a priest in Paris, December 1588, and the Society sent him to Belgium.[3]

---

[1] Welford, 87.

[2] For an excellent account of this poem, and an edited text, see Kilroy 1, 58–88, and 185–207.

[3] Knox, 189, 193; Jessop, 129..

In Belgium he first served as one of the missioner-chaplains to the soldiers fighting under Parma's command in the Low Countries. They included Sir William Stanley's regiment. During this period, for some unexplained reason he visited Flushing, a town held mostly by the English. There, not too surprisingly, he was captured, and held for ransom in prison. His brother Michael slipped out of England and succeeded in having him released by paying the ransom.

He remained in Brussels until October, 1591, when he was sent to the Jesuit novitiate at Tournai. Then, in mid-1592, he went to Bruges, and while he was at Bruges he lent a hand in the translation of Persons's *News from Spayne and Holland.*[1] From Bruges he went into Spain to help Fr. Persons with the English seminaries at Valladolid and Seville.

In June 1593, when Persons invited him to go to England, he accepted. *En route* north he visited the Spanish court, fund-raising for the college at St. Omer that Persons intended to found, and had an audience with King Philip II.

Here, then, was a Jesuit priest bound for England who had served as chaplain to the Spanish forces in the Low Countries, and who knew all the people in Brussels and Antwerp whom the English government considered a hive of conspirators. He had even been at the Spanish court and talked with the king, and he was a familiar friend of Fr. Persons. Even worse, he had assisted in the translation of a book by Persons. Did it not occur to Persons that if a priest with Walpole's *curriculum vitae* fell into English hands, he would be in for an exceptionally rough time?

Walpole's journey was doomed from the start. There seems to have been no system of planning or preparation in place. He was left entirely to his own devices. When he eventually set about finding a passage to England, he discovered that no French ships were making the voyage because London was in the grip of the massive plague outbreak of 1592–4 that killed over 17,000 people. Meanwhile word of Walpole's intention had spread. Two young men who had been overseas illegally and who wished to return home attached themselves to him. One was Edward Lingen, who belonged to a wealthy family in Herefordshire, and the other was Walpole's own brother, Thomas. Both men had been officers in Sir William Stanley's regiment, and Lingen had even been a pirate.

When Lingen heard of a small pirate fleet fitting out at Dunkirk, Walpole secured passage with them, stipulating (as he thought) that he

[1]Rea 1.

should be put ashore on the coast of Essex, Suffolk, or Norfolk. About 20 November 1593 they embarked, and sailed immediately into rough weather. By 3rd December they were off the English coast, but much farther north than Walpole had hoped. On the 4th they were off Flamborough Head in Yorkshire, and Walpole, who had had enough of the sea, asked to be put ashore.

They came ashore at Bridlington. Walpole did not know his way about Yorkshire, and to make things worse, under the Earl of Huntington's presidency the Council of the North had the Yorkshire coast closely watched. The trio made the mistake of staying together, and within hours of landing they were captured. On about 8 December they were examined for the first time in York, and committed to prison. There Walpole remained until Huntington sent him to London on 25 February 1594.

Huntington's original intention was to arrange for a gaol delivery and trial on 24 January, but he ran into a legal difficulty when the lawyers told him that there was no law under which they could prosecute Lingen and young Walpole for fighting with the Queen's enemies overseas. They could not even prosecute Lingen for his piracies. Huntington therefore wrote asking the Privy Council for a special commission,[1] but the Council, running into the same legal problems, did not send him a special commission. Instead, as Jessop puts it, they sent a special commissioner—Richard Topcliffe.

He arrived in York about 20 January, and took part with Huntington in an examination of Lingen on 21st.[2] On 25 January he wrote a long report from York, as the Queen had instructed, to Lord Keeper Puckering. His letter tells us that the Queen had personally sent him to York, also that although she had instructed him to report back to her through Puckering, he intended to report personally to her as soon as possible.[3]

From Topcliffe's letter we also learn that although Henry Walpole and Edward Lingen resisted Topcliffe's and Huntington's questioning, young Thomas Walpole told them everything he knew. In particular he told them that Henry Walpole had brought twelve letters into England with him, plus nine slips of parchment which were, in effect, safe con-

[1]BL Ms. Harl. 6996, No.28.

[2]NA/SP12/247/17 (21 Jan. 1594). Topcliffe has summarized the main points of the examination in the margin, signing his notes with his half-moon emblem, based on his coat of arms.

[3]NA/SP12/247/21.

ducts for anyone having dealings with Dunkirk and its pirates. When Walpole, Lingen, and young Walpole landed, Walpole saw to it that his brother buried the letters. Huntington, though, persuaded him to return to the seaside, and recover the letters from the place where he had buried them. Young Walpole did exactly that. Huntington, Topcliffe tells us, was so delighted with the recovery of the letters, that he jumped for joy. Huntington turned the letters over to Topcliffe, and together they carefully dried them before a roaring fire. Topcliffe included his copies of the parchment safe conducts with his letter to Puckering, attached to it by his characteristic pink thread.

Topcliffe, though, was not satisfied with young Walpole's freely volunteered information. He wanted to make Henry Walpole and Lingen talk as well, but that could not be done in York:

> Much more lieth hidden in these two lewd persons, the Jesuit and Lingen, which wit of man giveth occasion to be suspected, that labor of man without further authority and conference than his Lordship hath here can never be digged out.

In the margin he wrote, "This must be gotten by her Majesty's power and your wisdoms," and he added:

> The Jesuit and Lingen must be dealt with in some sharper sort above, and more will burst out, than yet or otherwise can be known.

He saw no point in prolonging his stay in York, and concluded his letter hoping that by the time he saw Puckering in a few days, the Queen would have given orders for Walpole and Lingen to be sent up to London. He then returned to London himself, taking with him all the important documents. It seems that as long as Topcliffe was in Yorkshire, he was in charge of the case.[1]

The order to transfer Walpole to London did not come as quickly as Topcliffe hoped; it was not until 25 February that Huntington sent him and his brother south. Then, a couple of weeks later, on his own initia-

---

[1]Huntington to Burghley, 23 February 1594 (Ms. BL Harleian 6996, f.72, printed in Pollen 1, 240–1: "Upon Monday next the Jesuit Walpole and his brother shall be sent towards London, and before they go I will examine them both again, which I will send with all the examinations and papers that be here remaining. But I think Mr. Topcliffe had all with him, or the true copies...."

tive he sent Lingen and John Ingram to London as well. Lingen was examined there on 14 March.[1]

*****

Topcliffe, however, had plenty to occupy him in the interval between his departure from York and the arrival of Walpole in London. On 18 February he presided over the execution of another seminary priest, William Harrington. He was one of six sons of William Harrington, a gentleman of Mount St. John, Yorkshire, and was about twenty-eight at the time of his trial and execution. He was ordained at Rheims in Lent 1592, and had been in England for about a year when Justice Young arrested him in May 1593 in the rooms of Henry Donne, John Donne's younger brother, at the time a law student in the Inns of Court.[2]

When Young examined him, 21 May, he refused to say that he was a priest. Henry Donne, though, identified him as a priest, and said that he had heard his confession.[3] At the next sessions, in June, he was removed from Bridewell to Newgate, and brought to trial, indicted of treason under the statute of 1585 for being ordained a priest overseas, and then coming into England. The trial, conducted in two episodes, proved to be an unusual one.[4]

Having pleaded "Not guilty," Harrington refused to be tried "By God and the country," choosing instead to be tried by "God and the Bench." His reason was that he would not put the guilt of his death on a "jury of simple men." "The bench," he said, "were or should be wise and learned, and thereby know whether the law were a just law and himself culpable: and other trial he would have none." When the court told him he would receive "present judgment," he said he was prepared for it.

His stand on the point must have puzzled, perhaps impressed the court. He was sent back to Newgate. There Mr. Attorney and Mr. Solicitor examined him, and committed him to the Marshalsea prison where he remained, sometimes close prisoner, sometimes enjoying the liberty of the house, for about seven months. In July, shortly after the aborted trial, he wrote a long, eloquent letter to Lord Keeper Puckering, a fellow

[1] Huntington to Puckering, 8 March 1594 (BL Ms. Harleian 6996, f.78, printed in Pollen 1, 241–2; *CSPD*, 1591–1594, 258 [NA/SP12/248/24: 14 March 1594]).

[2] For good accounts of Harrington, see Simpson 4 and Morris 3.

[3] Young's examination is in NA/SP12/245/14 .

[4] The details of Harrington's two trials are from the contemporary account in Stonyhurst Ms. Anglia 1.No. 77.

Yorkshireman whom (to judge from the opening sentences of the letter) he or his family knew well.

His arguments had no effect on Puckering, who merely endorsed the letter, "Harrington's, the Jesuit's, letter to me."[1] On 15 February 1594 he was taken once again to the Newgate sessions, and once again he refused to be tried by a jury. When the Recorder told him he was mistaken if he thought that refusal would save his life, Harrington replied that he knew that very well:

> He knowing that after the Jury should pronounce him guilty, yet the Judge must give sentence, meant therefore to free the jury and to lay all the guilt of his death on the Judge and bench.

A remarkable exchange then took place.

> "Then," said the Recorder, "it is manifest you are a priest, and come into England with traitorous intent, and therefore I will give judgment."
>
> "My intent, said Mr Harrington, "in coming into England was and is no other than St John Baptist's was in coming to Herod; and as he told Herod it was not lawful for him to marry his brother's wife, so I tell my loving countrymen it is not lawful to go to church and to live in schism and heresy. So if I be a traitor, St John was a traitor, his case and mine being all one."
>
> Upon this the Recorder gave judgment as in case of treason, whereat he was nothing dismayed.
>
> Then said the Lord Chief Justice unto him, "You are a young man, and the Queen is merciful. Go but to church, and you may live."
>
> Mr Harrington turned him to the people, and prayed them to note, "What goodly treason [it] was: if he would go to church he should live; but because he would not so do, he must die."

They then took him back to Newgate to await execution, which took place at Tyburn the next Monday, 18 February.

---

[1]NA/SP12/245/66. Harrington, of course, was not a Jesuit. An attempt to "turn" him might underlie this letter. Harrington had first gone to the seminary at Rheims in 1582, 16 years old, moving to the Jesuit novitiate at Tournai in 1584. Ill-health brought him back to England almost immediately. He was arrested, but not imprisoned, being sent back to Yorkshire to his father instead. When the former demoniac girl Friswood Williams was interrogated in 1598 and 1602 during bishop Bancroft's inquiry into the exorcisms of 1585–6, she said that a priest called Lister had married her to Harrington in the Marshalsea prison in 1586, that she had lived with him off and on, and become pregnant by him. The story is unbelievable for a number of reasons, the chief ones being that Harrington was neither in prison at the time nor anywhere near London, and that Friswood Williams, besides being a liar, had become a government spy by 1590–91. Had there been an attempt, after his first trial, either to blackmail him or damage his character? The Catholics had their revenge for this story by saying that Friswood became Bancroft's mistress, and had a child by him (Brownlow 2, 78, 374 & n; Anstruther, 149).

For some time now, the government had been executing priests in company with ordinary felons, and when Harrington's hurdle arrived at Tyburn with him on it, there were ten men and thirteen women waiting to be hanged first, a striking example of the casual savagery of the Tudor penal code. While the executioners were hanging these people, a minister began to dispute "questions in divinity" with Harrington, who told him that if he would keep to one subject he would answer him.

At that moment, Topcliffe, who must have been there all along, interrupted them, saying that this was neither the time nor the place to argue divinity. Since he had heard that Harrington was a gentleman, he wished him instead to acknowledge his treason, and ask the Queen's forgiveness.

Topcliffe's presence at this execution is surprising. It was not the execution of an important person (like Parry, for instance), and since he had neither arrested nor interrogated Harrington, and seems not to have been present at the trial, he had no personal interest in the case. No doubt he had heard a good deal more about Harrington than the mere fact that he was a gentleman. If he had heard about Harrington's performance at his trial, his presence at the execution was probably intended to make sure that nothing of the kind happened on the scaffold. That would certainly explain the interchange that now took place between them.

Replying to Topcliffe's challenge, Harrington said he had done nothing to offend the Queen. With that they put him immediately into the cart with the halter round his neck, and the following dialogue took place:

Harrington. O my loving countrymen, I thank you for your pains and patience in coming hither to bear witness of the manner and cause of my death...

Topcliffe. You are not at Rome, and this is no place to preach.

Harrington. Why, may I not speak?

Topcliffe. Yes, if you will speak to those three points: that is to say, anything that tendeth to the good of her Majesty's person, the good of the realm, or the reforming of your conscience. I have authority myself sufficient to save you, the sheriff, too. Hope for mercy, therefore, and tell us plainly what you know about the west country, where you have been living and conversing.

Harrington. I know nothing, but your mercy is worse than the Turk's. They keep the body in subjection, but seek not to destroy the soul: you are never content until you have sent both body and soul to the Devil. You are a bloodsucker, and I pray God to forgive you.

Topcliffe. Thou liest. Didst thou not say that the Queen was a tyrant?

Harrington. I say nothing of the Queen, except that I never offended her. But of you I say you are a tyrant and a bloodsucker, and no doubt you shall have blood enough. As long as you have halters and hands to hang us you shall not want priests. We were three hundred in England. You have put to death a hundred. The other two hundred are left. When they are gone two hundred more are ready to come in their places, and for my part I hope my death will do more good than ever my life could have done.

At that moment a gentleman called out asking what religion Harrington was dying for. "No more of that!" shouted Topcliffe, "He dieth for treason, and not for religion," and ordered the cart to be drawn away. The executioners cut Harrington down immediately; he fought with the hangman until they subdued him, and proceeded to dismember and kill him.[1]

Topcliffe's intervention had certainly not silenced Harrington, whose contempt for him emerged in what were probably the last words he spoke to him: when Topcliffe called him a traitor, Harrington replied, "Your words are no slanders—I think no man makes any account of them." After that, the best Topcliffe could do was to order that the place be cleaned of blood and other remains.to ensure that the Catholics would acquire no relics.

Henry Donne, in whose chamber Harrington was captured, was imprisoned in the Clink. His father had placed £500 with the City of London, to be paid to him on his twenty-first birthday. Almost twenty-one, he was moved from the Clink to Newgate in the summer of 1593, when the plague was known to be present among the prisoners. Henry Donne caught the plague, and so died in Newgate. As the author of the Stonyhurst manuscript writes, the move to Newgate was "in all likelihood contrived of purpose...to make him away to defeat him of his money," which stayed with the City.

*****

At the time of Harrington's second trial and execution, the Privy Council and its legal advisers were winding up an investigation into allegations by a quintet of Irish rascals that they had been hired by certain exiles (Sir William Stanley, his lieutenant Giacomo Franceschi, Hugh Owen the intelligencer, and the Jesuits Holt and Archer plus a priest called Sherwood) to murder the Queen. Two of these characters, John Daniell and his assistant Hugh Cahill, were "promoters." Daniell had

---

[1] The live mutilation, strongly implied in the Stonyhurst manuscript, is spelled out in John Stow's account of the execution. See Challoner, 197.

started out by working for Essex,[1] but he and Cahill were now in the pay of the Cecils.[2] William Polewhele, whose arrival and arrest in England, December 1593, seem to have prompted the inquiry, may have been another promoter: he gave evidence with Daniell at Patrick Cullen's trial to the effect that Sir William Stanley and Hugh Owen had hired Cullen to kill the Queen.

Although all these men knew each other, the remaining pair, Patrick Cullen and John Annias, were merely freelance amateurs, and they were the only ones who suffered. Cullen was indicted, convicted, and executed for treason. Annias went to the Tower. He was still there in January 1596, when he wrote a petitioning letter to the Council, saying that he was an Irishman in great misery, with no clothes except two shirts which Mr. Lieutenant had given him, and proposing a wholly fantastic scheme to go to Spain and steal an important record book.[3]

Although there was no substance to any of their allegations, the Council took them seriously enough to issue instructions regulating the entrance of Irishmen into the country from overseas, and restricting access to the court.[4] Topcliffe, as one would expect, had a role, though a minor one, in these inquiries. On 21 February, at Burghley House in the Strand, he heard Hugh Cahill's long confession, and wrote it out in his own hand.[5] The important part of this confession, from Topcliffe's point of view, was that two years earlier, Cahill had actually met Henry Walpole and the Irish Jesuit, James Archer in Calais on their way to Spain, and had even stayed in the same inn, called La Plume Blanche. In Cahill's version of the plot against Elizabeth, Fr. Archer was one of its

---

[1] About three years earlier, Essex had recommended Daniell as sergeant of the pantry, and Topcliffe, no doubt acting for the Cecils, had blocked the appointment by calling Daniell a papist (NA/SP12/235/28).

[2] On 27 February, immediately after the conclusion of the inquiry, Robert Cecil requested a warrant for money to be paid to "certain Irishmen," but the Queen refused to sign it until she was assured that none of it would go to Daniell (NA/SP12/247/96). When Daniell himself asked Cecil for financial help, August 1595 (NA/SP12/253/62), Cecil quickly procured him a pension of £40 a year. Daniell's letter of thanks, 6 October (NA/SP12/254/12) included an offer of further service, and enclosed a letter from one Piers Wale, lately come from Rome, and now a prisoner in Bridewell: "Wale calls himself my cousin: I would not have spared him if he had been my brother. I am for her Majesty's service without respect of persons." One understands the Queen's initial reluctance.

[3] NA/SP12/256/33.

[4] NA/SP12/247/66 (17 February).

[5] NA/SP12/247/78.

original inventors who, meeting Cahill in Calais, rebuked him for not being in England about his business.

As for Walpole, although he was not accused of inventing the plot, Cahill presented him as an enthusiastic proponent of it. He had "very earnestly" desired Cahill to perform the promise he had made to Frs. Holt and Archer, and to Hugh Owen. He knew, moreover, what Cahill's undertaking was because Fr. Archer and Hugh Owen had told him all about it, and he would pray to God for Cahill's success for, as Cahill heard him say at Calais, "he went about a good deed."

Then for good measure he added a description of Walpole, whom he knew well, having seen him celebrate Mass at Brussels, and threw in Edward Lingen and young ThomasWalpole as well:

> And he saith that Fr. Walpole the Jesuit was a short well-set, thick black man, full of black hair very like a Spaniard, and about 33 or 34 years old, and that Jesuit, this examinate saith, hath a brother called Thomas Walpole, who served Sir William Stanley, a strong black-set man. And he thinketh that he knoweth one Mr Lingen that also served under Sir William Stanley's regiment, and a reasonable tall young gentleman.

Cahill ended by saying that on arriving in England he had immediately done his duty, and gone straight to the Lord Treasurer with the whole story. What a performance! Topcliffe had no need of torture on this occasion—one can almost hear him asking his questions: "By the way, do you know Edward Lingen, too?" For his own purposes, he added a marginal note (not entirely legible) about Walpole's clothes:

> This father Walpole did wear at Calais a side cloak of English cloth of mingled colors with a hood, with silk buttons [........] cassock of black cloth, and [.....] hose with lace of black silk and buttons, and he exchanged his doublet that was of dark colored hollands fustian with a doublet of Walkens alias Scudamore striped with copper or silver, being canvas. And this examinate [i.e., Cahill] changed his cloak of mingled gray color with a cloak of dark color of Fr. Archer's, and his doublet of chamois skins with a doublet of Archer's....Walpole had a rapier of an Englishman, gilt, and a dagger for his own....

Sure enough, at Walpole's first interrogation, Topcliffe asked him about this swapping of clothes.

For Henry Walpole, the implications of Cahill's "confession" were sinister. In two separate declarations, John Daniell, Cahill's minder and boss, repeated his story of meeting Frs. Walpole and Archer at Calais, adding in the second declaration the damning refinement that they had "persuaded him to come over secretly."[1] A paper written out in the summer of 1594 shows Attorney-General Coke making notes and memoranda for Walpole's indictment from the examinations of Cullen, Polwhele, Annias, and others, bearing on "the nature and atrocity of his treason."[2] It hardly mattered that everyone in the government's inner circles knew that accusations made by the likes of Cahill, Daniell, Polwhele, and the rest were rubbish. This was the kind of evidence they needed, and the Cecils were prepared to pay for it.

When Huntington sent Walpole south on 25 February, the inquiry into the Daniell-Polewhele plot was finished, and by the time he arrived, a few days later the plot attributed to the Queen's physician, Roderigo Lopez had come to a climax with Lopez' conviction on 28 February. Walpole was sent to the Tower, and there he remained close prisoner for two months before the questioning began. On 27 April, Topcliffe, accompanied by Edward Drew, Recorder of London, and Attorney-General Edward Coke, put Walpole through the first of nine recorded examinations, a process that lasted until sometime after 17 June. Topcliffe and Recorder Drew were present at all the interrogations except one, which was conducted by Attorney-General Coke alone. Justice Young was present for four sessions, Francis Bacon and Miles Sandys for three. Robert Beale, Sir Michael Blount, William Daniel, Thomas Fleming, and Sir Henry Killigrew each attended one or two. The final, very long examination has no examiners' names attached.[3]

It was obvious from the start-up in York that Walpole was fitted neither by training nor temperament to withstand intensive, let alone aggressive interrogation. Like Edmund Campion before him, but unlike Robert Southwell, he made the mistake of answering their questions. At his first examination in the Tower he began by answering openly and candidly the questions asked, which were focused upon his travels in Spain and his coming to England. At the second examination, however, he refused to name the people he had been advised to be in contact with in Ireland and England, even though he must have known that the names were known to his interrogators from the letters he had brought into England, and which they had recovered through the betrayal of his brother, Thomas.

[1]*CSPD*, 1591–94, 438 (21 February), 442–3 (25 February).

[2]*CSPD*, 1591-94, 553 (SP12/249/135). The Calendar dates Coke's notes to August, 1594, but with a query.

[3]Pollen 1, 244–69 prints the surviving examinations from the State Papers.

By the fifth examination, 13 June, a full-dress occasion with eight examiners present, no doubt in anticipation of major revelations, Walpole had broken down:

> Craving humbly pardon of all my actions contrary to the proceedings of her most excellent Majesty in this her realm, and casting myself down at your worships' feet, I do intend to declare all things which do come to my mind that might be prejudicial to the estate of the realm, whereof I wish now I had taken more intelligence, from which I withdrew myself for fear of entangling myself, being subject unto strangers with their courses.

By the end of that session, Walpole was casting himself down at her Majesty's feet to be disposed of as it should please God to inspire her, desiring to serve her all the days of his life, and to conform himself to her godly laws, and never more to be subject to the Pope or any of his adherents. "All this," Topcliffe wrote in the margin, "was confessed and written voluntarily by Henry Walpole himself, and shewed unto us by himself."

For the examiners, the remaining four sessions were a dotting of the i's and a crossing of the t's as Walpole told them everything he knew. Fortunately, he knew very little. No matter how keen Topcliffe was to know where Henry Garnet was to be found, Walpole could not tell him because he did not know. Consequently, as a final manuscript of notes gathered by Francis Bacon from the examinations of Boste and Walpole reveals, the examiners learned nothing they had not already known, either from their own intelligencers or from the letters that Walpole brought with him. It was not exactly news to the likes of Topcliffe, Bacon, and Coke that several of their agents were suspected, and it cannot have surprised them that responsible people in the Low Countries thought that the English had sent an agent to kill the Cardinal Archduke Albert, governor of the Spanish Netherlands.[1] The best Francis Bacon could say about that was that if it were true, then the affair had been badly handled, and had "purchased slander without fruit."

There can be no doubt that, according to the confessions, Topcliffe broke Walpole. The question is, how complete was the break? How much credence are we to place in those later confessions? According to them, Walpole abjured his allegiance to Papal authority, and undertook to conform to the Queen's laws. In two articles on those later confes-

---

[1]Walpole's original sentence reads, "The prior of the Carthusians told me that he had heard that there was one in the Cardinal's house employed to kill him, but he knew not which it was" (Pollen 1, 264, who identifies the Cardinal as Archduke Albert, 268).

sions, W.F.Rea argued that they were forged, and that the motive had been to use them to demoralize other Catholics, priests in particular. Rea's case for forgery in the last two pages of the last confession is so strong that I think we can take it as proved.

The case turns upon the impossibility of Walpole's statement, made in the last confession, that he had contributed to the English translation of Persons's book against the 1591 Proclamation, written under the name Philopater.[1] That final confession (no.9), lacking the examiners' signatures, was already sufficiently anomalous to raise doubts, and although it would be difficult to sustain an argument for wholesale forgery in confessions 5–8, if the presence of forgery in Confession 9 is a fact, then the probability of it in others is extremely likely.

After all, if Henry Walpole had really renounced the Pope's jurisdiction and agreed to conform himself to the Queen's laws, the government would never have tried, condemned, and executed him. They were desperate for just such concessions from a priest of Walpole's standing. One concludes that either his concessions were wrung from him by torture, and therefore temporary, or else that they were a fiction invented by his examiners and foisted into his confessions. Similar fictions were circulated about Edmund Campion, and as John Gerard tells us, Justice Young tried to shake his resolve by just such a bogus report of Robert Southwell's change of heart and mind. Gerard was not taken in for a moment, even though Young was prepared to swear to the truth of his lie on the Bible.[2]

Nonetheless, anyone accepting the confessions has to ask, how did Walpole's interrogators break him as completely as they did? Augustus Jessop assumed that they had used torture. Fr. Pollen, looking at the handwriting of the confessions, and in particular at the signatures, is not sure about that, even though the handwriting deteriorates in the later confessions. Both he and Jessop inferred that the real torturing took place during the long period between the end of the interrogations in June and Walpole's removal to York for trial in April 1595. That is very possible. As we have seen, Council torture warrants could be used with a degree of freedom—although it is hard to fathom why anyone would have continued interrogating Henry Walpole under torture after that last recorded confession. If, however, the truth of the matter is that the final

---

[1]Rea 1 & 2, 277–9.

[2]Gerard, 75. John Ingram wrote warning his fellow-prisoners not to believe any reports of concessions by him under torture. See above, 261.

confession is a forgery, and there are forged statements in the other confessions, if, in fact, Walpole refused to answer as Topcliffe wished, then there is no mystery at all about the continued torture.

That there was torture, and a good deal of it, is beyond doubt. Topcliffe had threatened Walpole with torture in London while they were both in York, and the only reason he had Walpole moved to London was to find out what he really knew by torturing him under the Queen's authority. Secondly, someone told Fr. John Gerard, S.J., that Walpole had been tortured, and in his autobiography Gerard wrote that he could well believe it:

> For when he was taken back to York to be executed in the place where he was arrested on his landing in England, he wrote out with his own hand an account of a discussion he had with some ministers there. Part of it was given to me later with some meditations on the passion of Christ which he wrote in prison before his own passion. I was hardly able to read what he had written, not only because he wrote in haste but because his hand could barely form the letters. It looked like the writing of a schoolboy, not that of a scholar and a gentleman.[1]

Gerard's informant told him that Walpole had been tortured fourteen times.

Thirdly, a witness to Walpole's condition when he arrived for trial in York, whose words are reported in a letter by Fr. Holtby, leaves the matter in no doubt at all:

> Good Sir, I thought it my duty both to him of whom I have to write, and to yourself, to send you word of that which I have understood of Fr. Walpole by a gentleman who was his schoolfellow and familiar friend in Cambridge, and lately fellow prisoner with him in York, who having conference with him there hath told me what himself was there an eye-witness of. First for his usage in the Tower, he would not tell him any further but that he was diverse times (my friend thinks six or seven) upon a torture, I think by his description somewhat like that of Fr. Southwell's, by which means both his thumbs were lamed so that he had not the use of them. He was not upon the rack.[2]

Walpole's torture, then, was the manacles, and John Gerard adds the detail that, "as they tortured him more often than they wanted known, they did not do it in the ordinary public chamber," but in his room. Fr.

[1]Gerard, 105.

[2]Stonyhurst Ms. Anglia I.83, an account of the deaths of Fr. Walpole and Alexander Rawlins, a seminary priest.

Holby's correspondent said that Walpole was reluctant to talk about his experiences in the Tower, and that although he said he was not on the rack, and was tortured with the manacles seven times, he would not tell any more. What else Topcliffe did to Walpole we do not know.

Towards the beginning of April 1595, about a year after he was first taken to the Tower, the Council sent Walpole back to York for trial. The jury was impanelled on 3 April. At the ensuing trial there was no mention of any confessions, let alone of concessions made under torture, from which one can only conclude there were none. Walpole conducted himself with great courage and considerable legal skill—after all, he had been a lawyer. Inevitably the jury, as instructed by the judge, found him guilty of the indictment: that he had left the realm without license, had been ordained overseas, and returned to England to exercise his priestly function. Sentencing, though, was delayed until the trial of another priest, Alexander Rawlins, was completed. A weekend then intervened, and Rawlins and Walpole were both executed in York on Monday, 7 April 1595.[1]

It seems that Henry Walpole's imprisonment, trial, and execution raised a wave of sympathy for him in Yorkshire that was sufficient to neutralize any hopes the government had of whipping up anti-Catholic feeling. As Henry Garnet wrote to Claudio Aquaviva, Walpole's skill in argument as well as his manifest personal holiness defeated Huntington, and his speech from the scaffold drew tears from a crowd of two thousand.[2]

*****

By the time the Queen and the Council sent Topcliffe north to handle the case of the two Walpoles and Edward Lingen, he had become very powerful in his chosen sphere of action. Just to run over some of his actions in the preceding years reminds one just how powerful he was. In 1590 he drafted his own warrants for the imprisonment and torture of Christopher Bales, and in 1592—if its style is evidence—he wrote the warrant authorizing him to turn Robert Southwell over to the Lieutenant of the Tower. By 1589–90 he was imprisoning and torturing privately in his Westminster house. He even reversed orders issued by the Council. As far back as 1586–7, he had arrested William Watson even though he

---

[1] For an account of the trial, see Jessop, 297–307. The dates given here are the Old Style (Julian) dates. Some authorities use the New Style (Gregorian) dating, 13 & 17 April.

[2] Caraman 2, 199–200.

was under order of banishment, and at about the same time, when Thomas Clifton was turned over to him to be banished, he put him in the Marshalsea instead. In May 1594, encountering a man called Edward Chester being conducted to Bridewell, he re-wrote the order to include forty stripes. He told William Harrington on the scaffold that he had the power to save him.

All his activities in 1594 to early 1595 were predicated on his personal power. In London on the night of 15 March 1594, a tremendous nocturnal raid on suspected Catholic houses took place that had the entire city in an uproar. Henry Garnet, always well-informed, attributed the planning of the raid to Topcliffe. There was "such hurly-burly," he wrote to Persons, "as never was seen in man's memory: no, not when Wyatt was at the gates." It is not every "simple freeholder," as Topcliffe liked to describe himself, who can turn a capital city the size of London upside down.

One of the people Topcliffe hoped to catch in that raid was John Gerard, S.J. The house in Golden Lane that he and Garnet had been using was indeed raided, but fortunately, acting on a premonition by Garnet, neither of them was there that night. Instead the raiders caught four laymen, among them Garnet's servant, Richard Fulwood and the musician John Bolt, who had in his possession manuscript copies of Southwell's *Saint Peter's Complaint* and Walpole's poem on Campion.[1] Bolt, who later went into exile, was in real danger of torture to disclose the sources of his manuscripts, but he was saved by the intercession of Lady Penelope Rich, Sir Philip Sidney's Stella.

A month later, 23 April, tipped off by a false servant in the Wiseman household, they caught John Gerard at the same house in Golden Lane. He was first taken to the house of the pursuivant who caught him, then after a couple of days, to the Counter in the Poultry.[2] There, a few days later, Topcliffe and Young came to examine him.

Topcliffe, in court dress, and carrying a sword, began by assuming that his name and reputation would intimidate Gerard: "You know who I am? I am Topcliffe. No doubt you have heard people talk about me." He then slapped his sword on the table.

These tactics had no effect on Gerard except that instead of replying mildly and deferentially, he was intentionally rude. Himself a gentleman by birth and upbringing, Gerard understood that the only way to deal

[1]Caraman 2, 186–7; Gerard, 55.

[2]Gerard, 65–71,

with a man like Topcliffe was to take the upper hand. His attitude made Topcliffe extremely angry, and before he and Young left (ordering Gerard's gaoler to put him in irons), he threatened him with torture: "I will see that you are brought to me and placed in my power. I will hang you up in the air and will have no pity on you; and then I shall watch and see whether God will snatch you from my grasp." Gerard's reply to that was to tell Topcliffe that he could do nothing unless God allowed it.[1]

One suspects that despite Gerard's bravado and real courage he was fortunate never to find himself in Topcliffe's hands. He was tortured in the Tower, but not by Topcliffe, survived, and made a remarkable and dramatic escape. After his escape, Topcliffe, who remembered him well, wrote a description of him:

> John Gerard the Jesuit is about 30 years old, of a good stature, somewhat higher than Sir Thomas Leighton: and upright in his pace, and countenance somewhat staring in his look, or eyes: curled haired by nature, and black-ish, and not apt to have much hair of his beard (I think). His nose some-what wide and & turning up; blubbered lips turning outward, especially the over-lip most upward toward the nose. Curious in speech, if he do now continue his custom. And in his speech he flowereth, and smiles much, and a faltering, or lisping, or doubling of his tongue in his speech.[2]

This description, misdated to 1583 in the Calendar, was written some-time after Gerard's escape from the Tower, 4 October 1597. Topcliffe sent it to the Council in a letter warning that Gerard and Richard Blount (a priest trained at the English College, Rome) were preparing to leave England secretly from Dover or Rye "with the Lord Ambassador." When Gerard did escape from England in 1606, it was indeed "with the Lord Ambassador" [of Spain], but by then Topcliffe had been dead two years.

The interest of Gerard's description of his encounter with Topcliffe is that it communicates well Topcliffe's sense of his power and authority. At about the same time, the Montagus' servant Robert Barnes felt the malign edge of Topcliffe's power when Topcliffe, wishing to acquire his property for Anne Bellamy and Nicholas Jones, accused him of various treasons and felonies, arrested him, and committed him to the Gatehouse. He even had Barnes's window nailed up to make his impris-onment more complete.[3]

---

[1] Gerard's original was written in Latin. This translation is by Philip Caraman.

[2] NA/SP12/165/21. This is another document signed with Topcliffe's arms, three cre-scent moons.

[3] Pollen 1, 362; Hatfield 62/79 (23 July 98).

A little later, in August 1594, that same personal authority allowed Topcliffe, backed by the Queen, to make sure that William Randall, the exiled English mariner whose ship had blown ashore in a storm, should stay imprisoned in England, and to order the Lord Keeper to inform the Queen of Randall's wife's access to her shoemaker.[1] When Topcliffe intervened in June 1595 on Earl Gilbert's behalf in the matter of his former servant, Nicholas Williamson, he was still making the same assumption of authority, even though by then the Council had taken back his commission.[2]

In November 1594, he achieved a masterpiece of shameless self-assertion when he sued his former ally and employee, Thomas Fitzherbert, in the court of Chancery for the £3,000 owed to him under Fitzherbert's bond if he successfully prosecuted to death his father, uncle, and cousin, William Bassett. Henry Garnet tells the story in a letter to Robert Persons:

> Topcliffe and Tom Fitzherbert pleaded hard in the Chancery this last week; for whereas Fitzherbert had promised and entered into bonds to give £3000 unto Topcliffe if he would prosecute his father and uncle to death, together with Mr. Basset, Fitzherbert pleaded that the conditions were not fulfilled, because they died naturally, and Basset was in prosperity. Basset gave witness what treacherous devices he had used to entrap him; and Coke, the Queen's Attorney, gave testimony openly that he very well had proved how effectually Topcliffe sought to inform him against them, contrary to all equity and conscience: so that all the court flouting Topcliffe, the matter was put over to secret hearing, where Topcliffe had the upper hand.[3]

Not surprisingly, this case, unlike Fitzherbert's attempt to regain Padley,[4] has left no track in the records, and one is not surprised to hear that the suit was "put over to secret hearing." One would like to know, too, how it came about that "Topcliffe had the upper hand" in that secret hearing. He tells us himself in one of his letters that the Queen had seen to it that he won his previous suit with Fitzherbert, and so held on to the Fitzherbert manor of Padley.[5] Did the Queen intervene for

---

[1] See above, 183–5.

[2] See above, 216–18.

[3] Foley, 4.49–50.

[4] See above, 210.

[5] Topcliffe to Gilbert, earl of Shrewsbury, 20 February 1604: "I can prove good Queen Elizabeth entreated your Lordship's favor and assistance, under nine of her councillors'

him again against Fitzherbert? It seems likely. "Secret hearing" or not, however, Topcliffe never saw any of the money because by then Fitzherbert was in severe financial trouble himself.

All in all, as 1594 turned into 1595, Topcliffe's position will have seemed invulnerable to him and to virtually everyone else. He had made one serious mistake, however, the kind of mistake that is rooted in a man's character and upbringing: he had trodden, careless and unsuspecting, on a very powerful set of toes. As a result, when his downfall came, it took him completely by surprise.

*****

---

hands in the defense of my right unto Padley, when you were first earl" (Talbot Papers, Vol. M [Lambeth MS 3203], f. 184).

Thirteen

"A Dishonest Man"[1]

Topcliffe was a tremendous snob. In the 1580s he was involved in a suit with Lord Chief Justice Wray over a lease of the tithes and profits of the prebend of Corringham and Stowe in Lincolnshire, where his own estate of Somerby lay. He petitioned the Queen successfully to have the matter referred to the Privy Council. The Lord Chief Justice, he said, was not only having the corn threshed, but was engaged in a corrupt attempt to try the cause himself:

> And by such means I, my housekeeping and my credit yet overthrown, who have lived and served divers years before his Lordship set foot in Lincolnshire, as my ancestors had done and served their sovereigns as noble gentlemen before, and when his Lordship's grandfather served the Lord Conyers as a morrow-mass priest, and vicar of East Witton.

Nor was Topcliffe making this up. Lord Campbell, in his *Lives of the Chief Justices of England*, found two accounts of Wray's forbears in the Heralds' College. The first said that he was the son of Thomas Wray of Richmondshire by the daughter and heir of Richard Jackson. The second said that he was the natural son of Sir Christopher Wray, vicar of Hornby, by a wench in a belfry, and that he was brought up to the law by his reputed father's brother, a servant of the Lord Conyers of Hornby.[2]

Opinion has now verified and corrected the first version: Sir Christopher Wray, we are told, was born in the parish of Bedale, Yorkshire, the third son of Thomas Wray, seneschal of Coverham Abbey, Yorkshire, and his wife Joan, daughter and coheir of Robert Jackson of Gatenby, Yorkshire.[3] Since Topcliffe said nothing about the father's origins, but

---

[1]BL Ms. Harleian 6998, f.185.

[2]Campbell, 1.236–7.

identified the grandfather as "a morrow-mass priest," his version may be still correct; but whatever the version, Topcliffe found it hard to believe that a man of origins as obscure and dubious as Christopher Wray's, Lord Chief Justice or not, would have the crust to intrude himself into the Topcliffes' ancestral territory.[2]

In 1591, Lord Keeper Sir Christopher Hatton died, and for a while the Keepership was in commission. Then on 28 May 1592, the Queen knighted Mr. Sergeant Puckering, swore him in as a Privy Councilor, and appointed him Lord Keeper.

Puckering was another Yorkshire man. He was the eldest son of William Puckering of Flamborough and his wife Anne, daughter of John Ashton of Great Lever Hall, Bolton, Lancashire. To most people, this will seem like a respectable enough background, but once again Topcliffe was not impressed.

He has left nothing as plain-spoken as his remarks about Wray, but it is evident from the style of some of his letters to Puckering that he had little respect for him. His assumption of social superiority will have had a lot to do with that—a condescending tone towards Puckering seems to have come naturally to Topcliffe. Here he is reporting on the affair of the Scotsman's murder of Crow, the Queen's guard:

> It were not amiss if it pleased your Lordship to write unto her Majesty hereof, for I dare say that her Highness will take it well, and so will my Lord Chamberlain also, for none knows the Scottish causes better than he, and none can better decipher their knavery to their king than his Lordship...If your Lordship send down by any post when packets pass northward your letter to my Lord of Huntington, endorse a letter to me at my house at Somerby, commanding the post of Scrooby to convey it to me six mile from me....[3]

The implications of those sentences are extraordinary, starting with the opening, "It were not amiss...." Topcliffe is telling the new Lord Keeper his business, in the process letting him know that other people—the Queen, the Lord Chamberlain, and Topcliffe himself—understand these matters in ways that he has yet to learn. Then he orders the Lord Keeper

---

[3]*ODNB*.

[2]A "morrow mass" was the first mass of the day, celebrated very early, hence by no means in liturgical prime time.

[3]NA/SP12/243/9 (11 September 1592).

to be in touch with him by letter, and explains how he can do that. The patronizing tone will not have been lost on Puckering.

When the Queen and the Council sent Topcliffe north to handle the Walpole arrest, the Queen told him, very correctly, to report his findings to the Lord Keeper. Because he always obeyed the Queen, Topcliffe did that by writing a letter which he began by telling Puckering that he was writing because the Queen had "chiefly referred" him to Puckering "in this my travail," and he ended by saying:

> I beseech your lordship to show to her Majesty all that the worst-affected subjects in the north gaze and look after: the justice and doings of her Majesty and the Lord President, sitting in her seat as her justice: the countenancing of whom in this and like services in these parts will make traitors appalled. And so must I say, with all truth and humility to her Majesty at my return, when she shall vouchsafe to hear me; or else I shall not discharge the oath I have avowed to her Majesty, nor the duty of a true Englishman.[1]

What that passage told Puckering was that Topcliffe was writing to him as a matter of form. The person for whom he really worked, and to whom he preferred to report, was the Queen—and sure enough, when Huntington wrote to Puckering from York on 12 February, having spent several days chatting to Topcliffe, he spelled out, no doubt intentionally, the true state of the case:

> I have no doubt but afore this time Mr. Topcliffe hath waited on her Majesty, and after been with your lordship.[2]

"*After*"? Puckering took sufficient note of that sentence that he underscored it in the manuscript. If we put ourselves into Puckering's mind, we shall see what he was thinking: "It's not just Topcliffe who thinks he can bypass me; Huntington is one of them, too." It must have been the last straw for Puckering when the William Randall affair blew up, and Topcliffe ordered him to inform the Queen immediately of Randall's wife's access to her shoemaker. If he didn't, said Topcliffe, he would tell her himself.

There was nothing Puckering could do about any of this except fume. He was not a courtier like his predecessor Hatton, the two Cecils,

---

[1] NA/SP12/247/21 (25 January 1594).

[2] BL Ms. Harleian 6996, No.35, f.68, printed in Pollen 1, 239.

Huntington, and Topcliffe himself, and so he was not in the habit of enjoying easy, familiar access to the Queen. He was, though, a lawyer, and he knew how to watch and wait. That is exactly what he did—and it turned out that there was a lot to watch.

Topcliffe had a cousin, James Rither or Ryder, almost as well-born as himself, who had inherited the much-encumbered estate of Harewood with its castle in the county of Yorkshire. Rither is a puzzling figure. He was born in 1536, so was just four years younger than Topcliffe. His father had been an esquire of the body to Queen Mary, and the younger Rither had been sworn esquire of the body to Elizabeth. In the mid-1570s he was one of the clerks to the court of Star Chamber.[1] Then in the later 1580s he was a member of Parliament (Appleby) and a justice of the peace, writing letters to Burghley, whom he seems to have known.

Archbishop Sandys of York, though, described him as "a sour and subtle papist" who used his position as a justice to favor the Catholics, and by the 1590s his fortunes had taken a sharp turn for the worse. In 1592 he was in Newgate for debt, and petitioning Burghley for his release.

Some time before June 1593, one Hugh Hare of the Inner Temple, lent Rither money, and when Rither failed to pay him, attempted to take possession of Harewood castle. A regular battle then took place there between the defenders, led by Rither's son, and the forces of the under-sheriff. Hare's attempt to take the castle failed, but one of the defenders was shot dead.[2] In 1594, Rither himself was again in prison for debt, this time in the Fleet. He died 4 September 1595, and to pay his debts his heir had to sell Harewood.[3]

Even though he was either a Catholic or a Catholic sympathizer, he was on good terms with his cousin Topcliffe, who took to visiting him at the Fleet. Lord Keeper Puckering and Lord Treasurer Burghley had recently set up new orders for the operation of the Fleet prison. There was a good deal of grumbling about the new orders, and some of the prisoners had petitioned Puckering to bring back the old orders. Puckering, therefore, had an interest in the prison's affairs. Somehow he heard,

---

[1]In the mid-1570s he signs a deposition as clerk in STAC5/T.10/29 (Richard Topcliffe v. John Proctor, Thomas Backhouse).

[2]There are accounts of this affair in the records of the Star Chamber case which followed, NA/STAC 5/H.2/33.

[3]There is a summary life of Rither by Irene Cassidy in Hasler, 3.315–16.

probably from the head keeper, that Rither, backed by his cousin Topcliffe, was causing trouble. He decided to find out just what Rither had been saying, and what the pair of them had been up to.

To do this he drew up a short set of simple questions for one of his clerks to put to some of the prisoners beginning, probably, with Rither himself, who was questioned on 8 April 1594.[1] Puckering's questions do not mention Topcliffe—they did not have to:

> 1. What have you heard James Rither say in contempt of the Lord Keeper or any other Privy Councilor since he and the Lord Treasurer issued the orders for the prison? What have you heard him say about the orders?
> 2. Have you heard James Rither advise any of his fellow prisoners to appeal to the Queen from the courts of Star Chamber and Chancery because there was no justice to be had in those courts? Have you heard him say that some special friend of his would present their suits to her Majesty?
> 3. Have you heard James Rither discussing the Lord Keeper's administration of justice? If so, what have you heard him say about it?
> 4. What sums of money have you heard that James Rither has got out of Mrs. Jane Shelley under pretense of procuring her liberty by some friends of his? Do you know who those friends are? Do you know what reason he gave her why she should disburse so much money?[2]

Rither, then, had been telling his fellow-prisoners that if it was justice they wanted, it was a waste of time to petition the Lord Keeper and the Council. They should petition the Queen directly instead, and—what was more—he knew people who would take their petitions straight to her. He had been wheedling money out of another prisoner, Jane Shelley, as well.

Questioned, Rither denied everything except taking money off Mrs. Shelley. He had done that, he said, because she asked him to find someone to procure her liberty, and also because she was "a very simple gentlewoman" who needed protection from "such lewd persons in the prison, as did daily practice to abuse her simplicity and to deceive her."

The two surviving prisoners' responses tell a different story. Thomas Fitzherbert, who by now had no reason to be loyal to Topcliffe, said that Rither would not join the petition to Puckering to bring back the old orders because, "he knew my Lord Keeper well enough, for he had

---

[1] Ms. Harleian 6998, f.180.

[2] Ms. Harleian 6998, f.192 (modernized and abbreviated).

tasted already too much of his bitterness." As for the new orders, "The warden had paid dearly for them, and...he would have his Cousin Topcliffe move the Queen's Majesty of them, and put the warden out of his office." According to Fitzherbert, the real reason for Rither's dislike of Puckering and another councilor, Lord Buckhurst, was that they had taken Hugh Hare's part in the Star Chamber suit that followed the fight or riot at Harewood Castle.

Fitzherbert also confirmed the rumor that Rither had been telling the prisoners not to bother petitioning the Council or the courts, but to petition the Queen instead, "saying that his Cousin Topcliffe should be a mean for them to her Majesty." As for Mrs. Shelley, he had heard from several people that during the past year Rither, Topcliffe, and others had taken over £100 off her by pretending to procure her release, and by telling her that Puckering and Waad (a clerk to the Council) were her enemies.[1]

Patrick Sacheverell, the other prisoner whose replies survive, had nothing to say about the orders or Rither's opinion of Puckering, but he told the same story about Cousin Topcliffe's access to the Queen. Rither, he said:

> was very earnest with this examinate about a cause he had in the Star Chamber, and willed him to prefer his petition to the Queen's Majesty, saying he would be a mean to prefer his suit, which he refused. Also in a suit that Thomas Taylor had in the Star Chamber, and Richard More had in the Chancery, he procured the said Taylor and More to come into his Chamber in the Fleet before his Cousin Topcliffe, and there willed them to prefer their several petitions to the Queen's Majesty, affirming that Mr. Topcliffe should procure the right honorable the Countess of Warwick to deliver the same to her Majesty, and himself, Mr. Topcliffe, would do his best therein.[2]

According to Sacheverell's testimony, Topcliffe himself was offering his services, and of course the implication is that money was changing hands: Topcliffe was selling access to the Queen.

[1] Ms. Harleian 6998, f.193.

[2] Anne Dudley, née Russell, Ambrose, Earl of Warwick's 3rd wife was the eldest daughter of Francis Russell, 2nd Earl of Bedford. Like Topcliffe, she was probably in the Queen's service before her accession, and as an extraordinary gentlewoman of the privy chamber who was intimate with the Queen was thought to be an effective means of transmitting petitions and letters. Topcliffe knew her and her family well. See above, 46.

Sacheverell is even more interesting on the subject of Mrs. Shelley. He knew that Rither and Topcliffe had had £40 in gold from her, and Mrs. Shelley herself told him, without naming a sum, that "they had too much." Then one day, as he was standing under the vine in the Fleet garden, he saw Rither and Topcliffe take Mrs. Shelley into Rither's chamber, and he overheard their talk:

> Mr Topcliffe did threaten her with many evil words, saying he could procure her utter undoing; and Mr. Rither replied that her life lay in Mr. Topcliffe's hands, and that he the said Topcliffe was the man that could do her good; and Mr. Topcliffe charged her that she had deceived him in saying that she had divers goods, as jewels and other things in her Counter, being in her chamber in or near Holborn, which he could not find.[1]

Before her arrest, Mrs. Shelley had been living in Holborn, and if Sacheverell was right—and why would he not be?—Topcliffe had gone ferreting in her lodging for jewels "and other things."

Mrs. Shelley was a wealthy woman. Born Jane Lingen, she had inherited a large property in Herefordshire and Shropshire which went as jointure to her husband William Shelley. He had been tried and convicted of treason, and sentenced to death. Although the sentence was remitted, he remained in the Tower, and all his property was in attainder. The Queen was allowing Mrs. Shelley the relatively small sum of £200 a year out of her property, and of course it was not paid on time very often.

Not surprisingly, Mrs. Shelley considered her husband to be the cause of her troubles, and—as people often did—she consulted astrologers, one of them a fellow of Gonville and Caius College, Cambridge, to find out whether her husband would be executed, live, or die of natural causes. Unfriendly people then told the authorities that she was inquiring about the Queen's death. That was why she was arrested and committed close prisoner to the Fleet. She was certainly subject to exploitation there, both by the warden and an unsavory character called Ben Beard, who appears in the State Papers as a would-be spy, and who claimed to be related to her husband. Rither and Topcliffe, it seems, saw no reason why they should not join in the action.[2]

---

[1] Ms. Harleian 6998, f.194.

[2] Mrs. Shelley was not "a very simple gentlewoman." She was released some time by the end of 1594, and continued to live in London. Her husband died in 1597, and after the payment of £11,000 (£1,000 to Lord Howard of Effingham, £10,000 to the Exche-

It is a measure of Topcliffe's standing at court, and with the Queen and Council, that even now Puckering took no action, although one imagines that he must have talked privately to one or two fellow-councilors. After all, Topcliffe's disdain for the Council was not newly acquired. Back in 1591 before Puckering was a councilor, Topcliffe had told Thomas Pormort, "that he did not care for the Council, for that he had his authority from her Majesty." Puckering, meanwhile, continued to wait.

Interestingly enough on 27 November 1594, the Council wrote instructing the Warden of the Fleet prison to restore the prison's old orders, and to see to it that abuses and customs newly raised, and not agreeable with the old orders, "be utterly extinguished and suppressed."[1] Whether that change came about through the prisoners' petition or through Topcliffe's back-stage lobbying of the Queen does not appear. One suspects that Topcliffe's intercession would carry more weight than the prisoners' petition.

*****

On 6 April 1593, after eight months' imprisonment in the Tower, Robert Southwell, S.J. wrote a long, eloquent letter to Sir Robert Cecil, acknowledging that he was a priest of the Society of Jesus, and asking that he might be either released or brought to trial.[2] No response to Southwell's letter survives, although Henry Garnet who knew that the letter had been written, and who paraphrased what he knew of it, said that Cecil's reply, "worthy of such a noble councilor," had been that "if he longed for hanging so much, he might obtain it soon enough."[3] Garnet's informants also told him that Topcliffe was forever urging the Council to bring Southwell to trial so that he could acquire the

---

quer) his properties were put in trust for the heir. Mrs. Shelley then set about recovering her own property from the wreck of her marriage, and with the accession of James I, she succeeded, with the result that she had a large income of £3,000 out of which she easily paid her recusancy fines. She proved to be an astute and generous businesswoman. When she died childless in 1610, her heir was her cousin Edward Lingen, the same man who had come ashore with Henry Walpole at Flamborough. There is a good deal of material about her and her husband in the State Papers, handsomely summed up and narrated by Wainewright, q.v.

[1]APC, 25. 520.

[2]Brown, 77–85.

[3]Brown, xl.

Bellamys' property, "and so endow his virtuous bride." Garnet heard, too, that Topcliffe, the "most sordid of men," had so frightened the Queen with warnings of the dangers of priests and Catholics, "that she herself was wont frequently to ask when there would be another execution, since none had occurred for some time."[1]

There was indeed no execution of a priest in London for a year after William Harrington's death in February 1594 (although four priests and four laymen had been executed outside London). Then on 18 February 1595, by special warrant of Sir Robert Cecil, Robert Southwell was transferred from the Tower to the underground cell in Newgate called Limbo to be brought to trial, which followed on 20 February. Sir John Popham was the judge, Sir Edward Coke was the prosecuting Attorney-General, and Topcliffe was present in his usual capacity as a kind of free-lance assistant prosecutor.

No-one knows why the Council decided to try Southwell when it did. Christopher Devlin, his biographer, suggests that it was because Southwell's defense or explanation of the doctrine of equivocation gave them a justifying excuse. Equivocation certainly made up an important part of Attorney-General Coke's case for the prosecution, and yet it seems unlikely that it alone would have driven a decision to bring him to trial so late in the day.

No Jesuit had been killed in England since the execution of Edmund Campion had done so much damage to the Queen's reputation overseas, but if Garnet's information was correct, and Topcliffe had succeeded in frightening her enough, it would have been in character for Elizabeth to respond by taking vengeful action—as in 1569, 1586, and 1588—on the nearest available victim. Garnet's account, sent in a letter to Claudio Aquaviva, alleges that:

> By cunning contrivance, [Southwell's] enemies secured that the smallest audience possible should be present; for neither the gaoler nor anyone else received notice the previous day what they were about to do; and in order to divert the crowd from the Court at Westminster, they ordered that a notorious highwayman should be hanged at Tyburn at the very time.[2]

A brief account of the trial and execution sent to Verstegan at Antwerp agrees with Garnet, adding the detail that the both the trial and the secrecy were arranged, "by the instigation of the bloody Topcliffe."[2]

---

[1]Caraman 2, 194, 182, quoting Garnet to Aquaviva, 22 February and 20 June 1595.

Southwell had suffered permanent injury during his torture, and was in such poor condition that he asked the Newgate keeper to stay near him should he need help because, "as a result of his bitter tortures, his sides were not strong enough for him to shout." During the trial, therefore, speech was difficult for him. Nonetheless, two remarkable exchanges took place which had the effect of driving Topcliffe and Attorney-General Coke into unbecoming rages.[3] The first occurred after Chief Justice Popham ordered Southwell to keep quiet until Coke had finished speaking. Here is the anonymous eye-witness's account:

> Mr. Southwell replied, and besought that he might answer forthwith, because he could not carry it so well in mind, by reason that his memory and senses were much impaired through Mr. Topcliffe's means, under whose hands he protested, of his soul, and as he expected very shortly to answer it before Almighty God, he had been ten times tortured so extremely that the least of them was worse than ten executions.
>
> The Chief Justice said he never knew that he was so tortured.
>
> The Attorney-General said that he never knew that ever he was racked, and Topcliffe said that he was never upon the rack.
>
> Whereunto he answered, "I confess that I was never racked, but you have new kinds of tortures worse, I think, than the rack," and began to express the mode of them, but he was presently interrupted by the Chief Justice, who said it was lawful to use such tortures, and hath been so used by all nations.[4]
>
> He answered, "I confess it to be lawful, and that other nations have the like use; but when by torture nothing can be got out, I wish there might be some measure there lest a man in the end, by extremity of pain, be driven to desperation."
>
> Then they cried out, "Show the harm you have had by your tortures."
>
> He answered, "Let a woman [in childbirth] show her throes."

Topcliffe's response was to embark upon a long, blustering defense of

---

[2]Foley, 1.377.

[2]Verstegan, 223.

[3]There are two contemporary accounts of the trial, both at Stonyhurst. The first and more detailed, Ms. Anglia A.ii.1, *A Brief Discourse of the Condemnation and execution of Mr. Robert Southwell, Priest of the Society of Jesus,* is anonymous; Foley prints it, 1.364–75. The second, Ms. Anglia A.vi, is by a secular priest, Thomas Leake, and it is printed in Pollen 1, 333–7. The best modern account is in Devlin 1, 306–16.

[4]An extraordinary statement from the Bench, and an indication of the collapse of all standards of decency in English public life under Elizabeth I. Torture *was* unlawful in England, and could only be used, as we have seen, under the fiction of the royal prerogative, thus immunizing the torturers from prosecution.

himself, saying he had the Council's letters authorizing him to do as he did, but he was interrupted by Coke who said that Topcliffe had no need to excuse himself and, turning to Southwell, said, "Think you that you shall not be tortured? Yes, we will tear your hearts out of a hundred of your bodies."[1] The proceedings then deteriorated into a shouting match between Topcliffe and Coke until Chief Justice Popham restored order. If, according to Leake, at some point Southwell managed to say to Topcliffe, "Thou art a bad man," he had succeeded in making a major point in that court.

The second important exchange took place when Coke called his only witness, Anne Jones, née Bellamy, to testify that Southwell had taught her that "if upon her oath she were asked whether she had seen a priest or not, she might lawfully say no, though she had seen one, keeping this meaning in her mind, that she did not see any with intent to bewray [betray] him." When Southwell tried to explain the reasoning that underlay the doctrine of equivocation, they continually shouted him down until he directly challenged Coke, saying either that Coke should acknowledge equivocation to be no crime, or else Southwell would prove him to be no good subject or friend of the Queen.

Coke took the bait:

> "Suppose," said Mr. Southwell, "that the French King should invade her Majesty, and that she (which God forbid) should by her enemies be enforced to fly to some private house for her safety, where none knew her being, but Mr. Attorney; and that Mr. Attorney's refusal to swear, being thereunto urged, should be a confession of her being in the house (for I suppose that also if Mr. Attorney in this case should be examined and should refuse to swear that he knoweth that her Majesty is not there, with this intention not to tell them), I say, Mr. Attorney were neither her Majesty's good subject nor friend."

Chief Justice Popham said that Mr. Attorney should refuse to swear, to which Southwell answered, "That were by silence to betray his sovereign." Once again, the trial deteriorated into noise and shouting, with Coke calling Fr. Southwell "boy priest," and with Topcliffe "railing" until Popham told him to be quiet (One would like to know just what Topcliffe's "railing" consisted of).

---

[1]Coke is famous for discovering the English constitution and its protections under James I. It is one of the odder facts of history that under Elizabeth I Coke, a nasty piece of work, had never heard of it.

Since the indictment was brought on the basis of the 1585 statute making it treason to come into England as a priest, from the legal point of view, all this discussion of equivocation was irrelevant noise. A guilty verdict was inevitable. Nonetheless, the government liked to have more substantial grounds than that for killing a priest, and instead Southwell had succeeded in exposing the barbarity and the unreason of the entire prosecution. Popham seems to have understood this. While the jury was consulting, he ordered Southwell removed from the bar to rest himself, and even—virtually unprecedented—offered him some refreshment. But Southwell refused, and asked permission to remain.

When he was asked after the verdict whether he had anything to say he merely answered, "I pray God forgive all them that any way are accessory to my death." Even then, at the very end, Topcliffe could not resist taunting him, "saying he found him hidden in the tiles of the house," to which Southwell answered that, "It was time to hide when Mr. Topcliffe came."

Robert Southwell's trial and death are extremely well documented, and there can be no doubt that from the standpoint of the Queen and Council, the trial and its outcome could not be considered a success. They had their death sentence according to the statute, and the Queen would have her execution, but they had failed to "bring home" the charge of treason, and Southwell's demeanor throughout had engaged the sympathy of the onlookers. In Elizabethan London, moreover, news of an event like that spread very quickly by word-of-mouth.

This is probably why the scene of the execution, which took place the next day, 21 February, was the occasion for a piece of characteristic royal back-peddling. Topcliffe had captured and interrogated Southwell; he had supervised his imprisonment in the Tower, and he had been a participant at the trial. If Garnet's informants were right, he even bore some of the responsibility for the trial's taking place when it did. Yet he was not present at the execution in his usual capacity as observer and master of the ceremonies. His absence was most unusual, and the only explanation for it is that the Queen had forbidden his attendance.

The courtier who took his place as observer was Charles Blount, 8th Baron Mountjoy, governor of Portsmouth, a successful soldier and a man in favor with the Queen. He was undoubtedly present by royal command, and if we infer his instructions from his behavior, he was told to ensure as humane a death as possible in the circumstances.

Southwell, again, behaved impeccably. He made a graceful speech in which he prayed for the Queen, and prepared himself to die. When they drove the cart away, and the executioners, who were under the orders of the under-sheriff and unaware of any change in procedure, stepped forward to cut him down alive, Mountjoy and his entourage commanded them to stop. When the under-sheriff renewed his order, Mountjoy intervened again. The hangman then did his best to ensure that Southwell was dead before he took him down, and treated the body with notable and unusual courtesy.

Finally, when the hangman held up the head as was customary, saying, "God save the Queen: here is the head of a traitor!" silence greeted his words, and the crowd bared their heads. The angry under-sheriff said, "I see there are some here who have come, not to honor the Queen, but to reverence a traitor," to which Mountjoy replied, "I cannot judge of his religion; but pray God, whensoever I die, that my soul may be in no worse case than his."[1]

Diego de Yepes, author of the Spanish *History of the English Persecution*, published four years later in 1599, tells a peculiar story about Southwell's last hours. After the sentence had been passed, a nobleman went to the prison, and commanded Southwell to tell him truly, as he prepared to die, whether it was true that he had come to England to separate the Queen's subjects from their obedience. Southwell replied that he had never had any wish to bring harm to the Queen or anyone else; and that his sole purpose in coming to England from Rome was to administer the sacraments and to attend to the welfare of souls. He prayed God to enlighten the Queen and her Council, to give them the grace to know their errors, and not to impute the guilt of his death to them.

After the execution—which the nobleman must have attended—he went to the Queen and told her all that happened at the Father's death, praising him, and expressing wonder at his "rare parts." In reply the Queen told him, rather brusquely it seems, that she knew all about that, and that he had been deceived with false reports ("falsas relaciones") that the Father had come into England to disturb the kingdom. She was greatly saddened by his death, and especially so since she had seen a book that he had written on various pious subjects, both for his own recreation and to teach poets to use their gift as they should to the honor of God and virtue.

---

[1] Pollen 1, 337 (Leake's version). The version in *A Brief Discourse* is, "A Protestant lord wished that whenever he died, his soul might go with his" (Foley 1, 375).

Pierre Janelle and Christopher Devlin accept this story, Devlin suggesting that the nobleman was Mountjoy himself, who had shown the Queen the book she mentions. Yet there is no hint of the story in the extant manuscript accounts of Southwell's last hours, and it is surely a very unlikely one. In February 1595, the only book by Southwell that was generally available was *Mary Magdalen's Funeral Tears*, and even if the Queen had seen it, it is unlikely that she would have known that "S.W." who signed the introductory material was Southwell. The advice to poets which she quotes might have come either from Southwell's long poem, *Saint Peter's Complaint*, or from the letter, "to His Loving Cousin," that Southwell prefixed to the collection of his lyric poems. *Saint Peter's Complaint* was circulating in manuscript, and the lyric collection may have begun to circulate, too; but possession of such manuscripts was very dangerous, as the musician John Bolt and his patrons the Wiseman family had recently found out. Who in his right mind would have given the Queen Southwell's poetry to read in manuscript? The lyric collection included a poem treating Mary Queen of Scots as a martyr, and even *Saint Peter's Complaint* has passages that would have caused an ominous pursing of the royal lips.

The story postdates the execution, and probably by a fair interval since the "book" to which the Queen's words refer is surely *Saint Peter's Complaint, with Other Poems*, published anonymously a couple of months later in the spring of 1595. The effect of the story is to deflect blame for Southwell's unpopular death away from the Queen to the Council, and that was probably its intention. One of Verstegan's informants, writing in May or June, sent him a different version of the same shift in royal policy:

> You will marvel with me at the news which I now shall send you: there is now very great hope given that the Queen will proceed so mildly that none shall be troubled for their conscience so they give not otherwise just cause of offense. This is given out by some in principal authority...They endeavor to persuade the world that these hard courses were against the Queen's mind. This course is thought to proceed of fear and cowardice— they may perhaps think to profit more by this than by rigor. You know the story of the wind and the sun that strove who should pluck the passenger's cloak from his back, and the warm sun did it.[1]

This letter writer was skeptical both of the news and the motives behind

---

[1]Verstegan, 242–3.

its dissemination, although there was indeed no execution of a priest in London until 1598, when the persecution resumed. Executions of both priests and laymen continued without interruption, however, in the provinces, in York especially. Four laymen were hanged there in 1596, having been tricked by a minister into encouraging him to become Catholic. Two laywomen, Mrs. Ann Tesse or Tesh and Mrs. Bridget Maskew were condemned at the same time, and sentenced to be burned alive. Although reprieved, they remained in prison in York Castle for seven years until the Queen's death, after which James I pardoned them.[1]

*****

Topcliffe had been busy in the weeks before the Southwell trial. In January he had ridden "over foul roads" on the Queen's orders to attend to the affair of Thomas Gravener in Northampton. Shortly after that, he committed young James Atkinson to Bridewell, and about three weeks later he and Nicholas Jones killed him there under torture. In early February he was writing to Cecil about a young man he was grooming as an agent, and a few days after that he learned that William Randall's wife was lodging with the Queen's shoemaker, and told Lord Keeper Puckering to tell her so immediately.[2]

After Robert Southwell's death on 21 February, though, Topcliffe's appointment book emptied, and we hear nothing of him until 13 April, Palm Sunday. On that day, according to Topcliffe's own words, Lord Treasurer Burghley, acting on the Queen's orders, committed him to the Marshalsea prison on behalf of the whole Council.

There is no official record of this event.[3] We owe detailed knowledge of it to three letters that Topcliffe wrote, starting two days after his committal. First, he wrote to the Queen on Tuesday, 15 April, and again on Good Friday, 18 April. Both these letters were rejected, and so on Easter Monday, 21 April, he wrote to the Council, enclosing copies of his letters to the Queen.[4]

With the execution of Henry Walpole at York on 7 April, Topcliffe's official casebook was at last completely empty, and so the long-patient

---

[1]All these cases are documented in Challoner, 227–33. See also Morris, 3.89 and n.

[2]See above, 186–7; 253–5; 183–5; Hatfield 25/27.

[3]The relevant Council registers are missing.

[4]The letters survive in Puckering's papers, Bl Ms Harleian 6998, ff.184–87v.

Puckering decided to make his move. He did it very cleverly. There was no formal hearing of any kind. Two or three days before Palm Sunday, as members of the Council were assembling for a meeting, Topcliffe, a frequent visitor to the Council, came walking through the Council chamber. Out of the blue, Puckering asked him a question that was undoubtedly meant to be provocative.

Topcliffe had sued Thomas Fitzherbert for his £3,000 in Puckering's own court of chancery. Puckering knew all about the case, that it had been "put over" to a private hearing and decided in Topcliffe's favor. His question that so riled Topcliffe must have concerned the outcome of the case, for Topcliffe replied, "If I may have ordinary justice I shall recover £3,000 of Fitzherbert."

Puckering immediately took offense. He interpreted the words to mean that he, the Lord Keeper, had not done Topcliffe "ordinary justice," and in response he told him that he had spoken dishonestly, and that he was a dishonest man. He then put another, even more provocative question: "How could [you] deserve to have a bond of a prisoner of £3,000?" By now Topcliffe's easily-roused temper was up, and his reply was as indiscreet as it was angry:

> I had that bond, and the other gift three years before Fitzherbert was a prisoner, and I had deserved it as well as some had done for whose favor £10,000 had been given.

This reply was a reference to the bribe that had been paid some five years earlier to save John Fitzherbert's life. Topcliffe's point, therefore, was well taken: he had accepted an offer of £3,000 to take John Fitzherbert's life, and some councilors had accepted £10,000 to save it. Meanwhile, the man was dead of natural causes in prison. He had done his job and they had done theirs. Why all the fuss? As one can imagine, the Councilors did not care at all for the implied comparison. "Offense was taken," as Topcliffe says, "and this was construed to be meant: that I said that some councilor of them had taken £10,000."

Puckering, of course, had been neither Lord Keeper nor Councilor when the bribe was given. Yet he seems to have taken all Topcliffe's remarks personally. Topcliffe, bull-headed to the end, offered immediately to say in writing "by how many I meant it," but the Council, as one would expect, refused his offer. By now he had insulted the whole Council as well as Puckering, and he seems to have left the chamber.

The Queen had not been present during these exchanges. Either she now joined the Council or Burghley and his son Robert as acting secretary informed her of what had taken place. There must have been a good deal of discussion. Puckering will have put some of his cards on the table, and one or two of the other councilors were no doubt happy to see Topcliffe reined in.[1] Whatever the truth of his remarks, he had spoken contemptuously of the Queen's Council, individually and collectively, in the Council chamber, and some kind of disciplinary action was inevitable.

The upshot was that on Palm Sunday he was summoned to appear formally before them, and told at the Council table that it was the Queen's pleasure he should be committed to prison.

Rumors of his impending fall had quickly begun to circulate. As he told the Council after they committed him:

> It was given out abroad two or three days before I was committed, that I was committed, and wagers offered to be laid thereof in sundry places of note.

One Councilor's sardonic reply to that was, "He was a prophet that so gave out." The Catholics were overjoyed. Richard Verstegan thought it possible that the Council had imprisoned Topcliffe to make a scapegoat of him "because the people are very moved by the maltreatment and death of Fr. Southwell."[2] There is no sign of anything of the kind in Topcliffe's letters, and as we have seen, Puckering had been watching him for at least a year. Yet it is probable that the Queen's unhappiness over the bad publicity from the Southwell trial and execution was a factor in Puckering's decision to make his move when he did. One minor consequence of the committal was that James Rither finally wrote a rather grudging letter of apology to Puckering, 30 April.[3]

*****

On Good Friday, Fr. John Gerard, S.J., a prisoner in the Clink prison whom Topcliffe had interrogated two or three times, was surprised when the head keeper came banging on his door early, almost catching Gerard and his Catholic friends at their Good Friday devotions. The reason for

---

[1] It seems likely that jokes about him had begun to circulate among Essex's followers. Back in 1594 at the time of the Lopez trial, Anthony Standen had written to Anthony Bacon praising Essex because he eschewed "our Topcliffian customs" (Jessop, 111).

[2] Verstegan, 232.

[3] Ms. Harleian 6998, f.190.

the keeper's visit was to deliver a message from Topcliffe. It seems that the keeper had visited him, and their short conversation about Fr. Gerard had ended with Topcliffe sending Gerard his good wishes from the Marshalsea. Gerard sent a return message to the effect that he was in prison for the Catholic faith, and he wished Topcliffe were in prison for the same reason.[1]

If Topcliffe's intention was to give the impression that his imprisonment was a temporary misfortune patiently borne, the letter he wrote to the Queen that same day told a different story.

Topcliffe had first written to the Queen on the Tuesday after his committal, 15 April, giving her his version of the questions asked in the Council chamber, and his answers. It is (for Topcliffe) a subdued letter. Even so, there is an assumption of familiarity in it. Here he is, tackling the subject of his insult to the Council:

> Therefore I wish that when I had unknown poison given to me at Newgate at a dinner presently after I had given my sharp evidence against Bellamy's wife, then indicted, then that my tongue had lost power to speak for a year rather than I should have given to your princely conceit the least cause of offense for any evil meaning of mine that might be construed against the meanest counselor of your majesty's. For the almighty God knoweth, I have ever honored your choice, and themselves, and the Lord Keeper particularly; as your sacred majesty doth know my true and plain affection to his Lordship.

That was not, strictly speaking, true. He had told Thomas Pormort "That the Archbishop of Canterbury was a fitter councilor in a kitchen among wenches, than in a Prince's court," and the Queen certainly knew that. Yet she will also have known that when he wrote "I have ever honored your choice," he meant it, because in his mind she could do no wrong. There is an implication that these were matters about which she had talked to him.

A more overt reference to his familiar relationship with her appears at the letter's end, when he brings up his reference to the £10,000 bribe, which the Councilors had construed, naturally enough, to mean that one of them had taken the bribe:

> And to your Majesty, as to my goddess, I will explain it, whensoever my service to crime [?] shall deserve that I may be admitted to your most joyful presence.

[1]Gerard, 100–1.

That sentence suggests that he was expecting to be back on his old foot-ing at court very soon. When the week ended with no response, he wrote again, "this Good, or Evil Friday," 18 April, the day of his greeting to John Gerard. This second letter is a great deal less subdued:

> In my words, their Lordships and I differ not; but in meaning we differ. And therefore there is error in their or in my meaning, for which I wish that there lay a writ of error, or trial for my life with mine equal, or that I had lost my left hand, upon condition that your majesty had heard me speak, my words were so clear from thought of evil or fault in my heart. But when I said at that table, that it was given out abroad two or three days before I was committed, that I was committed, and wagers offered to be laid thereof in sundry places of note, then a councilor told me, that he was a prophet that so gave out.
>
> But that prophet was not my judge, for if he had been, or were, he would judge me from hence to Tyburn, to which place I have helped more traitors than all the noblemen and gentlemen about your court, your coun-cilors excepted. And now by this disgrace, I am in fair way, and made apt, to adventure my life every night to murderers. For since I was committed, wine in Westminster hath been given for joy of that news, and in all pris-ons rejoicings; and it is like that the fresh dead bones of Father Southwell at Tyburn, and Father Walpole at York (executed both since Shrovetide) will dance for joy: and now at Easter, instead of a communion, many an *Alleluia* will be sung of priests and traitors in prisons, and in ladies' closets for *Topcliffe's* fall, and in farther kingdoms also.

Those sentences were not written for one of his sympathetic "instru-ments" or mates, but for the Queen of England, and he ended by telling her that but for his committal to prison, he would have captured yet another priest on Palm Sunday.

Despite his message to Fr. Gerard, he was not taking his imprison-ment patiently. In the letter he wrote to the Council on Easter Monday, he complained that out of fear of poison he had been forced to become his own cook, and that every day he had to confront an Irish murderer whom priests had sent to kill him, "and yet he is not the worst of the Papists that daily front me with envious eyes." Reduced to essentials, his letters to the Queen, and to the Council, if they would listen to him, were saying, "You know who I am and what I have done. Get me out of here!"

And of course, they did listen to him. It is not known when Topcliffe was released, but he was not in for long. By 10 May, Verstegan heard from England by a letter dated 3 May that Fr. Walpole had been sent for execution to York, and that "Topcliffe is released out of prison, so that

Barrabas is freed, and Christ delivered to be crucified."[1] Topcliffe must have been out of the Marshalsea very soon after he wrote to the Council, probably in a few days at most, but he left the prison with less power than he entered it for, as Verstegan reported later, "Topcliffe is released out of prison, but his commission is taken from him."[2]

Topcliffe had operated under a "blanket" commission, empowering him to operate freely with no restriction of time or place. Without it he was powerless, and he never recovered it. It seems, from a letter to Burghley, written 19 June, that the Council had issued letters to a group of "commissioners," including Topcliffe, instructing them to examine certain "harborers and receivers of Jesuits." There was some delay in beginning the commissioners' work because the Lord Chief Justice (Sir John Popham) was away from London. When he returned, Topcliffe duly presented himself and his letter to Popham and Recorder Fleming. When they found that the letter concerned a commission under the broad seal, they sent him to Puckering as Lord Keeper of the Seal. Puckering then sent him to "Mr. Watson's office," either to receive a new commission or to have his old one returned to him, which he could then present to Chief Justice Popham.

At Mr. Watson's, he learned that Burghley (who was keeper of the Privy Seal) had the commission all along, whether the old one or a new one Watson did not know. Hence the reason for Topcliffe's letter to Burghley:

> I thought therefore to be so bold as to trouble your Lordship now to know your pleasure, if you have either [seal]: or if you will please to send either to the Lord Chief Justice (the new commission, if the same be finished, or else the old commission) to be used in this service, as in his wisdom and the residue they shall see cause, matters of some weighty service depending of their having of one of those commissions forthwith, or else the service will be delayed.[3]

And he added a postscript: "It may please your Honor I think the old commission is in the Council chest: and so thinks the Lord Keeper."

These days we would say that Topcliffe was being given the run-around. He received no new commission, and so could no longer freely

---

[1] NA/SP12/252/15: Verstegan, 233–4.

[2] Verstegan, 242.

[3] Hatfield 33/9.

hunt, capture, and interrogate priests and recusants anywhere in England. No evidence survives to explain why the Council, evidently with the Queen's agreement, decided to rein him in so completely. Had it dawned on them that they had created a monster? Probably not. It is more likely that the Council, resenting his insubordination, had decided rather late in the day that he was too big for his boots. The two councilors responsible for pressing that view of the matter were probably Puckering and Archbishop Whitgift. For Essex it will have been enough that he worked in cooperation with the Cecils.

Nonetheless, although Topcliffe lost his commission, he never lost favor either with the Queen or with the Cecils. His successful intervention on the Earl of Shrewsbury's behalf in the Williamson affair took place shortly after his release; and a letter written to Lord Burghley by a distressed prisoner in August 1595 reveals that the Lord Admiral had turned the man's case over to Topcliffe almost immediately after his release.[1] But the most striking evidence of Topcliffe's continuing influence is revealed by the fate of a petition against him that the Bellamys sent to the Council.

As news of Topcliffe's fall spread it occurred to Richard Bellamy's brother Thomas that now was a good time to strike back. He therefore presented a petition to the Council on behalf of his brother Richard and his family. Hearing of the petition, Topcliffe asked to see it, and wrote a series of responses.[2] He then obtained letters from the Council addressed to the two chief Justices (of Queen's Bench and Common Pleas), the Chief Baron of the Exchequer, the Master of Requests, Sergeant Drew, and Attorney-General Coke, instructing them, or any three of them, "to hear, examine, and certify...what truth they could find in the said petition." These letters were written about 20 May.

Three weeks later, 11 June, Thomas Bellamy petitioned the Council again, and from his second petition we learn what happened both to him

---

[1]The prisoner was one George Ellis, and he was writing to beg Burghley to "deliver [him] out of the hands of merciless Mr. Topcliffe." He had been in prison 15 or 16 weeks, which takes us back to the end of April 1595. The Lord Admiral had committed him, but then turned the case over to Topcliffe. He was still in the Fleet in March 1596, having been convicted in Star Chamber of forging Council warrants (BL Lansdowne Mss. 79, No. 93; 80, No. 38).

[2]Topcliffe's responses to the Bellamys' petition are in BL. Harleian Ms. 6998, f. 23. None of the responses answers to the subject of the petition, i.e., the debauching of Anne Bellamy.

and his first petition. When Thomas went to see the Lord Chief Justice and the others, they told him "they had no letter" from the Council. What happened then makes fascinating reading:

> Upon the which answer by them received, I resorted unto her Majesty's court to inform your Honors thereof; and meeting with Mr. Topcliffe I asked him of the said letters: who forthwith went unto the right honorable the Lord Chamberlain, and complained. Whereupon I was sent for to come before him, who laid nothing to my charge, but because I did come within the court, and so sent me to the Marshalsea, commanding irons to be laid on me.

No wonder Bellamy wrote a second petition. He ended it by asking either for a hearing before the Council, or for a mediator to be appointed. He begged the Council that true justice might be ministered, and that in the meantime, according to the Council's accustomed charity, "the poor prisoners" might be relieved by release on bond.[1] A note that Richard Bellamy appended to the Lansdowne copy of the original petition on a separate sheet backs up his brother's statements:

> In tender consideration that all in the said petition is true, and for that your honorable letters cannot be got out of Mr. Topcliffe's hand to cause a certificate of the petition, as also of their hard imprisonment of long time sustained, with the great charge of £3 a week unto your said petitioner, and the great danger of this extreme hot weather unto close prisoners, in most humble wise beseecheth your Honors even for God's sake even prostrate at your Honors' feet, their speedy delivery upon bonds or otherwise if his Brother Thomas be not able to prove as he hath in the said petition set down...[text breaks off][2]

What happened to Thomas Bellamy is not known. He received no reply to his second petition for the simple reason that the Council never saw it. It survives among the Hatfield manuscripts belonging to the Cecil family, endorsed by Robert Cecil's secretary, "Tho. Bellamy, prisoner in the Marshalsea to my Master" even though it was a petition addressed to the whole Council.

Why is Bellamy's second petition among the Cecils' manuscripts, and why is it misleadingly endorsed? The presumption is that Robert Cecil, like Topcliffe and the Lord Chamberlain, did what was necessary to

[1]Hatfield 32/94.

[2]BL Ms Lansdowne 73, No.47.

silence Thomas Bellamy's complaints. It is fascinating to see them all going through the charade of pretending to answer him. Topcliffe pretends to ask for an enquiry into the truth of the first petition, and the Council goes through the motions of sending out instructions to an array of important people—only the letters are either never written or never delivered, or if they are, the recipients pay no attention to them. When Bellamy goes to Court to inform the Council, he meets Topcliffe, and asks him what became of the letters. Topcliffe then turns him over to Lord Chamberlain Hunsdon as a Catholic within the verge of the court, thus giving Topcliffe and Hunsdon the opportunity to add Thomas to the list of imprisoned Bellamys. Hunsdon not only commits him to the Marshalsea, but orders him put in irons as well.

The reason Topcliffe got away with this kind of thing was that he had the Queen and the rest of the inner court circle in his pocket. All this, moreover, happened when he was supposed to be in disgrace. Thomas Bellamy miscalculated; for here is Topcliffe hobnobbing with the Council as if nothing had happened, and the Council is colluding to protect him. It looks as if the removal of his commission came about because Lord Keeper Puckering, having bided his time, saw an opportunity in the wake of the Southwell trial to provoke a showdown with him. Archbishop Whitgift, whom Topcliffe had also insulted, will have raised no objection, and the rest of the Council—the two Cecils, Hunsdon, Howard, and Heneage among them—would have seen how the wind was blowing. If that is what happened, then the removal of the commission represented neither a real change of policy nor, as the Catholic writers hoped, a withdrawal of favor from Topcliffe himself. His demotion, however, did represent a change of tactics, if not of policy. With the exception of John Gerard, tortured in the manacles in the Tower, April 1597 (by William Waad, Solicitor-General Fleming, and Francis Bacon, but not by Topcliffe), Henry Walpole proved to be the last priest tortured under Elizabeth I. When the persecution resumed in London, Topcliffe had no part in it.

*****

Fourteen

The Twilight of a Torturer

Apart from fending off the Bellamys and trying to recover his commission, Topcliffe remained relatively inactive for the rest of 1595. One reason for that, besides the loss of his commission, will have been the misfortunes of his son, Charles.

Charles Topcliffe, probably in his early thirties at the time, was a soldier. He had served in the Low Countries under the command of his kinsman Lord Burgh, becoming for a while the marshal of the Brill. In 1596 he took part in the Cadiz expedition, and a year later in 1597 he was with Lord Burgh at the first battle of the Blackwater Fort in Ulster.

In the Easter term of 1595, either while Topcliffe senior was in prison or shortly after he was released, Lord Burgh ordered Charles to accompany Elizabeth Brydges of the Queen's privy chamber to Westminster Hall for the hearing of her case in Chancery against her uncle, William, Lord Chandos. After spending about two hours in Westminster Hall, Charles was leaving when the under-sheriff of Middlesex, William Venables, waylayed him, intending to arrest him for debt.

As Charles later told his father, the under-sheriff neither identified himself as an officer nor produced either writ or warrant for the arrest. Charles, therefore, thought he was being attacked. So he slipped out of his cloak, and went for safety to the house of Mr. Morris, the Queen's attorney for the Court of Wards, and stood there knocking at the door for a while.[1]

Meanwhile Venables, very angry, went back into Westminster Hall, gathered a small party of men armed with halberds, and set off intending to search for Charles at his father's Westminster house; but seeing him

---

[1] Charles's account of this affair, written out by his father, is preserved in BL Ms. Additional 12508.

standing in doublet and hose at Mr. Morris's door, he shouted in a rage, "Art thou here? I will have thee now, or one of us shall die. Strike him down, strike him down!" and drew his sword. Seeing himself in danger for his life, Charles drew his rapier, and asked Venables to "let him pass," adding that "he would not be taken like a villain (i.e., as if he were a thief), for he served the Queen's Majesty in the Low Country in a place of charge." Paying no attention, Venables ran upon him with drawn sword, receiving as he did a small wound from the point of Charles's rapier, a little above the knee in his thigh.

Just then Mr. Morris's door opened, and Charles ran in to escape the armed men with the halberds. Venables followed him, shouting to his followers, "Kill Topcliffe if you find him! Strike him down!" What happened then does not appear in Topcliffe senior's account. Presumably Venables made his arrest. When Topcliffe senior intervened later, Venables told him to his face that he wished all the generation of the Topcliffes hanged.

Venables, however, had received a wound. He did not take proper care of it, and the "little prick above [his] knee" became infected. Ten months later he died of the infection.

In 1595 no-one, Protestant or Catholic, wished to die with a burdened conscience, and William Venables—if old Topcliffe's report is true—acknowledged on his deathbed that he had been wrong to attack Charles as he did:

> This William Venables was accounted a furious fellow in his rage, and a man full of passion: as he himself did confess upon his death-bed to two persons of credit, saying to this effect, *videlicet*: the devil was of me for to have to do with Charles Topcliffe. For I had once given him over, and meant not to have sought him out again and to have followed him; but as the devil would needs have it, I went in again from him into Westminster Hall, having given him over, and then I did take three or four with halberds and bills to go to search for him, and in my way (as the devil would) I did see Charles Topcliffe standing at Mr. Morris door, knocking, and I did fly to him, and would needs press upon the young man with my weapon in my hand. And Charles Topcliffe did entreat me not to meddle with him, but I thought to take him if he had been the devil, and so pressing upon him myself and my company, his chance was to hurt me with a little prick above my knee with his rapier.

This, though, was not the end of the affair. Venables had a brother, John Venables, and a brother-in-law, Thomas Bland, with whom he shared the office of under-sheriff in rotation year by year.[2] After their brother died, the remaining two kept up the attack on Charles Topcliffe. It turned out that the Venables were friends of the Bellamys and because "old Topcliffe had so sore plagued and persecuted their friends the Bellamys," they would never give over, they said, until "they had hanged the young dog for the old cur's sake." Bland is reported as saying that he was going to be revenged on old Topcliffe because it was through him that several of the Bellamys had been hanged.

A Middlesex coroner's jury, therefore, was prevailed upon to find that Venables's death was wilful murder, a verdict that put Charles Topcliffe in danger of his life. Intervention by the Queen and Council then saved him. Although no record of the proceedings survives in the published Middlesex records, the council gave him a warrant that allowed him "to pass and to travel" freely on the Queen's service and on his own business "without any arresting, attaching, suing, molestation, vexation or any other kind of trouble or disquieting of him in any sort, manner or case or cause whatsoever, or by whose means soever." Even so, Venables's wife and brother disregarded this warrant, and sued Charles "unto an outlawry upon an appeal of murder." In response the Council, gravely irritated, issued yet another, more emphatic warrant.[2]

As late as January 1602 Robert Cecil, who evidently liked Charles Topcliffe, was chiding his father because he was not seeing to it that his son was "cleansed" while he was alive to see to it.[3] When the Queen died in March 1603, Charles's warrant lapsed, but with Robert Cecil's help he renewed it in the new reign, and eventually received his pardon in 1605.[4]

Charles Topcliffe was apparently the victim of a conspiracy intended to hurt his father through him. It had begun twelve years earlier in 1583–4 when (according to his father's account) his cousin Henry Topcliffe and an associate called Francis Woodhouse, "two lewd cosening fellows," conned him into signing a bond for Henry in the amount of 400 marks (i.e., £266, 13 shillings, and 4 pence) guaranteeing

---

[2]Bland had been under-sheriff in 1593, when one of the Westminster bailiffs objected to his encroachments upon the liberty of Westminster (BL Ms.Lansdowne 74, Nos. 29 & 30.

[2]Hatfield 190/19 (before 20 Aug. 1604. Charles Topclyffe to Robert, Lord Cecil.

[3]Hatfield 84/36 2 Jan. 1602, Robert Cecil to Richard Topcliffe.

[4]*Hat. Cal.*,17.356. 7 August 1605. Lord Chancellor Ellesmere to Robert Cecil, now earl of Salisbury: "...The reasons contained in your letter for Topcliffe's pardon give me full satisfaction and therefore if it be called upon I will seal it and send it to you as you require."

the payment of a debt to Woodhouse of 200 marks (£133/6s/8d). These were very large sums of money—William Shakespeare's most expensive purchase, the Blackfriars Gatehouse, cost him £140.

It turned out that there was no debt in the first place. The object of the two "cosening fellows" was to dispose of the bond for ready money, but they could find no-one to take it, perhaps because in 1583–84 Richard Topcliffe was already gaining a reputation as an efficient policeman with very good connections. With old Topcliffe in prison, though, and deprived of his personal authority, the pair went into action. They found "a decayed merchant" called William Robinson to take the bond and pursue it as a debt. Henry Topcliffe, being in touch with his cousin, knew that he would be in Westminster Hall, and arranged for Venables to make the arrest.

This Henry Topcliffe belonged to a junior branch of the family living at Horstead in Norfolk. His father was John Topcliffe of Horstead, the son of Edmund Topcliffe, Richard Topcliffe's father's half-brother by the grandfather's second marriage. It will be remembered that when young Richard Topcliffe "sued his livery" and entered upon his inheritance in 1553, Edmund, John, and another relative, Lionel, of Buxton, Norfolk, sued him for a share of his grandfather's estate. The case was dismissed in November, 1560, but it must have left bad feeling in the family, no doubt exacerbated by Topcliffe's well-publicized later activities. In fact, the Norfolk Topcliffes were probably Catholic in sympathy.[1]

Five years later, Edmund, the son of Lionel Topcliffe of Buxton, went traveling in Europe with a friend, John Fitzwilliams. They went as far as Venice, when their money began to run out. So they returned home, coming to port in Cornwall from La Rochelle on a ship called The Blessing. Sir Nicholas Parker, the deputy lieutenant of Cornwall, was suspicious because they had left England without license, and had told the ship's bosun they had been at Rome, but now denied it. Even more suspicious, Edmund Topcliffe had been traveling under the name Richard Cornwallis. Asked why, he said that:

> Indeed the cause thereof was only for his safety; for that he well knew his own name, by reason of the place of his uncle Mr Richard Topcliffe, would not be so gracious in foreign parts as the name of Cornwallis.[2]

[1]For the Topcliffes of Horstead, see Rye, 290. The Horsted Topcliffes' lawsuit is in NA/REQ 2/22/105 and NA/C78/41/28, 26.

[2]Hatfield 79/50, 52, 57 (17 May 1600). The pair had wanted to visit the adventurer Sir Anthony Sherley in Persia, and carried letters to him from his father and Sir Francis Vere

That episode not only tells us what the Norfolk Topcliffes thought of cousin Richard, but that they probably had Catholic leanings as well.

As for Henry Topcliffe, one concludes that there must have been collusion between him and Venables. Venables's part in all this was that he was a friend of the Bellamys, and his determination to be revenged on their behalf against old Topcliffe explains his rash and violent behavior. It was foolish of him to attack, without provocation or warning, a soldier armed with a rapier. The Council's subsequent intervention to protect Charles is another sign that Topcliffe's quarrel with some members of the Council had not affected his personal standing with either the Queen or the Cecils.

By the time Venables's widow and brother instituted proceedings against Charles Topcliffe, he was out of the country, having joined the Anglo-Dutch expedition against Cadiz under the command of Lord Admiral Howard and the Earl of Essex. The fleet sailed in June 1596 with two major objectives: first, to do as much damage as possible to Spain's ability to mount another invasion attempt against England, and second, to bring enough plunder and loot back to cover costs, to pay the soldiers and sailors, and to enrich the Queen, the commanders, the officers, and even a few lucky soldiers.

When the victorious fleet returned, although they brought back a great deal of loot, there was not as much as had been expected. Inevitably, a good deal of recrimination and what we now call Monday morning quarter-backing took place. In all this one Wilson, a disgruntled soldier, himself guilty of appropriating some of the money, tried to put the blame for its disappearance on Charles Topcliffe. Fortunately for Charles, Robert Cecil, whose handling of the thefts from the Madre de Deus ("The Great Carrack") in 1592 had demonstrated his capacity for ferreting his way through this kind of thievery, was able to exonerate him.[1]

Again, one suspects that his father's demotion had given people in the Essex circle who had no love for the Cecils or their friends an opportunity to take advantage of Charles, who seems to have been entirely too trusting. It would be hard to exaggerate the dislike of Essex's supporters for the Cecilians. Francis Davison, writing to his father William Davison (the scapegoated secretary of state whose position Burghley and Walsingham had used to secure the execution of Mary, Queen of Scots)

---

at The Hague.

[1] For a summary of Cecil's memorandum in which he exonerates Charles Topcliffe, see *CSPD 1596–97*, 280–81.

is vitriolic on the subject of Robert Cecil's confirmation as principal secretary while Essex was away from England on the Cadiz expedition:

> My noble lord [of Essex], I doubt not, being rooted in her Majesty's favor
> and countenance by so great an enterprise as this his journey hath fallen
> out to be, will be able himself to ride out both this and any other storm.
> But whether he shall be able to bring in any of his friends to strengthen
> him (of which all the world thinks he hath need) or keep out his greatest
> enemies, who will seek by all possible means to overthrow him, I neither
> see nor hope for.

Knowing that his letter might easily be intercepted, he then goes on to
mock Cecil's humpback, bent shape, and "bumbasted legs" (i.e., padded
calves), calling him a viper and a pigmy. In a second letter he describes
Cecil's confirmation as, "the late instalment and canonization of the ven-
erable saint."[1] It is in the context of that mocking contempt for Robert
Cecil that the younger Davison, reporting on some English conspirators
en route via Spain, invented the word *Topcliffizare* to describe
Topcliffe's methods. There would be no need, he said, "either to
informare or *Topcliffizare*, being an office to which I have no great
stomach."

Not for the first time, one feels sorry for Charles Topcliffe. If
Davison's opinions were representative of the people around Essex, then
the younger Topcliffe's situation in a force commanded by Essex cannot
have been an easy one. In one of Charles's statements it appears that, to
his surprise, Essex himself had taken a dislike to him.[2]

After Cadiz, Essex conferred over sixty knighthoods, among them his
personal servant Gilly Merrick, and the Privy council clerk Anthony
Ashley, both of them guilty of major thefts from the Cadiz plunder.[3] In
the normal way of things, Charles Topcliffe, a well-connected, experienced and successful soldier, would have been a candidate for one of those
sixty-odd knighthoods; but Essex was not about to endorse the father's
associations and activities by knighting his son or even by treating him
decently.

An interesting personal detail that emerges from Topcliffe's letter to

---

[1]6 November 1596 (Birch 2.185–86, also 2.204).

[2]*CSPD, 1595–97*, 278: "I am sorry my General, the Earl of Essex, whom I honoured so,
conceives wrong of me, and puts a hard construction on my words and doings. I would
be thought honest, if a fool" (Charles Topcliffe to Secretary Cecil, 20 September 1596:
Calendar paraphrase).

[3]The list of knighthoods is in Folger Ms. V.b.142, f.21v.

Robert Cecil about his son's post-Cadiz troubles is that he was lame: he began the letter, "musing in my lame case," and signed off, "At Mr Wayer's house near the church, with my crutches...."[1] The lameness, however, was a temporary affliction.

*****

About six months after his release, Topcliffe began to resume activity, but in a much smaller way. In January 1596, he sent Puckering a final report on William Randall, the English Dunkirker whose ship had gone ashore in 1594, and asked him to let the Queen know the particularities: "my simple opinion being that if such men be spared for any respect, traitors will take heart to multiply in abundance."[2]

In January 1595 he had contributed to a set of documents on the priests imprisoned at Wisbech Castle, complaining that they were living well, entertaining servants, friends, and visitors "as if they were in a free college, and no prison." So when a priest called Tilletson who had escaped from Wisbech by going over the wall with a rope was recaptured and sent to the Gatehouse prison in March 1596, Topcliffe, by now back in London from Lincolnshire, was given the job of questioning him, but the larger inquiry into underlying conditions at Wisbech was left to Waad and Coke.[3] On 5 March, he and Stanhope (civil lawyer and chancellor of the diocese of London) moved a priest called Hothersall from the Gatehouse to Bridewell, and in June he, Mr. Solicitor Fleming, and Chief Justice Popham committed another priest, John Wilson, to the Gatehouse.[4] On 31 July 1596, he was included in a commission to search houses in the city. In August he presented Robert Cecil with comments appended to a list of the priests held in the London prisons.[5]

Those comments, offered as evidence of his knowledge of the subject, give one the impression that he was angling for work. They can be interesting, too. He claimed to have prevented George Hothersall from committing suicide. After his removal to Bridewell, "He did his endeavor to murder himself, and to cut his throat with a thin potshard most terribly;

---

[1] Ms. Hatfield 44/65 (Tuesday 7 Sept 96).

[2] BL Ms. Harleian 6998, f.214.

[3] BL Ms.Harleian 6998, f.222; *CSPD 1595–97*, 194.

[4] Anstruther, 383; MS Hatfield 43/41.

[5] Ms. Hatfield 43/41.

but," says Topcliffe, "by diligence, I procured him to be cured of this hurt." He diagnosed two of the priests, Tilletson and Hawkesworth, as potential informants, and of Robert Barwise or Barrows, alias Wallgrave, he wrote, "if I may proceed against him in Michaelmas term, I dare well promise to take one or two of the worst of those priests and practicers." He must have known that Barwise was already informing on his fellow-priests. He thought John Gerard, S.J., might be "used...to do service," but of course he was proved wrong about that.

In any case, Cecil did not bite. Instead, he and other Councilors started using him again for what we would call ordinary police work. They began by instructing him, along with Francis Bacon, to examine a man reported to the council as a suspected spy by the Earl of Essex and the Lord Admiral. He had been poking about among the ships at Plymouth, so they sent him up to London. Bacon and Topcliffe cleared him of the charge.[1]

In August, the Council issued Topcliffe a warrant to arrest a groom of the chamber called Maddox, along with his brother. He had been passing himself off as a Messenger of the Chamber, or pursuivant, so Topcliffe was to bring him before the Council, and to search his house with the constable as necessary.[2] Three months later, the Council wrote to the Recorder of London (now John Croke), Topcliffe, and Richard Skevington (a Middlesex justice) requiring them to examine a group of gipsies. A band of about eighty gipsies had been wandering from county to county until the Norhamptonshire authorities rounded them up, and sent some of the "leaders" to the council in London. Topcliffe and his companions were to examine them upon a set of articles drawn up by the Lord Chief justice. If they found themselves unable "by fair means to bring them to reveal their lewd behavior, practices, and ringleaders," then they were to transfer them to Bridewell, and put them to the manacles, "whereby they may be constrained to utter the truth in those matters concerning their lewd behavior."[3]   The gipsies' fate is unknown.

Two more police cases rounded out the next year, 1597. The first case was a nasty murder. The body of Richard Anger or Aunger, an elderly reader of Gray's Inn who had been missing for a month, was found float-

---

[1]*APC*, 25. 449 (10 June).

[2]*APC*, 26. 120. On 3 May this same year, 1596, the Queen issued a proclamation against "divers dissolute and audacious persons" impersonating messengers of the chamber, or pursuivants (*STC* 8249).

[3]*APC*, 26. 325 (21 November 1596).

ing in the Thames. "Certain skillful chirurgeons," examined the body and concluded that he had not drowned, but had been first murdered, and then thrown into the river. Suspicion fell on one of his sons, Richard Anger junior, and a porter of Gray's Inn, Edward Ingram.

On 17 November, the Council wrote to Topcliffe and four others, requiring them to examine the son and the porter. If they were unable to bring them to confess the truth of "this horrible fact" by ordinary means, they were to put both of them to the manacles in Bridewell, "that by compulsory means the truth of this wicked murder may be discovered and who were complices and privy to this confederacy and fact."[1]

The examinations, whether torture was used or not, were successful. The son and his wife Agnes Anger "put themselves guilty" to murdering the old man by strangling him, and were sentenced to be hanged. The porter put himself on the jury, and was found innocent.[2]

The year 1597 ended with the Council writing, 1 December, to Topcliffe and six others, asking any two of them to examine a man called Travers. He was in in Bridewell for stealing a standish (an inkwell) belonging to the Queen. He had been arrested on the evidence of witnesses, but was persisting in denial. The Council wanted a confession: "If he shall not declare the truth by your persuasion, then put him to the torture of the manacles." Either this was a very valuable inkwell, or else Elizabeth I, like her half-sister Mary, had little mercy for people who stole her personal property.[3]

*****

Topcliffe's most unusual police assignment in 1597 involved him in an episode of theatre history. In July, the Earl of Pembroke's Men, playing at Francis Langley's Swan theatre on the Bankside, put on a play by Thomas Nashe and Ben Jonson called *The Isle of Dogs*.[4] The play proved to be very offensive to the authorities. On 28 July the Lord Mayor and Aldermen of the City of London seized the opportunity to send the Council one of their letters asking for the suppression of the theatres, and the same day the Council—independently it seems—issued

---

[1] *APC*, 28. 187 (17 November 1597).

[2] Jeaffreson, 1.241.

[3] *APC*, 28. 165 (1 December 1597).

[4] There are many accounts of this incident. The standard account is in Chambers, 2.453, 4.131–2. See also Ingram, 167ff., and Nicholl 1, 242–56.

an order to the justices of Middlesex and Surrey not only to suppress all performances, but to "pluck down" the theatres as well. Their order does not mention the play; it merely says that the Queen has acted because "there are very great disorders committed in the common play-houses both by lewd matters that are handled on the stages and by resort and confluence of bad people." Nonetheless, Philip Henslowe, who owned and operated the Rose theatre on Bankside knew that performing *The Isle of Dogs* had caused the restraint.[1]

The Council, meanwhile, had set about finding and punishing those responsible for the play. They had three of the actors, Gabriel Spencer, Robert Shaw, and Ben Jonson arrested and put in the Marshalsea prison. They knew that Jonson was a writer of the play, and that his fellow-writer was Thomas Nashe. They sent a pursuivant, Ferris, to arrest Nashe, but he must have had advance warning of trouble, because he had skipped town and gone home to Norfolk. No doubt he remembered what had happened to poor Thomas Kyd a few years earlier.[2] Ferris (probably the officer in charge of arresting the other three as well) contented himself with raiding Nashe's lodging and taking his papers. Most of the acting company decamped, too, and went on tour. By September they were performing in Bristol.[3]

On 15 August, the Council wrote to Topcliffe, Thomas Fowler, Richard Skevington, Dr. Fletcher, and Mr. Wilbraham, requiring them to examine the three prisoners in the Marshalsea. By now they all knew what the play was about, and why it was "seditious." The council wanted to make sure that everyone responsible for the "lewd and mutinous misbehavior" of writing and acting the play should be punished. They also wanted to know what copies were in existence, and who had them.

All the addressees of the Council's letter (except Wilbraham) had experience of the torture room.[4] Even so, there is no hint in the

---

[1]Chambers, 4.321–3; 3.454.

[2]Kyd had been arrested and tortured as part of an attempt to find the authors of inflammatory libels against foreigners posted in London. Two Council warrants authorized the city authorities to use torture. The first, 16 April 1593, concerned a person already arrested; the second, 11 May, concerned people to be arrested and questioned, and specified Bridewell as the place. In both cases the torture would have been the manacles. Torture probably hastened Kyd's early death at 35 in August 1594 (*APC*, 24. 187, 222; Freeman, 181–3).

[3]*APC*, 27. 338 (15 August 1597); Chambers 2.133.

[4]Fowler and Skevington were Middlesex magistrates. Dr. Giles Fletcher was Remembrancer of London, and Thomas Wilbraham worked for Robert Cecil.

instructions of "aggressive" interrogation. On the contrary: the examiners were encouraged to extend the possibility of "favor" to the prisoners in return for their cooperation.[1]

The interrogators found out nothing of any importance. Jonson later told Drummond of Hawthornden that his keeper had warned him of spies in the prison, and he bragged that he said nothing to his interrogators except "Ay" and "No." There were no more arrests, and on 8 October the Council issued warrants for the release of the prisoners. Shortly after, on 11 October, as Henslowe had expected, playing resumed at the Rose.[2] There was no official lifting of the restraint, and no theatres were pulled down.

William Ingram, the historian of Francis Langley and his Swan theatre, thinks the *Isle of Dogs* affair was a storm in a teacup, and that Topcliffe was responsible for it. Professor Ingram based this conclusion on a sentence in a letter of reference that Topcliffe wrote on 10 August to Robert Cecil about one of his agents. Cecil knew the man, and had previously used his services, but had come to distrust him. Topcliffe, attempting to restore his man to Cecil's good graces, sent him to Cecil with his testimonial letter, which contains the reference to the play:

> And I have lifted up his heart again with letting him know that her Majesty is so well pleased with him, and your Honor also, for the proof he lately made to me of his loyal heart, to be the first man that discovered to me that seditious play called *The Isle of Dogs*, in his opinion as a venemous intent and a preparative to some far-fetched mischief.[3]

That sentence could certainly imply that Topcliffe's agent was the authorities' informant, through Topcliffe, about the play. The letter, though, is not about the play; it is about the agent, who has taken a lonely house for himself, his wife and children, fit for him and Topcliffe to carry out a number of unspecified purposes together. What those purposes were, we do not know, but they seem to be more important than the seditious play, and the letter gives one the impression that Topcliffe was once again angling for re-employment.

It is unlikely that Topcliffe initiated that much trouble over a play all by himself at that stage of his career, although since the play is described as seditious and slanderous, he would have taken a keen interest, as the

[1] *APC*, 27. 338.

[2] *APC*, 28. 33.

[3] Hatfield 54/20.

Queen's personal policeman, in finding out about it. Although the bearer of his letter was the first to tell him about the play, the sentence suggests that he heard about it from a number of people. Another implication of the sentence is that the play was a topic of conversation in governing circles.[1]

What, one wonders, was so offensive about this lost play? The answer to that question lies probably in the figurative implications of the title. In Elizabethan times, the Isle of Dogs was an expanse of marshy land east of London, enclosed on three sides by a huge meander of the Thames. It faced Greenwich and its royal palace on the south bank of the river. Until Dutch engineers drained and protected it in the seventeenth century the isle was an odorous, unsanitary waste, washed over by raw sewage floating down river from the city.

A pair of linked references to the isle will give a hint of the play's probable drift. First, Thomas Nashe himself, mocking Gabriel Harvey in *Strange News* (1593):

> Broom boys, and corncutters, (or whatsoever trade is more contemptible) come not in his way, stand forty foot from the execution place of his fury, for else in the full tide of his standish he will carry your occupations handsmooth out of town before him, besmear them, drown them; down the river they go *Privily* to the Isle of Dogs with his Pamphlets. (Sig.D4v)

The implication is that Harvey's pamphlets are only good for toilet-paper, and end up with all the other sewage at the Isle of Dogs.

The second reference is from the third Parnassus Play, *The Return From Parnassus, or The Scourge of Simony*, written shortly after Nashe's death in 1602. The speaker is Ingenioso, a character who embodies aspects of both Robert Greene and Nashe:

> Faith, *Academico*, it's the fear of that fellow, I mean the sign of the sergeant's head, that makes me to be so hasty to be gone: to be brief, *Academico*, writs are out for me, to apprehend me for my plays, and now I am bound for the Isle of Dogs...Our voyage is to the Isle of Dogs, there where the Blatant Beast doth rule and reign, renting the credit of whom it please.[2]

---

[1]Topcliffe's agent has now been identified as William Udall, a thoroughly unreliable, projecting rascal despite Topcliffe's testimonial. See Misha Teramura, "Richard Topcliffe's Informant: New Light on *The Isle of Dogs*," *Review of English Studies* 68 (Feb. 2017): 44–59. A few months later Udall, writing to the Earl of Essex about a planned raid on the Blackfriars Gatehouse, suggested that Topcliffe had given the residents advance warning; and in 1600 a man called Henry Knowles was warning Robert Cecil that Udall, whom Topcliffe trusted, was planning to deceive him (*Hat.Cal.*, 8.74 (1 March 1598); 14.141–2 (18 October 1600).

The first sentence sounds like a reference to Nashe's experience with his play; the second is probably a reference to the play itself. If the Blatant Beast from the 6th Book of Spenser's *Faerie Queene* rules the Isle of Dogs, then the play portrayed a society, no doubt a court society, dominated by lies, slander, and detraction. To complete the picture, and supply the inference, one has only to visualize the royal palace itself and the court sitting on the opposite bank of the river, the Isle's mirror-image.

If the play's satire was aimed at London and the court as a place of moral filth, pestered by spies and informers, then it is very likely that an important influence on its two young authors will have been Sir John Harington's recent pamphlet, *A New Discourse of a Stale Subject, Called a Metamorphosis of Ajax* (1596). Ostensibly that pamphlet is a witty fantasia on the whole subject of Elizabethan sanitation, recommending Harington's invention, a flushing water-closet, to clean the place up. Approached allegorically or figuratively it is also an unsparing attack on what Harington considered the moral filth of contemporary England, in particular the activities of spies, informers, and "promoters" used by people like Topcliffe and his associate Justice Richard Young. Harington actually named Young in the autograph marginalia that he wrote into presentation copies intended for certain friends.[2]

Like Harington, Nashe and Jonson will have treated their theme figuratively; but no matter how cleverly indirect the approach, readers and spectators in both cases would understand the implications, that the real subject was what Harington called "the quintessence of a stink." One sees why, if the Queen was implicated in the play's satire, Topcliffe started talking to Robert Cecil about it. It is no wonder, either, that both the pamphlet and the play caused trouble for their writers with the Queen and Council. Nashe in particular was in deep trouble. He had already made himself unpopular with the government because of his attack on the memory of Leicester (among other things) in his pamphlet *Pierce Penniless*. His career never really recovered from the disaster of *The Isle of Dogs*.

---

[2] *The Three Parnassus plays (1598-1601)*, edited by J.B. Leishman (London: Nicholson & Watson, 1949),

[2] For the significance of Harington's autograph marginalia, and the real meaning of his *Metamorphosis*, see Kilroy 1, 89–96, who prints Harington's note on Justice Young, recently dead: "*Tamquam stercus, memoria impiorum,* ("the memory of the unjust is as shit"). In 1595–6, though, Harington would not have dared to attack Topcliffe even privately, whatever he thought of him.

*****

Half a dozen ordinary criminal cases spread over a year was not enough to keep Topcliffe occupied, and besides he had other, long-standing business to attend to. He had still not found a way of maintaining Anne Bellamy and her husband Jones. As we saw, having failed to bully Richard Bellamy into giving him the farm called Preston, he had decided that his best option was to have Anne Bellamy incriminate one of her family's friends, a gentleman called Barnes, and so acquire his property for the pair.

Even a Tudor court would not indict Barnes on Anne Bellamy's gossip alone, so Topcliffe set about trying to force people who knew the man to inform against him, giving evidence that he had associated with seminary priests and Jesuits, that he had relieved priests, and procured masses to be said, etc. That was why, in quest of evidence against Barnes, Topcliffe had raided Lady Montagu's houses, and arrested her old Marian chaplains, and why, on the basis of confessions forced out of old Robert Gray by the threat of torture, he had arrested Barnes himself, and proceeded to arrest and torture old Mr. Garnet's servant, James Atkinson, in Bridewell.

When the Council imprisoned Topcliffe at Easter 1595, Atkinson was recently dead under torture; and Barnes was in close imprisonment in the Gatehouse, deprived of light and warmth, but still refusing to incriminate himself. Topcliffe had turned his attention to one of Barnes's servants, Michael Thompson. Thompson had refused to betray his master, and there for a moment matters lay.

Like any normal person, Thompson, after his encounter with Topcliffe, was "never quiet in mind, but said he thought he should have run out of his wits." Some time during that summer of 1595, therefore, he began writing letters to the Council in defense of his master, attempting to expose Topcliffe's methods. The result was an appointment to meet with the Council in London in Michaelmas Term. Inevitably, Topcliffe, newly out of prison, heard about this, and made arrangements for Thompson to be arrested. Lord Keeper Puckering, of all people, gave him a warrant to commit Thompson close prisoner to the Clink. Evidently Puckering, having made his own personal point about Topcliffe's infringements upon his authority, was not about to earn the ill-will of the Queen, the Cecils, or his fellow-councilors by standing in the way of Topcliffe's pursuit of Catholics.

Thompson in prison could not hurt Topcliffe, but neither could he be used against Barnes; Topcliffe, therefore, turned his attention to two more of Barnes's servants, a married couple called John and Joan Harrison. To give himself a pretext for arresting them, he put out the story that they were not married, that Harrison was a seminary priest, and that Joan Harrison was a common woman whom Barnes and the priest called Davies or Winkefield shared between them. He then began by arresting the wife, and putting her in Bridewell.

Joan Harrison was in Bridewell five months without giving evidence against her master. The Council then released her in response to her petitions, and so Topcliffe arrested her husband, and put him in Bridewell, too. His intention, once again, was to bully Harrison into incriminating his master, but like his wife, he refused. Mrs. Harrison, having successfully petitioned the Council on her own behalf, then wrote to them for her husband in February, 1596.

It appears from the Council's response that she had been a frequent complainer to them, also that Topcliffe had indeed accused her husband of being a seminary priest. Now Mrs. Harrison was asking that her husband should not be kept in prison without just cause, that he should be examined and, "upon certificate thereof made [to the Council] be proceeded with accordingly." The council thought her request was reasonable, and gave orders for John Harrison to be examined.[1]

His examination took place on 3 March 1596, and it is obvious from the questions that Topcliffe was in charge. There was no mention now of Harrison being a priest or of Mrs. Harrison being a common woman. That story had merely been a pretext for arresting the two of them. The examination first established that Harrison was Catholic (of which he made no secret) and that he had served Barnes for eighteen years. The serious questions which followed were all intended to show that Barnes had been in company with priests and Jesuits at the Bellamys' house and in Lord Montagu's house at Cowdray. Like James Atkinson and Michael Thompson, John Harrison found the courage to deny all knowledge of any evidence that would incriminate his master.[2]

We learn more of Harrison's treatment from Barnes's speech at his trial. Having arrested him on the pretense that he was a priest, Topcliffe first took him to the Bishop of London, at that time Richard Fletcher, where he did his best to force him to accuse his master. When Harrison refused, Topcliffe—no doubt in a rage—bound his hands with a cord and pulled him through the streets to Bridewell where he gave orders for

---

[1]*APC*, 25. 241 (27 February 15960.

[2]Harrison's examination is preserved in NA/SP12/256/71 (3 March 1596).

him to be put in irons and given no bed. When his examination produced no evidence justifying either an indictment of himself or his master, Topcliffe made sure that he remained in prison, even although his wife continually petitioned the Council for his freedom.

John Harrison died in Bridewell, sometime in the late spring or the summer of 1596, leaving his wife and children behind him. "And this," said Barnes at his trial, "is the third person dying in this bad cause, by Mr. Topcliffe's means." The other two were James Atkinson and Mrs. Bellamy, all three of them martyrs for their faith by Topcliffe's means.

*****

John Harrison's case, like Michael Thompson's, reveals that despite Topcliffe's loss of his commission he was still free to arrest people and, with a little ingenuity, commit them to prison. A pair of letters that the Council wrote to the keeper of the Gatehouse about his treatment of Mr. Barnes explains how he was doing this.

At about the same time that Joan Harrison wrote petitioning the Council for her husband, Robert Barnes wrote to Puckering, complaining about his treatment at Topcliffe's hands. He had been kept, he said, almost two years close prisoner, without light or warmth, and ten days in irons.[1] The Council's very prompt response had been to order the keeper of the Gatehouse to allow Barnes "the liberty of the prison."[2]

Topcliffe, though, told the keeper to disregard the Council's order, and so they wrote to him again:

> We understand that notwithstanding commandment given you that one Robert Barnes should have the liberty of the prison in your safe custody in the Gatehouse, yet by Mr. Topcliffe's direction he is still kept close prisoner, whereat we do not a little marvel. We require and charge you therefore to permit him to have the liberty of the house according to our said former commandment, and to require Mr. Topcliffe to come forthwith to attend upon us. Hereof fail you not.[3]

"Whereat we do not a little marvel" is strong language for the Council. A mere three days later, they wrote again, expressing themselves even

---

[1] Ms. Harleian 6998, f. 24, written Jan–Feb 1596.

[2] The head keeper at the Gatehouse was named Parlour. His two chief under-keepers were Pickering and Stanwardine Passy. Nicholas Jones was for a time an under-keeper at the Gatehouse.

[3] *APC*, 25. 237 (25 February 1596).

more strongly on the same subject. They began by saying that they had checked to see that this time their order had been obeyed, and that Barnes had been released from close imprisonment, "whom you had, as we perceive, shut up close contrary to our former commandment by Mr. Topcliffe's sole direction." They then proceeded to "require and command" the keeper "not to receive any prisoner by the warrant or commandment of any one private man *mentioned in the Commission under the Great Seal for the examination of prisoners, &c*" [my italics]. Before receiving any such prisoner, the keeper was to notify the Council. "Hereof fail you not," they concluded.[1]

This second letter tells us that when the first order came to release Barnes from close imprisonment, Topcliffe had not merely said to the Gatehouse keeper, "Pay no attention to them. I'm in charge here." Even Topcliffe would not have dared to do that. Instead, although he had lost his personal commission, he claimed authority to imprison as one of a number of people named in a still-valid general commission issued under the Great Seal. The Council, therefore, removed that authority too.

Topcliffe had acted upon a technicality, and that he had the nerve to do so reveals him still enjoying the kind of backing and favor that mattered. There must have been a division on the Council over him and his methods that he felt confident enough to exploit.

Even now he did not give up his pursuit of Barnes. As he later told Barnes in the presence of other people, "he never took any Papist in hand but he brought him to the gallows, or kept him in perpetual prison." He therefore launched another attack on Barnes through his Montagu connections. On 20 June 1596, two items of Topcliffian business came before the Council. The first was a letter to Topcliffe's neighbor, Roger Dallison, owner of Laughton, a small property just north of Gainsborough, whose servants had carried out a poaching raid on Topcliffe's manor, Somerby. The second was a letter directed to "Mrs. Browne," instructing her to deliver one of her servants, Anthony Fletcher, into the custody of the bearer, Nicholas Jones, yeoman of her Majesty's chamber, "whom we have made special choice of for that purpose." A note in the margin of the Council register tells us that, "These two letters following were brought ready drawn and signed to the Clerk of the Council by Mr. Richard Topcliffe, Esquire."[2]

This note is hardly believable: Topcliffe was still conducting his own

---

[1] *APC*, 25. 254 (28 Feb. 1596).

[2] *APC*, 25. 480–81 (20 June 1596).

business in his own words through the medium of the Queen's Privy Council, and the illiterate rascal Jones had come up in the world. He was now a yeoman of the Queen's chamber, empowered to bring a prisoner to London. Nor was he bringing him before the Council; he was required merely to arrest him and take him wherever he wished, presumably to Topcliffe, who was still using the power of the Council to arrest and interrogate as he pleased.

How had this come about? The event that allowed this reversion to former practice may have been the death, 30 April, of Lord Keeper Puckering. He had not been a particularly distinguished Lord Keeper, but he had had strong views on correct legal practice and the respect due to himself and his office.[1]

Anthony Fletcher had been one of the people named in the Council's letters authorizing Topcliffe to raid Lady Montagu's houses back in 1593. He had not been caught. When Topcliffe and Jones threatened James Atkinson in the late summer of 1593, it was to Fletcher that Atkinson wrote his intercepted letter of warning. In Topcliffe's mind, therefore, Fletcher was another servant who could incriminate Barnes, and the "Mrs. Browne" to whom he now wrote was one of Lady Montagu's daughters-in-law, probably Mary Dormer Browne, the 1st Viscount's eldest son's widow. Yet even though this letter was couched in threatening terms,[2] there is no evidence that Topcliffe and Jones ever succeeded in laying hands on Anthony Fletcher.[3]

Having failed completely to incriminate Barnes through the evidence of his neighbors and servants, Topcliffe now conspired to exploit the feature of the penal laws that made relieving a priest a felony, and by doing so to kill three recusant birds with one stone, one of them being

---

[1] Puckering's contemporary, Sir Roger Wilbraham, left an acid comment on him: "One said by Puckering L. Keeper: he was acquainted with him very familiarly, & had neither great learning nor wealth till that advancement, but now he perceived the operation of a L. keeper's place was to purchase a manor every month" (*The Journal of Sir Roger Wilbraham*, ed Harold Spencer Scott [Camden Miscellany, Vol .10: London: Offices of the Royal Historical Society, 1902], 9).

[2] "And you will foresee that he shall not start away or eloigne himself as heretofore he did, as though any place or person were privileged not to give a reckoning of their doings when good occasion falleth out."

[3] After his wife's death, in 1609 Anthony Fletcher entered the English College, Rome, under the alias Blackwell. He took the oath 2 May 1610, received minor orders the next June, was ordained subdeacon and deacon in December, and ordained priest 18 December 1610. He left Rome for England in September 1612. "A man of great virtue and prudence" (Foley , 6.253). See also Questier, 315.

Robert Barnes. The other two were the Catholic ladies imprisoned with him in the Gatehouse, Mrs. Bellamy and Mrs. Wiseman, and Topcliffe's fellow conspirators in this operation were certain members of the Council and the Secretary of State.

The third of these prisoners, Mrs. Jane Wiseman, was the widow of Thomas Wiseman of Braddocks, Essex. The family was strongly Catholic. Her four daughters became nuns, and two of her sons became Jesuits. Encouraged by John Gerard, S.J., who was for a time the family's chaplain, she made her properties into safe houses for the protection of priests and the celebration of Mass. A servant, John Frank, then betrayed the family. The houses were raided, and Mrs. Wiseman was imprisoned, probably in 1593. Being in the Gatehouse, she saw a good deal of Topcliffe, although he seems to have played no part in the raids on her houses.[1]

There was a fellow called Blackwell who hung about the prison, doing small errands for Mrs. Wiseman. She, Mrs. Bellamy, and Barnes provided him his dinner every day, plus enough to take home for his family. Unknown to the prisoners, this man was one of Topcliffe's spies or instruments. Topcliffe, extremely well-informed about priests in London, imprisoned and otherwise, knew that there was a priest in the Clink Prison suffering from a hurt leg. He thought it would be an excellent stratagem to arrange for this man's release, and then after a lapse of time to quiet any suspicions the priest might have, to have his agent Blackwell take him to the Gatehouse. There the kindly Catholic ladies would treat his sore leg, and all three Catholic prisoners would fraternize with him. All three could then be indicted for relieving a priest, and sentenced to death.

The priest was a Welsh Franciscan, John Jones, known to the prisoners only as Mr. Buckley. The published accounts of this man's ministry and dealings with the prisoners contain inaccuracies, partly because of

---

[1]For Mrs. Wiseman, see Gerard, 51–4, and the account of her in the Chronicle of St. Monica's (Hamilton, 81–4), which includes an amusing story of her time in the Gatehouse: "Upon a time her friend Topcliffe passed under her window, being mounted upon a goodly horse going to the Queen, and Mrs Wiseman espying him thought it would not be amiss to wash him a little with holy water, therefore took some which she had by her, and flung it upon him and his horse as he came under her window. It was a wonderful thing to see; no sooner had the holy water touched the horse, but presently it seems he could not endure his rider, for the horse began to kick and fling that he never ceased till his master Topcliffe was flung to the ground, who looked up to the window and raged against Mrs. Wiseman calling her an old witch who, by her charms, had made his horse to lay him on the ground, but she with good reason laughed to see that holy water had given him so fine a fall" (Hamilton, 83–4).

the lack of documentary information, but mostly because Topcliffe—except for Barnes's revelations at his trial—covered his tracks so expertly.

Fr. Gerard dates Jones's arrival in England sometime in 1592, then gives him a few months working with him out of his London safe house, then a few months on his own before he was arrested. Fr. Garnet gives him three years' work before his arrest, then two years in prison in the Clink, where he reconciled the lay martyr John Rigby ca.1596–97. As for his dealings with the Gatehouse prisoners, Garnet thought that Jones made his own way to the ladies in the Gatehouse from "motives of piety." Fr. Pollen, who knows that he was lured into going there by Topcliffe, thinks the visit took place on 3 January 1596; but that is a year too soon.

All the mysteries of Jones's dealings with the prisoners are cleared up by the chronology of events as Barnes narrated them at his trial, and by a remarkable letter that Topcliffe wrote to his fellow-conspirator, Robert Cecil. The letter, which survives among the Hatfield papers, is similar in tone to the letter that Topcliffe wrote to the Queen about the capture of Southwell. There is the same assumption of familiarity, the same breezy jocularity, and the same confidence that his correspondent will enjoy a little skullduggery:

> Right Honorable: It may seem strange that I sue to have a traitorous friar delivered out of a prison to a better lodging or friend. If I seek that favor for any other purpose for him but to take a traitor tenfold weightier then himself, and to deliver him to you, & him again also whom I seem to favor thus now, let my allegiance be then charged with corruption and falsehood two days after Candelmas day next. I do not name the party for secrecy, which is all in all.
>
> When I have the letter signed, I will set down a larger condition, and part of this service, and name all parties whom I have named to you before, and put forth to trial him that your honor and I have long suspected to be but a double dealer. He is by this letter signed put to the touchstone and last trial and refuge; and good surety shall be a piece of a pledge, but my allegiance most of all.
>
> The man that I require to have this favor for a while was taken by Mr. Justice Young four or five year since, and he can do no more hurt if he have this liberty than I am sure he doth in prison. And so humbly end, loath to trouble any councilor for secrecy sake but yourself. This present Thursday, your honor's at commandment,
>
> Ric: Topcliffe:
>
> I will show your honor the letter, when I have the Lord Keeper's hand, who liketh of the device; and two or three other councilors' hands at the

letter, else stay it upon my allegiance. No gain should force me to do this.[1]

It is not often that one catches a senior government official red-handed in a crime. This letter is obviously a follow-up to a conversation in which Topcliffe told Robert Cecil that he planned to trap Robert Barnes into relieving a priest by releasing Jones alias Buckley, and having his agent Blackwell take him to the Gatehouse pretending that he was a layman. There the ladies would treat his leg, and there Barnes, too (Topcliffe's primary object), would assist him. With any luck, they might even arrange to have a mass said in the prison. Although Topcliffe does not name names for secrecy's sake, "which is all in all," there was only one imprisoned friar in London whom Topcliffe was interested in for his purpose; and Robert Barnes is the double-dealer whom Topcliffe now means to put to the touchstone.

Once again, and with Cecil's complicity, Topcliffe has written his own warrant for Jones's release. One notices, too, with a special kind of relish, that the new Lord Keeper, Thomas Egerton,[2] is in on the trick, and that Topcliffe is sure that two or three other Councilors, suitably approached, will sign his letter. The remainder of the Council will be left in happy ignorance. So, with a warrant written by himself, and signed by Cecil, the Lord Keeper, and two or three other Councilors, Topcliffe will put his plan in action.

Blackwell, who had seen Mrs. Bellamy make a cerecloth to dress a wound one day, told her that a Catholic gentleman he knew had hurt his

---

[1]Ms. Hatfield 57/108 (22 December 1596). The letter is undated. Someone has endorsed it 22 December 1597; but since Barnes tells us that Blackwell brought Jones to the Gatehouse on 3 January 1596 (i.e., 1597 new style), the real date of the letter was 22 December 1596.

[2]Egerton was the bastard son of Sir Richard Egerton, a Cheshire landowner, and a servant girl called Alice Sparke. He was raised by Thomas Ravenscroft of Flintshire, whose daughter was his first wife. His father paid for his education, and he became an able lawyer, who put together a good practice with the patronage of the Stanleys and other regional magnates. As a young man he was a Catholic, but saw the error of his ways, and as a rising star in state service he became Burghley's means of countering Stanley influence after Ferdinando Stanley succeeded his father as earl of Derby. To quote Christopher Devlin: "Egerton...seems almost to have stepped into Ferdinando's skin. He got his Chamberlainship [of Chester: a hereditary Stanley office], his private papers, his books, his manor of Brackley, his unfortunate widow (who seems to have had no choice), and the wardship of his daughters...all this without any personal rancour; he was simply serving Cecil to check every path to the succession" (Devlin 2, 104n). The one cheering note in Egerton's rather depressing career of ingratiation and self-aggrandizement is that the dowager countess, who had been very happily married to Ferdinando Stanley, made Egerton's personal life hell.

leg, and could not afford to pay a doctor to look after it. Would she look
at it? She agreed, and the next day, 3 January 1597, Blackwell brought
Jones, calling him Buckley, to the Gatehouse. The time was "towards
evening." Mrs. Bellamy dressed the hurt leg, but her ointment hurt so
badly that the patient could not go home that evening. Blackwell asked
Barnes if "Buckley" might stay the night in his room with him. Without
his keeper's consent, said Barnes, he could not. So Blackwell went off
to see the keeper (probably Stanwardine Passy), and came back with the
keeper's instruction that Mr. Buckley should stay over night with
Barnes. Barnes, unwilling to annoy the keeper, agreed.

The next morning Blackwell returned with meat, bread, and a bottle
of wine at Buckley's expense. They all dined together, after which the
man they knew as Buckley left, and they never saw him again.

Topcliffe now had his case, but it was a risky one. Judges and juries
did not always like to hang men merely for being priests, and they would
certainly not like the idea of hanging three lay people because they
looked after someone's hurt leg, and had dinner with him, not knowing
that he was a priest.

Nothing now happened for six months until Midsummer, when
Blackwell announced to Mrs. Wiseman that he had become a Catholic.
She asked him who made him one? Blackwell told her it was Mr.
Buckley, the man with the sore leg. He was a priest and a friar. He and
two other priests had said mass at his house, and tomorrow he would
bring all his church stuff so that Mr. Buckley could say mass for them
all. "If he be a friar and a priest," replied Mrs. Wiseman, "be not so
hardy, for thy life, to bring him hither; for I have promised unto Mr.
Pickering, my keeper, that I will bring no person of danger hither to
endanger his house."

Even so, it seems that Topcliffe accused them all to the authorities for
arranging a Mass, but Barnes later told the court that they had successfully denied Blackwell's tales before Mr. Attorney and Mr. Solicitor,
and that Mr. Solicitor had assured Mrs. Wiseman that she would come to
no harm from Blackwell's lies. After that, Blackwell came less often to
the prison, but when he did he brought Catholic stuff—beads, grains,
medals and such—in hope that they might accept some of it. Eventually,
at the end of November, he brought "a book of pardons." He tried hard
to persuade Barnes to copy it out in his room, but of course the potential
victims knew what the plan was: as soon as Barnes took the book,
Blackwell would signal Topcliffe, watching at his window, and
Topcliffe would have caught Barnes, book in hand, and charged him
with treason.

Topcliffe's next move was to arrest Stanwardine Passy, Barnes's keeper, as a traitor for permitting a mass to be said in the prison, and for allowing a priest to stay over night in Barnes's chamber. Very shortly afterwards, he had Jones/Buckley arrested again, and then forged a letter, supposed to be written by Blackwell, asking the prisoners to send aid to his friend Mr. Buckley. Recognizing Topcliffe's style in the letter, they would have nothing to do either with it or with Blackwell.

By now we are in the early months of 1598. Mrs. Bellamy, having died in the prison, drops out of the narrative. Topcliffe has ordered Mrs. Wiseman and Barnes into close imprisonment despite the Council's now two-year old instructions to the contrary. Ever since the "relieving" of Jones a year earlier, Topcliffe, with the complicity of the Council, had been delaying trial as he attempted to strengthen his case. Finally, on the last day of Candlemas Term, he preferred indictments against Mrs. Wiseman, Barnes, and Jones alias Buckley, and the trials took place 30 June–3 July. The charge against Mrs Wiseman and Barnes was that they had "feloniously received and comforted" two priests, John Jones and George Hothersall.[1] Jones was charged simply with being a priest "under the statute."

Mr. Justice Fenner was the trial judge. Mrs. Wiseman pleaded not guilty, but being unwilling that the jury should incur the guilt of her death, refused jury trial, and was sentenced—as was usual in such cases—to the *peine forte et dure*, i.e., to be pressed to death or, as the marginal note (in Latin) puts it, "to be crushed." Jones, too, refused to put himself on the jury, and was sentenced out of hand to be hanged, drawn, and quartered. Barnes pleaded not guilty, and after a good deal of legal maneuvering as he tried his best to have his case heard by the law officers, he put himself on the jury, "knowing that his life was gone, notwithstanding his innocency."

There were only two witnesses against him, Blackwell and Topcliffe. Blackwell told the court that he brought Jones alias Buckley to the Gatehouse, that he stayed there two nights, and said two masses in Mrs. Bellamy's chamber for Mrs. Bellamy, her two daughters, Mrs. Wiseman, Barnes, and Passy. Barnes was the server, and gave Jones a piece of gold plus money towards the hire of a horse. Barnes denied all this, and when he asked permission to question the priest (who was present of course), Judge Fenner ruled that the priest's testimony was inadmissible

---

[1]Topcliffe had moved Hothersall from the Gatehouse to Bridewell in March 1596. The long note he wrote about him in August makes no mention of anyone "relieving" him in the Gatehouse. See above, 313.

because "he was a party," and because "he was dispensed withal, to swear any falsehood."

Then Topcliffe said that Passy, who was not present, described the mass in his confession. He then produced a red vestment the priest was supposed to have worn, and Barnes said that he never saw it in his life, and that Topcliffe had coerced Passy into his confession. So the trial proceeded, a legal farce if ever there was one, until Barnes, most unusually, asked permission to speak for himself. Judge Fenner permitted this, and Barnes began: "The first original of all my troubles proceeded from Anne Bellamy, the daughter of Richard Bellamy, of Uxendon, in the county of Middlesex...."

Barnes's speech must have lasted a good hour as he revealed, in circumstantial detail, the whole sordid story of Topcliffe's dealings with the Bellamys, starting with Anne Bellamy and the arrest of Fr. Southwell. At one point towards the end, the judge intervened to warn Barnes that he was doing himself no good:

> Here Mr. Justice Fenner said, I laid many subtle practices to be done by Mr. Topcliffe, but it did but make my cause to be the worse, to speak against so good a statesman, and that it would hurt my cause the more.

Even so, Barnes was not to be deflected. He carried his story to its conclusion in the present moment, and when the judge "exclaimed" against Mrs. Bellamy and her house, Barnes told him that she and her house had nothing to do with his indictment.

The verdict, inevitably, was "guilty." One last clash took place between Barnes and Topcliffe after the sentencing. When Judge Fenner told Barnes that if he conformed himself to the Queen's proceedings, i.e., conformed to the state church, he could have mercy, Barnes replied that he was a Catholic. Then, perhaps because a condemned felon's property was forfeit to the Crown in any case, Topcliffe told the judge that he would beg the Queen's mercy for Barnes. Barnes's answer was peremptory: "I had proved directly that he would have had my living for his woman Jones's wife, and as for my pardon, I wished him not to trouble himself for it, for I would none of his begging."

The judge thought that Barnes was refusing the Queen's mercy. Not at all, Barnes replied: he had tasted of her justice, now he appealed to her mercy—but not by his adversary's means. These replies drove Topcliffe into one of his rages. He wished, he said, that he had Barnes alone to spend his blood upon him—but no-one seems to have paid attention to him. Barnes prayed that God would forgive the jurors for their false verdict; the judges rose, and the prisoners were carried back to prison.

On 12 July, John Jones was taken on a hurdle to be hanged at St. Thomas Watering. This is the place where Chaucer's pilgrims paused with their host, Harry Bailey, on the first stage of their journey. It was named after a brook or spring dedicated to St. Thomas, but by the sixteenth century it had become the Surrey place of execution. It was two miles out of London, on what is now the Old Kent Road.[1]

Topcliffe was present. Jones's first act was to clear Mrs. Wiseman and Barnes of either giving him money or hearing a Mass in his presence. Topcliffe, doing his best to contradict him, seems to have been reduced, finally, to accusing Jones of saying his own private prayers in secret while he was with them. Topcliffe's attempts to persuade the crowd that all priests, Jones included, harbored wishes for the Queen's death, produced one last moment of drama when Jones said:

> that he assuredly believed that both he himself with all other priests and Catholics would be more ready to suffer much more for the good of the Queen than Master Topcliffe would; further he told him, with great resolution, that his cruelty only hath been sufficient to make her odious to all the priests in Christendom.

The hangman, by the way, had forgotten the rope, so that everyone was kept waiting for an hour. When the moment of death came, Topcliffe, most unusually, saw to it that Jones was allowed to hang until he was dead before being cut down.[2] He then supervised the placing of the quarters on poles in St. George's Fields, and by the wayside on roads into Newington and Lambeth. He put the head over the pillory in Southwark.[3]

John Jones was the first priest to be executed in London since Fr. Southwell's death in February, 1595, and the last priest over whose

---

[1]For the best account of Jones's death, see *The Rambler* N.S., XI, 52–54, which prints a document preserved by the Carthusians. Pollen 1, 362–75 gives an excellent summary, and prints the legal documents.

[2]One has to wonder, once again, whether instructions from the Queen, the Council, or both, were responsible for this uncharacteristic act of mercy. If so, Barnes's speech had had an effect.

[3]A last, gruesome detail. The Carthusian document says that the face was so attractive that it was drawing crowds, so the "officers"—whoever they were—disfigured it (*Rambler*, 54). Some young men removed the head and the quarters. They were caught and imprisoned, but one of the quarters made its way to the convent at Pontoise where Jones had made his profession and where it remained until the Revolution.

execution Topcliffe would preside.

The death sentences on Mrs. Wiseman and Robert Barnes were never carried out. Fr. Gerard simply says that the Council remitted Mrs. Wiseman's sentence motivated partly by fear that its barbarity would shock people, and partly by greed. Had she been pressed to death for refusing trial, her property would have gone to her son. Otherwise, her property went to the Crown. The version in the Chronicle of St. Monica's says that her son bribed someone with access to the Queen to put in a word for his mother. When the Queen understood for how small a matter she was to be put to so cruel a death, she rebuked the judges, and forbade the execution. One suspects that Fr. Gerard's more realistic account is the correct one. In both versions the Crown kept the property.[1]

The Queen reprieved Barnes, too. We learn this from a begging letter written to Secretary Cecil by the Protestant poetaster and rascal Henry Lok on the very day of John Jones's death. He told Cecil that Mrs. Wiseman was his aunt, and suggested he be put in charge of her, and given her living (£68 per year) in order to look after her. He wanted Barnes's living, too:

> The priest today dying hath charged his soul with clearing her and Barnes for ever knowing him a priest, hearing him say mass, or so much as praying with them, for which they were indicted: by which (her Majesty being in mercy likely to be moved to save Barnes's life also, as she hath by his reprieve given hope of) if it would also please her majesty to bestow...on me the benefit of Barnes's living (which with his death is lost) I should I trust appear thankful for your Lordship's mediation...His estate whilst he liveth is held worth £140 a year, which might both relieve him somewhat and satisfy my present wants.[2]

Mrs. Wiseman may have been Henry Lok's aunt, but she would not have welcomed the thought of being under his thumb for the rest of her life.[3] The Loks—or Locks or Lockes—were an extremely well-to-do, very Protestant family, and why the disgusting Henry Lok should have been unable to make a living is one of life's lesser mysteries. When last heard of, he was in debtors' prison.

Two weeks later, Lok wrote again to Cecil, very upset to hear that the Queen was accepting Topcliffe's version of the Wiseman-Barnes case.[4]

---

[1] See Gerard, 53; Hamilton, 83.

[2] NA/SP12/268/3 (12 July 1598).

[3] See the note at the end of this chapter.

He thought it unfair that he should have such a powerful rival in the scramble for Barnes's property, especially a man so much better off than he, whose service, Lok said, had already earned him £1000 more than Lok would ever make. He need not have worried. Henry Lok received none of Barnes's income, and Topcliffe received none of Barnes's property. And so ended Topcliffe's attempt to pay off Anne Bellamy.[2]

Mrs. Wiseman and Robert Barnes remained in prison for the last five years of Elizabeth I's reign, Mrs. Wiseman in the Gatehouse where, according to the chronicler of St. Monica's, Topcliffe continued to harass her. In early 1603, Barnes was one of sixteen priests and four laymen imprisoned in Framlingham Castle and listed as sent into banishment. Barnes, though, seems to have avoided banishment.

With the accession of James I he and Mrs. Wiseman were both pardoned. She was finally able to live out of prison again, although (again on the evidence of the chronicler), she "wanted not good occasions to exercise patience by one that was allied to her, a most perverse, fantastical woman who used her very ill." In 1609 her daughter Jane became the first prioress of St. Monica's Augustinian convent, Louvain. Mrs. Wiseman died in 1610.

As for Mr. Barnes, his property was returned to him, but his Catholicism exposed him to the penalties for not attending the state church. In 1610, two men, Augustine Griggs and Thomas Pinckney received the benefits of Robert Barnes's recusancy. In other words, his fines were diverted to their use.[3]

*****

A Note on Mrs. Wiseman's Parentage

No-one knows who Mrs. Wiseman's parents were. *ODNB* thinks that her father was a Tudor soldier of Welsh origin called Cuthbert Vaughan, but this is a mistake. Henry Lok, son of Anne Lok (or Lock or Locke), claimed that Mrs. Wiseman was his aunt.

The chronicler of St. Monica's tells us that Mrs. Wiseman's maiden name was Vaughan, that her father was of an ancient Welsh house, and

---

[4]NA/SP12/268/10 (26 July 1598).

[2]Apart from a few payments covering the movement of prisoners (a cost always met by the government), Topcliffe received no pay, and failed completely to recoup his expenses at his victims' expense.

[3]Hamilton, 84; Challoner, 268–9; Anstruther, 176–7; *CSPD James I, 1603–1610*, 29, 581.

that her mother was of the "blood royal." Her parents died while she was young, and she was left a ward. During her wardship she had to fend off a number of marriage proposals, but she had a maternal uncle, Mr. Gwynneth, who kept an eye on her. He was a priest, and was briefly in prison when the religious changes came; nonetheless it was he who made the match between her and Mr. Wiseman that turned out so well for them both.

Henry Lok's mother, Anne, shared Mrs. Wiseman's maiden name. She was the daughter of Stephen Vaughan, a London merchant in the time of Henry VIII. She had two siblings, Jane and Stephen, about whom virtually nothing is known. Stephen Vaughan's first wife was a lady of Welsh origins, Margaret Gwynneth. Vaughan was a keen Protestant.[1]

When Margaret Vaughan died in 1544, Stephen Vaughan may have missed her business-like ways, but his choice of Margery Brinkelow, widow of Henry Brinkelow, as a second wife could imply that he felt the need of a more committed Protestant in the family. Stephen Vaughan died in 1549.

If Mrs. Wiseman's maternal uncle's name was Gwynneth, then it seems to follow that Henry Lok's grandmother, Stephen Vaughan's first wife Margaret Gwynnethe, was his sister. If that was so, then it also follows that Jane Wiseman's sister was the fiercely Protestant poetess Anne Lok, bosom friend of John Knox, and wife (after her first husband's death) of the Puritan Edward Dering whom Elizabeth I disliked so much. Anne Lok was no doubt the relative, "a most perverse, fantastical woman," who proved to be such a nuisance to Mrs. Wiseman after her release.

Mrs. Wiseman, then, was the daughter of Stephen Vaughan, and Margaret Gwynnethe. The chronicler of St. Monica's does not tell us how she managed, given her family background, to become an English Catholic heroine. That story remains to be told.[2]

---

[1]For a previous mention of Stephen Vaughan, see above, 80.

[2]To see the current state of thinking about Mrs. Wiseman's background, see *ODNB*, s.v., "Jane Wiseman," "Cuthbert Vaughan," and "Anne Lock." For the chronicler of St. Monica's account, see Hamilton, 81. The best recent account of Anne Lock and her family is in Susan M. Felch (ed.), *The Collected Works of Anne Vaughan Lock* (Arizona Center for Medieval and Renaissance Studies, Tempe, AZ., 1999), xvi–xxxvi.

Fifteen

Finale

Robert Barnes had tried hard to have his case heard by the law officers: The Lord Chief Justice (Sir John Popham), Mr. Attorney (Edward Coke), Mr. Solicitor (Thomas Fleming), Francis Bacon, and the Recorder of London (John Croke). They had already examined him more than once; they knew the whole case, and had decided to bail him. Topcliffe, operating through the Council as always, had prevented this from happening by continually promising an indictment. When the trial day finally came, Mr. Attorney, despite Mr. Justice Fenner's promise, was not present. His excuse—which Barnes understood, but regretted— was that his wife had died just a few days earlier. Mr. Solicitor was present, and Francis Bacon tried to attend, but the Chief Justice told him there was no room for him.[1] Barnes, left with no alternative, "put himself on the jury," and, as he said, knew that his life "was gone."

An Elizabethan jury might find a murderer innocent; two juries even found a pirate innocent. But juries knew better than to find Catholics innocent. A Staffordshire jury had done just that, and found themselves summoned to London to explain "their disordered proceedings."[2]

Consequently, when Barnes made his remarkable speech to the court exposing Topcliffe's behavior, he had little thought of saving his life. Like Thomas Pormort before him, he had decided to expose the criminality of the government's chief agent, and in doing so to bring truth, of however limited a kind, to the judicial heart of a society rotten with lies. The extraordinary thing is that he was allowed to do it, and one would love to know why. Mr. Justice Fenner was not the cleverest man on the

---

[1] "Mr. Bacon...coming into the court...would have sitten under my Lord Chief Justices's feet, his Lordship said he were best be gone; for there was not room for him then."

[2] *APC* 13.256 (12 November 1581).

bench. A few years later Robert Cecil, worried about finding suitable candidates to replace an aging bench of judges, said of him that, "Justice Fenner will never run mad with learning."[1] Even so, it is unlikely that the judge lost control of the trial, and in any case the Lord Chief Justice was present as well.

Barnes's speech was one of a number of surprising developments in this case. The Council's response to the Harrisons' petitions had been a surprise, too, and their prompt response to Barnes's own petition to Lord Keeper Puckering was even more surprising. At the very least one has to conclude that there was division on the Council over Topcliffe and his methods. The sheer length of Barnes's speech, though, leads one to wonder whether there was not a powerful source of influence operating that enabled him to speak.

Michael Questier goes as far as to think that Barnes's speech was the Brownes' revenge for Topcliffe's raid on Lady Montagu's houses in 1593, and that it was only allowed because Topcliffe was now "the ditched activist whose enthusiasms were no longer either officially palatable or necessary."[2] Barnes had been part of the Browne entourage for a long time, and he was a close associate of the second Viscount Montagu. One understands why the dowager Lady Montagu and the second Viscount might exert whatever influence they had in Barnes's favor, but even so, on their own they were in no position to influence the court.

If we look for causes that set the stage for Barnes's speech, we should begin with Topcliffe himself. His age (he was in his 67th year in 1598), his cavalier attitude to the Council, and his run-in with Puckering, followed by the loss of his commission, all formed a prelude to his exposure by Barnes. There were also changes in the membership of the Council. All the older members of the earlier Councils had gone except William Cecil (b. 1520), who would die in August, and Charles Howard, the Lord Admiral (b.1536), appointed in 1584. After him the two senior members were Lord Buckhurst (b.1536) and John Whitgift, the Archbishop of Canterbury (b.1530), both appointed in 1586. Four councilors had been appointed in 1596–7, so that in 1598 the Council was different from the one Topcliffe began working with in the early 1580s.

Nonetheless, the speech remains an anomaly in its time and place. Even if the ultimate influence that allowed it emanated from the Queen

[1] *CSPD 1601–03*, 285.

[2] Questier, 247.

herself and the Cecils, the reason for allowing it remains a mystery. Robert Cecil, after all, along with the Lord keeper and certain other councilors, had been a party to the entrapment of Barnes and Mrs. Wiseman. Perhaps the Queen decided that for once she would not defend Topcliffe from the consequences of his own behavior; if she did, he never forfeited his personal standing either with her or the Cecils. As we learn from Henry Lok's letters to Robert Cecil, the Queen accepted Topcliffe's version of the case, even if she decided upon reprieves for Barnes and Mrs. Wiseman.

It would be a mistake, too, to interpret Topcliffe's exposure as signalling a shift in policy. The enforcement of the penal laws, and the associated executions of priests and lay-people, which had never stopped in the provinces, resumed in London in 1600. Between John Jones's death in 1598 and the Queen's death, 24 March 1603, there were thirty executions, nineteen of priests and eleven of lay-people. Some of those executions were notably cruel, especially those of John Rigby, a young layman (St. Thomas Watering, 21 June 1600), Mark Barkworth, OSB, and Mrs. Anne Line (Tyburn, 27 February 1601).

There are two explanations of the renewed persecution, one rather complex, the other very simple. The more complex explanation places it in the context of the affair of the Appellant priests, sometimes called the Archpriest controversy, which grew out of a quarrel among the imprisoned priests at Wisbech Castle over the management of their affairs, and the regulation of their lives. It included a pamphlet war between the rival parties, plus appeals to Rome, and came to focus upon anti-Jesuit feeling among some of the secular priests. Hearing of the troubles, the Queen and Secretary Cecil instructed Richard Bancroft, the Bishop of London, to exploit the quarrel in the interests of the state. Bancroft, who had demonstrated his knack for counter-insurgency ten years earlier by his handling of the Puritan outbreak associated with the Marprelate pamphlets, went to work. He encouraged the appellant pamphleteers, put them up in his palace, gave them access to the press, and encouraged their party's visits to Rome.

When word of Bancroft's activities leaked out, the Puritans, who had a well-funded, behind-the-scenes organization of their own, were infuriated to hear that their arch-enemy was dealing with Catholics in ways that were undoubtedly illegal under current law. They did not know that he was acting under instructions from the Queen, or that his purpose was to divide and demoralize the Catholics, even, perhaps to have the Jesuits withdrawn from England. So they began making threats of their own against members of the Council as well as Bancroft.[5]

William Sterrell, the Earl of Worcester's secretary who wrote news reports for Fr. Persons under the pen-name Anthony Rivers, S.J., reported that the renewed persecution was a response to the Puritans, motivated by fear.[2] The proclamation, 5 November 1602, issued from Richmond Palace in the Queen's name, "For Proceeding Against Jesuits and Secular Priests, their Receivers, Relievers, and Maintainers," was certainly intended to let everyone know that, whatever the rumors, the Queen and Council had no sympathy with priests of any kind, Appellant or otherwise.[3]

That is the more complex explanation. The simpler explanation is that, as the wording of the Proclamation explains, the recent slight relaxation in the enforcement of the laws had allowed Catholics in general as well the Appellant priests to get above themselves. And since it had also irritated the keener Protestants, potentially an extremely dangerous element, the obvious thing to do now was to resume enforcement of the law. That, no doubt, is why Lord Chief Justice Popham was the chief agent of the renewed severity.

Sterrell, as always extremely well-informed, thought the Queen was of two minds about the enforcement. When Popham, the day before three priests were to be executed (Tichborne, Watkinson, and Page, S.J.) waited upon her to know her pleasure, she told him that "she wished him to proceed, adding that she beshrewed his heart if he spared them or any other of their coat." Yet when Popham, on circuit at Bury, wished to put four more priests to death, the Queen forbade it.[4]

Whatever the reason for the renewed persecution, Topcliffe had nothing to do with it. His commission was gone, and so he arrested and interrogated no more priests, and—as far as we know—he attended no more trials and executions. Not that he was altogether out of business: the Council still used him from time to time. For instance, in a "privy search" in early 1599, he captured two men suspected "by some secret intelligence" of involvement in "some dangerous practice against the person of her Majesty and the state." The Council then commissioned him and Sir John Peyton, Lieutenant of the Tower, to commit them to

---

[5]For a brief summary account of Bancroft's manipulation of the Appellants and his simultaneous work against the Puritans, see Brownlow 2, 67–75.

[2]Foley, 1.30.

[3]For Sterrell/Rivers on the proclamation (*STC* 8295) see Foley 1, 47.

[4]Foley 1, 30, 57.

Bridewell for examination, "using such means of torture by the manacles as you shall find needful."[1]

At about the same, operating with a warrant from Robert Cecil, Topcliffe arrested an informer-spy called Thomas Harrison whom, it seems, he had been watching for some time. Most recently Harrison had been teaching handwriting in Kent, but he claimed to have worked in France for Walsingham. His response to being arrested was a very angry letter to Cecil, protesting innocence, and offering to go spying in Douay. Topcliffe thought he was a double agent—and he probably was.[2]

As late as May 1602, the Council commissioned Topcliffe to arrest a man called Richard Skinner, and turn him over to Chief Justice Popham. Skinner, whoever he was, was supposed to have threatened the Queen: hence Topcliffe's involvement. When Popham questioned him, he denied saying he would kill the Queen, but the remarks he acknowledged and wrote out upset Popham quite enough: "It is matter not fit for any honest heart to conceive much less for my tongue to speak or hand to write."[3] This was the last of Topcliffe's political assignments.

*****

Although the Queen and the Court of Chancery had confirmed Topcliffe in possession of the manor of Padley, he never lived there. When the Earl of Shrewbury's people captured the two priests at Padley in 1588 along with Sir Thomas Fitzherbert's brother John, the earl took possession of the manor, and made arrangements with the Council to administer it on behalf of the crown. The Queen and the Council asked his successor, the seventh earl, to acknowledge Topcliffe's right, but Earl Gilbert paid no attention. His "servants and possession-keepers" were still resident at Padley in 1604.

John Fitzherbert's youngest son, Anthony, had been taken in the first raid on Padley, and put in Derby gaol. Six months later his father joined

---

[1]*APC*, 29. 428 (4 January 1599).

[2]*CSPD 1598–1601*, 117 (5 November 1598); 168 (14 March 1599); Hatfield 59/52 (6 February 1599). Harrison was an interesting character who began his career as a Walsingham operative at the time of the Babington Plot which, he said later, Walsingham, Phelippes, and Bernard Maude invented. He also said that he and Thomas Phelippes forged the documents that doomed Mary Stuart and the plotters (Martin, P, 53–4).

[3]*CSPD, 1601–03*, 192 (21 May 1602). A man called Foster was in trouble, 25 June 1601, for a scandalous "ballett or libell in print betwixt a Papist and a Protestant," which someone called Mr. Skinner had given him (Jeaffreson, 1.272).

him in the gaol, and they were both there for the next two years until old
George Shrewsbury sent John Fitzherbert to prison in London, where he
shortly died. In May 1591, Anthony wrote to the new Earl of
Shrewsbury, offering to conform to the Church of England, and asking
him to intercede with the Council for his release.[1]

This is one of those letters written to be shown, on the writer's behalf,
to other people who are in a position to help him besides the recipient.
Although written as if to Earl George, who had died six months earlier,
its recipient was Earl Gilbert, whom we have already seen assisting an
imprisoned priest and his harborer. We know that Topcliffe had no confidence in him as a catcher of recusants, and so it is not surprising to find
him going quickly to work on Anthony's behalf, who was soon out of
prison, and able to resume his standing as one of the earl's entourage.
When Robert Bainbridge of Derby wrote to Burghley, January 1592,
enumerating Earl Gilbert's Catholic friends and kin, Anthony Fitzherbert
was one of the people on the list, described as "the most noted dangerous
recusant in all Derbyshire...long time a prisoner in Derby gaol." Bainbridge thought the earl had "entertained" him in London.[2]

Derby gaol was a disgusting place, "most odious for many causes,
with the loathsome and unsavory smells," as Anthony wrote. To have
survived it as long as he did, he had a strong constitution, and it is no
wonder that he asked to be released for reasons of health. Yet they were
not his only reasons. It appears from his letter that he and the earl had
been having conversations about his situation. It even seems likely that
the earl had advised him on the contents and approach of his letter. In
the course of those conversations, Anthony had told the earl about "some
other more special and particular causes" besides his health that would
be served by his release, and if we judge by his later activity, it is not
hard to guess what they were.

His brother's treachery was well-known in Derbyshire and Staffordshire, and by the time Anthony wrote his letter from prison, Thomas
Fitzherbert had already "sold" Padley to Topcliffe. Then in October
1591 Sir Thomas Fitzherbert died in the Tower, and Thomas the
younger, having been able, with Topcliffe's help and the Queen's, to
defeat his uncle's attempts to exclude him, inherited the Fitzherbert patrimony. Quite soon it became obvious that he was embarked on a

---

[1]Talbot, Vol. H (Lambeth MS 3199), f. 289 (21 May 1591).

[2]*CSPD 1591–94*, 174 (SP12/241/25), 25 January 1592. Cox 2, 272–3, prints the entire
document.

course, partly criminal and partly stupid, that would ruin the family's property and himself as well.

As early as 1592, one of his tenants was complaining to the Council that Thomas Fitzherbert had evicted him, his wife and family, from their dwelling, and torn the house down. A few months later a Nottingham-shire man complained that Fitzherbert, assisted by a gang of about sixty, had stolen lead and lead ore from him; and even though some of the gang had been prosecuted at the Derbyshire assizes, and Fitzherbert had been ordered to return the stolen material, he was now threatening to sell it. It seems that he had deluded himself into thinking that because of his connection with the Queen through Topcliffe he could count on her pro-tection, "whereby he supposeth himself to be exempt from suit of law."[1]

He must have defied the local justices whom the Council instructed to deal with him, because in November 1592 they sent a pursuivant to Norbury to arrest him and bring him to London to appear before them. Anticipating a difficult arrest, they told their messenger "in case of need to require aid."[2]

As we know, by 1594 Thomas Fitzherbert was in the Fleet Prison. By then he had broken with Topcliffe, whom he no longer needed, and had unsuccessfully sued him for the return of Padley. Topcliffe had sued him in return for payment on the £3,000 bond. He was in the Fleet until 1596–97. By then, in need of cash, he was selling and mortgaging the family's property, including their chief properties, Norbury and Hamstall Ridware.

In early 1598, in response to more complaints of violence and debt, the Council again issued warrants for his arrest; but he had taken refuge in the city liberty of Coldharbor, was claiming exemption from arrest, and offering violence to anyone who attempted to serve a process on him. For the time being, the Council took no further action. Instead, they instructed the Attorney-General, the Solicitor-General, and Francis Bacon to inquire into the charter, if any, that warranted the liberty of Coldharbor, and to advise them of their findings accordingly.[3]

The inquiry took some time, because it was nearly a year before the Council, acting upon the advice of the legal authorities, issued an open warrant to all officers for Fitzherbert's arrest. The Court of King's

---

[1] *APC*, 23. 72–3 (28 July 1592); 165–66. (3 September 1592).

[2] *APC*, 23. 314 (19 November 1592).

[3] *APC*, 28. 410 (18 April 1598); *APC*, 28. 424 (27 April 1598).

Bench had issued a writ of attachment to the sheriffs of London which, of course, he had ignored—a course of action that produced strong language from the Council:

> The said Thomas Fitzherbert being of very evil name and fame...lurketh and lodgeth secretly in diverse places in and near to the said city of London, thinking...by the occasion of some privileged places to continue still in his said evil demeanor, whereby her Majesty's process cannot be served and executed so duly and justly as [it] should....

The officers, therefore, are to enter any place, privileged or not, arrest him on sight, and commit him to prison until he find good and sufficient sureties for his good behavior.[1]

By then the heir of the senior branch of the Fitzherbert family was a common criminal, and Anthony Fitzherbert, out of prison, was the only member of the family in a position to take defensive action against him. As long as Topcliffe had his commission and the backing of the Queen and Council, there was little that Anthony could do unless—as seems likely—he was able, in conversations with Earl Gilbert, to decide upon a strategy for Padley. A further legal complication loomed because the next heir, in the event of Thomas Fitzherbert's death, was their brother Nicholas, a canonist living in Rome, who became Cardinal Allen's secretary. Nicholas had been attainted of treason *in absentia*, and so any property that might come to him was escheated to the Crown.[2]

With Topcliffe commissionless, and his brother a fugitive from the law, Anthony could act. When his brother began mortgaging and selling properties, 1596–97, Anthony, insofar as he could, began buying them back. (Where, as a younger son, he found the money to do this, is something of a mystery.) Topcliffe, meanwhile, knowing about Thomas Fitzherbert's crimes and "unthrifty bargains," and hearing about Anthony's attempts to restore his family, set about trying to make sure that the Fitzherbert properties would all fall to the crown, bringing in, as he put it, £1,000 a year to the Queen. Anthony Fitzherbert's response to that idea, so Topcliffe told Cecil in a letter written from Somerby, was to threaten him with exposure by complaint to the Queen and Council. "I am threatened," he wrote:

---

[1]*APC*, 29. 614–15 (26 February 1599).

[2]Thompson Cooper (*DNB*) dates the attainder 1 January 1580. An inquisition of 11 June 1604, disposing of the remainder of the manors of Padley &c. as may accrue to the King, gives the date as 1 Jan 1589 (Camm 2, 58n, 66n). Topcliffe, writing to Cecil, 11 October 1600 (Hatfield 250/20) claimed responsibility for the attainder.

with many deep and deadly revenges of my body and name; and now that I am here absent from the Court and term about the greatest business that ever I had...they...boast that they will sting me with slanderous cries and complaints in my absence both to her sacred Majesty and to the Lords at the Council table.

He ended by asking Cecil for his accustomed protection.[1]

By now Anthony Fitzherbert was living at Norbury, and so Topcliffe decided to take more vigorous action himself. Thorne, his old agent for recusant business in Derbyshire, had died in 1595, and so he had to work at a distance.[2] He informed the Sheriff and Under-Sheriff of Derbyshire that Norbury was a nest of traitors, and suggested that they keep an eye on the house and its occupants. The result was that the Sheriff raided the house, and found nothing. A friend at court then let Topcliffe know that Anthony and a man called Bamford had lodged a strong complaint with the Council to the effect that Topcliffe had "procured the high Sheriff of Derbyshire...to search and ransack their houses for Jesuits, Seminary priests, and traitors, and greatly to their reproach and discredit."

Topcliffe, of course, no longer had the authority to do such a thing, and his only justification was to say that he never intended that the Sheriff should actually do anything. He then bragged about his long record of service, and suggested that the Sheriff was a Fitzherbert friend who used the raid to warn the recusants of impending trouble. And once again he had to ask Cecil for his protection.[3]

Six months later he made one last attempt to persuade Cecil to give him a commission that would set him free to do as he wished in Derbyshire. In December 1601, he wrote a long letter from his house at Somerby, telling Cecil about two "monstrous traitors" who had come to his attention. The first was a former member of the Queen's guard, John Petty. The second, more interesting traitor was an unnamed "base clown" from the Derbyshire High Peak district who had dared to "sting with his tongue the sacred fame even of her Majesty."

---

[1] Hatfield 250/20 (11 Oct 1600).

[2] According to one Catholic memorialist, Thorne made an edifying end: "Thorne, the pursuivant, a most bad persecutor, lying on his deathbed, said: 'Now Queen Elizabeth cannot answer for me, nor Topcliffe, nor Thomas Fitzherbert do me any good.' He wished he might speak with a priest specially, whom he had sought much for, and that he should both come and go safely. In the end, he said he was condemned for persecuting the Church of God" (Foley 3, 227).

[3] One can piece together this whole episode from Topcliffe's letter to Cecil, Hatfield 86/88 (11 June 1601).

A witness, perhaps a local person, perhaps one of Topcliffe's network of informants, had reported this man's talk at third hand. On a recent visit to court, Topcliffe had passed the base clown's words on to the Queen, and she had instructed him to apprehend the man discreetly.

Topcliffe's next move was to find the original witness, and take down the exact words of the original offense, which, to his satisfaction, proved "more evil and odious" than the reported version. Word of Topcliffe's interest having reached the offender, he had prudently removed himself from the district. Since Topcliffe had only one witness against the "clown," to proceed against him successfully he would need real authority, not only to arrest him, but to take him to his house where "with mild usage (yet I hope)...he will utter the truth of all things needful."

In short, he needed his commission back along with his freedom of interrogation and torture. He therefore asked Cecil to solicit the Queen for a commission of the kind that he had in Cecil's father's time, "under the seal of the Council Table:"

> Then shall I think myself strongly armed against this proud vaunting slanderer, or any such monstrous viper, amongst those mountains in the Peak, if he lurk within the devil's den (usually called the Devil's Arse); or against his traitorous lawyer (against whom I have perilous proofs under his hand of disloyal persuasions), and for believe me (Noble Sir) there are in the parish where this clownish viper doth dwell above 100 persons no one of whom [any] loyal subject doth know to be christened...in which parish there have been harbored above 100 seminary priests and Jesuits whom I can name. And if it be needful to root up some one proved weed in this winter season (for example sake) such as this monstrous Clown is... then, when I have my commission, I am apter and readier to adventure any danger than to follow any Christmas delights or other pleasures. For inspeakably hath her blessed Majesty bound me with her sacred conceit, and her defense of my own credit (the comfort of a true gentleman) in all desperate times, such as I have lived in, who have lived to see six rebellions, and am therefore now more willing to become a faithful watchman to my sovereign, like a freeholder of England.[1]

He even sent Cecil, by the hand of his son Charles, an example of his old commission. His description of the monstrous clown's parish sounds suspiciously like his former descriptions of Norbury and Padley. With a new commission in hand, he would be down on them both like a ton of bricks in no time.

---

[1]Hatfield 90/2 (14 Dec. 1601). It seems that the people in the High Peak would not even go to the Church of England to have their children christened.

After a few weeks' delay caused by the Christmas doings at court, Cecil replied. The Queen, he said, had authorized the enclosed warrant for the man's arrest. There was no new commission. The tone of Cecil's response, while kindly, suggests that even in giving him the warrant he and the Queen were humoring the old man.[1] Whether anything came of this last foray into Derbyshire is unknown, but for the time being the Fitzherberts and their tenants continued unmolested.

*****

For the last eighteen months of the reign Topcliffe seems to have been at home in Lincolnshire. All his later letters are signed from Somerby, usually from "my solitary Somerby." He was dependent for court news on messages from friends or associates, and his conversation with the Queen about the "monstrous clown" in the fall of 1601 was probably the last conversation he had with her.

Eighteen months later, she would be dead. In those last months of the reign, her health declined steadily. Although, as one would have expected, she dealt ruthlessly with the Earl of Essex after his failed—and desperate—attempt at displacing Robert Cecil, his death left her in a profound melancholy. Two years later, the death of her kinswoman and friend Lady Nottingham in February 1603 plunged her into a depression from which she never emerged. In those last months she began to worry about loss of memory and concentration, and found it impossible to discuss matters of state with her Councilors. There were physical troubles as well: a persistent pain in her arm, and several falls.

In that last summer of 1602, she wanted to make a progress into the west, but the Council knew she was in no condition to make such a demanding journey, and they were so jittery about the possibilities should she die that they did not want to be away from London for so long. By the year's end her moods became so unpredictable that most of the Councilors and the nobility stopped coming to Court. Secretary Cecil never stopped trying to keep her happy and pleased with him, and the old Lord Admiral was always welcome; but the rest, except for the officers of the household, kept out of the way.

The Queen died on Thursday, 24 March 1603. In Robert Carey's famous account, she made a good end, attended by her chaplains and Archbishop Whitgift. The Archbishop first examined her upon her faith, and she answered him by raising her hand and moving her eyes. He then

---

[1]Hatfield 84/36 (2 January 1602).

prayed with her until his knees were sore—after all, he was older than she was—blessed her, and made to leave, but the Queen signed for him to stay, which he did, until the end.[1]

Soon after the Queen's death, in London Robert Cecil proclaimed James VI of Scotland King of England as James I, and Robert Carey was galloping north to Edinburgh with the news on a well-prepared express ride. By Saturday night, 26 March, Carey was in Edinburgh,[2] and very soon James and his family, accompanied by a horde of courtiers, began the slow trek south to wealth, a milder climate, and a far more stable country than Scotland had ever been. For a short time—and it proved to be very short—it seemed as if a new age might have been inaugurated. At some time in those happy early months of the new reign, Anthony Fitzherbert did a very clever thing: having already bought Norbury, he now bought back from the Crown, at a cost of £1,200, the escheat attaching to the estate because of his brother Nicholas's attainder for treason. He probably had the Earl of Shrewsbury's help in bringing this off—Earl Gilbert had been a Privy Councilor since June 1601.

As for Topcliffe, his mistress and protectress was gone, and by now he knew that he could no longer count on his family's old affinity with the Earls of Shrewsbury. He made one last attempt to reinstate the relationship by sending a generous contribution to the earl's entertainment at Worksop House for James's Queen, Anne of Denmark, on her journey to London.

Less than a week after Elizabeth I's death, on 30 March, the Earl of Shrewsbury wrote from his room at Whitehall Palace to his agent Mr. Harper, saying that he would soon be "in the country" and would very likely be entertaining the King at Worksop. Would Mr. Harper let all his friends in Derbyshire and Staffordshire know? He ended his brief letter with the welcome news that, "All things here are well, and nothing but unity and good agreement, God continue it. Amen, Amen, Amen!"—and added a postscript: "I will not refuse any fat capons and hens, partridges, or the like if the king come to me."[3]

---

[1]Nicholls prints Carey's account, Nicholls 1, 3.605. The scene had been very different when the Council first sent the Archbishop and other clergy to her earlier in her last sickness. As Elizabeth Southwell's narration tells us, at the sight of them, "she was much offended, cholerically rating them, bidding them be packing, saying she was no atheist, but knew full well that they were hedge priests and took it for an indignity that they should speak to her" (Loomis, 486).

[2]For Carey's ride, see Nicholls 2, 1.33–6, 55–6.

[3]Ms. Folger X.d.428.116.

The earl's house at Worksop, which no longer survives, was a very grand new one built by his father to the designs of Robert Smythson. The King arrived there, 20 April, and stayed for one night, leaving after breakfast the next day. The earl's friends brought him so much food in response to his message that after the King left, "there was such store of provision left, of fowl, fish, and almost everything, besides bread, beer, and wine, that it was left open for any man that would, to come and take."[1] There is no sign of Topcliffe's presence either at Worksop or during the Nottinghamshire and Lincolnshire phases of the King's journey.

Two months later, the Queen, accompanied by her children, Prince Henry and Princess Elizabeth, followed her husband, taking the same route, which brought her to Worksop 19 or 20 June. This time Topcliffe was prepared. On 15 June, he dispatched a generous contribution to the entertainment at Worksop, along with an explanatory letter. He seems not to have gone to Worksop himself, although the phrase at the end of his letter, "ready to ride towards Doncaster" implies either that he planned to join the people attending the Queen, or that he hoped to be invited to do so.[2]

In his letter he tells the earl candidly that he hopes his gifts will restore their old friendship:

> Right honorable, the duty that I have so long carried to your noble house, and the honest love I professed to you in your youth can (in me) hardly yet be slacked, which had taken such hold in my heart; and so have I showed likelihood divers times since I found many shows of alteration in your Lordship: But I will still be plain Topcliffe: and if I could do any thing to prove that the ancient honor I determined to you is not of my part given over by any unkindness offered to try me, you were like to find me more honest than a number of flatterers and soothers.

Hearing, therefore, that the Queen was coming to Worksop, "for old love" he sends:

> The best, and highest fallow deer that is in Somerby Park, or (I think) that is in Lincolnshire, wild-fed;
> 4 pies of the best stag that I have seen (of a wild deer) in Whitsun week, baked by a cook that learned cunning in your noble father's house when the Scottish Queen did remain with that earl.

[1] There is an account of the King's visit in *The True Narration of the Entertainment of his Royall Maiestie, from the Time of his Departure from Edenbrough; till His Receiving at London* (1603: *STC* 17153), printed in Nicholls 2, 1.85–7.

[2] Talbot Ms. 708, f. 141 (Lambeth Palace), 15 June 1603.

"If I had known the certain day of the Queen's coming," he adds, he would have sent "some young heronshaws out of the nest, which, well boiled, is excellent meat, cold or hot, and better than roasted."

Heronshaws, or young herons, were a specialty with Topcliffe. A month ago, he says, he could have provided a hundred that are now flown, but if the earl would really like to have some for the Queen's visit, all he has to do is give his orders to the bearer, and he will bring them, live. Then at the last minute, he changed his mind, and added a marginal note saying that he was sending eight young herons, new killed.

People were still eating heron and crane well into the seventeenth century, and the reason for Topcliffe's enthusiasm and expertise on the subject is that at Somerby he raised herons himself in a specially-built mew. He included with his letter detailed instructions telling the earl how to build his own heron mew: "A way to make heronshaws breed in any place where there is timber woods growing, either of oak or ash, where crows may breed."[1]   The earl, moreover, would be in good company: Sir Thomas Gresham had built a heron mew out of ships' masts in his fish-ponds, and it could be a profitable interest, too—a former pensioner of the Queen's, Francis Harvey, told Topcliffe that he made two hundred marks (over £130) a year out of his herons.

This is a rather sad letter because Topcliffe is not only trying to revive a lost friendship; he is trying hard to write as one country gentleman to another about country matters of interest to them both: judging the quality of the deer in one's park, taking pride in one's cook and his stag pies, and raising herons for the table. This is the Topcliffe Gilbert Talbot originally knew, before he disappeared into the state's torture rooms. It is a role that Topcliffe suspects the earl will not find convincing, and so he tells him three times in one letter that he is acting as a plain friend, as plain Topcliffe, and that he is no flatterer, no "fawning cur:"

> but being, and bearing for my cognizance, a gentle white hound, sitting ready and gazing, with his tail upon his back, to abide all trials.

He signed off, "At my solitary house Somerby, ready to ride towards Doncaster...Your Lordship's plain, and faithful well-wisher, Ric: Topcliffe."

One wonders what kind of "Thank you" the earl sent to Somerby. He probably sent the deer, the herons, and the pies to his cooks, and put the letter aside.

---

[1]Talbot Ms. 708, f. 143 (Lambeth Palace).

Topcliffe wrote his last, distressed letter to the earl from his "solitary Somerby" on 20 February 1604, having heard, presumably from one of the earl's agents, that he was about to lose whatever right he still had in Padley manor:

> Now give me leave (I beseech your Lordship) to be somewhat tedious in a cause that doth concern mine undoing, because I did receive no answer from your Lordship of my last letter sent you by Mr. Fenton, one who honoreth you, and seemeth to love me; for I was then loath, and still am so, that any person but a well wisher to us both should know that your Lordship (whom I have honored half a hundred years above all men now living, and under whose forefathers my ancestors have made proof of their loyal affections to their sovereigns, and true love to the Earls of Shrewsbury) should now go about to offer to heave me (with your strength) out of Padley, a delightful solitary place in which I took threefold the more pleasure for the nighness of it unto three of your chief usual houses, where I thought that I should (in my old days) take comfort in your Lordship's presence in any time of discomfort such as time doth breed.[1]

The earl, he said, used to enjoy his letters and his company well enough in the days when his position enabled him to intercede with the Queen on his behalf when local difficulties were causing him trouble at court. As examples he mentions the complaining tenants of Glossopdale, and the problem the earl had inherited with Mrs. Britten, the companion of his father's old age, and—as we have seen—he could have mentioned the far more dangerous Williamson affair. As for Padley, for which he had paid dearly, it was not part of the original Fitzherbert patrimony; and not only had Thomas Fitzherbert assured it to him and his heirs but, as the earl knew, the Queen herself had assured his right to the place.

Topcliffe, assuming that the earl intended to keep Padley for himself, went on to tell him that in that case there were two abuses at Padley needing immediate reform, and that they had been especially bad "since the time of these contentions, and never so foully as in these two times that your Lordships' servants and possession-keepers have been resident there." First, people had been spoiling the woods: "Those few, pleasant, and needful woods of all sorts, great and small, that raveners have left unspoiled, woods being so dainty in that place," should be preserved from destruction. Second, as many as eight or ten households of riff-raff were living there, "fugitive traitors, whoremongers, bawds, and like abominable persons...like a Sodom or sanctuary of filthiness," and the

---

[1] Talbot Ms. M (Lambeth MS 3203), f. 184 . This and the previous letter are reproduced in full, in the original spelling, in Appendix 2.

earl, following his father's example, should clean them out. The implication is that squatters had occupied the house.

The reference to "these contentions" and to the earl's twice installing "possession-keepers" implies that Topcliffe had tried to move in, and found his servants' entry blocked. Obviously, he had resented that, and their reports of conditions there. He signed off hoping to receive "by the bearer" a plain statement of a kind that would allow him to continue honoring the earl.

How the earl defeated Topciffe's title to Padley does not appear in the documents, but he did, and the property went back to the Fitzherberts. One can only presume that neither Topcliffe nor his son was in a position to sue for the property in Chancery against so powerful and wealthy an opponent.

So ended Topcliffe's attempt to bring down the Fitzherberts, and with it his friendship with Earl Gilbert. Nine months later, on 21 November 1604,[1] he died at his solitary Somerby, having just passed his seventy-third birthday. He was buried, like his father and grandfather, in the Lady chapel of Corringham church, the last of his family to be buried there.

*****

---

[1]According to an Inquisition post mortem, taken 15 Jas I, i.e., 24 March 1617–23 March 1618 (NA/C142/360/59).

Sixteen

Epilogue

By a nuncupative will given near the point of death, Topcliffe left all his property (except the life tenancy of a farm, which he bequeathed to his bailiff) to his son Charles, who inherited a severely encumbered estate. Like Sir Francis Walsingham, Richard Topcliffe had funded his operations on the Queen's behalf out of his own pocket, and spent himself into near-bankruptcy. Charles Topcliffe's first act was to sell Somerby to an Alderman Jones of London, who seems to have done little or nothing with the property. In a survey of 1616, the house is described as "an ancient capital house...moated about, much decayed, and so are the orchards, gardens, etc." By 1628–9 the owner was Sir Edward Hussey, Bt. The estate eventually came into the possession of a family called Beckett, whose last representative was Miss Mary Beckett. When she died about 1920, Somerby passed to her sister's husband, Sir Henry Hickman Bacon. In 1922, Kelley's *Directory of Lincolnshire* described the house: "an ancient mansion of brick, said to have been erected about the time of Queen Elizabeth, and originating as a farm house, has been enlarged at various times and now forms a mansion of considerable extent, situated in a park of about 80 acres, adorned with numerous groups of stately trees and approached from the high road by a carriage drive half a mile in length, through plantations." By then, though, the old house was riddled with dry-rot and wood-worm brought on by damp, cold and neglect. Sometime in the 1920s, the Hickman Bacons pulled it down. Excavations at Somerby in the 1950s revealed that what people had thought were remains of a Roman settlement was in fact the lost village of Somerby, destroyed by the Topcliffes in favor of sheep farming.[1]

In June 1603, Charles Topcliffe had been present at Worksop for the Queen's visit, for which his father sent gifts of food. He wrote a congratulatory letter from Worksop to Robert Cecil, now Lord Cecil, complimenting him upon his young son's behavior there during the visit. It appears from that letter that Charles was in service with Cecil, who was shortly to secure his pardon for the death of Venables, the Middlesex sheriff. Charles also hoped to be taken into the service of the Earl and Countess of Shrewsbury; but one can see why, after the earl's final break with his father the next year, nothing came of those arrangements.[2]

The unfortunate Charles Topcliffe, inheritor of a blighted name and a ruined estate, is last heard of in prison for debt in 1611.[3]

Anthony Fitzherbert's conformity to the Church of England, having ensured his release from prison, was short-lived. After recovering much, though by no means all, of his family's property, he paid his recusancy fines, and continued to live at Norbury. Whether, as Bede Camm suspected, he had to pay Earl Gilbert a good price for the return of Padley does not appear: one hopes not. He died early in 1613, having made his will on Christmas Eve, 1612. He left all his property to his wife, Martha, appointing her his executrix. His treacherous brother died ca. 1614, having performed one last decent act by releasing all claims to the family's properties to Anthony's widow.[4]

Anthony's son Sir John Fitzherbert succeeded him. When he died without issue in 1649, the Fitzherbert patrimony passed to the junior branch of the family, descended from Sir Thomas Fitzherbert's brother William, and resident at Swynnerton Hall, Staffordshire. Norbury, therefore, was no longer the family's primary residence, and declined into a farmhouse. The Fitzherberts eventually sold the property in 1881 after owning it for over 750 years. The family is still at Swynnerton Hall, rebuilt after destruction by the Puritan army in the Civil Wars.

---

[1]There is an account of the estate in Dennis C. Mynard, *Excavations at Somerby, Lincs., 1957*. Reprinted from *Lincolnshire History and Archaeology*, 1. 4 (1969): 63–91.

[2]Hatfield 187/79 (21 June 1603), To the right honorable my especial good lord The Lord Cecil; Talbot Ms. 706, f. 164 (Lambeth Palace), Charles Topcliffe to the Earl and Countess of Shrewsbury, "This Tuesday in Easterweek" (otherwise undated).

[3]*Hat. Cal.* 21. 324 (1611); *CSPD 1611–1618*, 72 (1 Sept. 1611), Charles Topcliffe to Robert Cecil, now Earl of Salisbury with whom, it seems, he was still in service.

[4]Camm 2, 64, 68–9.

They are still Catholic, and the head of the family now holds the title Baron Stafford.

Padley Hall no longer exists. After the family sold it in 1657, it fell into ruin, and its stones were sold for building. All that remains of what had been a splendid, extensive fifteenth-century house is the former gate-house and chapel, used for many years as a barn and cow-shed. Charles Cox, visiting in the 1880s, found Padley, which had seen a murder and a suicide in the eighteenth century, a sad place: "A curse seems to cleave to the spot, as though the very spirit of Topcliffe impregnated the place."[1]

In 1892 the first pilgrimage to Padley took place in memory of the martyred priests, Robert Ludlam and Nicholas Garlick, whom the Earl of Shrewsbury arrested there in 1588. The pilgrimage, organized under the auspices of the Guild of Our Lady of Ransom, became an annual event, drawing hundreds of Catholics from the Midlands and the Peak. In 1931 Monsignor Payne of St. Mary's, Derby, made arrangements for the diocese of Nottingham to buy the property, and the restored, reconsecrated Chapel was reopened on 13 July 1933 with a Mass celebrated by Monsignor Payne and served by two representatives of the Fitzherbert family.

During the excavations that accompanied the restoration, the restorers uncovered a large rectangular stone. An architect, Sir Harold Brakspear, visiting the site to see how the work was going, noticed the stone, and told the restorers, "There's your altar. Dig it out and turn it over, and you will find the crosses." Sure enough the stone with its five crosses incised on the obverse side proved to be the original Padley altar stone, buried to hide it from the Protestant desecrators.[2]

Catholic writers on these matters use hard words of George Talbot, 6th Earl of Shrewsbury, who captured the priests at Padley, imprisoned John and Anthony Fitzherbert, and supervised the raid on Norbury. As we have seen, old George Shrewsbury, left to himself, would not have done anything of the kind. The Fitzherberts were a part of his affinity, therefore his friends, and he would have continued to turn a blind eye to their recusancy. Topcliffe, himself a member of the Talbot affinity, knew that very well. One can pick up a hint of Topcliffe's suspicion of the earl's reliability from the peculiar tone of the letter he wrote him

---

[1] Cox 1, 249.

[2] Reports on the Padley pilgrimages and the purchase and restoration of the chapel can be found in *The Tablet*: pilgrimages (20 July, 1907; 23 July 1921); purchase of Padley (9 January 1932); restoration (22 April 1933); reopening (22 July 1933); finding of the altar stone (9 September 1933).

from the 1578 progress, enclosing instructions for catching a priest in his home territories.

Shrewsbury was no fool. He saw through Topcliffe easily enough, but he also saw what had happened to the Percies, the Nevilles, and the Howards, and he knew what was required of him if he was to remain in favor with the Queen and her Council. His appropriation of Padley, moreover, which kept it out of the hands of the Crown, proved in the long run to have been a means of preserving it for the family. At some point in the last couple of years of his life, he let Topclife know what he thought of him.

Topcliffe made a huge miscalculation when he thought that, operating with the Queen's backing, he could destroy the Fitzherberts with Shrewsbury's compelled assistance, and still maintain his own position in the Talbot affinity. The Fitzherberts, with Gilbert Talbot's help, survived the struggle. Topcliffe did not.

*****

What, though, of the English people at large? What was the effect on them of Topcliffe's years of incessant activity enforcing the government's religious policy, and to what extent did he determine its outcome?

No responsible historian now denies that when Elizabeth I came to the throne in 1558, the country was overwhelmingly Catholic. The Protestants were a small minority. John Foxe, speaking of the persistence of the London Protestant congregation in Queen Mary's time, said that its numbers varied from 40 to 200. In a city of over 150 parishes, that is a tiny number.[1]

Elizabeth I and her first principal Secretary, William Cecil, had both presented themselves as Catholics under Queen Mary—and so had Richard Topcliffe—but once she succeeded to the throne, she and Cecil were determined that the country should no longer be Catholic. She seems to have wanted a restoration of her father's kind of national but "Catholic" church, whereas Cecil certainly wanted some kind of Protestantism; but no-one knows what actually went through their minds. They must have thought that the royal will, backed by legislation from a carefully picked Parliament, would ensure the people's obedience, whatever their preferences, and whatever the outcome of the compromises between the two people at the top.

[1]Hughes, 3.55.

Parliament duly enacted the statutes of Supremacy and Uniformity re-establishing the Henrician form of state religion, and requiring the people's submission to it in fairly stringent terms. The Queen signed the statutes into law, and she and her Council immediately set about enforcing the laws' provisions, suppressing Catholic belief and observance. When it became increasingly obvious that the people as a whole had little enthusiasm for either the royal Supremacy in religion or for worship in the royal church, the result was a steady increase in the severity of the enforcement, especially after priests trained in the Douay-Rheims seminary began arriving in the 1570s.

Penal law succeeded to penal law, culminating in the statute of 1585, which made it high treason for any Jesuit or seminary priest to be in England at all, and felony for anyone to harbor or relieve a priest. The penalties of the statute of *Praemunire*, i.e., loss of land and goods, were imposed on all who contributed to the overseas seminaries, plus a fine of £100 for each offense on people who sent children overseas without licence.

By the time Parliament enacted the statute of 1593, forbidding Catholics to travel more than five miles from their homes, the state was treating English Catholics, in principle a majority of the population, as undesirable aliens in their own country, deprived of all rights as subjects. Like Hamlet's Denmark, their own country had become a prison to them. Nor did the government, from time to time, hesitate to describe the intended effect of the enforcement of their policy as "terror."

At this point, some numbers and anecdotes will be useful. In every one of the 30 years between 1569 and 1599 an English subject was put to torture, the overwhelming majority of them for religious reasons. Of the 171 cases so far traced in those years, Topcliffe took part in 47, or 27%.[1] Apart from 3 cases in 1582, though, Topcliffe's known torturing activity in religious cases was confined to the 7 years from 1588 to 1595. The total number of cases found in those years is 70. Topcliffe was probably responsible for 34 of them, or half.

In every year between 1581 and 1603 an English subject was put to death under the penal laws outlawing Catholicism. The Catholic Church has now canonized or beatified 179 English and Welsh subjects who died under those laws in the 33 years between 1570 and 1603. In his really busy years, a mere 7 out of the 33, Topcliffe attended at least 37 executions. Given a number like that, it is hardly surprising that "the

---

[1] For details, see Appendix I.

contemporary Catholic complaint literature seethed with hatred for Topcliffe."[1]

Yet however energetic and committed he may have been, Topcliffe was not a unique phenomenon. The repression was in process before him, and it continued after he was dead under James I. In the Elizabethan years, in addition to the 179 deaths officially recognized by the Church, another 190 or so people whom we know about died either on the scaffold or in prison, and the real numbers of prison deaths are certainly much higher than that. An Elizabethan prison sentence was always likely to mutate into a death sentence, either because the circumstances of imprisonment were so appalling, or because the authorities left prisoners to die there. A lot of women died in prison because the people in charge, the Queen in particular, balked at executing them publicly for religion.

The northern prisons under the regime of Henry Hastings, 3rd Earl of Huntington, were particularly bad, and the officers serving under him were free to abuse Catholic prisoners. Several Marian priests in northern prisons died because of the filth. When John Pearson, an elderly Marian imprisoned at Durham, was taken sick there, the keepers put him in with a gang of thieves, who tormented him by relieving themselves as he was trying to eat. He died there. Another Marian, Jeffrey Stephenson, close prisoner in the Ousebridge prison, York, was moved to Hull after three years, and there, "being thrust down into a low vault...by reason of cold and noisome vapours and damps, [he] lost the use of all his senses, and so shortly died."[2]

The most pathetic of the old priests who died in the York prisons was John Almond, a Cistercian monk who had taken his vows in Henry VIII's time. By the time of his last move to prison in Hull he was "blind and crooked with old age." When he became helpless, unable to take care of himself, the keeper refused to allow two fellow-prisoners to look after him. He died of starvation and neglect.[3]

In all these cases we find people acting with what in American law would be called "a depraved indifference to human life." The worst of them all was another York case. A pair of sheriffs, John Wedall and Leonard Beckwith—let us remember their names—put a group of Catholic women into a filthy cellar-room of the Kidcote prison, without bed-

---

[1]Questier, 245.

[2]Morris 1, 3.315, 301.

[3]Foley 3.247–8.

ding, on a winter's night. They knew, moreover, that the room, where another prisoner had just died, was infected. Within three days, Mary Hutton, Dorothy Vavasour, and Alice Oldcorne had taken sick and died.[1]

Filth and depraved indifference were by no means unique to Huntington's north. In London, Hopton as Lieutenant of the Tower put a young Catholic layman called John Cooper into a filthy room in the Beauchamp Tower. When he took sick, Hopton took away his bed, and left him to die on the stone floor.[2]

Sometime about 1575, on the opposite side of the country, up in the north-west, the Church of England's bishop of Chester noticed that Richard White or Gwyn of Overton near Wrexham was not attending the church.[3] He persuaded White to conform, but when White encountered a priest and changed his mind, his troubles began in earnest. By 1580 he was in serious difficulties with the authorities for no reason whatever except that he was a Catholic and would not attend the local church. In mid-1580, they imprisoned him at Ruthin, with hand bolts on his arms and huge bolts on both heels.[4]

After three months they offered him a pardon if he would go to the church. At Christmas time they moved him to prison at Wrexham, and at the Wrexham assizes in May, Sir George Bromley, chief justice of Chester, ordered that he should be carried to church by force. When his irons made a noise, they put him in the stocks, and indicted him for creating a nuisance during divine service. He was indicted again in September because he owed £140 in fines for not attending church, and 100 marks (£66) fine for his forced attendance. When he told Bromley that he had sixpence towards the fines, the enraged justice sent him back to prison with double irons.

So it went on, assize after assize. In May 1583 White and two other prisoners, John Hughes and Robert Morris, were transferred to the custody of the Council of the Marches, along with a pair from Flint gaol, a priest called John Bennet, and Harry Pugh, a layman. In November 1583, all five were tortured under the authority of the Council at Bewdley and Bridgnorth, where they were "laid in the manacles." These

---

[1]Morris 1, 3.317.

[2]Challoner, 18.

[3]The bishop in 1575 was William Downham,. William Chaderton succeeded him in 1579.

[4]The full account of this case is to be found in Burton-Pollen, 127–44.

administrators of the Welsh Marches were well ahead of Topcliffe in their use of the manacles, and Richard Atkyns, the Council's attorney-general, even anticipated Topcliffe's personal methods by torturing White in his own house.

This case, an example of coarse and stupid bullying by English officials in Wales, came to a predictable climax when White, Hughes, and Morris were sent back to prison in Wrexham, where they were arraigned 9 October 1584, accused of high treason under the Act of Supremacy. Morris was acquitted. White and Hughes were found guilty. Hughes was reprieved, but White was sentenced to be hanged, drawn, and quartered on the following Thursday, 15 October. On Tuesday the 13th he was told that if he would acknowledge the Queen to be supreme head of the Church within her dominions, he would be discharged of all his troubles. He refused.

Like most of the Wrexham people, the local gaoler, a man called Coytmor, was sympathetic to the prisoners. When they returned from the Council to Wrexham, he let them out of gaol on parole. As a punishment the local authorities forced him to be White's executioner. The poor man, having never done anything like it before, bungled the job, and White's death was unspeakably horrifying.

The only purpose of such a performance was to terrorize the local population into conformity. The Council's picked man for such proceedings in that neighborhood was the Bishop of Chester, William Chaderton, a protegé of the Earl of Leicester, appointed in 1579. They had written to him, 4 July 1581, congratulating him on his "proceedings against such persons as have been convented before you, for their obstinacy in matters of religion, and not coming to the church." A pair of ladies, it seems, had skipped our of Chaderton's jurisdiction into the neighboring diocese of Lichfield and Coventry. The Council assured him that they had instructed the bishop there, William Overton, to find them, and either reduce them to conformity himself or proceed against them:

> Which kinds of proceeding we trust will so terrify the rest, as we hope that, if his Lordship shall do his duty in that behalf (whereof we doubt not), they and other like disposed persons will not attempt to do the like hereafter.[1]

In pursuit of the policy of "terrifying the rest," scenes of appalling cruelty and inhumanity like Richard White's death were enacted all over

---

[1] *APC*, 13. 122 (4 July 1581), corrected from Peck 3, 106.

England.[1] They had their effect. By 1603 the fines, whippings, imprisonments, torturings, and executions had persuaded the majority of the English and Welsh people to conform themselves to the state church. The conformity was not enthusiastic. When James VI of Scotland acceded to the throne in 1603, there was a brief relaxation of the enforcement of the penal laws, in particular the fines. The resulting increase in Catholic numbers and practice alarmed the government so much that Robert Cecil saw to it that a more stringent enforcement resumed. He also saw to it that others took over Topcliffe's work—one of them was Sir Anthony Ashley, who wrote to tell Cecil, "I have supplied with good success Mr. Topcliffe's office, and have apprehended John Digby at a house where he meant to sup this evening about 8 o'clock...."[2]

The interest of Topcliffe's brief but extraordinary career as Elizabeth I's chief policeman is that it reveals dramatically the complicity of the Queen and her closest advisers in the worst cruelties and corruptions that accompanied their determination to uproot and destroy the country's religious and social traditions. It was a disgraceful episode in the long, initially successful, but ultimately failed struggle of the Crown and Parliament to eradicate Catholicism in England in the name of the social and religious changes that they called, in self-congratulation, "the Reformation."

*****

For the English people at large, however, a great deal more than a change in religion alone was involved for, to speak constitutionally, the whole operation—as we saw in chapter 2—was dishonest and illegal from the beginning. Magna Carta not only forbade torture and summary proceedings; in its very first item it guaranteed the liberty of the Church (the speaker, of course, was King John, and he was speaking, however reluctantly, not only for himself but for his successors):

> We have, in the first place, granted to God, and by this Our present Charter confirmed for Us and Our heirs forever—That the English Church shall be free and enjoy her rights in their integrity and her liberties untouched. And

---

[1] The worst scenes were enacted outside London, where amateur executioners were pressed into service, e.g., the deaths of John Sandys at Gloucester (Burton-Pollen, 220–21), Joseph Lampton at Newcastle (Challoner, 190), and John Rigby at St. Thomas Watering (Worthington, B4v–C1).

[2] *Hat. Cal.*, 18. 40 (1 February 1606).

that We will this so to be observed appears from the fact that We of Our own free will, before the outbreak of the dissensions between Us and Our barons, granted, confirmed, and procured to be confirmed by Pope Innocent III the freedom of elections, which is considered most important and necessary to the English Church, which Charter We will both keep Ourself and will it to be kept with good faith by Our heirs forever.

There is not much wiggle-room in that opening clause of the Great Charter, and by the time of the Tudors, as everyone knew, the Charter had the force of a constitutional document. It was part of the statute law of the country, its provisions repeatedly confirmed and defined.

Schoolchildren in England used to be told that the "Reformation" was a popular event, and that the only people damaged by it were the Pope and some lazy monks and nuns. This was not true. When Henry VIII succeeded his father, England was a small but rich country, its people well paid, well clothed, and well fed. After 20 years of Henry's extravagance, bankruptcy of the royal treasury was a real possibility. The King needed his subjects' wealth, and since about a third of it was in the custodianship of the Church, the only effective way to get his hands on a fair piece of it was to expropriate or—as we would now say, "nationalize"—the Church. And that, in defiance of the law of his kingdom, is what he did.

The wealth of the Church was a kind of massive trust fund held in a diversified portfolio of over 800 religious houses, 17 dioceses, over 10,000 parishes, about 100 colleges, over 100 hospitals, and over 2,000 chantries, not to mention free chapels, almshouses, and guilds. Besides providing the religious services of the Church, these institutions educated the young, took care of the sick, the indigent, and the old-aged, and provided hospitality for travelers. All over England, too, they employed teachers, musicians, sculptors, painters, glaziers, and stone-masons in large numbers. At the level of the parish, local management was in the hands of the parishioners. As we learned a few years ago from Eamon Duffy, in the process of taking care of their church and managing its business even the parishioners of the tiny parish of Morebath in Devonshire had accumulated a considerable communal property, both material and cultural, which was all taken from them by the "Reformation," even down to the altar linens.[1]

In the first stage of the Reformation, Henry VIII seized the property of

[1] Eamon Duffy, *The Voices of Morebath* (New Haven & London: Yale University Press, 2001). See especially Chapter 6, "Morebath Dismantled," 111–51. The altar linens go on p.150.

the religious houses. The seizures of diocesan and parochial wealth followed under Edward VI and Elizabeth I, and by the time the process was complete, as William Cobbett wrote nearly two hundred years ago, the English people's patrimony was gone. As we would put it, a huge, unprecedented transfer of wealth had taken place from the Church and the people into the hands of the Crown, its servants and friends. The immediate consequence was the loss of a kind of intellectual and cultural autonomy in the towns and villages of England that would never be seen again. No longer would ordinary people in parishes large and small be commissioning local sculptors and artists to decorate their churches and guild chapels, as in Shakespeare's Stratford-upon-Avon. But the most devastating social consequence was the appearance, by the end of the sixteenth century, of unprecedented pauperism and beggary everywhere in the country.

Equally devastating to the quality of English life was the loss of the people's constitutional protection from the misbehavior of an outlaw or criminal government, and the consequent development of a savage penal code.[1] William Cobbett wrote his *History of the Protestant Reformation in England and Ireland* in the 1820s in large part to find an historical explanation for the miseries of laboring English people in his time. That was why, in his 4th paragraph, he wrote:

> The "REFORMATION," as it is called, was engendered in beastly lust, brought forth in hypocrisy and perfidy, and cherished and fed by plunder, devastation, and by rivers of innocent English and Irish blood...as to its more remote consequences, they are, some of them, now before us in that misery, that beggary, that nakedness, that hunger, that everlasting wrangling and spite, which now stare us in the face....[2]

Peter Cochrane, introducing his online edition of Byron's friend Cam

---

[1] When William Harrington was executed, 18 February 1594, ten men and thirteen women were hanged that same day (See above, 268). The numbers of people judicially killed under the Tudors are mind-boggling. For an attempt at estimating some numbers, see Francis Barker, "A Wilderness of Tigers: *'Titus Andronicus'*, Anthropology and the Occlusion of Violence," in *The Culture of Violence: Tragedy and History* (Chicago: Chicago University Press, 1993), 143–206. William Harrison, writing in his *Description of England*, attributed 72,000 executions of "great thieves, petty thieves, and rogues" to Henry VIII which, if true, puts him in the Mao and Stalin class (Harrison, 246).

[2] William Cobbett was an English Protestant farmer, journalist, writer, and Member of Parliament. The best version of his remarkable book, *The Protestant Reformation in England and Ireland*, is the revised edition, with notes and preface, by F.A.Gasquet (London: Burnes Oates & Washbourne, 1934). For easy cross-reference Cobbett numbered the paragraphs of his book.

Hobhouse's diary, has this to say of the state of English politics in Cobbett's and Hobhouse's time:

> It's important to understand that the English political system in Hobhouse's time was, before 1832 and even after, so bizarrely unfair and illogical—so overtly corrupt—that to be against it did not qualify a person as a radical. With a government which made so clear its estimate of the English people as a menace to be contained for the sake of England, one could reconcile constitutional radicalism and social conservatism with a perfectly clear conscience."[1]

The originating cause of that state of affairs, as Cobbett knew, was in the shredding of English constitutional law in the Tudor sixteenth century. The suspension of the English people's statutory and constitutional rights began under Henry VIII and was rendered permanent in the long reign of his daughter Elizabeth. There is no better example and proof of that statement to be found than in the activities of Richard Topcliffe, torturing so freely, with his royal mistress's encouragement, in the Tower, in Bridewell prison, and even in his own basement.

*****

[1]Peter Cochrane, "Introduction," *The Diaries of John Cam Hobhouse*, vii. Published online at https://petercochran.files. wordpress.com /2009/12/00-introduction.pdf

Appendix I

I. The Tortures, 1558–1603: General

In the case of warranted tortures, the date is the date of the warrant. In the other cases, the date is the reported, sometimes approximate date of the torture. More warrants would have survived if the privy council registers were complete.

W = Warrant. l =lay. p = priest

1–2. 15 Mar 59	Pitt & Nicholas, thieves; To be tortured if they deny the fact (W: *APC* 7. 66–7; to Sir Richard Blount, Lt).
3. 13 Apr 61	Bishops of London and Ely recommend torture of a priest, Haverd, arrested leaving England (Hughes, 3.255; Stowe, 126)
4. 22 Jun 65	Nicholas Heath, l. "To use some kind of torture unto him, so as it be without any great bodily hurt" (W: *APC* 7.222; to Lord Scrope).
5. 28 Dec 66	Clement Fisher, l. "To feel some touch of the rack" (W: *APC* 7.319; to Mr. Justice Welsh, Sir Gilbert Gerard, AG, others).
6. 18 Jan 67	Rice, bucklermaker. To be tortured if he will not confess. Accused of thieving (W: *APC* 7.324; to Lt. and others).
7. 28 Nov 69	Thomas Wood, p. Threatened with the rack by Henry Knollys and others (Heath, 84; *CSP Dom. Eliz.* lix.43).
8. 20 Jun 70	Thomas Andrews. Accused of murder; to be brought to the rack (W: *APC* 7.367), and to be racked (W: *APC* 7. 368; to Mr. Justice Southcote).
9. 25 Jun 70	John Felton, l (W: *APC* 7.373; to Sir Thomas Wroth, to take him to the Lieutenant of the Tower.).
10. 29 Apr 71	Charles Bailly, l (Heath, 98–100; Edwards1, 42). Threatened with rack by Burghley, put on the rack by Lt.
11. 26 Oct 71	John Leslie, Bishop of Ross, threatened with the rack (Edwards 1, 50).
12-13. Sep –Oct 71	Lawrence Bannister, Norfolk's land-agent, & l of his secretaries, William Barker (Heath, 101–3); the rack at the tower: Sir Thomas Smith & Dr. Thomas Wilson.
14. 3 Jul 72	An anonymous Englishman, racked at Berwick by Lord Hunsdon (Heath, 104).
15. 1 Apr 73	George Browne and others. Suspected of murder; to be brought or put to the rack (W: *APC* 8.94; to the Master of the Rolls, Justices Southcote and Manwood).

16. 29 Nov 74   Humphrey Needham, l. "To be brought to the rack without stretching his body" (W: *APC* 8.319; to Thomas Randolph, Henry Knollys, Thomas Norton).

17. 6 Feb 75   Henry Cockyn, a bookseller. The Tower; "to put him in fear of the rack" (W: *APC* 8.336; to Sir Owen Hopton, Lt.).[1]

18. 25 Oct 76   Thomas Wells, suspected thief. Sir Owen Hopton, Lt., and William Fleetwood, Recorder to "bring him in fear thereof" (W, carelessly written: *APC* 9. 222).

19. 4 Dec 77   Thomas Sherwood, l. "To assay him at the rack" (W: *APC* 10.111; to Sir Owen Hopton, Lt., Gilbert Gerard, AG, John Bromley, SG, Fleetwood, Recorder).

20. 4 Nov 78   Harding. To be "brought to" the rack (W: *APC* 10.373; to Hopton, Lt.).

21. 4 Nov 78   John Sanford. To be "put to" the rack (W: *APC* 10.373; to Hopton, Lt.).

22–23. 11 Jun 79   Harvey Mellersh and Robert Wintershall. Suspected of murder; to be dealt with "by shew of some terror to be offered unto them," by dungeons, short diet, finally by the rack, with implication of use if necessary (W: *APC* 11. 157-8; to Justice Southcote, Lt., Sir Thomas Browne, Robert Livesey).

24. Dec. 80   Stephen Brinkley's servant, racked (Kilroy 2, 190).

25. 9 Dec 80   Humphrey, a boy. Accused of complicity in robbing Sir Dru Drury: "some slight kind of torture," e.g., whipping, to be used (W: *APC* 12.275–6; to Thomas Townsend, Henry D'Oyly, William Bleverhasset).

26. 15 Dec 80   Robert Johnson, p (DT).

27. 15 Dec 80   Ralph Sherwin, p. Also 16 Dec 80, early 81 (DT).

28–30. 24 Dec 80   John Hart, p., James Bosgrave, p., John Pascal, l. "to bring them unto the tortures, and by terror thereof wring from them the truth of such matters as they shall find most necessary to be discovered" (W: *APC* 12.294; to Hopton, Lt., Sir George Carey, Gilbert Gerard, AG, John Popham, SG).

31. 31 Dec 80   Henry Orton, l. (and John Hart threatened) (DT).

32. 3 Jan 81   Christopher Thomson, p (DT, Anstruther, 350).

33. 14 Jan 81   Nicholas Roscarrock, l (DT, *ODNB*).

34. 15 Jan 81   Jerome Stevens, l. Threatened with the rack (DT).

35. 10 Feb 81   2George Dutton, l. Threatened with torture (DT).

36. 3 May 81   Alexander Briant, p. Also 6 May (?) 80 (DT; W: *APC* 13.37; to Hopton, Lt., Norton, and Dr. John Hammond).

[1]Cockyn was suspected of being a link in Mary Stuart's chain of communication with Scotland (Heath, 95–6).

37. 22 Jun 81   Unknown visionary Catholic girl. To be "secretly whipped" in Chester to reveal imposture (W: *APC* 13.98; to the Bishop of Chester, William Chaderton.)

38. 30 Jul 81   Edmund Campion, p. Also 14 August, 31 October: "to deal with him by the rack" (DT; W: *APC* 13.146; to Hopton, Lt., Robert Beale, Norton).

39. 30 Jul 81   Thomas Myagh, l. An Irishman: "deal with him by the rack as they shall see cause" (W: *APC* 13.147; to Hopton, Lt., Norton).

40. 14 Aug 81   John Colleton or Collington, alias Peters, p. The Tower, to "put them in fear of the torture" (W: *APC* 13.147, 171–2; Hopton, Lt., Beale, Hammond).

41. 14 Aug 81   Thomas Ford, p. The Tower; first threatened, then 29 Oct 81 the real thing: "put them unto the rack" (W: *APC*, 13.171, 249; to Popham, AG, Thomas Egerton, SG, Hammond, Thomas Wilkes, Norton).

42. 14 Aug 81   John Paine, p. Also 31 Oct 81 (DT; W: *APC* 13.172; to Hopton, Lt., Hammond, Beale).

43. 29 Oct 81   John Shert,[1] p. (Challoner, 48; W: *APC* 13.249; to Popham, AG, Egerton, SG, Hopton, Lt., Hammond, Wilkes, Norton).

44. 29 Apr 82   Thomas Alfield, p. "That they put him to the rack, and by the torture thereof draw from him such things as he shall be able to say" (Burton and Pollen, 147; W: *APC* 13.400–1; to Hopton, Lt., Randolph, Hammond, Thomas Owen).

45–7. 8 Aug 83   Clinton, Atkinson, Pursar, l (pirates). The Tower: "you may travail with them by the terror and torture of the rack." (W: Heath, 111, to Drs. Aubrey, Jones, Caesar, deputy judges in Admiralty).

48. 16,19 Nov 83, 2 Dec   Francis Throckmorton, l. The Tower, racked; also 2 Dec (DT). On 19 Nov, according to Graves, 269, Walsingham brought Norton in as an expert (Heath, 125; Edwards1, 91.)

49. 24. Nov. 83   Edward Arden, l. The Tower, racked (DT; Heath, 126).

50. 25 Nov. 83   Hugh Hall, p. The Tower (Heath, 126).

51–55. Nov 83   John Bennet, p., John Hughes, Robert Morris, Harry Pugh, Richard Gwyn, or White, l. All tortured by the Council of Wales at Bewdley & Bridgnorth (Burton-Pollen, 127–44; Challoner, 103–4).

56. Nov. 83   John Somerville, l. The Tower (Martin R, 334, but no definite evidence, hence doubtful)

---

[1] At his execution, Shert said that he had been "racked and tormented" (Challoner, 48). He may have been tortured under the warrant of 29 Oct 81 which names Campion and Ford, "and others, prisoners in the Tower," with instructions to "put them unto the rack."

57. 11 Dec 83   Roger Dickenson tortured in Bridewell, "where he was very barbarously used" (Pollen 2, 84; Anstruther, 103).[1]

58–59. 12 Feb 84   William Shelley, l., Pierpoint, l (SP 12/168/14).

60. Mar 84   Jasper Heywood, p. The Tower (Flynn, 125).

61–2. May 85   Thomas Alfield, p., Thomas Webley, l. The Tower; racked (Challoner, 106; Burton-Pollen, 151). See No. 44.

63. Jul 85   Edward Atslowe, l (Verstegan, 102; *ODNB*).

64. 1585–86   Hethfield, a Newcastle merchant (Burton-Pollen, 527).

65. 10 Apr 86   Matthew Beaumond. Accused of robbery (W: *APC* 14.56; to Hopton, Lt., McWilliams, and Young).

66. 17 Apr 86   William Wakeman. Accused of robbery (W: *APC* 14.62; to Hopton, Lt., McWilliams, and Young).

67. 13 May 86   Pynder alias Pudsey.[2] Accused of Felonies (W: *APC* 14.107–8; to Hopton, Lt.).

68. ca.26 Aug 86   John Ballard, p. The Tower, the rack (Pollen 3, clxii, 161, 167).

69 Sep 86   Bartholomew Bellamy, l. Racked, died in the Tower (Morris, 2.49).

70–79. 23 Dec 86   The Babington Plot aftermath: ten to be re-examined with torture as necessary: Edward Windsor, Edward Bentley, Ralph Ithell, Anthony Tuchenor, Thomas Habington, Jerome Payne, Sampson Loane, Henry Foxwell, Thomas Heath, Thomas Tipping (W: *APC* 14.271; to Hopton, Lt., Popham, AG, Egerton, SG. Miles Sandys, Owen).

80. 24 Apr 87   Andreas von Metter, l. For "matters concerning the state:" the Tower, "the accustomed torture of the rack as often times as they should see cause" (W: *APC* 15.51; to Hopton, Lt., Mr. Daniel, and Young).

81–82. 7 Jan 88   John Staughton, l., Humphrey Fullwood, l. For "practices against the state and government...to be put to the rack" (W: *APC* 15.330; to Hopton, Lt., Randolph, Killigrew, and Young).

83. 14 Jan 88   Roger Ashton, l (W: *APC* 15.334–5: to Hopton, Sir Edward Waterhouse. William Waad, Owen, Young).

84. 16 Feb 88   George Stoker, l (W: *APC* 15.365; to Hopton, Lt,. Sir Thomas Bodley, Waad, Owen, Young. Tower, rack).

85. 14 Mar 88   William Deeg, l. Tortured and hanged by Caudwell and Thorne in Staffordshire (Foley, 3, 227).

86. 24 Jun 89   An anonymous goldsmith accused of robbery. Bridewell: "the torture of the House in such sort and measure as you...shall think fit" (W: *APC* 17.310; to Young).

---

[1]No reference in Pollen, hence a doubtful case.

[2]Nos. 65–7 were accused of theft; all three were racked under warrant of 13 May. The rackers were Hopton, McWilliam, and Young.

87–9. 24 Aug 89	Hodgkiss (or Hodgkins), Valentine Sims, Thornlyn. These three are Marprelate cases (W: *APC* 18.62: to Fortescue, Master of the Wardrobe, Rokesby, Master of St. Katherine's, and Recorder Fleetwood).
90. late 1588–89	Richard Randall or Randolph, l.
91. 1589?	William Norton, l. (Bridewell, the manacles: Verstegan, 9).[1]
92–96. Apr 90	Four unnamed robbers plus William Browne, a butcher. The butcher to be especially dealt with: the rack and the manacles in Bridewell (W: *APC* 19.69–70; to Young).
97. 20 Jul 91	Hacket, l. Bridewell. "A most pestiferous and seditious person...the manacles and such other torture as you shall think good" (W: *APC* 21.300: to Owen and Young).
98. Jan. 92?	Anthony Skinner, l. (Verstegan, 57).
99. Jan 92	Nicholas Fox, p. "By ill usage is dead in the Tower" (Verstegan, 49; Anstruther, 123).
100. 4 Jun 92	Owen Edmunds. An Irishman accused of "matter concerning the state (W: *APC* 22.512: to Sir George Carey, Young. Bridewell: "put him to the torture accustomed in such cases").
101–103. ca.23 Dec 92	Richard Webster and Gratian Brownell, schoolmasters, threatened, Robert Faux, l. tortured. Bridewell, the manacles: Richard Young (NA/SP12/243/93; Morris, 3.34n.; Pollen 1, 213–15).
104–106. 8 Feb 93	Urmstone, recusant from Lancashire, Edward Bagshaw and Henry Ash, recusants arrested in Derbyshire. To be taken to Bridewell from the Gatehouse for interrogation: "in case of need to pinch them with the torture as in such cases is accustomed" (W: *APC* 24.56; to Young and Ellis).
107. 16 Apr 93	Anon, a libeller (W: *APC* 24.187; to the Lord Mayor; Heath, 118).
108. ca.12 May 93	Thomas Kyd, l. Bridewell, the manacles; under a general warrant for torture in Bridewell, Kyd not named (W: *APC* 24.227: to Sir Richard Martin, Anthony Ashley, and Alderman Buckle; Freeman, 181–3).
109. 1593–4	John Annias, Irishman. Put in the manacles by Justice Young "until he was almost dead" (NA/SP/12/247/33, cited by Edwards, *Plots*, 197, n.11).

---

[1]The authority for Richard Randall's torture by the manacles is Robert Southwell, who also names Norton, who may have been William Norton, one of a group of Oxonians arrested on the French ambassador's ship, September 1585 (*CSPD 1581–90*, 266-68). According to a Cecil operative called Anthony Hall, Randall (or Randolph), who was caught up in the proceedings against the Earl of Arundel, April 1589, was a professor of law (Strype 1, 4. 233).

110–11. 1594.	Richard Fulwood and Nicholas Owen, John Gerard's men. The manacles (Gerard, 72).[1]
112. 26 Feb 94	Tinoco, a Portuguese. "Put to the manacles" (Harl. 871, f.42v; Handover, 117).
113. 25 Feb 94	Roderigo Lopez, Portuguese Jewish physician. Threatened with the manacles, possibly tortured (Ibid., Green, 269, Edwards 1, 226).
114. 1595	Richard Williams (Verstegan, 239).
115–16. 12 Nov 95	Gabriel Colford, l., Thomas Faulkes, l. Bridewell, the manacles (W: *APC* 5.73: to Thomas Fleming, SG and Waad).
117. Jun 95–Nov 96	Thomas Dowlton, l. "Little Ease," "standing stocks," 20 lashes "upon the trosse" in Bridewell; committed by Stanhope for the High Commission (Caraman, *Weston*, 243–4).
118. 25 Jan 96	John Hardy. "A Frenchman, come into the realm for no good purpose...the ordinary torture there in Bridewell" (W: *APC* 25.179–80; to Wilkes and Waad).
119. 28 Feb 96	Hodges, a thief. Bridewell, the manacles (W: *APC* 25.251: to Sir Richard Martin).
120–24. 19 Dec 96	The 5 Oxford conspirators: Bartholomew Steer, James Bradshaw, Richard Bradshaw, John Ibill, Robert Burton (W: *APC* 26.373–4: to Edward Coke, AG, Thomas Fleming, SG, John Crooke, Recorder, Fancis Bacon).[2]
125. 3 Feb 97	William Thompson. "A very lewd and dangerous person...a purpose to burn her Majesty's ships;" the Tower, to be put to the manacles and the torture of the rack (W: *APC* 26.457: to Berkeley, Lt.: letter to Coke, AG, Fleming, SG, Bacon, Waad).[3]
126. 13 Apr 97	John Gerard, p. "Cause him to be put to the manacles and such other torture as is used in that place" (W: *APC* 27.38; to Sir Richard Berkeley, Lt., Fleming, SG, Bacon, Waad).
127. 17 Apr 98	Valentine Thomas, l. For "matters concerning greatly the estate;" Bridewell, the manacles (W: *APC* 28.406; to Fleming, SG, Bacon, Waad, Waad to apply the torture).

[1]Nicholas Owen was to die under torture, 2 Mar 1606 (Gerard, 201 and n.).

[2]Steer and James Bradshaw seem to have died under torture. Burton, Edward Bompass & R. Bradshaw were indicted 24 Feb 96. Burton and Bradshaw were convicted of treason 11 Jun, and sentenced to be hanged, drawn, and quartered. Bompass disappeared from the record; he too was probably dead (Walter, 128, n.131).

[3]According to John Annias's confession, January 1594 (NA/SP12/237/33) Thompson had been imprisoned previously, ca.1592. At that time, Young had tortured him with the manacles.

128. 19 Oct 98   Edward Squire, l. The Tower; the rack. Lt (Peyton), Coke, AG, Fleming, SG, Bacon, Wade (Heath, 134–6).[1]

129. Aug 99   John Lillie, l. The Tower, the manacles, Waad in charge (Gerard, 156; Anstruther, *Vaux of Harrowden*, 202).

130. 14 Apr 01   Thomas Howson, l. For seditious libels; Bridewell, the manacles (W: *APC* 31.281; to Waad and Thomas Fowler).

131. 1601   Thomas Hackshot, l (Challoner, 260; Anstruther, 358).

132. 1580–1600   Thomas Pounde, Jesuit lay brother. "Periodically tortured," subjected to "the Widow's Mite," a torture device in Newgate (*ODNB*; Foley, 3.588).

II. The Tortures, 1582–1603: Topcliffe's Cases

1. Feb 82   Edward Osborne, p. Threatened with "Sir Owen Hopton's school" (Alfield, Sigs. E3, F1; Anstruther, 261–2).

2. 5 Mar 82   Anthony Fugatius, a Portuguese gentleman: after 2 years in prison and "the most cruel rackings, being at the point of death (for he was old and broken by sufferings), was privately removed on a litter, & shortly died" (DT).

3. Aug 82   John Jetter, l. The Tower, racked (DT; Pollen 2, 221–5).

4. ca. Oct 82   William Carter, l. The Tower, "nearly killed on the rack" (Pollen 1, 27; *CRS* 4.75; *ODNB*; see above, 121, 141).

5. 1588, spring?   Thomas Felton, l. Bridewell, the manacles (Challoner, 139).

6   1588, summer   William Watson, p. Bridewell, the manacles (Anstruther, 373; *ODNB*).

7   Aug 88   Margaret Ward. Bridewell, flogging and the manacles; crippled (Pollen 1, 323, 327).

8. 8 Sep 88   Tristram Winslade, l. Captured in the Spanish ships (W: *APC* 16.273; to Hopton, Lt., James Dalton, Topcliffe.[2]

9. ca.23 May 89   George Nichols, p. Bridewell, the manacles, (Challoner, 157; Pollen 1, 168; Anstruther, 252).

10. 25 May 89   Richard Yaxley, alias Tankerd, p. Bridewell, the manacles, then committed close prisoner to the Tower, only Topcliffe to have access to him; racked or threatened with the rack (Challoner,1 57;Pollen 1, 168; W: *APC* 17.205; 25 May 1589; to Hopton, Lt.).

11. 3 Dec 89   Francis Dickenson, p. Bridewell, the Manacles (Pollen 2, 314, 322; Anstruther, 102).[3]

---

[1]Squire's two associates, Stanley and Richard Rolls, were said to have been "sore racked" as well (Heath, 136).

[2]Winslade was released after torture, 24 Feb 89 (APC, 18, 387).

12. 3 Dec 89, Miles Gerard, p. Bridewell, the manacles (Pollen 2, 314; Anstruther, 130).

13. Jan–Feb 90 Christopher Bayles, p. Bridewell, the manacles and worse (See Pollen 2, 290) for nearly 24 hours (Pollen 1, 178–9; Pollen 2, 289–90; W: NA/SP12/230/57; to Topcliffe and Young).

14–17. Jan–Feb 90 John Bayles, Henry Gurney, Anthony Kay, John Coxed, l. Bridewell, "such torture as is usual" (W: NA/ SP12/ 230/57; to the Keeper of Bridewell, Topcliffe and Young).

18. Jan–Feb 90 Nicholas Horner, an old man, a tailor. Condemned on Topcliffe's evidence for making a jerkin for a priest; Bridewell, the manacles (Pollen 2, 227–31).

19. Apr 90 Edward Jones alias Hughes, p. Bridewell, the manacles; also "tormented in Topcliffe's house by the privy parts" (Verstegan, 9; Pollen 1, 184, 291; Pollen 2, 290).

20–22. 9 Aug 90 Richard Fitzherbert, Richard Twyfford, Martin Audley, l. (W: APC 19. 370: to Topcliffe, Daniell, Fuller, Brainthwait, Thos. Waad: to examine them "strictly and severely").

23. 10 Jan 91 George Beesley, p. Chained in Topcliffe's cellar, racked in the Tower, put in "Little Ease;" Pollen 2, 303, 291; Pollen 1, 203; W: APC 20.204; to Blount, Lt., Killigrew, Beale, Fletcher, Topcliffe).

24. 10 Jan 91, Robert Humberson, l. The Tower, "Little Ease" (W: APC 20.204; to Blount, Lt., Killigrew, Beale, Fletcher, Topcliffe).

25–6. Feb–Jun 91 Roger Dickenson, p., Ralph Milner, l. The Marshalsea and Bridewell, the manacles (Pollen 2, 90, on the authority of Thomas Stanney, S.J.). Also see No.4.

27–8. 31 May 91 Robert Thorpe, p., John Watkinson, l (John Cecil in Pollen 1, 202–3).

29. Sep 91 Thomas Pormort, p. Bridewell, Topcliffe's house, the manacles; he suffered a rupture (Pollen 1, 200, 292; Anstruther, 280).

30–31. 24 Oct 91 Brian Lacey, l., and Eustace White, p. Bridewell, "the manacles and such other tortures as are used in Bridewell," Topcliffe in charge of the interrogation (Pollen 1, 292; W: APC 22.39–40; to Fletcher, Topcliffe, Brathwaite, Young).[2]

32. 27 Oct 91 Thomas Clinton, l. Bridewell, the manacles (W: APC

---

[3]There is a detailed account of the torture ("caused him to be hanged up by the privy parts") in Fitzherbert, 6–6b.

[2]Eustace White described his torture in a letter to Henry Garnet (Pollen 2, 123-26).

		22.42; to Popham, AG and Egerton, SG, instructed to send for Topcliffe and Young).
33.	26 Jun 92	Robert Southwell, p. Topcliffe's house, the Gatehouse; the manacles (Devlin 1, 293–90).
34.	Oct 93	Robert Gray, p. Threatened with irons or manacles (Stonyhurst Ms. *Anglia* A.II.41).
35.	Mar 93–Jul 94	John Boste, p. The Tower, once in the manacles, four times on the rack, crippled (Challoner, 203; Morris, 3, 196).
36.	Mar 94	John Ingram, p. Racked in the Tower (Challoner, 204; Foley, 3.765; Pollen 1, 283; Anstruther, 183).
37.	May–Jun 94	Henry Walpole, p. The Tower, the manacles; his interrogators were Blount, Lt., Topcliffe, Coke, Bacon, Edward Drew, Killigrew, Beale, Young, Sandys (Challoner, 220, 222; Pollen 2, 245).
38.	1594–Feb 95	James Atkinson, l. Bridewell, Topcliffe's house; threatened, tortured, killed (Stonyhurst Ms *Anglia* A.II.41; Challoner, 221; Pollen 1, 287).
39–43.	21 Nov 96	Gipsies (W: *APC* 26.325: to the Recorder, Topcliffe, Richard Skevington).
44–5.	17 Nov 97	Richard Aunger, Edward Ingram, murder suspects. Aunger was suspected of murdering his father, Richard Aunger of Gray's Inn; Ingram, the porter of Gray's Inn, was an accomplice; Bridewell, the manacles (W: *APC* 28. 187; to Topcliffe, Recorder Crooke, Nicholas Fuller, Mr. Gerard, Mr. Altham.
46.	1 Dec 97	Thomas Travers, suspected of theft from the Queen. Bridewell, the manacles (W: *APC* 28.165; to AG, Recorder Crooke, Topcliffe, Sir Richard Martin, Fowler, Skevington, Mr. Vaughan).
47–48.	4 Jan 99	Richard Denton, Peter Cooper. "Privy unto some dangerous practice against the person of Her Majesty and the State;" Bridewell, the manacles (W: *APC* 29.428; to Sir John Peyton, Lt., Topcliffe).

III. Some Cases of Chronic Duress and Other Punishments

Little Ease

1.	12 Oct 71	Charles Bailly, l (Edwards 1, 43).
2.	14 Aug 82	Stephen Rousham, p., 18 months, 13 days (DT).
3.	13 Nov 83	Francis Throckmorton, l (Edwards 1, 91).
4.	1588	Thomas Felton, l (Challoner, 139).

5–6. 10 Jan 91   George Beesley, p., Robert Humberson, l (W: *APC* 20.204).

The Scavenger's Daughter

7.   10 Dec 80   Luke Kirby, p (DT).
8.   10 Dec 80   John Cottam, p (Bleeds at nostrils: DT).
9.   17 Mar 81   Thomas Myagh, l (Dick, 17).
10. 1 Sep 82   John Jetter, l (DT).
11. 4 Feb 84   Robert Nutter, p (Also 6 Feb; DT).

The Pit

12. 8 Feb 81   Thomas Briscoe, l (5 months: DT).
13. 6 Apr 81   Alexander Briant, p (DT).
14. 11 Jan 82   John Hart, p (then 19 Jun 83, 40 days: DT).
15. 7 Feb 82   George Haydock, p (5 days: DT).
16   7 Feb 82   Arthur Pitts, p (5 days: DT).
17. 22 Mar 82   Robert Copley, l (7 days: DT).
18. 23 Jul 82   Richard Slack, p (2 months "laden with fetters:" (DT).
19. 1 Sep 82   John Jetter, l (8 days: DT).
20. 23 Nov 83   Francis Throckmorton, l (DT; Edwards 1, 91).
21. 2 Feb 84   Robert Nutter, p (47 days; then 10 Nov 84, 2 months, 14 days: (DT).
22. 7 Feb 84   James Fenn, p. (6 days before execution; DT).
23. 7 Feb 84   Thomas Hemerford, p (6 days before execution; DT).
24. 7 Feb 84   John Nutter, p (6 days before execution; DT).
25. 13 Jun 84   Thomas Layton, l (DT).
26. 19 Jun 84   Thomas Worthington, p (2 months, 3 days; DT).
27. 27 Aug 84   William Aprice, l (23 days; again 24 Sep, 48 days; DT).
28. 16 Oct 84   William Crumlum, l (2 months, 24 days, again 7 Jun, 7 days; DT).
29. 4 Jun 85   Patrick Ady, l (4 days; DT).

Some Other Unpleasantnesses

30. 1578?   Thomas Bell, p (Hung by the feet for three days in York Castle, Camm, 570).
31. 17 Nov 77   Thomas Sherwood, l ("If the said Sherwood shall not willingly confess such things as shall be demanded of him, he is then required to commit him to the dungeon amongst the rats;" W: *APC* 10.94: Lt.; Camm, 240).

32.	Nov 80-Apr 81	Thomas Clifton, p (Manacled to the wall in an underground pit, Newgate; in Dec 86 he was "delivered to the custody of Mr. Topcliffe by the Lords' order," to be banished; but he stayed in Bridewell, where he was dead by 17 Mar 1593; *CRS* 2, 274; Anstruther, 80).
33.	27 Mar 81	Alexander Briant, p (Needles under nails; DT).
34.	21 Nov 81	Alexander Briant, p (Shackled 2 days; DT).
35.	21 Nov 81	William Filby, p (Manacled for cheerfulness; DT).
36.	1 Dec 82	John Hart, p (20 days in irons for disagreeing with Reynolds, a minister; DT).
37.	15 Feb 83	John Munden, p (20 days in iron fetters; DT).
38.	13 Mar 84	Thomas Stephenson, p (Fetters 39 days, no bed 27 days; DT).

IV. Women

Although the Elizabethan authorities only put three women to death under their penal laws governing religious conformity (Margaret Clitherow, Margaret Ward, and Anne Line, all three now canonized saints), they killed a great many more by imprisonment. This list, which is merely representative and by no means complete, will give a reader some idea of the régime's treatment of non-conforming women. Imprisonment was, in many cases, a death sentence. York, under the rule of the Earl of Huntington, was especially bad. Two sheriffs John Wedall and Leonard Beckwith, put Dorothy Vavasour, Mary Hutton, and Alice Oldcorne, after 7 years' in prison, into a cold, filthy room in the middle of winter without bedding, knowing that it was infected. All three were dead in a few days (Morris 3.316–17).

1.	25 Mar 86	Margaret Clitherow: pressed to death at York.
2.	30 Aug 88	Margaret Ward: hanged at Tyburn.
3.	27 Feb 1601	Anne Line: hanged at Tyburn.
4.	Sep 62	Elizabeth Sherwood: widow of Henry Sherwood, taken at mass in London, imprisoned, died in prison fourteen years later (Pollen 2, 7–8).
5.		Dame Isabelle Whitehead: nun, died York Castle, 18 Mar 87.
6.		Mrs. Ardington: imp. York Castle.
7.	Imp 77	Mrs. Ann Foster: York, in Ousebridge (1 year), where she died.
8.	Imp 77	Isabella Foster: daughter of Richard Langley; imprisoned York Castle, pregnant, died there 3 dec 87.
9.	Imp 77	Agnes Johnson: York, in Ousebridge (2 years), where she died.

10. Imp 77	Alice Williamson: York, in Ousebridge (2 years), where she died.
11. Imp. 77	Alice Simson: York, in Ousebridge (17 years as of 1594).
12. Imp. ca 78	Ann Landers: York, Ousebridge; released, reimprisoned ca. 1579, York Castle and Hull (5-6 years); moved to the Clink, London, Mar 79; died there 1589.
13.	Mrs. Philip Lowe: London, White Lion ("many years"); died Apr 88.
14.	Mrs Tremaine: Dorchester gaol, died.
15.	Mrs. Ursula Foster: Shrewsbury gaol, where she died in irons (Foley, 4.493).
16. imp.79	Agnes Fuister. York, Ousebridge (1-2 years), died.
17. Imp. 80	Dorothy Vavasour: York, Kidcote (7 years), died.
18. Imp. 80	Mary Hutton: York, Kidcote (7 years), died.
19. Imp. 80	Alice Oldcorne: York, Kidcote (7 years), died.
20–1. Imp. 80	Etheldred Wethereld, her maid Elizabeth Reade, & husband James: York (released on bonds within 4 years).
22. 29 Jun 85	Frances Webster: died in St. Peter's Prison, York (218).
23.	Also her mother, Mrs. Webster (Burton-Pollen, 275).
24. Imp. 85	Joan Vyze: Staffordshire county gaol (4 years), died there 1589 (Foley, 3.226)
25. Imp. 88	Mrs. Joan Lowe: condemned for receiving and relieving priests; reprieved, died in the White Lion prison, 7 Apr 89.
26. Imp. 96	Anne Tesse: York, condemned to be burnt; reprieved, imprisoned during pleasure.
27. Imp. 96	Bridget Maskew: York, condemned to be burnt; reprieved, imprisoned during pleasure.
28. Imp. 91	Mrs. Swithin Wells: London, died in Newgate, 1602.
29. Imp. Aug 86	Catherine Bellamy: Uxendon, died in the Tower, Aug 86.
30. Imp. 95	Catherine Bellamy: daughter-in-law of above, died in the Gatehouse prison, hounded to death by Topcliffe.
31. 99	Eleanor Hunt: sentenced to death for harboring Christopher Wharton, but reprieved, imprisoned during pleasure, where she died (Challoner, 238).
32. Jun 1600	Mrs. Norton: Durham, condemned to death, reprieved, imprisoned.
33.	Alice Pawlin: two years in Stafford gaol, where she died (Foley, 3.227).

V. The Torturers

The following necessarily incomplete list of torturers is striking both because it contains so many names and because a few names stand out as specialists in the business. Hopton, Lieutenant of the Tower from 1570 to 1590, is Topcliffe's only close rival for the sheer number of cases over which, as lieutenant of the Tower, he presided. He seems to have had no qualms about that aspect of his office.

Like the lieutenants of the Tower, the senior law officers (attorney general and solicitor general) found themselves in the torture chamber as part of their official duty. Of the Elizabethan holders of those offices, only Edward Coke and John Popham seem to have relished the work. It is surprising to see the Lord Mayor of London and an alderman appearing as *ex officio* torturers along with the recorders of the city; but once torture became a routine part of police work, the men responsible for keeping order in the city were bound to find themselves involved in it.

Of the rest, John Hammond was a civil lawyer employed, like Thomas Norton, Robert Beale and William Waad, by the Privy Council. Norton, who became notorious for his part in the racking of Edmund Campion and his fellow priests, had a short but enthusiastic torturing career. He is named as a torturer in only seven surviving warrants, but he was involved in at least twice as many cases. Beale and Waad, privy council clerks, went on to become professionals of the torture room, Waad in time becoming lieutenant of the Tower under James I, in which capacity he was responsible for the post-Gunpowder Plot tortures, which included the murder under torture of Nicholas Owen ("Little John"), the ingenious builder of hideaways. Richard Young was a justice of the peace and Customer of the Port of London. He is named in fifteen Council torture warrants, and became notorious in that role. Sir John Harington singled him out as representing the moral filth that needed to be cleaned out of Elizabeth I's court.[1] Francis Bacon's is a surprising name to find in this gallery: he appeared on at least five occasions, and seems to have been one of Topcliffe's friends.

By the time Sir Henry Killigrew joined the torturers as a gentleman-amateur, he had retired from a long and lucrative career of international trouble-making on behalf of the English government. The new *Oxford Dictionary of National Biography* makes

[1]Kilroy 1, 92–3.

no mention of his torturing activities—but then it also describes Beale[1] and Waad as diplomats and administrators, too. It cannot be sufficiently emphasized that under English law, unrepealed since 1215, torture is felonious assault, and death under torture is murder.

Altham, Mr.

Ashley, Anthony

Bacon, Francis (5)

Beale, Robert (6)

Berkeley, Sir Richard, Lt.

Bleverhassett, William (whipping)

Blount, Sir Michael, Lt. (7)

Blount, Sir Richard, Lt.

Bodley, Sir Thomas

Braithwait, Mr.

Bromley, John, SG

Browne, Sir Thomas

Buckle, Alderman

Carey, Sir George (2)

D'Oyly, Henry (whipping)

Caudwell

Chaderton, William, Bp of Chester

Coke, Edward, AG (3)

Cordell, Sir William

Crooke, John, Recorder (2)

Daniel, William.

Dalton, Mr. James

Drew, Edward

Egerton, Thomas, SG (3)

Ellis, Mr.

Fleetwood, William, Recorder (3)

Fleming, Thomas, SG (4)

Fletcher, Dr Giles. (2)

Gerard, Sir Gilbert, AG (3)

Gerard, William

Hammond, Dr. John (5)

Hopton, Sir Owen, Lt. (39)

Killigrew, Sir Henry (4)

Knollys, Henry

Livesey, Robert

Manwood, Mr. Justice

Martin, Sir Richard (4)

McWilliams (2)

Norton, Thomas (14)

Owen, Thomas (5)

Peyton, Sir John, Lt.

Popham, John, SG, AG (4)

Randolph, Thomas (3)

Rokesby, Master of St. Catherine's

Sandys, Miles, Mr. (2)

Scrope, Lord

Skevington, Mr. (2)

Smith, Sir Thomas

Southcote, Mr. Justice (3)

Thorne, Edward

Townsend, Thomas (whipping)

Topcliffe, Richard (51)

Vaughan, Mr.

Waad, William (8)

Waterhouse, Sir Edward

Mr. Justice Welsh

---

[1]In 1583, Beale, a former Marian exile, sympathetic to Puritan opinions, wrote a pair of pamphlets arguing against interrogation under oath in ecclesiastical cases. According to Archbishop Whitgift's notes, "In his said books, among many other points, he disputeth against her Majesty's authority to grant power by commission ecclesiastical, for to apprehend any, what malefactor soever he be, as Jesuit, Seminary Priest, recusant or other contemptuous and disobedient person...He condemneth (without exception of any cause) *racking* of grievous offenders, as being cruel, barbarous, contrary to law, and unto the liberty of English subjects" (Strype 2, 1.402–3). These principles, for which he deserves credit, did not keep him out of the torture rooms.

Fortescue, Master of the Wardrobe
Fowler, Thomas (2)
Fuller, Nicholas

Wilkes, Thomas Mr. (3)
Wilson, Dr. Thomas
Young, Richard (18)

VI. Topcliffe at the Kill

Observers from the court or the Privy Council were usually present at executions for treason. From 1582 onwards, Richard Topcliffe was a vocal participant in such executions, and became something of a master of the ceremonies at them.

1.	1 Jun 71	Dr. John Storey (Rowse, 191)
2.	30 May 82	William Filby. p.
3.		Luke Kirby, p.
4.		Robert Johnson, p.
5.		Thomas Cottam. p (Allen 1).
6.	2 Mar 85	William Parry, l (BL Addit 48027, f.244-246; Lansdowne MS 43, fol. 127*v*).
7–20.		The Babington executions, both days, fourteen men (BL Addit 48027, ff.263, 271).
7.	20 Sep 86	Anthony Babington, l.
8.		John Ballard, p.
9.		Robert Barnwell, l.
10.		Henry Dunne, l.
11.		Sir Thomsas Salisbury, l.
12.		John Savage, l.
13.		Chidiock Tichborne, l.
14.	21 Sep 86	Jerome Bellamy,l
15.		John Charnock, l.
16.		Robert Gage, l.
17.		Edward Habington, l.
18.		Edward Jones, l
19.		Charles Tilney, l.
20		John Travers, l.
21.	8 Oct 86.	John Lowe, p.
22.		John Adams, p.
23.		Robert Dibdale, p.
24–40.		The Armada hangings: present at sixteen out of twenty-six deaths.
24.	28 Aug 88	William Deane, p (Mile End Green): Hanged.
25.		Henry Webley, l (ditto): hanged.
26.		William Gunter, p (Theatre, Shoreditch): hanged.
27.		Robert Morton, p (Lincoln's Inn Fields): hanged.

28.		Hugh Moore, l (Lincoln's Inn Fields): hanged.
29.		Thomas Holford, p (Clerkenwell): hanged.
30.		James Claxton, p (Near Brentford) : hanged.
31.		Thomas Felton, l. (ditto): hanged.
32.	30 Aug 88	Richard Leigh, p (Tyburn): hanged.
33.		Edward Shelley, l (Tyburn): hanged.
34.		Richard Martin, l (Tyburn): hanged.
35.		Richard Flower, l (22 years old) (Tyburn): hanged.
36.		John Roche, l (Tyburn): hanged.
37.		Margaret Ward (Tyburn): hanged (Pollen 2, 304).
38.	5 Oct 88	John Hewett, alias Saville or Weldon, p (Mile End): hanged: he was fifteen minutes dying (Pollen 2, 309).
39.		William Hartley, p (The Theatre, Shoreditch): hanged.
40.		Robert Sutton, l (Clerkenwell): hanged (Morris 3.38).[1]
41.	4 Mar 90	Christopher Bayles, p (Pollen 2, 308).
42.		Nicholas Horner, l.
43.		Alexander Blake, l.[2]
44.	6 May 90	Edward Jones, p (Pollen 2, 308).
45.		Anthony Middleton, p (Pollen 1, 186).
46.	31 May 91	Robert Thorpe, p.
47.		Thomas Watkinson, l (CRS 5.200; Anstruther 353–4).
48.	1 Jul 91	George Beesley, p.
49.		Montford Scott, p (Pollen 2, 203, 302).[3]
50.	10 Dec 91	Edmund Gennings, p.
51.		Swithin Wells, l.
52.		Polydore Plasden, p.
53.		Eustace White, p.
54.		Brian Lacey, l.
55.		John Mason, l.
56.		Sydney Hodgson, l (Pollen 1, 205–7; Pollen 2, 106–15).
57.	22 Jan 92	William Pattenson, p (Verstegan, 40).
58.	21 Feb 92	Thomas Pormort, p (Pollen 1, 209; Pollen 2, 120)
59.	23 Jun 92	Roger Ashton, l (Pollen 1, 211).
60.	18 Feb 94	William Harrington, p (Stonyhurst Ms *Anglia* I.77).

[1]These three (38–40) were in the same cart, though hanged in different places.

[2]The case of Christopher Bayles and his two lay associates in death was a Topcliffe operation. His presence at the laymen's deaths is indicated by the detail that each had a "title" set on or over his head on the gallows: this was a Topcliffian practice (Pollen 2, 231, 291).

[3]Monford Scott's friends had obtained an order for his banishment from the council, but "when the time of his banishment was come, he was committed to prison again by Topcliffe, and afterwards brought to the Sessions, where for want of other matter Topcliffe signified that it was good policy to put him to death..." (Pollen 2, 291).

61.   12 Jul 98   John Jones, O.S.F. (Pollen 1, 373).

VII. Live Mutilations.

The death sentence for men in cases of treason required the victim to be hanged, cut down while still alive, dismembered, disembowelled, the heart removed, then beheaded and quartered. Historians who find themselves required to mention this obscene procedure frequently soothe their own and their readers' feelings by suggesting that in many if not most cases the victim was allowed to die before the full sentence was carried out.

Such was not, in fact, the case. Live mutilation and butchering was the norm, sometimes mentioned because of an unusually cruel or incompetent performance by the executioner, but always to be assumed unless an account specifically says that the victim was first allowed to die.

List A. Priests and laymen sentenced to hanging, drawing, and quartering, but allowed to die by hanging before mutilation.

1.   1 Dec 81   Edmund Campion, p (Camm, 352; Kilroy 2, 341).
2.   Ralph Sherwin, p (Camm, 395).
3.   Alexander Briant, p (Camm, 420).
4.   2 Apr 82   John Paine, p (Chelmsford: Camm, 442).
5.   28 May 82   Thomas Forde, p (Allen 1, 59).
6.   John Shert, p (Allen 1, 62).
7.   Robert Johnson, p (Allen 1, 66).
8.   30 May 82   William Filby, p (Allen 1, 69).
9.   Luke Kirby, p (Allen 1, 74).
10   Laurence Johnson, p (Allen 1, 81).
11.   Thomas Cottam, p (Allen 1, 83).[1]
12. 28 Nov 82   James Thompson, p (York).[2]
13. 21 Sep 86   Jerome Bellamy, l.
14.   John Charnock, l.
15.   Robert Gage, l.
16.   Edward Habington, l.
17.   Edward Jones, l.
18.   Charles Tilney, l.

[1]The mildness of the 1582 executions, compared to what went before and what came after them, was a response to the strong disapproval, at home and overseas, of the previous executions.

[2]Hanged only (Camm, 597).

19.		John Travers, l.
20.	c. Easter 87	Stephen Rowsham, p (Gloucester).[1]
21.	16 Mar 89	John Amias, p (York).
22.		Robert Dalby, p (York: Challoner, 153).
23.	1 Jun 91	Monford Scott, p (Fleet Street: Pollen 2, 303).
24.	10 Dec 91	Polydore Plasden, p (Pollen 2, 114).[2]
25.	17 Apr 94	Henry Walpole, SJ. (Stonyhurst Ms Anglia I.83[3])
26.	26 Jul 94	John Ingram (Newcastle: Morris, 3.212).
27.	21 Feb 95	Robert Southwell (Brownlow, 22)[4]
28.	12 Jul 98	John Jones, OSF (St. Thomas Waterings: Challoner, 235).
29.	Mar 1601	Thurstan Hunt, p (Lancaster: Pollen 1, 390).
30.	20 Apr 02	Francis Page, SJ. (Foley 1.431).

List B. Priests and Laymen cut down alive. [*] = specific record of live mutilation.

1.	10 May 66	William Blagrave, OP (Strype, I.1.342-3)
2.	8 Aug 70	*John Felton, l (*ODNB*)
3.	4 Jan 70	Thomas Plumtree, p (Durham: Camm, 159).
4.	1 Jun 71	*John Storey, p (Camm, 85–95).
5.	13 Jun 73	*Thomas Woodhouse, p (Camm, 199).
6.	29 Nov 77	*Cuthbert Mayne, p (Launceston: Camm, 219–20; Anstruther, 226).[5]
7.	3 Feb 78	*John Nelson, p (Allen 1, 116; Camm, 232).
8.	7 Feb 78	*Thomas Sherwood, l (Allen, 119; Pollen 2, 6
9.	30 Jul 81	*Everard Hanse, p (Allen 1, 102; Anstruther, 147).
10.	22 Aug 82	William Lacy, p (York: Camm, 576)
11.	22 Aug 82	Richard Kirkman, p (York: Camm, 588).

[1]Stephen Rowsham owed his relatively humane treatment at Gloucester to local horror at the "inhumane butchery" of John Sandys' death there the previous August. The local people and the cathedral clergy insisted that the officers not carry out the full sentence (Morris, 3, 42; Pollen 2, 333).

[2]Sir Walter Raleigh, who had tried to save him, evidently had the authority to insist that he be allowed to die by hanging.

[3]"They let him hang until he were dead."

[4]Southwell's case, like William Davies', is not certain. The sheriff wanted him cut down alive, but the onlookers, including Lord Mountjoy with a group of noblemen, wanted him dead. In response, the hangman pulled on the body to ensure death; but the knot had been clumsily tied, and so despite his willingness to cooperate in defiance of his superior, the outcome was uncertain.

[5]According to the far less circumstantial account in Allen 1, 108, "The sheriff's deputy...let him hang till he was dead."

12.	15 Mar 83	*William Hart, p (York: Challoner, 76).[1]
13.	22 Mar 83	James Layburn, l (Lancaster or Manchester: Pollen 2, 217–18).
14.	29 May 83	*Richard Thirkeld (York: Challoner, 83; Camm, 645).
15.	30 Oct 83	*John Slade, l (Winchester: Pollen 2, 62).
16.	2 Nov 83	* John Bodey, l (Andover: Pollen 2, 65).[2]
17.	11 Jan 84	William Carter, l (*ODNB*).
18–22.	12 Feb 84	*George Haydock. p (Challoner, 89; Anstruther, 159).
		*James Fenn, p (Challoner, 93; Burton-Pollen, 69–70).
		*Thomas Hemerford, p (Challoner, 94; Pollen 2, 253).
		*John Nutter, p (Challoner, 97).
		*John Munden, p (Challoner, 100).
23.	20 Apr 84	James Bell, p (Lancaster: Pollen 1, 74–8).
24.	20 Apr 84	John Finch, l (Lancaster: Pollen 1, 79–88).
25.	15 Oct 84	*Richard Gwynn or White, l (Wrexham: Challoner, 104; Burton-Pollen, 127–44).
26.	26 Nov 85	Hugh Taylor, p (York: Challoner ,106).
27.	2 Mar 85	*William Parry, l (BL Ms. Additional 48027, f.244).
28–9.	21 Jan 86	*Edward Stransham, p (Challoner, 111).
		*Nicholas Woodfen, p (Challoner, 111).
30–31.	20 Apr 86	Richard Sergeant, p (Challoner, 113)
		William Thompson, p (Challoner, 114).
32–3.	25 Apr 86	*Robert Anderton, p (Isle of Wight).
		*William Marsden, p (Isle ofWight).[3]
34.	3 Jun 86	Francis Ingleby (York: Pollen 2, 258, 304).
35.	8 Aug 86	John Fingley, p (York: Challoner, 115).
36.	11 Aug 86	*John Sandys, p (Gloucester).[4]
37–43.	20 Sep 86	*Anthony Babington, l.
		*John Ballard, p.
		*Robert Barnwell, l.
		*Henry Dunne, l.
		*Edward Jones, l.
		*John Savage, l.
		*Chidiock Tichborne, l.

[1] Camm's less circumstantial source writes that the crowd prevented the executioners from cutting Hart down alive (Camm, 631).

[2] "He [Slade] was cast beside the ladder, and afterwards cut down and quartered according to his judgment." "He [Bodey] was put beside the ladder, and quartered according to his judgment."

[3] "Underwent the extreme penalty" (Burton-Pollen, 210).

[4] "Most bloodily and beastly used" (Pollen 2, 333). See also Ibid, 336; Burton-Pollen, 321–2. Anstruther, 302, thinks Sandys may have suffered in 1587: "Indeed it is possible that he and Rowsham [whose suffering was mitigated because of the horror of Sandys' death] died together."

44–6. 8 Oct 86	John Lowe, p (Challoner, 116).
	John Adams, p (Challoner, 116).
	Robert Dibdale, p (Challoner, 117; Pollen 2, 285).
47. 8 Oct 86	*Robert Bickerdike, l (York: Challoner, 120; Burton-Pollen, 251–58).
48. 21 Mar 87	*Thomas Pilchard, p (Dorchester: Pollen 2, 261–4).
49. 23 Mar 87	Edmund Sykes, p (York: Challoner, 121–2)..
50. c. Easter 87	John Hambly, p (near Salisbury: Pollen 2, 268–9; Pollen 1, 140).
51. 27 Jul 87	*Robert Sutton, p (Stafford: Pollen 2, 325; Burton-Pollen, 305).
52. 8 Sep 87	*George Douglas, p (York: Burton-Pollen, 315).
53. 30 Nov 87	*Alexander Crow, p (York).[1]
54–6. 24 Jul 88	*Nicholas Garlick, p (Derby: Challoner, 131; Burton-Pollen, 347).
	*Robert Ludlam, p (Derby)
	*Richard Simpson, p (Derby)
57. 1 Oct 88	*William Way, p (Kingston-upon-Thames: Morris, 3.38; Burton-Pollen, 445).
58–64. 1 Oct 88	*Robert Wilcox, p (Canterbury: Challoner, 146).
	*Gerard Edwards, alias Edward Campion, p (Canterbury: Anstruther, 109; Burton-Pollen, 458).
	*Christopher Buxton, p (Canterbury: Challoner, 147).
	*Robert Widmerpool, l (Canterbury: Challoner, 147–8).
	Ralph Crocket, p (Chichester: Anstruther, 94).
	Edward James, p (Chichester: Anstruther, 94).
	John Robinson, p (Ispwich: Burton-Pollen, 505).
65. 31 Oct 88	Edward Burden, p (York: Burton-Pollen, 548)
66. 1588	*William Lampley, l (Gloucester: Morris, 3.43).
67–8. 5 Jul 89	George Nichols, p (Oxford).
	Richard Yaxley, p (Oxford: Challoner, 158).
69. 24 Sep 89	William Spencer, p (York: Challoner, 159)..
70. 4 Mar 90	Christopher Bales, p (Challoner, 160).
71–2. 30 Apr 90	Miles Gerard, p (Rochester: Anstruther, 130).
	Francis Dickenson, p (Rochester: Anstruther, 101–2).
73–4. 6 May 90	*Edward Jones, p (Pollen 2, 317; Pollen 1, 186).
	*Anthony Middleton, p (Pollen 1, 186).
75–8. 27 May 90	Edmund Duke, p (Durham).
	Richard Hill, p (Durham).
	John Hogg, p (Durham).
	Richard Holiday, p (Durham).[2]

[1]"Passing through the usual course of the ordinary butchery" (Challoner, 129.

[2]These four, ordained Sep 89, left Rheims 22 Mar 90, and landed together on the NE coast. They made the mistake of keeping together, aroused suspicion, were arrested, convicted and martyred together two months after setting out. Father Curry, S.J., wrote that

79. 31 May 90 Robert Thorpe, p (York: Challoner, 165–6).
80. 1 Jul 91 *George Beesley, p (Pollen, 2, 302).
81. 7 Jul 91 *Roger Dickenson, p (Winchester: Pollen 1, 292; Pollen 2, 95–6).
82–83. 10 Dec 91 *Edmund Gennings, p (Pollen 2, 109).
*Eustace White, p (Pollen 2, 114–15).
84. 1591 *William Pike, l (Dorchester: Challoner, 169; Pollen 1, 292).
85. 1592 Lawrence Humphreys, l (Pollen 2, 233–4).
86. 22 Jan 92 *William Pattenson, p (Challoner, 186–6; Morris, 3.49;[1] Pollen 2, 117).
87. 20 Feb 92 *Thomas Pormort, p (Pollen 2, 120[2]).
88. after 20 Feb 92 Richard Williams, a Marian priest (Burton-Pollen, 537; Pollen 1, 230–1).
89. 1 Jul 92 *Joseph Lambton, p (Newcastle: Morris, 3.226–7).
90. 7 Jan 93 *Edward Waterson, p (Newcastle: Challoner, 188).[3]
91. 5 Mar 92 James Bird, l (Winchester: Pollen 2, 231–2).
92. 20 Apr 93 Anthony Page, p (York: Challoner, 189).
93. 27 Jul 93 *William Davies, p (Beaumaris: Challoner, 196).[4]
94. 18 Feb 94 *William Harrington, p (Challoner, 197, quoting Stow).
95. 3 Jul 94 *John Cornelius, p (Dorchester: Challoner, 201
96. 24 Jul 94 *John Boste, p (Durham; Challoner, 599; Morris, 3.210).
97. 26 Jul 94 *George Swallowell, l (Darlington: Challoner, 208).
98. 6 Nov 94 Edward Osbaldeston, p (York: Challoner, 210
99. 7 Apr 95 Alexander Rawlins (York: Challoner, 218).[5]
100. 13 Aug 95 *William Freeman, p (Warwick: Challoner, 228; Pollen 1, 359).[6]

---

they "stoutly endured the extremity of suffering" (Pollen 2, 318; see also Anstruther, 107, 167,170, 172).

[1]"Cut down very lively, standing upright on his feet, and so quartered."

[2]"The priest was quartered after their manner."

[3]According to Fr. Holtby's account, though, printed in Morris, 3.230, "After being dead he was cut down, and his body bowelled and quartered."

[4]Challoner's very detailed account says that he was cut down "half hanged;" another, equally detailed account (Stonyhurst MS *Anglia* vii.9, printed in Pollen 2, 137–42) agreeing substantially with Challoner's version says, "He was pulled by the hangman to die, before he was taken down, the deputy sheriff asking often to break the halter before he was dead, for a colour belike lest he should be complained upon."

[5]Not certain. His companion in death, Henry Walpole, was allowed to hang until dead.

[6]In sentencing Freeman, the judge (Anderson) gave specific instructions for live mutilation, but whether the sentence was fully carried out is doubtful.

101–4. 29 Nov 96	George Errington, l (York).
	William Knight, l (York).
	William Gibson, l (York).
	Henry Abbot, l (York: Challoner, 229; Morris 2.243).
105. 4 Jul 97	William Andleby, p (York: Challoner, 232
106. 1 Apr 98	John Britton, l (Challoner, 233).
107. 15 Jun 98	Peter Snow, p (Challoner, 233).
108. 9 Aug 98.	Christopher Robinson, p (Carlisle: Challoner, 235).
109. 4 Sep 98	Richard Horner, p (York: Challoner, 236).
110. 1599	Matthias Harrison, p (York: Challoner, 236; Anstruther, 152).
111. 16 Jul 99	John Lion, l (Oakham, Rutland: Challoner, 236).
112. 13 Aug 99	James Dowdall, l (Exeter: Challoner, 236).
113. 28 Mar 00	Christopher Wharton, p (York: Challoner, 238; Anstuther, 377).
114. 21 Jun 00	*John Rigby, l (St Thomas Watering: Worthington, Sig. C1).[1]
115–16. Jul 00	Thomas Sprott, p (Lincoln).
	Thomas Hunt, p (Lincoln: Worthington, Sig. F4v).
117–18. 26 Jul 00	Edward Thwing, p (Lancaster).
	Robert Nutter, p (Lancaster: Challoner, 247–9).
119. 9 Aug 00	Thomas Palaser, p (Durham: Challoner, 250).
120. 18 Feb 01	John Pibush, p (St Thomas Watering: Anstruther, 274).
*121–2. 27 Feb 01	*Mark Barkworth OSB (Challoner, 256; Kilroy 1, 20–22).
	Roger Filcock, S.J (Challoner, 257).
123–4. Apr 01	Thurstan Hunt, p (Lancaster)
	Robert Middleton, p (Lancaster: Challoner, 259–60; Anstruther, 230–31, 179–81).
125. 22 Mar 02	James Harrison, p (York: Challoner, 260–1).
126–7. 20 Apr 02	Thomas Tichborne, p (Challoner, 264–5).
	Robert Watkinson, p (Challoner, 264–5).
128. 17 Feb 03	William Richardson, p (Challoner, 269).

[1]A sinister figure, "that sat under the judges" (Worthington, Sig.B2v) at Rigby's trial, and instructed the jury to find a verdict of treason might well have been Topcliffe.

Appendix II

1. Talbot Ms. 708, f. 141. *Richard Topcliffe to the Earl and Countess of Shrewsbury at Worksop Manor, from Somerby, 16 June 1603.*

Right honorrable, the dewty that I have So Longe Carryed to yor Noble howsse, & the honest Loove I professed to yow in yor yowthe, Can (In mee) hardlye yet bee sleckedd, whiche hadd tayken sutche hovlde in my hartte; & so have I shewd Likelyhoode dyvers tymes Synce I fovnde Many Shewes of Alteracion in yor Lordeship: Bvt I will still Bee playne Topclyffe: And If I colde do anye thinge To proove That the Ancyent hono^r I determyned to yo^w, Is not of my partte geven ove^r, By Anye vnkindnes offerred To trye mee, yow were like to fynde mee more honest, then a novmberr of flatterrers, & Soowthers — I hearinge that the Queenes Ma^{ty} that Now is, dothe Cvme To yor Lo^{ps} hovse To Woorsoppe parke shortlye, & As yett the tyme unknowen to mee, I (Not lyke a favninge Cvrre, Bvt Beinge, & Bearringe for my Cognizance A Gentill white hownde, Syttinge, Reddy, & Gayssinge wth his Taylle vpon his Backe, To Abyde all Tryalls)^1 do Sende to yor Lordeshipp for ovlde Loove, The Best, & Highest fallowe deare, That is in Svmerby Parke, Or (I thinke that Is in Lyncolneshire, Wildefedd) And I have Sentte yor Lordeshipp therewth iiij^{er} pyess of the best stagge, That I have Seene (of a wilde deare) In Whittsonweeke, Bayked by A^2 Cooke y^t Learned Cvnnimnge in yor Noble fathers howsse, when ye Skottish Q^{een} did remayne wth that Erlle [*caret*]. And if I hadd known the Certen day of thys good Q^{een} her Cvminge To yor Lordeshipp, I woulde have Sentte yor Lo^{pe} Svme yoinge Herronsewes ovt of the Neste, whiche well Boyled, Is

---

^{1}This was indeed his "cognizance." See illustration No.15, showing Topcliffe's coat of arms.

^{2}In the margin, a pointing hand, and a note to be inserted at the caret after "Erlle" below: "& I have Sent Also by hym Eight yoinge herronshews ovt of the Neast new kylled".

Excellent Meatte Covlde or hotte, & Better then Roasted / And If yor Lordeshipp like To have Some yoingoe hearronsewes Ageinst the day of ye Qs Cuminge to yow, If yor Lordeshipp will Commande this Bearrer To Bringe svme Qvicke hearronsewes To Woorsopp to yow, Svche, As Bee then vnflowen, I have Geven hym Chardge to Bringe to yor Lordeshp / Bvt a monethe passed, I Colde have Sent yow, A C, yt Bee flown And If I shovlde thinke, That yor Lordeshipp woolde tayke my Coortesye As A flatterye, I woovlde haytte my Selfe for doinge lyke a Gentill hownde As I am, In my hartte / And So Trvstinge yor Lordeshipp will Repvte mee, In hvmble Soarte, As doothe Becumme the parte of A playne frinde I Ende At my Solytarye howse Svmerbye Reddy to Ryde towoords dancastor, This wednesday the xvth of Ivne 1603:

yor Lordeshipss playne, &
faythefull well wysher,
Ric: Topclyffe

postscrt:—I wishe that sr Ihon
Skudemore were now
at woorsoppe parke

Enclosure:

A waye to mayke Heronseews breedd In any place wheare theare is Tymber woodes growinge, Eather of Oake, or Ashe, wheare Croows may breede

First yow must provide to mayke A Mewe of Poowlles, and Lattes, Lyke a Hawkes mew, In, and Neare, a Lyttell Ponde of water, Or water Brooke, Halfe of the Mewe to be wthin ye water, and halfe wthowte //

And yor mewe mvst be Twelue, or fowerteene yeardes in Bredthe, Every waye; And fyve yeardes of Heyght, That the Herons may have roovme boathe to walke In, To feede in, and to Pearke vpon Poowles, Sett a Crosse wthin the Mewe //

And yor Lattes mvst be sett so neare to gether, yt Neather foxes, Dogges, Cattes, Croows, Nor other vermyn may gett In to yor Mewe Eather to hurte yor herons, or to deceave them of theere meate, Nor ye herons to pvtt owt there hedes for hurtinge them //

And mayke a Dooare for there keper to go In, and owt at wth the^r meate /
And mayke Lyttell trowghes for there meate to be putt In, accordinge to
the Number yow wil bringe vp, for one yeare //

Then Provide halfe a skoare Cowple of yovnge heronesewes to be tayken
owt of ye Nest, and pvtt them Into yor Mewe, there fethers beinge hoale
And (for a while) Laye in there trowghes sume smalle Eylls, or other
smalle fishe (the Eylls nycked in theare backes y^t they Creepe Not a
waye) And they will presently fall to feedinge of them selues.

And after a Seavennight, or a forteennight yow may feede them wth
ssheeps Lyvers, or Oxe Lyuers, Guttes washed, Or any fleshe y^t is
Cheepe //

In this sorte yo^w mvst keepe yor herons in theare Mewe all ye first Summer / & the Next winter, feedinge of them dayly wth freshe meate, vntyll
all frostes and wynter weather be past; And then Pull vp ye Top of yor
Mewe And yor Herons will Pearke in yor Trees Neare vnto yor Mewe,
and flye vnto open Brookes, Ryvers, and waters, in ye cvntrey and feede,
Abowt Easter, or Springe of the yeare //

And They will resort hoame to ye place wheare they weare first
Nurrished, and they will breede theare abowt toow yeares after, and
Multiplie and Increase wonderfully.//

And yf Nestes (Bigger in Cvmpasse then ye Nestes of Croows, or
Roowkes, bee (By layinge of one Crowked styck over another) maide, It
will cumforthe, and Cherrishe them mvtche.

For so dyd Sr Thomas Gresham begyne and mayke a heronrye vpon
Mastes of Shipps, Sett In, and Neare vnto his fyshe Pondes At
Awsterlaye, Neare London, As I my selfe dyd See, and is well knowne,
vntill Gvnnes did dryve them away aft^{er} his deathe //

And francis Harvye of Essex a layte Pensioner to Q^{een} Elizabethe dyd
Confess to me, That he dyd mayke a Rent of his Herons yearly to the
valew of CC marks /

> yor Lordeshipps
> Ric: Topclyffe

Modernised

Right honorable, the duty that I have so long carried to your noble house, and the honest love I professed to you in your youth, can (in me) hardly yet be slacked, which had taken such hold in my heart; and so have I showed likelihood divers times since I found many shows of alteration in your Lordship. But I will still be plain Topcliffe; and if I could do anything to prove that the ancient honor I determined to you is not of my part given over by any unkindness offered to try me, you were like to find me more honest than a number of flatterers and soothers.

I hearing that the Queen's Majesty that now is doth come to your Lordship's house to Worksop Park shortly, and as yet the time unknown to me, I (not like a fawning cur, but being and bearing for my cognizance a gentle white hound sitting ready, and gazing with his tail upon his back, to abide all trials) do send to your Lordship for old love, the best and highest fallow deer that is in Somerby Park, or (I think) that is in Lincolnshire, wildfed; and I have sent your Lordship therewith four pies of the best stag that I have seen (of a wild deer) in Whitsunweek, baked by a cook[1] that learned cunning in your noble father's house when the Scottish Queen did remain with that Earl. And if I had known the certain day of this good Queen her coming to your Lordship, I would have sent your Lordship some young heronshaws out of the nest which, well boiled, is excellent meat cold or hot, and better than roasted. And if your Lordship like to have some young heronshaws against the day of the Queen's coming to you, if your Lordship will command this bearer to bring some quick heronshaws to Worksop to you, such as be then unflown, I have given him charge to bring to your Lordship. But a month passed, I could have sent you a hundred that be flown.

And if I should think that your Lordship would take my courtesy as a flattery, I would hate myself for doing like a gentle hound as I am in my heart. And so trusting your Lordship will repute me, in humble sort, as doth become the part of a plain friend, I end at my solitary house Somerby, ready to ride towards Doncaster, this Wednesday the 15th of June 1603:

> your Lordship's plain, and
> faithful well-wisher,
> Ric: Topcliffe

---

[1]In the margin, a pointing hand with words to be inserted after "Earl" below: "and I have sent also by him eight young heronshaws out of the nest new killed."

postscript:—I wish that Sir John
Scudamore were now at Worksop Park.

Enclosure:

A way to make heronshaws breed in any place where there is timber
woods growing, either of oak, or ash, where crows may breed.

First you must provide to make a mew of poles and laths, like a
hawk's mew, in and near a little pond of water or water brook, half of
the mew to be within the water, and half without.

And your mew must be twelve or fourteen yards in breadth every
way; and five yards of height, that the herons may have room both to
walk in, to feed in, and to perch upon poles set across within the mew.

And your laths must be set so near together that neither foxes, dogs,
cats, crows, nor other vermin may get into your mew either to hurt your
herons, or to deceive them of their meat, nor the herons to put out their
heads, for hurting them.

And make a door for their keeper to go in and out at with their meat.

And make little troughs for their meat to be put in, according to the
number you will bring up for one year.

Then provide half a score couple of young heronshaws to be taken out
of the nest, and put them into your mew, their feathers being whole and
(for a while) lay in their troughs some small eels, or other small fish (the
eels nicked in their backs that they creep not away), and they will presently fall to feeding of themselves.

And after a seven-night or a fortnight you may feed them with sheeps'
livers, or ox livers, guts washed, or any flesh that is cheap.

In this sort you must keep your herons in their mew all the first summer and the next winter, feeding of them daily with fresh meat until all
frosts and winter weather be past; and then pull up the top of your mew
and your herons will perch in your trees near unto your mew, and fly
unto open brooks, rivers, and waters in the country, and feed, about Easter or spring of the year.

And they will resort home to the place where they were first nourished; and they will breed there about two years after, and multiply and
increase wonderfully.

And if nests, bigger in compass than the nests of crows or rooks, be
(by laying of one crooked stick over another) made, it will comfort and
cherish them much.

For so did Sir Thomas Gresham begin, and make a heronry upon masts of ships, set in, and near unto his fish ponds at Austerley, near London, as I myself did see, and is well known, until guns did drive them away after his death.

And Francis Harvey of Essex, a late pensioner to Queen Elizabeth, did confess to me that he did make a rent of his herons yearly to the value of 200 marks.

        your Lordship's,
            Ric: Topcliffe.

2. Talbot Mss, Vol. M, f. 184 (Lambeth Mss., 3203). *Richard Topcliffe to the Earl of Shrewsbury, at Court or at his house in Broad Street, from Somerby, 20 February 1604.*

Right honorrable: Eare now, yor Lordeship hathe written to mee, That my longe letters have not beene tedyooss to yo^w to reade when I have written to you (Att leingthe) Comfortable newess of my Simple Services doone to yo^{ur} Lordesh^p ageinst yor Cuntry Enemyes,[1] how I did encounte^r there clamourooss complaynttes to o^r laite Queen (gone to God) in yor behalfe, desyringe mee to contynewe that kinde of Longe wrytinge: Now gyve mee leave (I besitche yor Lo^p) To bee Somwhat Tedyooss in a cawse that dothe concerne myne undoinge, because I did receave no answer from yor Lo^p of my Last Lre syntte yo^w By Mr. Fenton, One who honorrithe yo^w, and seemethe to loove mee, for I was then Loathe, & still am so, That any person, But a well wishe^r to us boathe shoulde knowe, That yor Lordeship (whome I have honorred halfe a hondreade yeares Above all men now lyvinge, and under whose forefathers my Aunceto^{res} have maide prooffe of the^r loyall affectyons to the^r Sovereignes, & trewe loove to the Erles of Shrewsburye) shulde now Go about To offer To heave mee (wth yor streinghthe) out of Padley, a delightfull Solytary playce In whiche I tooke threefoulde the more pleasure for the nighnes of it unto 3 of y^{or} cheeffe usuall howses, whe^r I thought That I shulde (in my oulde dayes) tayke comfortte in yor Lo: precence, In Any tyme of discomfortte, Sutche, As tyme dothe Breede: And as I did wryte therein, so now I trust That no practizinge Enemye of myne shall intiesse yor Lordesh^p To offer to mee that requytall for my Longe Lovinge yo^w, Eathe^r for the^r reveindges Ageinst mee or for the^r owne gayninges; For sutche feugetyve chaindge wo^{res} & Broakers do not wyshe Padley to yor Lordesh^p for dewty, or Loove, But for othe^r dyvicess // And if I hadd not knowen in my hartte, That There is a God, who will Cawlle myghtye, & meane, unto An accoumpt, how they heappe upp Lande, to Lande, Howses, To Howses, And also Townes, to Townes, & often Townes, To one howse, I culde have hadd foo^{r}ther footte houlde In Hadersedge, Norbury, Ridwayre, & In all those staytlye maners, & parkes, Then Anye purchazer As yett hathe // And, wth Bitterness of Sowlle sume purchazer will Buy his bargayne dearlye // For Padlaye, I did knowe That it was no partte of Fitzharbertes Auncyent

---

[1]In the margin: "At ye tyme when yor Lordeshy^{ppes} tennantes off Glossopdale, or Nell Britten, did Exclayme"

Inheritaunce, But gyven to Sr Thomas, & to him, by Dame Ane
Fitzharbert, And Thomas Fitzharbert did assewre it to mee & To my
heires, I dearly paienge for it, & for the resedewe adioyninge to It, partly
wth my pursse, wth Adventew^{res}, with Chardges, & wth above Seaven
yeares Toylle, & Travell for him. I therfore hoape, That yor Lordeship
(whome God hathe blessed wth so manye Thowsande poundes of staytlye
landes synce I did first knowe yo^w, And Synce yor Lo^p did first Loove
me, As Entyrelye as yow did any Gentillman in England (if Eather
wordes or writinge may bee beleeved) and of yor Loove I have founde
tayste; That yo^w will Contynewe yor good opynyon of mee, And Suffer
mee To enioye wth yor favo^r Padley, & the resedewe assewrid unto mee,
To whome I can proove Good Queen Elyzabethe Intreatted yor Lo^{ps} favo^r
& assistance, under :9:^{en} of her Counsellers handes in the defence of my
right unto Padley, when yo^w were fyrst Erle // And if yor lop will
vouchsayffe To Lett mee knowe yor resolvte Answe^r to that Lette^r last
sentt by Mr Fenton, By yor lett^r, I shall (with dewty) resolve my selfe to
that Coorsse of lyffe, whiche Shall Best Beecume Mee: for whiche
pvrposse, If yor Lordesh^p hadd stayed But toowe dayes Longer, I hadd
waytted upon you at Sheffilde, or at Woorsoppe to have desyred to
knowe whereunto to truste or To dispayre / And Of [......] fowlle Abuses
there vsed At Padley (whose fortune Sowev^{er} it shalbe to enioye it) It
woulde Bee a very honorrable, & charytable partte for posteryte, if yor
Lo: woolde Gyve chardge vnto Some Gentillman of discressyon who Is
neare adioynninge to that howse, ffor Refoormacyon of toowe foowlle
Abvsess whiche Bee vsedd in that howsse of Padlaye, synce the tyme of
theis Contencyons: & Never So fowllye As In theis toowe tymes Thatt
yor Lordeshipps servanttes & possessyon-Keepers have beene Resyant
there: The one Is, That those fewe, pleasant, & needfvll woodds of All
Sorttes, Greate, & Smale (That Raveners have Leaftte unspoyllede)
Maye bee now preservedd & kept frome distructyon (Wooddes Beinge
So daynty In that Playce): The othe^r Abuse Is, That viijth or Tenne
Contynewall fyers, & I thinke So many howssehovldes of inmayttes,
Svtche, & of So Badd Conversacyon As Spainished Clarke, & Chaindge
m^r Dawkyns, have beene knowen to bee, maye Not Bee Contynewally
Keptt, & Nvrreshedd there, As In tyme past, fewgetyve traytors,
Hoaremovngers, Bawddes, & lyke Abhomynable persons have hadd
habytacyon & Refuidge, Lyke A Soadome or Saynctuary of fylthyness //
Whereof If yor Lo^p hadd knowen, I dovbt Not Bvt yo^w would have Seene
Reformacyon, As yor honourr^s fathe^r mayde one prooffe In yor memorye
// And If yor Lo: will Resolve mee now directly & plainely By yor Lre.
By this bearre^r yor pleaso^r, & therin vnto what I shall trvst, I shall honor

yo^w the more, wishinge That I maye still have occacyon To hono^r yo^w most / from my Solitary Svme^rby ye xx^th of Febrvary 1603: [i.e. 1603/4]

yor Lordshi^ps Auncyent Honorrerr

As ye Lorde Godd dothe know:

Ric. Topclyffe

Modernised:

"Right honorable: Ere now, your Lordship hath written to me, that my long letters have not been tedious to you to read when I have written to you (at length) comfortable news of my simple services done to your Lordship against your country enemies:[1] and how I did encounter their clamorous complaints to our late Queen (gone to God) in your behalf, desiring me to continue that kind of long writing. Now give me leave (I beseech your Lordship) to be somewhat tedious in a cause that doth concern mine undoing, because I did receive no answer from your Lordship of my Last Letter sent you by Mr. Fenton, one who honoreth you, and seemeth to love me; for I was then loath, and still am so, that any person but a well-wisher to us both should know that your Lordship (whom I have honored half a hundred years above all men now living, and under whose forefathers my ancestors have made proof of their loyal affections to their sovereigns, and true love to the Earls of Shrewsbury) should now go about to offer to heave me (with your strength) out of Padley, a delightful solitary place in which I took threefold the more pleasure for the nighness of it unto three of your chief usual houses where I thought that I should (in my old days) take comfort in your Lordship's presence, in any time of discomfort, such as time doth breed. And as I did write therein, so now I trust that no practicing enemy of mine shall entice your Lordship to offer to me that requital for my long loving you either for their revenges against me or for their own gainings; for such fugitive change-workers and brokers do not wish Padley to your Lordship for duty or love, but for other devices. And if I had not known in my heart that there is a God who will call mighty and mean unto an account, how they heap up land to land, houses to houses, and also towns to towns, and often towns to one house, I could have had further foothold in Hathersedge, Norbury, Ridware, and in all those stately manors and parks than any purchaser as yet hath. And with bitterness of soul some purchaser will buy his bargain dearly.

---

[1] In the margin: "At the time when your Lordship's tenants of Glossopdale, or Nell Britten, did exclaim"

For Padley, I did know that it was no part of Fitzherbert's ancient inheritance, but given to Sir Thomas, and to him, by Dame Anne Fitzherbert; and Thomas Fitzherbert did assure it to me and to my heirs, I dearly paying for it, and for the residue adjoining to it, partly with my purse, with adventures, with charges, and with above seven years' toil and travail for him. I therefore hope that your Lordship (whom God hath blessed with so many thousand pounds of stately lands since I did first know you, and since your Lordship did first love me as entirely as you did any gentleman in England—if either words or writing may be believed—and of your love I have found taste—that you will continue your good opinion of me, and suffer me to enjoy with your favor Padley and the residue assured unto me; to whom I can prove Good Queen Elizabeth entreated your Lordship's favor and assistance, under nine of her councillors' hands in the defense of my right unto Padley, when you were first Earl. And if your Lordship will vouchsafe to let me know your resolute answer to that letter last sent by Mr. Fenton, by your letter, I shall (with duty) resolve my self to that course of life which shall best become me: for which purpose, if your Lordship had stayed but two days longer, I had waited upon you at Sheffield, or at Worksop to have desired to know whereunto to trust or to despair.

And of [......] foul abuses there used at Padley (whose fortune soever it shall be to enjoy it), it would be a very honorable, and charitable part for posterity if your Lordship would give charge unto some gentleman of discretion who is near adjoining to that house, for reformation of two foul abuses which be used in that house of Padley, since the time of these contentions, and never so foully as in these two times that your Lordship's servants and possession-keepers have been resident there. The one is, that those few, pleasant, and needful woods of all sorts, great and small that raveners have left unspoiled may be now preserved and kept from destruction—woods being so dainty in that place. The other abuse is that eight or ten continual fires, and, I think, so many households of inmates, such, and of so bad conversation, as Spanished Clarke and Change Mr. Dawkins have been known to be, may not be continually kept and nourished there as in time past; fugitive traitors, whoremongers, bawds, and like abominable persons have had habitation and refuge, like a Sodom or sanctuary of filthiness. Whereof if your Lordship had known, I doubt not but you would have seen reformation, as your honor's father made one proof in your memory.

And if your Lordship will resolve me now directly and plainly by your letter by this bearer your pleasure, and therein unto what I shall trust, I shall honor you the more, wishing that I maye still have occasion to honor you most. From my solitary Somerby, the 20th of February 1603 [i.e. 1603/4],

your Lordship's ancient honorer
As the Lord God doth know:
Ric. Topcliffe

Works Cited and Abbreviations

AC — Cooper, Charles Henry, and Thompson Cooper. *Athenae Cantabrigienses*. 3 Vols. Cambridge: Deighton, Bell, 1858–1913.

Adams 1 — Adams, Simon. *Leicester and the Court: Essays on Elizabethan Politics*. Manchester: Manchester University Press, 2002.

Adams 2 — ———. "Faction, Clientage, and Party: English Politics, 1550–1603." *History Today* 32 (1982): 32–39.

Adams 3 — ———, ed. *Household Accounts and Disbursement Books of Robert Dudley, Earl of Leicester, 1558–1561, 1584–1586*. Cambridge, New York: Cambridge University Press for the Royal Historical Society, University College London, 1995.

Alfield — Alfield, Thomas. *A true reporte of the death & martyrdome of M. Campion Iesuite and preiste, & M. Sherwin, & M. Bryan preistes, at Tiborne the first of December 1581. Observid and written by a Catholike preist, which was present therat. Wher unto is annexid cetayne verses made by sundrie persons*. London: R. Rowlands or Verstegan, 1582 [*STC* 4537].

Allen — Allen, William. *A Briefe Historie of the Glorious Martyrdom of XII. Reverend Priests*. 1582 [*STC*: 369.5]. Edited by J. H. Pollen. London: Burns & Oates, 1908.

Anstruther — Anstruther, Godfrey. *The Seminary priests: A Dictionary of the Secular Clergy of England and Wales 1558–1650, I. Elizabethan 1558–1603*. St. Edmund's College, Ware, [1968].

Anstruther2 — ———. *Vaux of Harrowden: A Recusant Family*. Newport, Monmouthshire: R.H.Johns Limited, 1953.

APC — Great Britain. The Privy Council. *Acts of the Privy Council of England. New Series, 1547–1631*. Edited by J. R. Dasent (vols. 1–32), H. C. Maxwell (vols. 33–34), J. V. Lyle (vols. 35–46). 46 vols. London, 1890–1964.

Bald — Southwell, Robert. *An Humble Supplication to Her*

Maiestie. Edited by R.C.Bald. Cambridge, UK: Cambridge University Press, 1953.

Baldwin   Baldwin, T.W. *Shakespeare Adapts a Hanging.* Princeton, NJ: Princeton University Press, 1931.

Bardon   *The Bardon Papers: Documents relating to the Imprisonment and Trial of Mary Queen of Scots.* Edited by Conyers Read. London: The Camden Society, 3rd Series, Vol. 17, 1909.

Bath   Royal Commission on Historical Manuscripts. *Calendar of the Manuscripts of the Marquis of Bath, Preserved at Longleat, Wiltshire.* 5 Vols. London: Printed for H. M. Stationary Office by Mackie & Co. Ltd., 1904–80.

Bayne   Bayne, C. G. *Anglo-Roman Relations.* Oxford: The Clarendon Press, 1913.

Bernard   Bernard, G.W., ed. *The Tudor Nobility* (Manchester and New York: Manchester University Press, 1992).

Bindoff   Bindoff, S.T. *The House of Commons: 1509–1558.* 3 Vols. London: Secker & Warburg, 1982.

Birch   Birch, Thomas. *Memoirs of the Reign of Queen Elizabeth from the Year 1581 till her Death.* 2 Vols. London, 1754.

Birrell   Birrell, T.A. "William Carter (c. 1549–84): Recusant Printer, Publisher, binder, Stationer, Scribe—and Martyr." *Recusant History* 28.1 (May 2006): 22–42.

BL   The British Library.

Bossy   Bossy, John. *Under The Molehill: An Elizabethan Spy Story.* New Haven: Yale University Press, 2001.

Breay   Breay, Claire. *Magna Carta: Manuscripts and Myths.* London: The British Library, 2010.

Brown   Brown, Nancy Pollard, ed. *Two Letters and Short Rules of a Good Life. By Robert Southwell, S.J.* Charlottesville: University Press of Virginia, 1973.

Brownlow   Brownlow, F.W. *Robert Southwell.* New York: Twayne Publishers, 1996.

Brownlow 2   ———. *Shakespeare, Harsnett, and the Devils of Denham.* Newark, DE: University of Delaware Press, 1993.

Burton-Pollen   Burton, Edwin H, and J. H. Pollen, eds. *Lives of the English Martyrs. Volume I. 1583–1588.* London: Longmans, Green and Co., 1914.

Camm   Camm, Dom Bede, O.S.B., ed. *Lives of the English Martyrs. Volume II. Martyrs under Queen Elizabeth.* London: Burns and Oates (Limited), 1905.

Camm 2   Camm, Dom Bede, O.S.B. *Forgotten Shrines.* Second edi-
              tion. London: MacDonald & Evans, n.d. [1936].
Campbell   Campbell, John Lord. *The Lives of the Chief Justices of
              England.* 4 Vols. 3rd. Ed. London: John Murray, 1874.
Caraman 1   Caraman, Philip. *A Study in Friendship.* St. Louis, MO:
              The Institute of Jesuit sources, 1995.
Caraman 2   ———. *Henry Garnet, 1555–1606, and the Gunpowder
              Plot.* London: Longmans, 1964.
Caraman 3   ———, ed. *The Other Face: Catholic Life Under Eliza-
              beth I.* New York: Sheed and Ward, 1960.
Cashman   Cashman, M. J. "Two Newcastle Martyrs." *Recusant His-
              tory* 10.4 (January 1970): 231–40.
Cashman 2   Cashman, M.J. "The Gateshead Martyr." *Recusant History*
              11.3 (October 1971): 121–32.
Challoner   Challoner, Richard. *Memoirs of Missionary Priests.* Edited
              by John Hungerford Pollen. London: Burns Oates &
              Washbourne, 1924.
Chambers   Chambers, E.K. *The Elizabethan Stage.* 4 Vols. Oxford:
              the Clarendon Press, 1923.
Chancery   *Calendars of the Proceedings in Chancery in the Reign of
              Queen Elizabeth.* Vol. I. Printed by command of his Maj-
              esty King George IV. 1827.
Clancy 1   Clancy, T. H. *Papist Pamphleteers.* Chicago: Loyola Uni-
              versity Press, 1964.
Clancy 2   ———. "Notes on Parsons's *Memorial.*" *Recusant His-
              tory* 5.1 (January 1959): 17–34.
Cole   Cole, Mary Hill. *The Portable Queen: Elizabeth I and the
              Politics of Ceremony.* Amherst, MA: University of Massa-
              chusetts Press, 1999.
Collections   *Collections for a History of Staffordshire.* Edited by the
              William Salt Archæological Society. London: Harrison and
              Sons, 1912.
Cox 1   Cox, J. Charles. "Norbury Manor House and the Troubles
              of the Fitzherberts." *Derbyshire Archaeological Journal* 7
              (1885): 221–59.
Cox 2   ———. *Three Centuries of Derbyshire Annals as Illustra-
              ted by the Records of the Quarter Sessions from Queen
              Elizabeth to Queen Victoria.* 2 Vols. London: Bemrose and
              Sons, 1890.
Cross 1   Cross, Claire. *The Puritan Earl: The Life of Henry Has-
              tings, Third Earl of Huntington, 1536–1595.* London:

Macmillan, 1966.

Cross 2 ———. "The Third Earl of Huntington and trials of Catholics in the North, 1581–1595." *Recusant History* 8.3 (October 1965): 136–46.

CRS Catholic Record Society.

CSPD Great Britain. The Public Record Office. *Calendar of State Papers, Domestic Series, of the Reigns of Edward VI, Mary, Elizabeth, and James I.* Edited by Robert Lemon (vols. 1–2), Mary Anne Everett Green (vols. 3–12). 12 vols. London, 1856–1872.

CSPF Great Britain. The Public Record Office. *Calendar of State Papers, Foreign Series, of the Reign of Elizabeth.* Edited by Richard Bruce Wernham. 23 vols. London: His Majesty's Stationary Office, 1950.

Devlin 1. Devlin, Christopher. *The Life of Robert Southwell, Poet and Martyr.* London: Longmans, Green, and Co., 1956.

Devlin 2. *Hamlet's Divinity and Other Essays.* London: Rupert Hart-Davis, 1963.

Dick Dick, William Robertson. *Inscriptions and Devices in the Beauchamp Tower, Tower of London.* London, 1853.

DNB *Dictionary of National Biography.*

Dodd Dodd, Charles, *The Church History of England. With Notes, Additions, and a Continuation by Mark Aloysius Tierney.* 5 Vols. New York: AMS Press, 1971.

Douay *The First and Second Diaries of the English College, Douay.* Edited by the Fathers of the Congregation of the London Oratory, with an introduction by T.F.Knox. London: David Nutt, 1878.

Dovey Dovey, Zillah. *An Elizabethan Progress: The Queen's Journey into East Anglia, 1578.* Frome, Somerset, UK: Alan Sutton Publishing Ltd., 1996.

DT Harrison, Brian A, ed. *A Tudor Journal: The Diary of a Priest in the Tower, 1580–85.* London: St. Pauls Publishing, 2000.

Dutton Dutton, Richard, Alison Findlay, and Richard Wilson, eds. *Religion, Region, and Patronage: Lancastrian Shakespeare.* Manchester and New York: Manchester University Press, 2003.

Edwards 1 Edwards, Francis, S.J. *Plots and Plotters in the Reign of Elizabeth I.* Dublin: The Fours Courts Press, 2002.

Edwards 2 ———, ed. and trs. *The Elizabethan Jesuits.* London: Phillimore, 1981.

Ellesmere Petti, Anthony G, ed. *Recusant Documents from the Ellesmere Manuscripts.* CRS 60 (1968).

Fitzherbert   Fitzherbert, Thomas. *An Apology of T.F. in Defence of Himself.* Antwerp, 1602.

Fletcher   Fletcher, Anthony, and Diarmaid MacCulloch. *Tudor Rebellions.* London and New York: Longmans, 4th edn., 1997.

Flynn   Flynn, Dennis. *John Donne and the Ancient Catholic Nobility.* Bloomington and Indianapolis: Indiana University Press, 1995.

Foley   Foley, Henry, ed. *Records of the English Province of the Society of Jesus.* 7 vols. in 8. London: Burns and Oates, 1877–84.

Foster   Foster, Joseph G., ed. *Register of Admissions to Gray's Inn, 1521–1889.* London, 1889.

Freeman   Freeman, Arthur. *Thomas Kyd: Facts and Problems.* Oxford: The Clarendon Press, 1967.

Gennings   Gennings, John. *The Life and Death of Mr. Edmund Geninges Priest. Crowned with Martyrdom at London, the 10. day of / November, in the year* M.D.XCI. Saint Omer: Charles Boscard, 1614.

Gerard   Gerard, John. *John Gerard: The Autobiography of an Elizabethan.* Trs. Philip Caraman. London: Longmans, Green and Co., 1951.

Gibbons   Gibbons, John, and John Fen, eds. *Concertatio ecclesiae Catholicae in Anglia.* Augustae Trevirorum, Henricus Bock, 1589.

Gillow   Gillow, Joseph. *A Literary and Biographical History, or Bibliographical Dictionary, of the English Catholics, from the Breach with Rome, in 1534, to the Present Time.* 5 Vols. London: Burns & Oates: New York, Catholic Publication Society, [1885–1902].

Graves   Graves, Michael A.R. *Thomas Norton: The Parliament Man.* Oxford, UK & Cambridge, MA: Blackwell, 1994.

Green   Green, Dominic. *The Double Life of Doctor Lopez: Spies, Shakespeare and the Plot to Poison Elizabeth I.* London: Century, 2003.

Greenslade   Greenslade, Michael. *Catholic Staffordshire, 1500–1850.* Leominster, Herefordshire, UK: Gracewing, 2006.

Guy   Guy, John. *Elizabeth: The Forgotten Years.* Viking, 2016.

H & L   Hughes, Paul L., and James F. Larkin, eds. *Tudor Royal Proclamations.* New Haven: Yale University Press, 1964–69.

Hacket   Hacket, Helen. *Virgin Mother, Maiden Queen.* London: Macmillan, 1995.

Hadfield   Hadfield, Andrew. *Edmund Spenser: A Life*. London and New York: Oxford University Press, 2012.

Hamilton   Hamilton, Adam, O.S.B., ed. *The Chronicle of English Augustinian Canonesses Regular of the Lateran, at St. Monica's in Louvain (Now at St. Augustine's Priory, Newton Abbot, Devon), 1548–1625*. 2 Vols. Edinburgh: Sands & Co., 1904–6.

Handover   Handover, P. M. *The Second Cecil: The Rise to Power of Sir Robert Cecil, 1563–1604, Later First Earl of Salisbury*. London: Eyre & Spottiswoode, 1959.

Harington 1   Harington, Sir John. *Letters and Epigrams*. Edited by N.E.McClure. Philadelphia: University of Pennsylvania Press: London: Oxford University Press, 1930.

Harington 2   ———. *A New Discourse of a Stale Subject, Called The Metamorphosis of Ajax*. Edited by Elizabeth Story Donno. London: Routledge and K. Paul, [1962].

Harington 3   ———. *Nugae Antiquae: Being a Miscellaneous Collection of Original Papers*. Edited by Thomas Park. 2 Vols. London, 1804. Rptd. New York: AMS Press, 1966.

Harington 4   ———. *A Tract on the Succession to the Crown*. Edited by Clements R. Markham. London: Printed for the Roxburgh Club by J.B. Nichols and Sons, 1880.

Harpsfield   Harpsfield, Nicholas. *A Treatise on the Pretended Divorce between Henry VIII and Catherine of Aragon*. Edited by Nicholas Pocock. Westminster: Nichols and Sons for The Camden Society, 1878.

Harris   Harris, P. R. "William Fleetwood, Recorder of the City of London, and Catholicism in Elizabethan London." *Recusant History* 7.1 (January 1963): 106–22.

Harrison   Harrison, William. *Elizabethan England*. Edited by Lothrop Withington. London: Walter Scott, [1876?].

Hasler   Hasler, P.W, ed. *The House of Commons 1558–1603*. London: Published for the History of Parliament Trust by Her Majesty's Stationary Office, 1981.

Hatfield   The Hatfield Papers.

Hat. Cal.   *Calendar of the Manuscripts of the Most Hon. the Marquis of Salisbury. Preserved at Hatfield House*. 24 vols. London, 1883–1976.

Hayden   Hayden, Cheryl. "Tristram Winslade—The Desperate Heart of a Catholic in exile." *Cornish Studies* 20.1 (1 May 2012): 32–62.

Haynes   Haynes, Alan. *Invisible Power: The Elizabethan Secret Services, 1570–1603*. New York: St. Martin's Press, 1992.

Haynes 2	Haynes, Samuel. *Affairs in the Reigns of King Henry VIII. King Edward VI. Queen Mary, and Queen Elizabeth, From the Year 1542 to 1570.* London: William Bowyer, 1740.
Heath	Heath, James. *Torture and English Law: an Administrative and Legal History from the Plantagenets to the Stuarts.* Westport, CT: Greenwood Press, 1982.
Hembry	Hembry, Phyllis. *The English Spa, 1560–1815.* Madison, Teaneck, NJ: Fairleigh Dickinson University Press, 1990.
Hicks	Hicks, Leo, ed. *Letters and Memorials of Father Robert Persons, SJ.* Vol. 1. *Introduction: Life up to 1588.* Catholic Record Society 39 (1942).
Hicks 2	———. *An Elizabethan Problem: Some Aspects of the Careers of Two Adventurers.* London: Burns & Oates, c. 1964.
Hicks 3	"The Strange Case of Dr. William Parry: the Career of an Agent-provacateur." *Studies: An Irish Quarterly Review* 37.147 (September, 1948): 343–62.
Hill	Hill, Geoffrey. "The Absolute Reasonableness of Robert Southwell." In *The Lords of Limit.* New York: Oxford University Press, 1984, 19–37.
Honigmann	Honigmann, Ernst. "The Play of Sir Thomas More and Some Contemporary Events." *Shakespeare Survey* 42 (1990): 77–84.
Howard 1	Howard, Henry, 14th Duke of Norfolk, ed. *The Lives of Philip Howard...and of Anne Dacres His Wife.* London: Hurst and Blackett, 1857.
Howard 2	Howard, E. Dick. *Magna Carta: Text and Commentary.* Charlottesville, VA.: University of Virginia Press, 1964.
Hughes	Hughes, Philip. *The Reformation in England.* 3 Vols. London: Hollis & Carter; New York: Macmillan Co., 1954–1956.
Hynek	Hynek , R.W. *The True Likeness.* London: Sheed & Ward, 1951.
Ingram	Ingram, William. *A London Life in the Brazen Age: Francis Langley, 1548–1602.* Cambridge, MA: Harvard University Press, 1978
Ives	Ives, E.W. *Anne Boleyn.* Oxford: Basil Blackwell, 1986.
James	James, Susan E. *Kateryn Parr: The Making of a Queen.* Aldershot: Ashgate, 1999.
Janelle	Janelle, Pierre. *Robert Southwell the Writer: A Study in Religious Inspiration.* New York: Sheed and Ward, 1935.
Jeaffreson	Jeaffreson, John Cordy, ed. *Middlesex County Records.* Volume 1, 1550–1603. Middlesex County Record Society. London, 1886.

THE QUEEN AND THE TORTURER

Jensen   Jensen, Phoebe. "Recusancy, Festivity and Community." In *Region, Religion and Patronage: Lancastrian Shakespeare*, edited by Richard Dutton *et al*. Manchester: Manchester University Press, 2003, 101–20.

Jessop   Jessop, Augustus. *One Generation of a Norfolk House*. 3rd Edition, revised. London: T. Fisher Unwin, 1913.

Jones   Jones, Norman. *Faith by Statute, Parliament and the Settlement of Religion, 1559*. London: Royal Historical Society; Atlantic Highlands, NJ: Humanities Press, 1982.

Kilroy 1   Kilroy, Gerard. *Edmund Campion: Memory and Transcription*. Aldershot, Hampshire, UK: Ashgate Publishing, 2005.

Kilroy 2   ———. *Edmund Campion: A Scholarly Life*. Farnham, Surrey, U.K: Ashgate Publishing Ltd., 2015.

Kilroy 3   ———, ed. *The Epigrams of Sir John Harington*. Farnham, Surrey, UK, & Burlington, VT: Ashgate Publishing, 2009.

Knox   Knox, T.F., ed. *The First and Second Diaries of the English College, Douay*. London: David Nutt, 1878.

L&P 4   Brewer, J.S., ed. *Letters and Papers, Foreign and Domestic, of the Reign of Henry VIII*. Vol. 4. London: Longman & Co., 1875.

LM   *The Letters and Memorials of William, Cardinal Allen*. Edited by the Fathers of the London Oratory, with an Historical Introduction by T.F.Knox. London: David Nutt, 1882.

Levin   Levin, Carole. *The Heart and Stomach of a King: Elizabeth I and the Politics of Sex and Power*. Philadelphia: University of Pennsylvania Press, 1994.

Lodge   Lodge, Edmund, ed. *Illustrations of British History: Biography and Manners in the Reigns of Henry VIII, Edward VI, Mary, Elizabeth, and James I*. 3 Vols. London: G. Nichol, 1791.

Loomis   Catherine Loomis. "Elizabeth Southwell's Account of the Death of Queen Elizabeth." *English Literary Renaissance* 26.3 (Autumn 1996): 482–509.

MacCaffrey   MacCaffrey, W.T. "Talbot and Stanhope: an Episode in Elizabethan Politics." *Bulletin of the Institute of Historical Research* 33 (1960): 33–75.

MacCulloch   MacCulloch, Diarmaid. *The Boy King Edward VI and the Protestant Reformation*. Berkeley, CA.: University of California Press, 2002.

Maddison   Maddison, A.R., ed. *Lincolnshire Pedigrees*. Vol 3. London: Publications of the Harleian Society 52 (1904).

Maisse   Maisse, André Hurault, Sieur de. *A Journal of All that was Accomplished by Monsieur de Maisse, Ambassador in England from King Henry IV to Queen Elizabeth.* Edited by G.B.Harrison and R.A. Jones. London: Nonesuch Press, 1931.

M&F 1   Martin, Patrick, and John Finnis. "The Identity of Anthony Rivers." *Recusant History* 26 (2001): 39–74.

M&F 2   ———. "The Secret Sharers: 'Anthony Rivers' and the Appellant Controversy, 1601–2." *Huntington Library Quarterly* 69.2 (June 2006): 195–238.

M&F 3   ———. "Thomas Thorpe, 'W.S.,' and the Catholic Intelligencers." *English Literary Renaissance* 33.1 (Winter, 2003): 3–43.

Martin   Martin, Christopher. "The Breast and Belly of a Queen: Elizabeth After Tilbury." *Early Modern Women* 2 (Fall, 2007): 5–28.

Martin, P   Martin, Patrick H. *Elizabethan Espionage: Plotters and Spies in the Struggle between Catholicism and the Crown.* Jefferson, NC: McFarland & Company, 2016.

Martin, R   Martin, Randall. "Rehabilitating John Somerville in *3 Henry VI*." *Shakespeare Quarterly* 51.3 (Autumn 2000): 332–340.

Mathews   Mathews, Nieves. *Francis Bacon: The History of a Character Assassination.* New Haven and London: Yale University Press, 1996.

McIntosh   McIntosh, Marjorie Keniston. *A Community Transformed: The Manor and Liberty of Havering-atte-Bower 1500–1620.* Cambridge University Press, 2002.

McCoog   McCoog, Thomas M., S.J. *English and Welsh Jesuits, 1555–1650.* Catholic Record Society, Vols. 74–5, 1994–95.

McGrath 1   McGrath, Patrick, and Joy Rowe. "Anstruther Analysed: The Elizabethan Seminary Priests." *Recusant History* 18.1 (May 1986): 1–13.

McGrath 2   ———. "The Imprisonment of Catholics for Religion under Elizabeth I." *Recusant History* 20.4 (October 1991): 415–35.

McGrath 3   ———. "The Marian Priests under Elizabeth I." *Recusant History* 17.2 (October 1984): 103–20.

MG   *The Master of Game.* By Edward, Second Duke of York. Edited by Wm.A. and F. Baillie-Grohman. London: Chatto & Windus, 1909.

Middleton   The Royal Commission on Historical Manuscripts. *Report on the Manuscripts of Lord Middleton, Preserved at Wollaton Hall, Nottinghamshire.* London: His Majesty's Stationary Office, 1911.

Montrose   Montrose, Louis. *The Subject of Elizabeth.* Chicago: Chicago University Press, 2006.

More   Henry More. *Historia Anglicanæ Societatis Iesu, ab anno salutis, M.D.LXXX ad DCXIX.* St. Omer, 1660.

Morris 1   Morris, John. *The Troubles of Our Catholic Forefathers.* 3 vols. 1872–77. Reprint, Farnborough, UK: Gregg International, 1970.

Morris 2   ———. "A New Witness about Blessed Edmund Campion." *The Month*, August 1893, 457–65.

Morris 3   ———. "The Martyrdom of William Harrington." *The Month*, April 1874, 411–23.

Motley   Motley, J.L. *The Rise of the Dutch Republic.* 3 Vols. London: Chapman and Hall, 1856.

Muir   Muir, Kenneth. *Life and Letters of Sir Thomas Wyatt.* Liverpool: Liverpool University Press, 1963.

NA   The National Archives, Kew, Richmond Surrey TW9 4DU.

Naunton   Naunton, Sir Robert. *Fragmenta Regalia. Memoirs of Elizabeth, her Court and Favourites.* London, 1824.

Nicholas   Nicholas, Sir Harris. *Memoirs of the Life and Times of Sir Christopher Hatton, K.G.* London: Richard Bentley, 1847.

Neale 1   Neale, John. *Elizabeth I and Her Parliaments 1584–1601.* London: Jonathan Cape, 1957.

Neale 2   ———. *The Elizabethan House of Commons.* London: Jonathan Cape, [1949].

Nicholl 1   Nicholl, Charles. *A Cup of News: The Life of Thomas Nashe.* London: Routledge & Kegan Paul, 1984.

Nicholl 2   ———. *The Reckoning: the Murder of Christopher Marlowe.* New York: Harcourt Brace, 1992.

Nichols 1   Nichols, John. *The Progresses and Public Processions of Queen Elizabeth.* 3 vols. London, 1823.

Nichols 2   ———. *The Progresses, Processions, and Magnificent Festivities, of King James the First.* 4 Vols. London: J.B.Nichols, 1828.

ODNB   *The Oxford Dictionary of National Biography.*

O'Rahilly   O'Rahilly, Alfred. *The Massacre at Smerwick.* Cork: Cork University Press, 1938.

Peck 1	Peck, D.C., ed. *Leicester's Commonwealth*. Athens, OH: Ohio University Press, 1985.
Peck 2	Peck, D.C. "'News from Heaven and Hell': A Defamatory Narrative of the Earl of Leicester." *English Literary Renaissance* 8 (1978): 141–58.
Peck 3	Francis Peck, ed. *Desiderata curiosa*. London, 1779.
Petti	Petti, Anthony. "Stephen Vallenger (1541–1591)." *Recusant History* 6.6 (October 1962).
Pollen 1	Pollen, J.H., ed. *Unpublished Documents Relating to the English Martyrs, 1584–1603*. CRS 5 (1908).
Pollen 2	———. *Acts of English Martyrs*. London: Burns and Oates, 1891.
Pollen 3	———. *Mary Queen of Scots and the Babington Plot*. Studies in Tudor Social History. Edinburgh: The University Press for the Scottish History Society, 1922.
Pollen 4	———, ed. "Official Lists of Catholic Prisoners during the Reign of Queen Elizabeth, Part II, 1581–1602." CRS 2 (1906), 219–88.
Pollen 5	———, ed. "Tower Bills." CRS 3 (1906), 4–29.
Pollini	Pollini, Girolamo. *L'historia ecclesiastica della rivoluzion d'Inghilterra*. Roma, 1594.
Questier	Questier, Michael. *Catholicism and Community in Early Modern England*. Cambridge: Cambridge University Press, 2006.
Rea 1	Rea, W.F. "The Authorship of 'News from Spayne and Holland' and its Bearing on the Genuineness of the Confessions of Blessed Henry Walpole, SJ." *Biographical Studies* 1 (1951–2): 220–30.
Rea 2	———. "Self-Accusations of Political Prisoners: An Incident in the Reign of Queen Elizabeth." *The Month*, November 1951, 269–79.
Read	Read, Conyers. *Mr. Secretary Walsingham*. 3 Vols. Oxford: the Clarendon Press, 1925.
Rowse	Rowse, A.L. "The Truth about Topcliffe," in *Court and Country: Studies in Tudor Social History*. Brighton, Sussex: Harvester, 1987, 181–210.
Rye	Rye, Walter, ed. *The Visitacion of Norffolk*. London: Publications of the Harleian Society 32 (1891).
Sander 1	Sander, Nicholas. Edited and augmented by Edward Rishton. *De origine ac progressu schismatis Anglicani, Liber*. Cologne, 1585.

Sander 2 | Sander, Nicholas. *Rise and Growth of the Anglican Schism.* Translated by David Lewis. London: Burns and Oates, 1877.

Sherman | Sherman, William H. *Marking Readers in Renaissance England.* Philadelphia: University of Pennsylvania Press, 2008.

Simpson 1 | Simpson, Richard. *Edmund Campion: Jesuit Protomartyr of England.* London: John Hodges, 1896.

Simpson 2 | ———. *Edmund Campion.* Revised, Edited & Enlarged by Peter Joseph. Leominster, Herefordshire: Gracewing, 2010.

Simpson 3 | ———. "A Biographical Sketch of Thomas Poundes." *The Rambler* 8 (New Series). July 1857. Part XLIII. 24–38, 94–106.

Simpson 4 | ———. "William Harrington." *The Rambler* 10 (New Series). July 1858. Part LV. 399–407.

Smyth | Smyth, C.H. *Cranmer and the Reformation under Edward VI .* Cambridge: Cambridge University Press, 1926.

Southern | Southern, A. C., ed. *An Elizabethan Recusant House.* London: Sands & Co., 1954.

Southwell 1 | "The Letters of Robert Southwell, S.J." Ed. Thomas M. McCoog, S.J. *Archivum Historicum Societatis Iesu* 63 (1994): 101–24.

SP | State Papers.

Stapleton | Stapleton, Thomas, ed. *Plumpton Correspondence.* London: J.B.Nichols for The Camden Society, 1839.

Starkey | Starkey, David, ed. *The English Court: From the Wars of the Roses to the Civil War.* London and New York, 1987.

STC | Pollard, A.W., and G.R.Redgrave. *A Short-Title Catalogue of Books Printed in England, Scotland, & Ireland and of English Books Printed Abroad, 1475–1640.* 2nd Ed., revd. London: The Bibliographical Society, 1976–1991.

Stephens | Stephens, Archibald John. *The Statutes Relating to the Ecclesiastical and Eleemosynary Institutions of England, Wales, Ireland, India, and the Colonies.* Two vols. London: John W. Parker, 1845.

Stow 1 | *Stowe's Memoranda. (Three Fifteenth-Century Chronicles with Historical Memoranda by John Stowe, The Antiquary.)* Edited by James Gairdner. London: The Camden Society, 1880 (NS. 28).

Stow 2 | Stow, John. *A Survey of London.* London, 1598 [*STC* 23341].

Stow 3 ———. *The Annals of England*. London, 1601 [*STC* 23336].

Strype 1 Strype, John. *Annals of the Reformation*. 4 Vols. Oxford: The Clarendon Press, 1824.

Strype 2 ———. *The Life and Acts of John Whitgift, D.D.* 3 Vols. Oxford: The Clarendon Press, 1822.

Swärdh Swärdh, Anna. *Rape and Religion in English Renaissance Literature. Studia Anglistica Upsaliensia* 124. Uppsala, 2003.

Talbot The Talbot Papers, Lambeth Palace Library.

VCH *Victoria County History.*

Venn Venn, John, and Venn, J.A. *Alumni Cantabrigienses*. Part I, 4 Vols. Cambridge: Cambridge University Press, 1922–27.

Verstegan Petti, Anthony G, ed., *The Letters and Despatches of Richard Verstegan.* CRS 52 (1959).

Wainewright Wainewright, John B. "William Shelley." *Notes and Queries.* 10th Series. 3 (10 June 1906): 441–3.

Walker Walker, Julia. "Reading the Tombs of Elizabeth I." *English Literary Renaissance* 26.3 (Autumn 1996): 510–30.

Walter Walter, J. "A 'Rising of the People'? The Oxfordshire Rising of 1596." *Past and Present* 107 (May 1985): 90–143.

Weir Weir, Alison. *The Life of Elizabeth I.* New York: Ballantine Books, 1998

Welford Welford, Richard, ed. *History of Newcastle and Gateshead.* Volume 3. *Sixteenth and Seventeenth Centuries.* London: Walter Scott, 1883–87.

Weston Weston, William. *The Autobiography of an Elizabethan.* Trs. Philip Caraman. With a Foreword by Evelyn Waugh. London: Longman, Green and Co, 1955.

Williams 1 Williams, Penry. *The Later Tudors: England 1547–1603.* Oxford: Clarendon Press, 1995.

Williams 2 ———. *The Tudor Regime.* Oxford: Clarendon Press, 1979.

Williams 3 Williams, Neville. *Thomas Howard, 4th Duke of Norfolk.* London: Barrie and Rockliff, 1964.

Worthington Worthington, Thomas. *A Relation of Sixtene Martyrs glorified in England in twelve monethes.* 1601 [*STC* 26000.9].

Yepes Yepes, Diego de. *Historia particular de la persecucion de Inglaterra.* Madrid, 1599.

Zurich   *The Zurich Letters.* Edited by Hastings Robinson for The
                Parker Society. Cambridge: The University Press, 1842.

Shakespearean quotations and references follow the text of *The River-side Shakespeare,* edited by G. Blakemore Evans (Boston: Houghton Mifflin, 1974). Citations from the *Calendar of State Papers (CSP Dom.)* give the volume and item number of each document calendared. This method of reference is interchangeable with references to the documents themselves (*NA/SP*). Unless otherwise indicated, quoted texts are modernized.

*****

Index of Names and Places

Adams, John, 129.

Adams, Simon, 38,

Afferton —, 51–2.

Agazario, Alfonso, 190.

Aldred, Solomon, 168.

Alfield, Thomas, 64–7, 102 & n, 103,105, 115, 263; distributes Allen's *Defence,* 122; arrested, tried, & convicted, 123.

Allen, William, 65, 66 & n, 87, 93, 96, 97, 98, 103, 104, 112–13, 120, 121, 125–6, 136, 141, 149, 167n, 176n, 201, 226n, 344; on Thomas Norton's imprisonment, 106–7; on Edmund Campion's torture, 108–9; Topcliffe's annotated copy of his *Modest Defence,* 121–2.

Almond, John, 356.

Anderson, Sir Edmund, 194–95, 223.

Anger, Richard, 314–15,

Annias, John, 271, 273.

Ap Rhys (Preece, Price), William, 137.

Aquaviva, Claudio, 23, 144, 173, 175, 193n, 277, 291 & n.

Archer, James, S.J., 270–2.

Arden, Edward, 148–9; his widow 246.

Arnold,Richard, 151.

Arundell, Lady, née Margaret Willoughby, 32n, 33 & n.

Ashley, Sir Anthony, 312, 359.

Ashton, Roger, 200–02.

Askew, Anne, 79.

Aston, Sir Walter, 158, 160.

Atkinson, James, 251–4, 321, 322; killed by Topcliffe & Jones in Bridewell, 254–5.

Audley, Martin, 206.

Aylmer, John, Bishop of London, 52, 118, 120, 236, 237.

Babington, Anthony, 15, 152, 236; the Babington Plot, 9, 127, 128, 129, 151, 165n, 166–8, 176, 208, 236–7, 339n.

Bacon, Anthony, 198, 299n.

Bacon, Sir Francis, 124,171, 185n, 273, 274, 305, 314, 335, 341.

Bagot, Richard, 154–58, 159, 160–61, 164; Topcliffe's letter to him, 155.

Bailly, Charles, 90.

Bald, R.C., 124.

Baldwin, T.W., 176.

Baldwin, William, S.J., 254.

Bale, John, 81.

Bales, Christopher, 190–93, 197, 277.

Bales, John, 190.

Bancroft, Richard, Bishop of London, 124, 268n, 337.

Barker, Edward, 128–9.

Barker, Francis, 361n.

Barkworth, Mark, OSB, 337.

Barnes, Robert, 124, 237–49, 251–55; arrested, 253; witness to Mrs. Bellamy's death, 258; his trial, 329–31; reprieved, 332; pardoned by James I, his property returned, 333.

Barnwell, Robert, 129.

Barwise, Robert, 314.

Barwys, John, 224 & n.

Bassett, William, 150, 206, 209, 210–11, 248, 249–50, 280,

Beale, Robert, 21, 22, 101, 121n, 208, 219, 273, 375–6n; interrogates Edmund Campion with

torture, 100.
Beard, Ben, 289.
Beckwith, Leonard, 356.
Bedingfield, Sir Henry, 58.
Beesley, George, 218–20.
Beilin, Elaine V., 80n.
Bellamy, Anne, 236, 237–44, 257, 293, 303n, 320.
Bellamy, Audrey, 237, 256.
Bellamy, Bartholomew, 236.
Bellamy, Jerome, 237.
Bellamy, Katherine (Mrs. Richard), 16, 240–1, 255–8, 322, 325–9, 330.
Bellamy, Katherine (Mrs. William), 236–37.
Bellamy, Mary, 259–60.
*Bellamy, Richard, 16, 236, 237, 241–2, 247, 256, 303; dies poverty-stricken in exile, 258.
Bellamy, Robert, 236n, 237.
Bellamy, Thomas (Richard's brother), 237, 240, 303–4.
Bellamy, Thomas (Richard's son), 237, 239, 255–6.
Belson, Thomas, 177.
Bennet, John, 357.
Benthall, George, 163–4.
Berden, Nicholas, 168.
Berkeley, Sir Richard, 20.
Bindoff, S.T., 30n, 31n, 33, 43. 49,
Birket, George, 238, 249.
Blackwell, Nicholas, clerk of the peace, 153– 60.
Blackwell, Nicholas, agent, 325– 9.
Blagrave, William, O.P., 84n.
Blake, Alexander, 192.
Bland, Thomas, 308 & n.
Blount, Charles, 8th Baron Mountjoy, 294–5.
Blount, Sir Michael, 209, 273.
Boleyn, Anne, 31, 33, 118, 124, 125.
Boleyn, Mary, 118, 124.
Bolt, John, 278.

Bolton, John, 84.
Bonner, Edmund, Bishop, 83.
Bosgrave, John, 95, 97, 98.
Bossy, John, 123, 130n, 168n.
Boste, John, 259–60 & n.
Bowcher, Matthew, 49n.
Brettam, George, 200.
Brettam, Henry, 200.
Briant, Alexander, 97, 98, 107; tortured by Thomas Norton, 103–5.
Briscoe, Thomas, 97.
Bristow, Richard, 236.
Bromborough, Edward, 97.
Bromley, Sir George, 357.
Brown, Thomas, alias Revell, 136.
Browne, Anthony, 1st Viscount Montagu, 94n, 249.
Browne, Edmund, 152, 153, 158– 9, 160.
Browne, Sir George, 250, 252
Browne, Magdalen, Viscountess Montagu, 247–50.
Browne, Mary Dormer, 323–4.
Brownlow, F.W., 129n.
Brudenell, Agnes, nëe Topcliffe, 241 & n.
Brydges, Elizabeth, 307.
Bull (the hangman), 196, 198–9.
Burbage, James, 174.
Burden, Edward, 175.
Burgh, Sir Edward, 31, 33.
Burgh, Thomas, 3rd Baron Burgh, 30 & n, 31 & n, 33, 43.
Burgh, Thomas, 5th Baron Burgh, 307.
Burnell, Edward, 50n, 93.
Buxton, 43, 46, 62–3, 250; Shrewsbury's development of, 46; Topcliffe's device etched in window at, 47.
Byrd, William, 65, 263.
Cahill, Hugh, 270–3.
Camm, Dom Bede, 85n, 90n, 93n, 146n, 149n, 151, 161n, 163, 170n, 206n, 207, 228n, 342n, 352.

Campion, Edmund, 15, 64, 93, 96, 97–106, 108–9, 115, 120, 125, 165, 236, 263; capture and transfer to London, 100; 1st and 2nd tortures, 100–01; 3rd torture, 102, 108–9.

Carey, Henry, 1st Baron Hunsdon, Lord Chamberlain, 94, 102, 184, 245, 284, 304–5.

Carey, Sir George, 95, 170.

Carey, John, 260–1.

Carey, Robert, 345, 346.

Carter, Jane, 121.

Carter, William, 107; arrested by Topcliffe, 118; indicted for treason, 121; tortured, 121, 140–41.

Cary (or Carew), Lady, 85–6.

Caudwell, Mr., 155

Cecil, John, 183n, 260n.

Cecil, Sir Robert, 22, 23, 24, 32, 51, 52, 185, 216–18, 247, 271n, 290, 297, 304, 309, 311–12, 313, 317, 336, 337, 339, 340, 342–5, 352, 359; *Isle of Dogs* affair, 315–19; conspires with Topcliffe to entrap Robert Barnes, 326–7.

Cecil, William, Lord Burghley, 9, 44, 50–1, 87, 88, 89, 90n, 91, 92, 101, 117, 128, 130–2, 166n, 168, 172, 183–4, 224, 232 250, 286, 302; composes the bogus *The Copy of a Letter*, 170–1; his *Antidote against Jesuitism* warns the Queen against Catholic revenge, 178; commits Topcliffe to prison, 297.

Chaderton, William, 357n, 358,

Chassagne, Girault de la, 123.

Chester, Edward, 178, 278.

Claxton, James, 173.

Clement V, Pope, 75.

Clement VII, Pope, 125.

Clifford, Margaret, née Russell, Countess of Cumberland, 46.

Clifton, Thomas, 128, 134, 278.

Cobbett, William, 361, 362.

Cochrane, Peter, 361–2.

Coke, Edward, 28, 216, 253 & n, 272–4, 280, 291–3, 303, 313, 335.

Colleton, John, 97, 98 100, 101; racked, 101.

Columbell, Roger, 152.

Comberford, Henry, 57, 84.

Como, Cardinal of, 130, 131.

Cooke, Robert, 165n.

Cooper, John, 357.

Copley, Anthony, 17.

Cottam, Oliver, 200, 201, 218.

Cottam, Thomas, 67, 95, 97, 98, 107, 117.

Cotts, Richard, 50.

Cox, Charles, 146n, 149n, 152n, 153n, 209, 340n, 353.

Cox, Richard, Bishop of Ely, 85, 86.

Coxed, John, 190.

Crane, Thomas, 97.

Cranmer, Thomas, 81, 82, 91, 92, 118.

Cranmer, Edmund, 91.

Creighton, William, S.J., 216

Cromwell, Thomas, 73, 79, 80.

Cross, Claire, 232n.

Cullen, Patrick, 271–2.

Curry, John, S.J., 175, 189, 193 & n, 197n, 250, 252–3, 255.

Dallison, Roger, 323.

Dalton, James, 169, 189.

Daniel, William, 253, 273.

Daniell, John, 270–3.

Davies, Richard, 240n, 241n, 321.

Davison, Francis, 311.

Davison, William, 311.

Deane, William, 65–6, 67, 146, 172, 173, 175.

Dee, Dr. John, 45.

Deeg, William, 155.

Dethick, Sir Gilbert, 164n.

Devereux, Robert, 2nd Earl of

Essex, 224, 270, 298n, 302, 311–12, 314, 318n, 345.

Devlin, Christopher, 10, 20n, 21, 23, 24,126, 179n, 182, 185, 239, 244, 247n, 291, 295, 327n; describes Topcliffe as a favorite, 185.

Dibdale, Robert, 129–30.

Dickenson, Francis, 178, 189–90, 197,

Dickenson, Roger, 142, 144, 220–1.

Digby, Everard, 139.

Digby, John, 138–40, 359.

Dolman, Alban, 95n.

Donne, Henry, 267, 270.

Donne, John, 199, 267.

Douglas, John, 244.

Dovey, Zillah, 55, 56, 59.

Downham, William, 359n.

Drake, Sir Francis, 123–4, 168, 169.

Drew, Edward, 253, 273, 303.

Drummond, William, of Hawthornden, 317.

Dudley, Ambrose, Earl of Warwick, 36, 37, 115, 185, 214.

Dudley, Anne, née Russell, countess of Warwick, 288 & n.

Dudley, Robert, Earl of Leicester, 36, 43, 44–5, 46–7, 62, 90n, 112, 115, 123, 138, 145, 148–9, 152, 164n, 166, 169, 175–6, 195n, 199, 214, 229, 319, 360.

Dutton, George, 96.

Dyer, Sir Edward, 226n.

Edward I, King, 29.

Edward III, King, 29;

Edward VI, 80, 81, 82n, 361; torture under, 80.

Egerton, Sir Thomas, 171n, 185n, 327 & n.

Elizabeth I, Queen, 16, 17–19, 21, 24–5, 28, 43, 44, 87, 92, 95, 106–7, 109–10, 119, 121, 124–6, 130–31, 134–5, 148, 151, 168, 174–5, 183–6, 215–18, 222, 224–7, 265, 271n, 290, 295–6, 330–2, 337, 338, 355, 361; Topcliffe's early service with, 33–36; Acts of Supremacy and Uniformity, 82–6; asks for 700 executions in the north after the 1569 rising, 36n; on progress to Norwich, 54–64; discusses "Popish beasts" with Topcliffe, 62–63; torture under, 80–1; asks Topcliffe to arrange assassination of Thomas Morgan, 132–33; her support of Topcliffe, 151, 163, 185, 208, 210, 241–4, 247–50, 280, 346; her response to danger, 176–7; last days and death, 345–6.

Ellis, George, 303n.

Ely, Humphrey, 97, 99.

Emerson, Ralph, 97, 123n.

Englefield, Sir Francis, 177.

Eyre, Sir Arthur, 146, 162.

Eyre, Thomas, 207.

Felton, John, 89.

Felton, Thomas, 142, 175.

Fenner, Edward, 329, 330, 335–6.

Fiennes, Edward de, Earl of Lincoln & Lord Admiral, 36.

Filby, William, 71, 99.

Finnis, John, 17n.

Fitzherberts, the, 146–7, 354–6.

Fitzherbert, Anthony, 153, 161, 339–43, 352.

Fitzherbert, Sir Anthony, 146.

Fitzherbert, John, 147, 153, 155, 160–1, 202, 207, 298.

Fitzherbert, Sir John, 147, 352.

Fitzherbert, Nicholas, 149, 342, 346.

Fitzherbert, Richard, 147, 160, 162, 202–6, 213.

Fitzherbert, Thomas, 16, 149–51, 160, 205–6, 209–10, 223, 248, 280–1, 287–8, 297–8; his criminal career, 340–2; death, 352.

Fitzherbert, Sir Thomas, 84, 146–7, 150–1, 151–2, 158, 162, 168, 170, 202, 207–9.

Fitzherbert, Thomas, S.J., 70, 149, 197.
Fitzherbert, William, 147, 149, 197n.
Fitzwilliams, John, 310.
Fleetwood, William, 64n, 65–6, 67, 89, 93, 94, 115, 194–5 & n, 229.
Fleming, Sir Thomas, 185n, 273, 301, 305, 313, 335.
Fletcher, Anthony, 251, 323–4 & n.
Fletcher, Giles, 219 & n, 227, 316.
Fletcher, Richard, 202, 321.
Flower, Richard, see Lloyd, Richard.
Ford, Thomas, 97, 98, 99n, 100; racked, 101, 102.
Fortescue, Sir John, 28, 77.
Fowler, Thomas, 316 & n.
Foxe, John, 92, 118, 120, 354.
Franceschi, Giacomo, 270.
Fuller, Nicholas, 189.
Fulwood, Richard, 278.
Gage, John, 209.
Gage, Robert, 129.
Garlick, Nicholas, 160–1, 353.
Garnet, Anthony, 251, 253, 320.
Garnet, Henry, 16, 20, 21, 23, 134, 150n, 207–8, 232, 254, 277, 280, 290, 291, 294, 326.
Gennings, Edmund, 227, 228, 229–30.
Gerard, Sir Gilbert, 89, 94, 95
Gerard, Fr. John, 22, 142, 173, 175n, 197, 275, 276, 278–9, 299, 305, 314, 325, 326, 332; tortured in the Tower, 19–20.
Gerard, Miles, 178, 189–90, 197.
Gérard, Balthasar, 165.
Giblet, William, 97.
Gifford, Gilbert, 167 & n.
Glanvil, Ranulph de, 75.
Goldwell, Thomas, Bishop, 83, 97.

Gravener, Thomas, 186.
Graves, Michael, 93n, 104, 105n, 107–8.
Gray, Robert, 151, 250, 252–3, 320.
Gregory XIII, Pope, 110, 130.
Grenville, Sir Richard, 170, 182.
Grey, Arthur, 14th Baron Grey de Wilton, 99, 181–2.
Grindal, Edmund, Bishop of London, 85.
Gunter, William, 172.
Gurney, Henry, 190
Guy, John, 77–8, 185n, 223.
Gwyn, David, 138.
Gwyn, Richard, see White, Richard.
Hackett, Helen, 58.
Hammond, Dr. John, 67, 94, 95, 99, 101, 103, 121n; interrogates Edmund Campion with torture, 100, 101, 102.
Hardesty, Robert, 177.
Hare, Hugh, 286, 287.
Harington, Sir John, 33–4, 226, 319.
Harpsfield, Nicholas, 116, 118–19.
Harrington, William, 267–70, 278, 361n.
Harrison, James, priest, 156–8.
Harrison, John, a priest, 174.
Harrison, John, a servant, 321–2, 336.
Harrison, Joan, 321–2.
Harrison, Thomas, 132, 168n, 339 & n.
Harrison, William, 175n, 361n.
Harsnett, Samuel, 124.
Hart, John, 95–6, 97, 98, 99, 118, 121, 141; keeps the "Tower Diary," 69n, 95, 102n, 104n, 105; his career, avoidance of torture and execution, and death in Poland, 110–13.
Hartley, William, 140, 174–5, 176.

Harvey, Gabriel, 318.
Hasler, P.W., 30n, 33n, 43n, 49n, 147n, 183n, 248n, 286n.
Hastings, Henry, 3rd Earl of Huntington, 232 & n, 259, 261–2, 265–6, 273, 277, 284, 285, 356.
Hatton, Sir Christopher, 134–5, 185n, 186, 226, 284, 285.
Haverd, Thomas, 85.
Hawkesworth, Robert, 314.
Haydock, George, 195n.
Heath, James, 22n, 27, 69n, 70, 180; on civil law and torture, 74–7.
Heath Thomas, 156.
Heathfield, Robert, 123n.
Heneage, Sir Thomas, 128, 134.
Henri III, King, 132–33.
Henry II, King, 74–5.
Henry III, King, 29.
Henry VII, King, 77, 87.
Henry VIII, 31n, 45, 46, 81, 83, 362, 363n, 364; his takeover of the Church, 77–9.
Hewitt, John, 174, 176, 192.
Heythe, Thomas, 237.
Heyward, Jasper, 91.
Hicks, Leo, Fr., 102n, 111n, 130–3 & n.
Higgens, Isaac, 135.
Hill, Geoffrey, 171.
Hobhouse, John Cam, 362.
Hodgson, Sydney, 227, 228, 230.
Holford, Thomas, 172.
Holland, John, Earl of Exeter, 75–6.
Holt, William, 272.
Holtby, Richard, S.J., 232 &n, 262, 276.
Hopton, Sir Owen, 52, 67 &n, 68, 69–70, 88, 89, 90, 94, 95, 96n, 136, 139, 169, 171, 201, 357; interrogates Edmund Campion with torture, 100–2.
Horner, Nicholas, 192–3.
Hothersall, George, 313, 329.

Howard, Anne, Countess of Arundel, 23.
Howard, Charles, Earl of Nottingham and Lord Admiral, 169, 302n, 311, 314, 336, 345.
Howard, Philip, Earl of Arundel, 58, 140.
Howard, Thomas, 4th Duke of Norfolk, 58, 88, 89, 90, 92.
H, P.W., a spy, 121.
Hughes, Philip, 78, 83n, 86n, 87n, 166n, 176n, 191n, 356n.
Humberson, Robert, 219.
Humphrey, Duke of Gloucester, 75.
Hunt, Simon, 193.
Hutton, Mary, 357, 373, 374.
Hutton, William, 261, 262, 266, 275n.
Hynek, R.W., 20n.
Ingram, John, 260–3.
Ingram, William, 315n, 317.
Jackson, Edward, 94.
Jacob, John, 142.
Janelle, Pierre, 295.
Jeaffreson, John Cordy, 49n, 241n, 315n, 339n.
Jerningham, Lady, widow of Sir Henry, 63.
Jetter, George, 68, 71.
Jetter, John, 68–71, 121.
Jewel, John, Bishop, 83, 84n.
Johnson, Lawrence, 67, 68, 97.
Johnson, Robert, 95, 96, 97, 98, 111.
Jones, Edward, 193–6, 197, 198, 202, 227.
Jones, John, OSF, 325–29, 331.
Jones, Nicholas, 238, 239, 241–8, 251–5, 279, 297, 320, 322n, 323–4; marries Anne Bellamy, 241.
Jonson, Ben, 315–17, 319.
Kay, Anthony, 190.
Kelley, Edward, 45.
Kemp, William, 97.
Killigrew, Sir Henry, 22, 219, 273, 375.

Kilroy, Gerard, 102n, 263n, 319n, 375n.
Kirby, Luke, 67, 95, 97, 98, 117 .
Knollys, Sir Francis, 131–2, 154, 177, 180, 182.
Kuin, Roger, 38n, 138n.
Kyd, Thomas, 316 & n.
Lacey, Brian, 227–30.
Lampley, William, 173.
Leake, Thomas, 23n.
Leech, John, 200.
Leigh, Richard, 173, 174.
Lesley, John, Bishop of Ross, 88.
Levin, Carole, 223n, 224n.
Lewis, William, 133.
Line, Anne, 339.
Lingen, Edward, 264–6, 272, 289n.
Lloyd, Richard, 173.
Lok, Anne, 333–4.
Lok, Henry, 332–3.
Lopez, Roderigo, 273.
Low, John, 129.
Ludlam, Robert, 160, 353.
Lumley, John, 1st Baron Lumley, 121
Magna Carta, Cap. 39, 28–9, 78n;
Mainey, Mrs., 128.
Maisse, M. de, 225–6.
Man, John, 137–8.
Manners, John, 152.
Manners, Roger, 105.
Markenfield, Thomas, 51.
Marshall, Ralph, 245.
Martin, Gregory, 120–21.
Martin, Patrick, 16n.
Martin, Richard, 173.
Martyr, Peter, 83.
Mary I, 81, 195, 230, 354; torture under, 80.
Mary, Queen of Scots, 87–8, 92, 165–8, 219n, 296, 311, 339n.
Maskew, Bridget, 301.
Mason, John, 227, 228, 230.
Mathews, Nieves, 27n.
Maude, Bernard, 167–8n, 339n.

Maxfield, Humphrey, 135–6.
Mayne, Cuthbert, 93, 165.
Merrick, Gilly, 312.
Middleton, Anthony, 193–6.
Mildmay, Sir Walter, 139, 180, 186, 225.
Mills, Francis, 130.
Milner, Ralph, 142n.
Mompesson, Laurence, 235.
Montrose, Louis, 61n, 223n.
Moore, Hugh, 172.
More, Henry, S.J., 243, 258.
More, Thomas II, 116–17.
Morgan, Thomas, 132–3,
Morris, Mr., Queen's Attorney, 307–8.
Morris, Fr. John, 108n.
Morton, Nicholas, 51, 53, 97, 98, 110.
Morton, Robert, 51–3, 55, 146, 172–3.
Morton, Samson, 51.
Munday, Anthony, 117, 118n, 182n, 245.
Munden, John, 180.
Musgrave, Robert, 200.
Myagh (Meagh), Thomas, 99–100.
Nashe, Thomas, 315–16.
Neale, J.E., 27n.
Needham, Humphrey, 92.
Nelson, John,165.
Neville, Charles, 6th Earl of Westmorland, 87, 92.
Neville, Edward, 130–31, 132.
Newall, William, a pursuivant, 130, 216n.
Nicholl, Charles, 27n, 127.
Nichols, George, 177.
Norris, Henry, 1st Baron Norris, 46.
Norton, Christopher, 38,
Norton, Richard, 38, 51. 66.
Norton, Thomas, 50n, 70, 90, 92–7, 98–100, 103–5; origins and career, 91–2; tortures without

specific warrant, 98–9; interrogates Edmund Campion with torture, 100–2; imprisoned, 105–6; attempted self-justification, 109; praised by the Queen, 109–10.

Oldcorne, Alice, 357, 373, 374.

Orange, William of, 165.

Orton, Henry, 96, 97, 98.

Osborne, Edward, 65–6, 67, 70.

Ostcliff, George, 97, 98.

Overton, William, 358.

Owen, Hugh, 270

Padley, 146, 147, 148, 153, 160–, 3, 205–6, 210, 280, 339–50, 352–3: establishment of the pilgrimage and restoration of the chapel, 353.

Page, Richard, 258.

Parker, Sir Nicholas, 310.

Parr, Queen Katherine, 31, 33.

Parry, William, 130–2, 166.

Pascal, John, 95, 96n, 97.

Passy, Stanwardine, 217, 253, 258, 322n, 328–30.

Pattenson, William, 235.

Paulet, Sir Amyas, 180, 186.

Pearson, John, 356.

Percy, Thomas, 7th Earl of Northumberland, 51, 87, 92,151.

Perrot, Sir John, 176n.

Persons, Fr. Robert, 21, 24, 66n, 90, 93 & n, 97–8, 102–5, 110–13, 121, 129, 150n, 175, 235, 236, 238, 246n, 263–4, 275, 278, 280, 338.

Peyton, Sir John, 338.

Phelippes, Thomas, 132, 168n, 209n, 341n.

Philip II, King, 168.

Pibush, John, 181.

Pierpoint, Mrs., 85.

Pius V, Pope, 51, 88, 110, 125.

Plasden, Polydore, 227–31.

Pollen, John Hungerford, S.J., 142, 175n, 220n.

Pollini, Girolamo, 31n, 33, 43, 119; Topcliffe acquires his

L'historia ecclesiastica, 124–26,

Polewhele, William, 276, 278.

Pooley, Robert, 170.

Popham, Sir John, 94, 95, 208, 291–3, 301–2, 313, 335, 338–9.

Pormort, Thomas, 221–5, 227, 235, 290, 300, 37.

Pounde, Thomas, 64n, 102, 108n.

Pritchard, Humphrey, 177.

Proctor, Thomas, of Cowpercote, 38–43,

Proctor, William, of Bordley, 41–2.

Proctor, Sir Stephen, 39n, 158n.

Puckering, Sir John, 126, 172, 184–5 & n, 244–5 255–8, 259, 265–6, 267, 320, 322, 336; Topcliffe's attitude towards, 284–5; Puckering's Topcliffe dossier, 286–7; moves against Topcliffe, 297–9; his death, 324 & n.

Pugh, Harry, 357.

Questier, Michael, 94n, 249n, 251n, 253n, 324n, 336, 356n.

Radcliffe, Thomas, 3rd Earl of Sussex, Lord Chamberlain, 57–61.

Raleigh, Sir Walter, 170, 181, 230–1.

Randall, William, 183–5, 279–80, 285, 297, 313.

Rastell, William, 125n.

Rawlins, Alexander, 276n, 277.

Rea, W.F., 280.

Redford, John, 216n.

Revell. See Brown, Thomas.

Rich, Lady Penelope, 278.

Rich, Sir Richard, 79.

Richard III, King, 77.

Ridcall,Francis, 151, 250.

Ridolphi, Robert, 88.

Rigby, John, 339.

Ripon, North Yorkshire, 79n.

Rishton, Edward, 97–9, 113.

Rither, James, 285–90, 299.

Rivers, Fr. Anthony, S.J., 16n, 338.
Robinson, William, 310.
Roche, John, 173.
Rollins, Hyder, 92n.
Rookwood, Edward, 57–62.
Roscarrock, Nicholas, 94, 96, 97, 98.
Rowland, Richard. See Verstegan.
Rowse, A.L., 30n, 31n, 35n, 67n, 107n, 186.
Russell, Bridget, Countess of Bedford, 46.
Russell, Francis, 2nd Earl of Bedford, 46.
Rylstone, Yorkshire, 38–42; Rylstone Church, riot in, 40–1.
Sacheverell, Patrick, 288–9.
Sackville, Lady, 85–6.
Sackville, Richard, 92.
Sander, Nicholas, 113, 118, 125n.
Sandys, Edwin, 286.
Sandys, John, 360n.
Sandys, Miles, 273.
Savage, John, alias Digby, 139.
Scott, Cuthbert, Bishop, 83.
Scott, Montford, 178, 220, 228.
Seymour, Edward, Duke of Somerset, 80, 91.
Shakespeare, William, 30, 124, 129n, 148, 164, 174, 193, 199, 210, 310, 361.
Shelley, Edward, 173.
Shelley, Jane, 287–9.
Shelley, William, 289 & n.
Shert, John, 97, 98, 99.
Sherwin, Ralph, 94–8, 106.
Sherwood, Elizabeth, 85n.
Sherwood, Henry, 85 & n.
Sherwood, Richard, 270.
Sherwood, Thomas, 86n, 89–90, 165.
Simpson, Evelyn, 199–200.
Simpson, Richard (priest),152, 161.
Simpson, Richard, 64n, 100, 101n, 102n, 108n, 166n, 267n.

Six Statues, The, 29–30;
Skeffington, Leonard, 69n.
Skevington, Richard, 314 & n.
Skinner, Richard, 339.
Smeaton, Mark, 73.
Smith, Otwell, 185n.
Smith, Sir Thomas, 90.
Somerby, Lincolnshire, 30, 55, 241–4, 245, 283, 284, 323, 342, 345, 347, 349–50, 351–2.
Somerville, John, 148.
Southwell, Elizabeth, 346n.
Southwell, Richard, 23,
Southwell, Fr. Robert, 102, 124, 144, 173, 175, 177, 183n, 193, 198, 221, 243, 256–7, 273, 276, 277, 297, 299, 301, 330; on the Babington Plot, 168; on torture in Bridewell & Topcliffe's house, 144, 179n, 191, 197; captured at Uxendon, 15–16, 241; tortured by Topcliffe, 19–22; by the Privy Council's interrogators, 22–23; moved to the Tower, 24–25; Anne Bellamy's role in his capture, 238–41; writes to Robert Cecil, 247, 290; trial and condemnation, 290–96.
Spencer, William, 177.
Spenser, Edmund, 181, 182 & n, 319.
Squire, Edward, 70.
Stafford, Sir Edward, 133, 139, 167n.
Standen, Anthony, 298n.
Stanhope, Edward, 313.
Stanhope, Sir Thomas, 215–17,
Stanley, Ferdinando, Lord Strange 224, 327n.
Stanley, Sir William, 166, 201, 263, 269, 270–2.
Stephen, King, 73.
Stephens, Jerome, 96.
Stephenson, Jeffrey, 356.
Sterrell, William, 16n, 338.

St. John, Oliver, 145n.
Stoker, George, 236n, 237.
Storey, Dr. John, 67, 126.
Stow, John, 85n, 86, 141, 270n.
Stubbs, John, 106, 107.
Sutton, Robert, 140n, 174.
Talbot, Elizabeth ("Bess of Hardwick"), Countess of
Shrewsbury, 45–7, 215.
Talbot,,George, 6th Earl of
Shrewsbury, 43–4, 50, 52–3,
146, 148, 164n, 186, 206–7,
353–4; develops the medicinal
waters at Buxton, 45–7; moves
against local recusants, 152;
arrests John Fitzherbert and
seizes Padley, 160–3; arrests
Richard Fitzherbert, 203–4,
206; breaks with Topcliffe,
205, 215; death, 213; correspondence, 44, 47, 49–50, 53–
4, 55–64, 101, 160, 162, 204–
4, 207.
Talbot, Gilbert, Lord, later 7th
Earl of Shrewsbury, 205, 354,
356; his association with
Topcliffe, 43, 47, 48, 55, 213–
15, 347–8; intervenes on behalf
of James Harrison, priest, 156–
7; succeeds his father, 213;
supports Anthony Fitzherbert,
341–2; privy councilor, 348;
keeps Topcliffe out of Padley,
210, 280n, 341, 350–2; correspondence, 37, 43, 48, 50n,
115, 156–7, 210, 213–15, 346.
Tesse (Tesh), Anne, 296.
Thompson, Michael, 255, 320–1.
Thorne, Edward, 153–6, 157, 159,
160, 162, 202–4, 205, 206, 207,
213; his death, 343n.
Thorpe (or Throwpe), Matthew,
54.
Thorpe, Robert, 221.
Throckmorton, Francis, 107.
Throgmorton, Sir George, 125n.
Thurland, Edmund, 52.

Tilletson, Francis, 313, 314.
Tippet, John, 93 & n.
Tiptoft, John, Earl of Worcester,
75–6.
Topcliffe, Charles, 307–12, 344,
351–2.
Topcliffe, Edmund, 310.
Topcliffe, Edmund, son of Lionel,
310–11.
Topcliffe, Henry, 309–10, 311.
Topcliffe, John, 310.
Topcliffe, Lionel, 310.
Topcliffe, Richard; 15–17, 18–19,
21, 24–5, 48, 53, 91, 115, 117,
128, 133, 354, 355–6, 362;
announces his capture of
Southwell to the Queen, 17–18;
described as a sadist, 27–8; his
family and upbringing, 30–2;
marriage, 32; begins his service
of Elizabeth Tudor, 32–34;
esquire of the body to Elizabeth
I, 35 & n, 36; raises and equips
30 horsemen to serve against
the Rising of the North, 1569,
36–7; carries letters between
Elizabeth and Leicester, 36–7;
serves the Dudley brothers, 37–
8; steward of the sequestered
Norton estates in Yorkshire,
38–43; his long-standing family connection with the Earls of
Shrewsbury, 43; manages an
alchemical scheme for
Burghley and Leicester, 44–5;
writes about a visit with
Leicester to Buxton, 45–7;
assists Lord Shrewsbury in his
case against his Glossopdale
tenants, 48; his houses burgled,
49; investigates Yorkshire robberies for Shrewsbury, 49–50;
arrests Robert and Ursula Morton, 52–3; emerges as an expert
on the Catholics, ca. 1578, 52–
4; writes a letter of news and
instructions to Shrewsbury

from the royal progress into East Anglia, 55–64; captures his first priest, 65–6; receives his first commission, 67, 115–16; tortures John Jetter, 68–71; searches for illicit books and manuscripts, 116–26, 135; raids William Carter's house, 118–21; working with Walsingham, 121, 123, 126–28; present at the Babington executions, 129; at William Parry's execution, 130–32; various arrests, 134–38; begins torturing with the manacles in Bridewell, 142–44; his campaign against the Fitzherberts, 146–64, 202–11; his bond with Thomas Fitzherbert, 149–50; his first surviving torture warrant, 169; role in the Armada hangings, 171–6; his period of greatest activity begins, 178ff.; tortures in his own house, 179; his devotion to Elizabeth I, 183–6; writes his own instructions and warrants from the Council, 24, 190–1, 323–4, 327; his mode of operation, 197–9; obscene tortures, 197; acquires Padley, 205–6; his letter to Gilbert Talbot on inheriting the earldom, 213–15; brags to Thomas Pormort about his closeness to the Queen, 222; seven of his prisoners executed in one day, 227–31; seduces or rapes Anne Bellamy in the Gatehouse, 237–44; sues Fitzherbert for his bond, 280–1; committed to prison, 297–9; writes to the Queen from prison, 299–301; attacked through his son Charles, 307–12; investigates *The Isle of Dogs,* 315–18; seeks to incrimi-

nate Robert Barnes, 249–58, 320–30; last conversation with the Queen, 344, 347; "heaved" out of Padley, 349–50; death, 350.

Tregian, Francis, 227n.

Tresham, Sir Thomas, 66n, 67, 102n.

Twyford, Richard, 206.

Udall, William, 318n.

Uxendon, 15–16, 236–40, 247, 258n.

Vallenger, Stephen, 68, 69–70, 120.

Vaughan, Stephen, 80, 334–5.

Vaux, William, 3rd Baron Vaux of Harrowden, 66n, 67, 129.

Vavasour, Dorothy, 357, 374.

Venables, John, 308,

Venables, William, 307–11, 352.

Vere, Edward de, Earl of Oxford, 85.

Verstegan, Richard, alias Rowland 20, 21, 24, 35n, 65, 66, 140, 179n, 202, 223n, 235, 246, 291, 296, 299, 301.

Waad, William, 21, 22, 143n, 201, 222, 228, 288, 305.

Waldgrave, Sir Edward, 85.

Walpole, Christopher, 263.

Walpole, Henry, 64–5, 124, 174, 176, 254, 271–3, 278, 289n, 300, 301, 305; career & capture, 263–6; interrogation and torture, 273–6; trial & death, 277.

Walpole, Michael, 264.

Walpole, Thomas, 264–6, 272.

Walsingham, Sir Francis, 22, 87, 90, 99, 106, 105–8, 109, 115, 123, 133, 139–40, 150, 165, 177, 236–7, 311; 339 & n; the Ridolphi Plot, 88n; protects John Hart, 110–12; & the Parry Plot, 131–2; manages the

Babington Plot, 129, 166–8; works with Topcliffe, 121, 126–8, 130, 134, 135, 180; Topcliffian behavior, 180–1; death, 180, 186.
Walter, Robert, 137–38.
Walton, Roger, 138–40.
Ward, Margaret, 143–44, 173.
Watkinson, Thomas, 221.
Watson, William, 143, 173, 277.
Webley, Henry, 172.
Webley, Thomas, 123.
Wedall, John, 356, 373.
Weir, Alison, 27n.
Wells, Swithin, 227, 228–30.
Wells, Mrs. Swithin, 228, 229, 374.
Weston William, Fr., 123n.
Wharton, Philip, 3rd Baron Wharton, 46.
Wharton, Sir Thomas, 85.
Whitchurch, Edward, 91.
White, Dorothy, 192n.
White, Eustace, 227–8, 231.
White, Richard, 144, 359–60.
Whitford, Richard, 69n.
Whitgift, John, Archbishop of Canterbury, 207, 235, 253, 302, 304, 338, 347; godfather to Thomas Pormort, 221, 222, 223–4; destroys Sir Thomas Fitzherbert's will, 209.
Wilbraham, Thomas, 316 & n.
Williams, Friswood, 268n.
Williams, Penry, 27, 28.
Williamson, Nicholas, 216–18, 280.
Willoughby, Sir Edward, 32.
Willoughby, Sir Francis, 32 & n, 148.
Willoughby, Sir Henry, 33n.
Willoughby, Margaret, 32n, 33.
Wilson, Thomas, 63, 94.
Winslade, Tristram, 169–70.
Wiseman, Jane, 243, 325 & n, 328; tried & condemned to *peine forte et dure*, 329; rep-
rieved, 332–3; her parentage, 333–4.
Wollaton, Nottinghamshire, 32.
Wolsey, Thomas, Cardinal, 77–8.
Woodhouse, Francis, 309–10.
Woodville, Richard, Earl Rivers, 76.
Woolley, Sir John, 259.
Worsley, a pursuivant, 130.
Worthington, Thomas, 135–36.
Wray, Sir Christopher, 158–9, 229, 283–4.
Wriothesley, Thomas, 1st Earl of Southampton, 79.
Wyndham, Edmund, 58.
Yaxley, Richard, 177.
Yepes, Diego de, 23, 295–6.
York, Rowland, 166.
Young, Richard, 22, 64n, 144, 169–70, 171, 191–7, 201n, 223, 227–8, 246, 253, 256, 267, 273, 278, 319, 326.
Younger, James, 222, 223n, 224, 228n, 229–30.

Printed in Great Britain
by Amazon

56915965R00235